To Paulana Vivian
with love and gratitude
Olga
November 4, 2012

# ❙❙❙ Modern Ladino Culture

INDIANA SERIES IN SEPHARDI AND MIZRAHI STUDIES

Harvey E. Goldberg and Matthias Lehmann, editors

# Modern Ladino Culture

## Press, Belles Lettres, and Theatre in the Late Ottoman Empire

Olga Borovaya

INDIANA UNIVERSITY PRESS

Bloomington and Indianapolis

This book is a publication of
Indiana University Press
601 North Morton Street
Bloomington, Indiana 47404-3797 USA
iupress.indiana.edu

Telephone orders   800-842-6796
Fax orders   812-855-7931

∞ The paper used in this publication meets
the minimum requirements of the American National Standard
for Information Sciences—Permanence
of Paper for Printed Library Materials,
ANSI Z39.48-1992.

Manufactured in the United States of America

Library of Congress Cataloging-in-Publication Data

Borovaia, O. V. (Ol'ga Vol'fovna)
Modern Ladino culture : press, belles lettres, and theater in the late
Ottoman Empire / Olga Borovaya.
p. cm.—(Indiana series in Sephardi and Mizrahi studies)
Includes bibliographical references and index.
ISBN 978-0-253-35672-7 (cloth : alk. paper)—
ISBN 978-0-253-00556-4 (e-pub) 1. Jews—Turkey—Intellectual life—19th century.—
    2. Jews—Turkey—Intellectual life—20th century. 3. Ladino literature—19th century
History and criticism. 4. Ladino literature—20th century--History and criticism.
    5. Ladino newspapers—Turkey. 6. Jewish newspapers—Turkey. 7. Jewish theater—
Turkey—History. 8. Turkey—Ethnic relations.  I. Title.
DS135.T8B68    2011
305.892'405609034—DC23    2011030436

1  2  3  4  5  17  16  15  14  13  12

To my parents,
with gratitude and admiration

You cannot find out what a man means by simply studying his spoken or written statements, even though he has spoken or written with perfect command of language and perfectly truthful intention. In order to find out his meaning you must also know what the question was . . . to which the thing he has said or written was meant as an answer.

—R. G. Collingwood, *Autobiography*

# ▌▌▌ Contents

# ❙❙❙ Acknowledgments

Having been trained as a Romance philologist, I would have never turned to history had I not met Steven Zipperstein who, aside from encouraging me, offered an exceptional opportunity to immerse myself in Jewish studies for which I am profoundly grateful to him. My full and joyful "conversion" to history, however, happened during the years of work and intensive conversations with Aron Rodrigue, the echo of which can be perceived on almost every page of this book. Aron Rodrigue's rigorous thinking, openness to new ideas, and astonishingly wide interests have been the major influence on my work, and this book would have not been written without his faith in me, immense support, and unwavering friendship.

I am also deeply grateful to Julia Phillips Cohen, my outstanding research assistant of many years, enthusiastic interlocutor, colleague, and friend who, in three different countries, shared with me the unmatched joys of reading the Ladino press.

I am greatly indebted to Daniela Blei, Dushan Djordjevich, Matthias Lehmann, Scott Lerner, Sergey Lyosov, Kenneth Moss, Avner Peres, Anat Plocker, and Maurice Samuels for offering their expertise in history, literature, and linguistics as well as their invaluable suggestions.

I warmly thank David Epstein, my indefatigable and resourceful voluntary assistant, who has made the most of every opportunity to do research for me in various continents and languages.

My warmest thanks go to Devin Naar, who promptly and generously answered my questions during the final stages of work on this book, when I had no access to libraries.

During the revision process, this book tremendously benefited from the insightful comments and stimulating questions of its first readers: Aviva Ben-Ur, Kenneth Moss, Aron Rodrigue, Maurice Samuels, and Sarah Stein.

The idea for the cover design, tastefully developed by Indiana University Press, belongs to Maurice Samuels. I am profoundly grateful to Angela Burton, managing editor at Indiana University Press, for her immense help and patience during the final months of production of this book.

It was always an immense pleasure to do research at the Ben Zvi Institute Library, some of whose materials are used in this book. I am particularly indebted to Dov Cohen, its renowned Ladino press expert, for his assistance and for sharing his vast knowledge. Earlier, my research was greatly facilitated by the library staff of the Center for Advanced Judaic Studies at the University of Pennsylvania and by Sonia Moss at the Green Library at Stanford.

None of this research would have been possible without the generosity of foundations and private donors. My project was supported by the Fulbright Scholar Program, the Primo Levi Fellowship (Andrew and Erna Viterbi), the American Academy for Jewish Research, the Memorial Foundation for Jewish Culture, and the American Philosophical Society, as well as by my faithful friends Ellen Bob and David Waksberg, David and Charlotte Epstein, and Ludwig and Carol Tannenwald.

# ❚❚❚ Note on the Translation, Transcription, Proper Names, and Dates

All translations in this book, unless otherwise indicated, are mine. The Bible is quoted from the New Revised Standard Version

In transcribing Ladino, I use the system adopted by the periodical Aki Yerushalayim with one difference: the letter yod representing the consonantal element in diphthongs is rendered here by the letter y (e.g., t*yempo*, not *tiempo*).

I spell the names of Sephardi literati as they or their contemporaries Romanized them (hence, *Alexandre Benghiat*). The names whose contemporaneous Romanized versions are not available are transcribed according to the general rules, with the exception of those widely used in scholarly works (e.g., *Fresco*, not *Fresko*). When a first name is taken from the Bible and therefore spelled in Ladino texts as in Hebrew, i.e., without vowels, I represent its Ladino pronunciation (e.g., *Shemuel*, not *Samuel* or *Shmuel*).

In the titles of Ladino periodicals and books, I capitalize only the first meaningful word (e.g., *El Jurnal israelit*) as is common in other Romance languages.

Turkish words and proper names are transliterated to ensure their correct pronunciation by English speakers (e.g., *Mejid*, not *Mecid*).

In transliterating Hebrew, I follow the Library of Congress rules with one exception: the letter het is represented by ch.

If a former Ottoman city had multiple names, all of them, including the current one, are indicated in parentheses when it is mentioned for the first time.

All dates, unless otherwise stated, are according to the Gregorian calendar.

# ▌▌▌  Modern Ladino Culture

# ▮▮▮  Introduction

## I

This book is the first study of the three forms of modern Ladino cultural production—the press, belles lettres, and theater—in their unity as a single cultural phenomenon produced by Sephardi Jews in the late Ottoman period. Having no counterparts in previous epochs, these three genres emerged in the second half of the nineteenth century as a result of westernization and secularization. They were imported by Sephardi westernizers from Europe but took root and developed in their own ways in the local culture. Since they were created by the same literati for the same audience and with the same intention, by examining each of them in isolation from the other two, one risks failing to see the new cultural movement in its entirety or to comprehend its place in Sephardi history. Nevertheless, this study is divided into three parts organized chronologically in the order in which the genres emerged, the press being the earliest one. However, this division, which is essential for my analysis, does not obscure the total picture because belles lettres is examined against the backdrop of the press which brought it into existence, and theater is discussed in the context of both the press, which played an exceptional role in its development, and belles lettres, the genre closest to it in terms of subject matter.

As I am not concerned with the aesthetic value of Ladino culture but, rather, regard its textual manifestations as a source on Sephardi history, this book will focus mainly on printed materials. For this reason, I will limit my examination of Sephardi Theater to Ladino plays and the representation of this cultural practice in the press. Furthermore, from a historian's standpoint, examining a Ladino text only within the framework of a single genre category or even in the context of the author's work as a whole is not sufficient. In my case studies, I will put Ladino novels, newspaper articles, and plays under analysis side by side with other contemporaneous publications, including rabbinic writings.

An in-depth examination of Ladino print culture is imperative for Sephardic studies as a field due to the extreme scarcity of available sources on the history of Ottoman Jews. All we have left is no more than a thousand Ladino texts, counting every periodical as a separate item, which is very little given that, by the turn of the twentieth century, there were about 250,000 Sephardi Jews in the Ottoman Empire.[1] A great number of handwritten documents, including communal records, private letters, and memoirs, perished as a result of the numerous fires, wars, and mass migrations. As for printed texts, their circulations were so small that already in the early 1900s publishers of some Ladino periodicals asked their subscribers to sell them a full run of their own newspapers, as theirs had disappeared. Many periodicals did not survive at all, and there are only a couple of pages left from some others. For this reason, another goal of my book is to offer new information on Ladino periodicals and their publishers, mainly gleaned from a close examination of their mastheads and announcements, or from other newspapers. Thus, before (and often instead of) posing the questions commonly asked by students of other literatures, a scholar of Ladino literature has to turn to the history of Sephardi Jews.

Writing about Ladino culture today is immeasurably easier than it was twenty years ago. In the early 1990s, the groundbreaking work by Esther Benbassa and Aron Rodrigue, *Juifs des Balkans* (Paris, 1993),[2] as well as Rodrigue's earlier book, *French Jews, Turkish Jews* (Bloomington, 1990), provided a new perspective on the history of the Ottoman Sephardi community, particularly its modern period, and set a frame of reference for further discussion of a wide range of related topics. A great number of publications on Sephardi history and print culture, not all of them academic, appeared in the 1990s in connection with the celebration of the five hundredth anniversary of the arrival of Iberian Jews in the Ottoman Empire. Many of these works, produced mainly by Spanish scholars, were dedicated to Ladino literature.

The most important and comprehensive of them is Elena Romero's *La Creación literaria en lengua sefardí* (Madrid, 1992) which—following the pattern of the first scholarly history of Ladino literature, Michael Molho's *Literatura sefardita de Oriente* (Madrid, 1960)—covers all genres of Ladino print culture produced between the early sixteenth century and the mid-twentieth. But, like Molho's work, rather than being a study of Ladino literature as a single cultural phenomenon, *La Creación literaria* is a collection of essays on individual genres that, as it appears, merely coexisted or replaced each other. In short, Romero is not interested in establishing synchronic and diachronic relations between different genres nor in placing the development of Ladino print culture in a historical context. Nevertheless, *La Creación literaria en lengua sefardí,* as well as Romero's other works and articles by some of her Spanish colleagues, contains a significant amount of information, mostly of encyclopedic character. No doubt, bibliographic lists and annotated editions of Ladino texts published by Elena Romero and Amelia Barquín,[3] many of them cited in this book, are useful for the study of Ladino print culture, yet it is time to shift the perspective and undertake an analytical investigation that asks historical questions.

The books on Ladino print culture produced in the United States by Matthias Lehmann and Sarah Stein are the first works that place the texts under analysis into a particular historical setting, which enables the scholars to uncover the inherent functions of the respective genres and move to the study of the intended readerships. Stein's book *Making Jews Modern* (Bloomington, 2003) for the first time examines Ladino newspapers in a historical context and analyzes their ideological agenda within the framework of the westernization and secularization under way in the Sephardi community.[4] Lehmann's elucidating study of vernacular rabbinic production, *Ladino Rabbinic Literature and Ottoman Sephardic Culture* (Bloomington, 2005), constitutes an important chapter in the history of Ladino print culture; it not only examines the Ladino *musar* (ethical treatise) as a genre but also discusses its role in shaping the audience for nineteenth-century secular literature.

The present book, sharing the historical premises of these two studies, continues the reconstruction of Ladino print culture from a different perspective. I will look at a number of texts created by Ottoman Sephardim in Ladino and French between the moment of the first attempt to establish a Ladino periodical (1842) and the Young Turk revolution (1908), which made censorship less repressive and guaranteed all Ottoman subjects freedom of expression. Since the Jewish communities in different Ottoman cities differed from one another in many aspects, I chose to focus only on the three largest centers of Ladino culture—Salonica (Saloniki, Thessaloniki), Istanbul (Constantinople), and Izmir (Smyrna).

Most extant Ladino newspapers, plays, and novels, which are mainly available only on microfilm, were incompetently bound; their typographic quality was usually rather poor; and some articles were cut out by readers. Hence, sometimes, one can decipher letters or words only from the context. This peculiar character of our sources, together with the scarcity of information even on well-known literati, accounts for the abundance in this book of modal verbs and phrases expressing uncertainty, such as "this must have been," "he would have known," and "it is likely." For the same reason, this study, like virtually all other works on Ladino print culture, no doubt contains a number of errors, but just as I have identified inaccuracies in the works of my predecessors, I hope that other scholars will correct mine.

## II

Ladino literature was produced in the Ottoman Empire and the successor states roughly between the mid-sixteenth century and the mid-twentieth by the descendants of the Jews who left the Iberian Peninsula as of the end of the fifteenth century. As is well known, on March 31, 1492, the Catholic monarchs, Ferdinand and Isabella, signed the Edict of Expulsion of the Jews from Spain and its possessions.[5] Jews were given three months to leave or convert to Christianity. By July 1492, there were no more Jews in Spain. A similar decree was issued in 1497 in Portugal, where a large number of Spanish Jews had fled.

Under these circumstances, most Sephardim chose to leave the peninsula, while others converted, hoping to return to Judaism later. However, the "new Christians" (*conversos*) in Spain and, after 1536, in Portugal became a constant target of the Inquisition, which accused them of secret Judaizing.[6] Unable to integrate into a hostile Christian society and fearing for their lives, many conversos managed to emigrate, joining the first refugees in Italy, North Africa, Holland, and the Ottoman Empire. In the absence of reliable statistics, scholars put the total number of Iberian refugees between 100,000 and 150,000.[7]

While openly returning to Judaism was dangerous in most parts of Europe and in the overseas Spanish colonies, the Ottoman Empire, which had the largest number of Sephardi exiles, allowed Jews to practice their religion freely and offered the Jewish community as a whole a great deal of autonomy.[8] The flow of Sephardi immigrants coming directly or indirectly from the Iberian Peninsula continued through the first decades of the eighteenth century, but the majority of ex-*conversos* settled in the Ottoman lands in the sixteenth century and the early seventeenth. Scholars disagree about the number of Iberian Jews who arrived in the Ottoman Empire after 1492, but the most realistic estimate, based on the Ottoman censuses, puts it at around 60,000.[9]

In the sixteenth century, the largest Sephardi communities and the leading centers of Jewish printing were those of Salonica and Istanbul. The first printing press in the Ottoman Empire was established in Istanbul by Spanish exiles, the brothers David and Samuel Ibn Nahmias, in 1493.[10] The first press in Salonica was founded in 1512 by Yehuda Gedalia, with type brought from Portugal.[11] The Soncino family, which came to Salonica from Italy, printed Hebrew books there in the 1520s, and in 1529 Gershom Soncino and his son Eliezer established a printing press in Istanbul. These presses printed a large number of Hebrew and Ladino books for those who had never stopped practicing Judaism but perhaps even more for the ex-*conversos* returning to normative Judaism.

Most *conversos* had secretly continued to practice some form of Judaism in the peninsula and western Europe, though often this was limited to a cautious observance of the Sabbath and avoidance of pork. Yet some crypto-Jews (marranos), as Yosef Yerushalmi points out, were "not so much unknowledgeable as they lacked systematic instruction."[12] It was crucial, therefore, to provide the refugees with means of quick acquisition of "ba*sic* Judaism," such as a Ladino translation of the Bible and the prayer books. Since most Sephardi immigrants had little or no knowledge of Hebrew upon arrival, Jewish males were expected to learn the language, a fact that accounts for a significant number of Hebrew grammars published in the sixteenth and seventeenth centuries.[13] But as soon as they learned the alphabet, they were able to read Ladino which, while being a Romance language, used a Hebrew script.[14] In his introduction to the Ladino version of Joseph Caro's *Shulhan Aruch*, reprinted in Venice in 1602, its publisher explains that the text is printed in "a Ladino of full [i.e., square Hebrew] letters with vowel-points, so that all can make use of it, even he who knows no more than the letters and the vowels."[15]

The first known Ladino book is *Dinim de shehitah i bedikah* (*The Rules of Ritual Slaughter and Inspection of Animals*; Istanbul, 1510), which was meant to ensure that even in exile the ritual slaughterers illiterate in Hebrew would have clear instructions for observing the laws of *kashrut*. It was followed by the book of Psalms (Istanbul, 1540) and the famous Constantinople Pentateuch in Hebrew, Greek,[16] and Ladino, published in 1547 by Eliezer ben Gershom Soncino, who also used square Hebrew letters with vowel signs. In 1568, only three years after the first Hebrew edition of *Shulhan Aruch*, its abridged Ladino version saw light in Salonica, and the following year, a major work of Jewish philosophical ethics, Bahya Ibn Paquda's *Hovot ha-levavot* (*The Duties of the Heart*), was translated into

Ladino and published in Istanbul. These and other Ladino translations and adaptations were the rabbis' response to the mass immigration of conversos, whose influx increased after 1536 when the Inquisition was established in Portugal.

Rabbi Moses ben Barukh Almosnino (c. 1518–1580), a famous Salonican preacher, a prolific author, and a prominent Jewish thinker, is the earliest known Ladino author in the Ottoman Empire. Though, like all Jewish authors, he mainly wrote in Hebrew, Almosnino also produced a number of works in the vernacular, only two of which had utilitarian purposes, the rest dealing with abstract matters. His *El Regimyento de la vida* (*The Regimen of Life;* 1564) is the first *musar* in Ladino and is mainly based on Aristotle's *Nicomachean Ethics.* Almosnino's *Crónica de los reyes otomanos* (*The Chronicle of the Ottoman Kings;* 1567)[17] was produced by its author independently of any other text and thus can be considered the first original narrative in Ladino. It is part history of the empire, part travelogue of Istanbul, which sought to introduce Sephardim to their new home and assure them that they could count on the sultan's protection. However, this book, a work of some literary value, was never published in the Ottoman Empire and thus had no influence on later Ladino literature.[18]

In the seventeenth century, a significant decrease of Iberian immigration, the mass migration of Jews within the Ottoman Empire, and the economic decline of Salonica, a major center of Ladino printing, undermined the status and role of the vernacular culture and had a negative impact on book publishing. In addition, "scholars suffered from the uncertainty of philanthropic backing, and had to cope with the erosion of the support network that had made much of their production possible."[19]

In the eighteenth century and the first half of the nineteenth, Ladino literature consisted mostly of rabbinic writings, now designed to reach the broadest possible audience of Ottoman Jews in order to teach them the rabbinic tradition, make accessible the Bible, whose calque translations had become incomprehensible, and replace the complex ethical works by Almosnino and Ibn Paquda, produced for an educated audience,[20] with straightforward guidance. Most scholars agree that the boom of vernacular rabbinic writings in the early eighteenth century responded to what was perceived as an educational crisis in the wake of the messianic movement around Shabbetai Zvi and reflected the rabbis' new educational ideal. The two most important eighteenth-century writers are Jacob Huli (1689–1732), author of the *Me'am Lo'ez,* often described as an anthology of Jewish knowledge in the form of a commentary on the Bible, and Abraham

Assa (c. 1710–c. 1768), a prolific translator and author of numerous works in Ladino.

According to Lehmann, *Me'am Lo'ez*, an "immense project of a comprehensive Bible commentary . . . marked the beginning of a flourishing vernacular literature in the eastern Sephardic diaspora . . . and provided a frame of reference for the considerable output of Ladino religious literature during the following two centuries."[21] The *Me'am Lo'ez* series, initiated by Huli's commentary on Genesis (Istanbul, 1730), was continued by ten other authors for more than a century and a half, the last volume coming out in 1899.

The very title, *Me'am Lo'ez*—literally, "from a foreign people"—indicates that it is written in a "non-Hebrew" language (*la'az*) and is, therefore, accessible to all Ladino speakers. In the introduction to his volume, Huli states that his goal is to explain the Pentateuch "to all men and women, as well as to the youth of Israel," although some people will make fun of his work, calling it "women's knowledge."[22] Assa's extensive translations, including that of the entire Bible (Istanbul, 1739–1744), had the same educational objective: to make the Jewish tradition accessible to Sephardim with little or no knowledge of Hebrew.

The vernacular rabbis'[23] major contribution to Ladino culture consisted in molding "a broad reading public which included social groups that had been all but excluded from printed Hebrew elite communication and that was the basis for the emergence of a Judeo-Spanish public sphere in the nineteenth century."[24] Furthermore, the educational efforts of the vernacular rabbis arguably shaped a particular reading practice that later facilitated the diffusion of Ladino periodicals and fiction.

Finally, rabbinic works, and *Me'am Lo'ez* in particular, introduced a simple style and a pattern of writing for the masses that combined instruction and entertainment. In the nineteenth century, this method of teaching was adopted by secular Ladino writers, who usually tried to make their serialized novels educational and educational newspapers entertaining. Sephardi Theater, moreover, explicitly aspired to replace rabbinic authority in the sphere of moral edification.

Another genre of learned Ladino literature that served didactic purposes was *coplas* (couplets). They were usually composed for Jewish holidays and special occasions, and in the late nineteenth century were sometimes used by the rabbis to criticize modern mores. While *coplas* as a genre go back to the pre-expulsion period, in the Ottoman Empire they began to be published only in the eighteenth century and were transmitted in writing, though some of them later entered the oral tradition.[25] The most famous eighteenth-century edition is *Coplas de Yosef ha-Tsadik* by Abraham de Toledo (Istanbul, 1732), consisting of four hundred quatrains.

The eighteenth century also saw the publication of the second known work of secular Ladino literature, *La Guerta de Oro* (*The Golden Flowergarden*, a calque of the Greek *anthologia*; Livorno, 1778). It was produced by David Attias, an Ottoman Jew born in Sarajevo who had spent most of his life in Livorno.[26] This unusual work, ranging from an introduction to the Italian language and the Greek alphabet to a treatise on physiognomy and thirty-four suggestions on educating children for a mother in the East, was the first book in Ladino to advocate secular education, the study of European languages, and acquisition of practical knowledge that would allow one to become rich. It was written for an Ottoman Jewish audience to promote the ideal of secular learning and European ways of living, and thus, if Almosnino's *Crónica de los reyes otomanos* may be considered an introduction for Iberian Jews to the Ottoman Empire, *La Guerta de Oro* served as an introduction for Ottoman Sephardim to Europe. Yet Attias's book also remained unknown in the empire. Perhaps it is not coincidental that neither of the first two works of secular literature found a publisher in the Ottoman Empire, where until the mid-nineteenth century book printing was controlled by the rabbis.

The emergence of the short-lived periodical *Sha'arei mizrach*, which appeared in Izmir in December 1845, marked a turning point in the history of Ladino print culture, which from then on was no longer monolithic, presenting one worldview. From that moment on, Ladino literature developed in two different directions, and its two branches, always aware of each other, began to compete for audiences. The rabbis responded to the acute decline in religiosity accelerated by westernization with an increased output of *musar* works. Earlier, their main foe had been ignorance; now, they had to battle an alternative worldview and a new lifestyle. But all the efforts of the vernacular rabbis notwithstanding, religious literature soon lost to its secular counterpart, which was thriving in the form of newspapers, novels, and plays.

## III

The title of the first Jewish periodical in Muslim lands—*Sha'arei mizrach* (*Gates of the East*)—symbolizes the new configuration of the Jewish world which, after the first close contacts between Ottoman and European Jews in connection with the Damascus and Rhodes blood libels of 1840,[27] was no longer divided into Sephardim and Ashkenazim. The Sephardi-Ashkenazi dichotomy was replaced with a new one: between East and West, that is, between the "*Orient*" and Europe. However, this development should not be interpreted as the end of Sephardi history,[28] but rather as the end of the European myth about Sephardi superiority and the beginning of a new phase in the history of Ottoman Jews. To be more precise, the image of Spanish Jews, the great scholars and rabbis of the mythical Sefarad,[29] was not damaged by the nineteenth-century reality, but which revealed to Ashkenazim that their eastern brethren had little to do with their legendary Iberian ancestors. Describing the dire situation of his coreligionists in Izmir in 1842, the editor of an Anglo-Jewish periodical notes with surprise, "The majority of the Jews are Sephardim, but they are much degenerated, possessing few of those traits of character that distinguish other members of their body" (*Voice of Jacob,* July 22, 1842, 175).

This realization brought into existence what Aron Rodrigue has called the "Jewish Eastern Question."[30] The "backward" and "degenerated" eastern Jews, kept in ignorance by their superstitious rabbis and not even having a language of their own, regularly appeared in the pages of all Jewish periodicals and were an object of harsh critique. Concerned about their own image, feeling responsible for their unfortunate non-European brethren, and believing in the magical power of emancipation, western Jews saw the cure in modern education, which they hastened to provide to the Jews in Islamic lands.

Ottoman Sephardim, grateful to their European coreligionists for their intervention in 1840, readily adopted this view, creating their own myth, described by Rodrigue as the myth of the "West,"[31] which became the key factor in their intellectual history through the early twentieth century. However, this myth, together with the European project of Jewish emancipation, was put to the test in the late 1890s by the Dreyfus Affair and the rising anti-Semitism in Hungary. And just like the myth of the *convivencia* in medieval Spain survived among European Ashkenazim, its modern counterpart, the unwavering faith in the possibility of integration into majority society, survived the trying reality of the 1890s in the minds of many Ottoman Sephardim. In other words, while European Jews hoped to re-create the lost paradise of religious harmony, Sephardi westernizers aspired to attain the golden age of Jewish existence allegedly already reached by their European coreligionists. Yet the 1880s–1890s witnessed the birth of a Jewish ideology that rejected the idea of *convivencia* in any form or place as unfeasible. The Zionist dream of a glorious future in a Jewish state was also embraced by some Sephardi intellectuals, but it should be emphasized that this ideology, like its universalist rival, became available to Ottoman Jews through the European-style schools and foreign press.

The most significant role, by far, in providing modern education to eastern Jews belonged to the schools established by the philanthropic organization Alliance Israélite Universelle (AIU),[32] founded in Paris in 1860 with the goal of supporting persecuted Jews throughout the world. By the early twentieth century, the Alliance had major influence on all Jewish educational institutions in the Ottoman Empire, including the most important talmudei torah, whose curricula now listed French and other secular subjects. By the eve of World War I, at the height of its influence, the organization had established 183 schools with 43,700 students of both sexes in "an area ranging from Morocco in the West to Iran in the East"; "each Turkish Jewish community had an Alliance school."[33]

The first book distributed among the students of the Alliance institutions, *Le Petit français,* begins: "France, our motherland, is a beautiful country." Later, the students were taught to revere this country as "the land of the Rights of Man, Hugo, Lamartine, the encyclopedists, and all the classics."[34] Nevertheless, since the intellectual roots of the Alliance's ideology lay in the *Haskalah* (the Jewish enlightenment), the organization's agenda by no means implied a rupture from the Jewish tradition but, on the contrary, attached great importance to teaching Judaism. The Alliance introduced the notion of the modern Sephardi Jew, who was expected to be an enlightened person with a thorough knowledge of Jewish history and tradition, a fluent speaker of French as well as Turkish, and a loyal Ottoman citizen. The curricula of the Alliance institutions were based "upon the one used in schools in metropolitan France, with the addition of instruction in local languages and in Jewish subjects such as Hebrew and Jewish history."[35] The language of instruction was French but, despite the fact that after a few years Ladino was officially banned, it continued to be used in the schools. Although the Alliance leaders realized that knowledge of Ottoman—the language of the bureaucracy, which was quite different from the quotidian Turkish—was indispensable for the Jews who wanted to become civil servants and make a career outside their community, it was never adequately taught. This was one of the reasons why only a few Sephardim achieved high positions in the state. At the same time, it was the graduates of the Alliance schools who produced the bulk of modern Ladino print culture. The impact of modern education on the development of the Ladino press is obvious: it began to flourish only in the late 1870s after a number of Alliance and other modern educational institutions had been founded and had prepared an audience eager to read newspapers and fiction.

The first steps of Sephardi Jews on the way toward westernization coincided with the beginning of the *Tanzimat* (Turk. "reorganization"; 1839–1876) and are best understood in its context. This was a series of reforms aimed at transforming an empire based on theocratic principles into a modern state.[36] The imperial Rescript of Gülhane, promulgated on November 3, 1839, guaranteed security of life, property, and honor to all Ottoman subjects, irrespective of religion. These westernizing measures were followed by the 1856 Decree of Reform and the Citizenship Law of 1869, which legally emancipated the non-Muslims. But the equality of all Ottoman subjects before the law was incompatible with *millet* (religious community) privileges, which is why the state called for a restructuring of the non-Muslim communities and implementation of "reforms required by the progress of civilization and the age."[37]

As a result of these measures, non-Muslims could no longer try civil, criminal, or commercial cases in their own courts. The reform legislation left to the millets jurisdiction only over family, inheritance, and divorce litigations, that is, matters concerning personal status. Consequently, they lost their juridical autonomy, and their religious leaders became paid state servants. "The new administrations were now explicitly hierarchical organizations with the laity having a major say in the running of communal affairs."[38] Thus the Jewish community, among others, moved toward secularization. This development had a major impact on the intellectual life of Ottoman Jews because, on one hand, the rabbis, whose power was now quite limited, felt the need to defend it by all available means, but, on the other, they could not effectively persecute their opponents without resorting to the state. Excommunication was becoming inefficient: instead of isolating the disobedient intellectuals, it made them even more famous among westernized Jews. Some of them played an important role in the creation of modern Ladino print culture.

## IV

Given the disagreement among scholars of Sephardi culture about some ba*sic* concepts, most importantly about the name and nature of the Sephardi vernacular, I will preface this examination of modern Ladino literature by defining a few terms used in this book and offering a brief overview of the language discussion relevant to my subject. For the purposes of this study,[39] I describe Ladino as an Ibero-Romance language used by Sephardi Jews in the Balkans and the eastern Mediterranean in the sixteenth century through the mid-twentieth. It is grammatically similar to fifteenth-century Castilian, while its vocabulary includes a significant number of words from other Romance languages, Hebrew, Turkish, and Balkan languages. For most of its history, Ladino was written in the variety of the Hebrew alphabet referred to as Rashi script.

It follows from this definition that in the debate about the time and place of Ladino's emergence I share the opinion held by, among other scholars, Moshe Lazar, according to whom "it was only after the Spanish Expulsion of 1492 that Ladino began to be a specifically Jewish language."[40] Indeed, the contention that it existed in the Iberian Peninsula before the expulsion as a Jewish language cannot be proven, because the evidence cited in support of this view is limited principally to the use of Hebrew terms referring to Jewish religious practices and to the avoidance of explicitly Christian terms.[41] However, many Hebrew loans were Hispanicized and often used by non-Jewish speakers, but later, with a few exceptions, dropped by Castilian. For instance, *malsin* (slanderer, informer) from the Hebrew malshin became part of Castilian as early as 1379 but was eventually dropped,[42] while *desmazalado* (ill-fated) from the Hebrew *mazal* is still used today, and *mazaloso* (lucky) also reappears from time to time. Hence, morphological adaptation of Hebrew words does not differ from the integration of all other loans and thus does not provide any ground for concluding that Spanish Jews had a language or dialect of their own.

My description of Ladino also indicates that I do not subscribe to what amounts to a quantitative approach to language development, as implied by Iacob M. Hassán's contention that Ladino became a separate language independent of Castilian only with the emergence of *Me'am Lo'ez*.[43] Romero, who supports this theory, describes the language used in the sixteenth century by Sephardi Jews of Salonica as "pre-Judeo-Spanish."[44] However, neither scholar defines the criteria on which these distinctions are based. No doubt, there is a significant difference between the texts produced in Ladino in different periods, which is true for all languages, but the use of multiple terms to refer to one language, depending on the period, only obfuscates matters.

From the moment a large group of Iberian exiles began to use their Romance vernacular in a different—not even adjacent—territory and in a different linguistic environment, it parted ways with Castilian in terms of further development. Therefore, it is legitimate to designate this language by a name of its own. The vernacular texts I have seen refer to it as romance, *ladino, espanyol (Levantino), judeo-espanyol*, and *jidyo* (and I have heard the term *espanyolit*). In this book, I will call it "Ladino"—the name preferred by most of its speakers after World War II—and its other names will appear only in direct quotations. Some scholars, among them David Bunis and Paloma Díaz-Mas, insist on calling the Sephardi vernacular *Judezmo* despite the fact that this word means "Judaism." For instance, Isaac Jerusalmi quotes one of Assa's poems, which uses the terms judezmo and ladino on the same page to refer to the religion and the language, respectively.[45] It is not only unnecessary to give yet another name to the Sephardi vernacular, but this name is not even linguistically justifiable.

Haim-Vidal Sephiha and his followers, in their turn, believe that the term "Ladino" is applicable only to the calque language of the translations of the religious Hebrew texts,[46] thus postulating the existence in the same speech community of two Romance languages or language varieties: one (Judezmo or Judeo-espanyol) for oral communication and the other (Ladino) for translations of sacred texts. But the fact that, due to the fundamental structural differences between Semitic and Romance languages, the Ladino translations were stiff and barely understandable even at the time of their first publication, does not provide grounds for differentiating between Ladino-vernacular and Ladino-calque. Jerusalmi rightly describes this artificial compartmentalization of Ladino as an "exercise in futility,"[47] simply because there are no criteria allowing one to make a distinction between the two varieties.

Hassán, on the basis of his analysis of Almosnino's *Crónica de los reyes otomanos,* suggests that it is more appropriate to speak of two literary styles rather than dialects.[48] I would add to this another argument. Since by the definition of Ladino-calque, no user could produce an utterance in it without having in front of him a text in another language (Hebrew), it cannot be considered a language or even a language variety but only a functional style (or register). It is noteworthy that both the vernacular rabbis and the editors of the first Ladino periodicals intuitively tried to reconcile the two registers in order to make their writings understandable to the least educated audiences and yet to go beyond the low style of quotidian communication.

From what has been said, it is evident that Ladino is a constant object of controversies, not because of its linguistic nature, which by itself would not generate such heated polemics, but for ideological reasons. These controversies are a continuation—at a new historical stage—of the passionate language polemic that started in the pages of the Sephardi press at the turn of the twentieth century.[49] For the participants in the debate, the question was whether Ladino could be considered a legitimate Romance language that, with some purification and refinement, should be used by Ottoman Jews, or whether it was a contemptible jargon to be supplanted by Turkish, Hebrew, or French, depending on the journalist's ideological affiliation. The reverberations of this discussion can still be heard in most descriptions of Ladino, even those produced by professional linguists, as they continue to operate within the parameters set by the Sephardi literati more than a hundred years ago.

With few exceptions, all discussions of Ladino in some form address the question of whether it is a language or a dialect, though none of the scholars has attempted to explain what is meant by these terms.[50] This is not surprising, since what is at stake here is not a linguistic term, but, presumably, a matter of national or cultural pride, especially in view of the fact that nowadays Yiddish is rarely described as a dialect of German. The use of the term Judezmo, intended to emphasize that Sephardim also speak a *Jewish* language, has the same unstated ideological motivation. When, as a consequence of the Holocaust, no monolingual speakers of Ladino were left, the language question lost its earlier relevance, but the subject has become more sensitive on the emotional level. For this reason, many authors once again have felt the need to legitimize and defend Ladino by claiming that "academicians . . . continue to be fascinated by the richness of Sephardi language"[51] and that it possesses a particular nobility.[52]

For a study of the modern forms of Ladino culture, the central issue is the evolution of the functions and status of Ladino in the earlier periods and their transformation in the nineteenth century. All I can say here with regard to its history is that, contrary to the common assumption, its functions and cultural prestige considerably changed in a nonlinear fashion, predicated on its interaction with other languages used by Ottoman Jews. The most significant sociolinguistic factor in the development of Sephardi print culture was diglossia. While it is almost impossible to find a study of Ottoman Jewry that does not mention diglossia, most scholars describe this community as polyglossic, emphasizing the fact that Sephardim spoke a few languages. Yet it is important to remember that diglossia presupposes not just the use of different linguistic codes for different social functions by the members of one speech community, but their use for *intrasocietal* (intracommunal) communication. Furthermore, according to Joshua Fishman's now classic definition, "bilingualism is essentially a characterization of individual linguistic behavior whereas diglossia is a characterization of linguistic organization at the sociocultural level," which means that diglossia and bilingualism may but do not have to co-occur.[53]

In addition, believe that the multilingualism of Sephardi Jews is generally overstated. To begin with, the linguistic situation, like many other circumstances, significantly differed from one Ottoman Jewish center to another and, of course, changed with time. Thus, speaking about the seventeenth and eighteenth centuries, Minna Rozen observes that in Salonica, where Jews formed the largest religious group, "a Jew could live his entire life without having to exchange more than a few sentences in a language other than Judeo-Spanish." But in Istanbul, where Jews formed a tiny minority and were "far more enmeshed with the ambient Muslim society than in any other place in the empire,"[54] they spoke more Turkish than anywhere else.

Needless to say, this was true mostly for men. Since women did not receive any formal education until the last third of the nineteenth century, few of them—and only those in well-off families—learned Hebrew. Besides, most Jewish women had limited contact with non-Jews, which left them monolingual.[55] Poor women from the working classes had to use co-territorial vernaculars for practical purposes, but this knowledge, certainly only oral, did not have to go beyond several phrases. As for men, a lot depended on their occupations, but, of course, in port cities Sephardim had more contacts with speakers of other languages than did those living inland. Port workers, merchants, and owners of coffeehouses had to speak the local languages, but often even rudimentary linguistic skills were sufficient, and this knowledge was always oral. In any event, the fact that Jewish men and some working-class women used local languages in their occupational activities, that is, for intergroup communication, had no impact on the linguistic situation within their own community.

Since, until the end of the nineteenth century, only Ladino and Hebrew were used by Ottoman Sephardim for internal communication, we are dealing with a classic case of diglossia: Hebrew was utilized for religious and other high-culture purposes, whereas the Jewish vernacular, Ladino, was the language of quotidian needs, spoken at home and at work. In written form, it was used in prayer books and for the education of the common people who were illiterate in Hebrew.[56] For about four hundred years, this relationship remained stable and nonconflictual due to the high status of Hebrew, a situation common to all Jewish communities around the world. Hebrew has always been the vehicle for canonized culture, regardless of whether it had a counter-register linguistically related to it or not.[57] In this connection, I would suggest that the word "jargon" was not necessarily used by Sephardim (or other Jews) in the pejorative sense, but often stood for a "non-Hebrew" language (la'az), including a Jewish vernacular. This is why even the most ardent proponents of Ladino, who aspired to confer to it high status, referred to it as "our jargon."

It is believed that knowledge of Hebrew in the Sephardi community was limited mainly to the intellectual elite. Though there are no statistics on

Hebrew literacy among Ottoman Jews, all indirect evidence indicates that the majority barely understood it. For this reason, prayer books had to be translated into Ladino even in the eighteenth century, long after the flow of *conversos* had stopped. The famous Istanbul publisher Jonah Ashkenazi, who printed Ladino prayer books, was concerned about his coreligionists not understanding their own prayers because "if one does not understand what one is asking for . . . what response is he going to get from Heaven?"[58] The low Hebrew literacy among Sephardi men is usually explained by the inadequate methods of teaching, poverty, lack of religiosity, and the fact that, unlike their counterparts in Eastern Europe, they spent only a short time, if any, at *yeshivas*.[59]

Indeed, Sephardi boys attended school (*meldar* or *talmud torah*) between the ages of seven and thirteen,[60] and not many of them continued education at yeshivas. In the nineteenth century, even the pro-western Ladino press often complained about the poor teaching of Hebrew in religious schools. For instance, the Istanbul periodical *El Jurnal israelit* published a letter signed by Barukh Mitrani, a well-known journalist and educator, who insisted that Hebrew should be taught in meldars by modern methods instead of having children repeat biblical verses "like squawking parrots" without any understanding of the words or grammar (January 24, 1868, 2). Most Alliance schools also taught Hebrew as a dead language, which prompted harsh critiques by the nationalist press.

Though the status of Hebrew was never challenged directly, starting in the second half of the nineteenth century, the process of secularization affected the prestige of the culture it represented, so that in the end its functions became limited to religious purposes, and it was essentially replaced by French as the language of high secular culture, the only culture in which the graduates of the Alliance schools in Salonica and within the borders of present-day Turkey could productively participate.[61] It is important to emphasize that the social status of French in the Sephardi community differed from its status in some European countries where, before World War I, it was used only by high society—into which one had to be born. The Alliance made schooling available even to the poor, thus encouraging the learning of French in all social groups.

By the early 1890s, young Sephardi intellectuals began to publish newspapers and write books in French. It is emblematic that the first Salonican journalist, rabbi Juda Nehama, who was fluent in French, communicated with his intellectual peers abroad in Hebrew, while his son, Joseph Nehama, who had a good knowledge of Hebrew, wrote to his Jewish friends in Europe in French and authored a few works, including a seven-volume history of Salonican Jewry, in this language. His colleagues Moïse Franco and Avram Galante also produced histories of Ottoman Jews in French. These works and, even more so, the Francophone periodicals, were intended for Sephardim fluent in French, which means that it became the language of intellectual exchange between members of the same speech community. In other words, by the end of the nineteenth century, French had assumed the function that earlier was assigned to Hebrew and that now could not be performed by any other language available to Ottoman Jews. Regardless of whether this new circumstance rendered the sociolinguistic situation polyglos*sic* (triglos*sic*), it was indicative of the impact of westernization and secularization on the Ottoman Sephardi culture.

In the nineteenth century, Sephardi literati contributed to the re-Romanization of Ladino by replacing syntactic Hebraisms with Gallicisms and by substituting Ladino words that contained Hebrew, Turkish, and Balkan elements with their Romance equivalents glossed in parentheses. *El Meseret,* a Ladino periodical directed by the prominent westernizer Alexandre Benghiat, recommends to those who want to improve their writing "not to use Turkish or Hebrew words and . . . little by little try to Gallicize [*frankear*] somewhat the basis [of Ladino]" (June 18, 1902, 4).[62] An example of how to do this is found, for instance, in Benghiat's own adaptation of Gulliver's Travels, published in the same periodical a year later. Benghiat introduces the Spanish verb *renunciar* (reject) to replace the Ladino *desvachar*—a fusion of the Spanish affixes *des-* and *-ar* and the Turkish root borrowed from *vazgeçmek.* But, since Ladino was always an object of ideological rather than philological debates, such substitutions were done ad hoc and, in the absence of any linguistic authority, no attempts were made to standardize the language. In any case, all efforts to save it were doomed.

The fact that the functions no longer performed by Hebrew were not taken up by Ladino demonstrates that, despite the increase in Ladino literary production, its prestige remained low and, unable to serve all purposes, it continued to be the language of mass culture. Thus it is incorrect to say that toward the end of the nineteenth century Ladino experienced a decline and that it was caused primarily by the "competition from internationally prestigious languages such as French and Italian, as well as from local languages such as Turkish, Greek, Bulgarian, and Serbo-Croatian."[63] Being a language of high culture, French did not have to compete with Ladino. As for Turkish and Greek, Sephardim were forced to learn and use them, which happened much later, in the twentieth century.

The death of Ladino has been explained by political developments, namely, the emergence of the nation-states replacing the Ottoman Empire, whose nationalist policies discouraged or even suppressed the use of minority languages, which soon lost their social prestige.[64] The Holocaust dealt it the last blow by eliminating more than a third of Ladino speakers and dislocating most of the rest. In 1999, the UNESCO Red Book Report on Endangered Languages classified Ladino as "seriously endangered," a language with between twenty and tens of thousands of speakers but without children among them.[65] Yet the death of Ladino also had a fundamental, intrinsic reason: it was never intended to be an all-purpose language, it failed to become the only language of Ottoman Sephardim and was eventually replaced by its fully functional competitors.

This kind of sociolinguistic development is not unique to minority languages in nation-states. The same UNESCO report defines Belarusian, one of the two official languages of Belarus, as a "potentially endangered" language which, albeit used by a large number of children, does not have a "prestigious status." According to a poll conducted in 1999, only 11.9 percent of Belarusians used this language, which had been losing to Russian, its more prestigious competitor. Nevertheless, 85.6 percent of the nation-state's population claimed Belarusian as their mother tongue.[66] This discrepancy demonstrates once again that poll respondents often identify a language as their own for ideological or political reasons. This is why the fact that, in 1927, 85 percent of the Jews in European Turkey declared Ladino to be their mother tongue[67] does not provide reliable information on how many Sephardim really used it at the time.

As even a cursory comparison with Belarusian shows, it is imperative to consider Ladino from a sociolinguistic perspective, not just as a Jewish language explicitly or implicitly Juxtaposed to Yiddish, but as a dying minority language that always existed in a diglossic relationship with at least one high prestige competitor: Hebrew, French, Turkish, or Greek. This study of modern Ladino culture will shed new light on its coexistence with Hebrew and French and will demonstrate that, roughly until World War I, Ladino did not experience any decline.

*Part 1*    The Press

# 〰〰〰 I

## The Emergence of Modern
## Cultural Production in Ladino:
## The Sephardi Press

The press was the earliest and the most influential form of modern Ladino print culture. Alongside European-style schools, it served as an essential medium for the westernization of Ottoman Jewry. Furthermore, it brought into existence Ladino belles lettres and played a crucial role in the development and conceptualization of Sephardi Theater. In addition, despite the poor condition of the extant Ladino periodicals, a thorough reading has allowed me to uncover a considerable amount of new information. For all these reasons, I will dedicate more space to the discussion of the Ladino press than to the other two genres.

In the late nineteenth century, the press had already begun to attract the interest of historians and bibliographers, and it continues to be the most discussed aspect of Sephardi intellectual life. The first among the numerous bibliographies of Ladino periodicals was Meyer Kayserling's *Biblioteca Española-Portuguesa-Judaica* (Strasbourg, 1890). But the most authoritative catalog to date is Moshe Gaon's *The Ladino Press* (1965), despite the fact that some new data became available after its completion.

A significant number of articles and dissertations on the Ladino press have appeared in recent years in Spain, France, Israel, and the United States, but only Elena Romero's *La Creación literaria en lengua sefardí* (1992) offers a systematic survey of the Ladino press, even though it is very brief and is organized in an encyclopedic form. Almost all other studies focus on one newspaper or one journalist.[1] This kind of work should certainly be continued, because such case studies, by filling at least some gaps, will eventually allow us to turn the collage we have been putting together into a more consistent, albeit always tentative, picture of the Ladino press.

Yet the amount of available information already allows us to move to the
next level of investigation and pose several vital questions that have not
been dealt with before, as well as rethink certain conventional assumptions.

The first of these assumptions that I will challenge is the implicitly accepted notion of the Sephardi press as a single entity that emerged in the
1840s in Izmir and reached its peak on the eve of World War I in Salonica.
Instead, I will suggest that the Ladino press had multiple beginnings and,
under different sociocultural and historical circumstances, it could have
evolved in various other directions (though, in any case, it would have
served as a vehicle of modern ideas). Undoubtedly, it is the influence of
Franco-Judaism spread by the Alliance schools that in the 1870s defined
the ideological emphasis and content of Ladino periodicals now taken to
be Sephardi journalism par excellence. Thus, instead of offering another
version of a single history of the Sephardi press, I will sketch a few discon-
tinuous histories of its beginnings.[2]

I will also deal with some questions, the answers to which are usually
taken for granted: Were Ladino periodicals indeed available to the Sephardi
masses? How many people did they really reach? What were the factors
affecting their availability? Were the literacy rates as high as some scholars believe? What was the role of the press control mechanisms and what
were the limits of the so-called rabbinic censorship in the era of secularization? Finally, I will continue the discussion of the Sephardi audience and
its reading practices begun by Matthias Lehmann with regard to the *musar*
literature.

Between 1845 and 1939, approximately three hundred Sephardi periodicals, many of them short-lived, appeared in the Ottoman Empire and
its former territories.[3] The majority came out in Salonica (105), Istanbul
(45), Sofia (30), and Izmir (23), most of them after 1908.[4] Another fifteen
Sephardi publications intended mainly for Ottoman Jews were published in
the Habsburg Empire, in Vienna and Zemun (Semlin). It must be emphasized that these statistics are approximate, and we will never have the exact
numbers. Yet scholars are, no doubt, aware of all long-lasting publications.

Most Sephardi newspapers appeared in Ladino, but approximately
twenty of them, including those published in Egypt, came out in French,
and a few were bilingual. The newspapers that combined Ladino with
one or more other languages either had particular ideological agendas or
were aimed at specific audiences, usually rather assimilated bilingual communities. For instance, the Ladino-Turkish *Jeride-i Lisan* (Journal of the
[Turkish] Language) encouraged Sephardim to learn Turkish, the Ladino-
Hebrew *El Jidyo* (The Jew) promoted Zionism, the Ladino-Bulgarian *La*

*Boz de Israel* (Voice of Israel) targeted Bulgarians, and the Ladino-Arabic *El Mitsraim* (The Egypt) addressed Egyptian Sephardim. In this book, I will examine only monolingual Ladino and French newspapers.

## The First Beginning of the Ladino Press

Scholars agree that the Ladino press emerged in the aftermath of the Damascus Affair, more precisely, the blood libels in Damascus and Rhodes in early 1840. In both places, Jews were accused of murdering Christians to use their blood for ritual purposes and were imprisoned and tortured. Having learned about this through Jewish leaders in Istanbul, French and British Jews, acting jointly, managed to save the prisoners, achieve their exoneration, and obtain a denial of the blood libel from the sultan.[5] These events demonstrated the importance of information for building international Jewish solidarity, which led to the unprecedented rise of the Jewish press in various parts of the world.[6]

Yet there is a more immediate connection than scholars used to assume between the two blood libels and the birth of the first Ladino periodical in 1845. While it cannot be established whether Sir Moses Montefiore, a key figure in resolving the Damascus crisis, and Rafael Uziel, the editor of the first Ladino periodical, met during the former's brief stay in Izmir in October 1840,[7] it is certain that the great English philanthropist was aware of the paper's emergence and closure. Moreover, he was among those who had welcomed Uziel's plan to establish a Ladino periodical in Izmir three and a half years earlier, in May 1842.

The first Ladino newspaper, *Sha'arei mizrach* (Gates of the East, 1845–1846), was published by Rafael Uziel, a merchant of Italian extraction and a resident of Izmir, in close association with Isaac Pincherle, an Italian merchant also residing in Izmir, and his brother David, a lawyer who spent most of his time in London and belonged to the same Sephardi congregation, Bevis Marks, as Moses Montefiore.[8] While there is some information on the Pincherle brothers, nearly nothing is known about Uziel,[9] and, until now, scholars were in disagreement even about the identity of the first Sephardi journalist. Were Rafael Uziel and Isaac Pincherle two different people or the same person?[10] An analysis of *Sha'arei mizrach* and the contemporaneous European Jewish press puts an end to this discussion.[11]

Rafael Uziel undoubtedly belonged to a Franco family. Francos were foreign merchants—mainly Italians, Jews among them—who lived in the Ottoman Empire but were protected by their respective governments.[12] In the nineteenth century, many Francos and their descendants, such as

Abraham de Camondo in Istanbul and Moïse Allatini in Salonica, played a crucial role in the development of Jewish education and the Jewish press. A note in *Les Archives Israélites* directly points to Uziel's Italian origins by referring to him as Raphael Uziello (312). Furthermore, the book stamp printed on number 16 of his periodical (which by that time had a second, Ladino title, *Las Puertas del Oryente*) says, "Le Porte dell'*Oryente* / Raffael Uziel."

Regardless of where he was born, Uziel's first language must have been Italian. Some of his readers complained that his Ladino was "incorrect," apparently referring to a great number of Italianisms in his articles (no. 1, 2; no. 4, 32). A thorough linguistic analysis of *Sha'arei mizrach* undertaken by David Bunis demonstrates a strong Italian influence at all levels, and even establishes certain features characteristic of the Venetian or Livornese dialects.[13] *Sha'arei mizrach* has other peculiarities pointing to its editor's European background. Thus, number 16 is dated 2 Heshvan 5607, but the masthead also indicates the Christian date, November 4, 1846, which means that Uziel converted the Hebrew date to the Gregorian calendar, which was not introduced in the Ottoman Empire until 1916.

Uziel's paper has another curious feature: proper names and such words as "sublime puerta" And "sultan" are often capitalized. The editor replaces the first Rashi letter of the word with a square one of a bigger size, like those used for the headings. He does not do this consistently from issue to issue, but when he does he follows the rules of most Romance languages. Though Uziel does not explain this odd practice, it was most likely an attempt at Europeanizing Ladino. We do not know where Rafael Uziel received his education, but it is obvious that he studied in Europe. He must have spent some time at the *talmud torah* in Livorno, as he knew it well enough to compare it with the one in Izmir (no. 6, 41).

The Pincherle brothers, members of a prominent Triestine family, came to Izmir in 1929. That year, Isaac established his company, I. Pincherle & Co. (*Der Orient*, August 8, 1840, 245), which played an important role in the 1840s in helping the city to recover after the Great Fire of July 1841. In fact, the only time Uziel mentions Isaac Pincherle is precisely in this connection. In issue number 5 of *Sha'arei mizrach*, he speaks of "the honorable Isaac Pincherle, a merchant established in Izmir, a man of much good, known for his kind deeds at the time of the fire" (33).

Isaac Pincherle was not only a respectable merchant but also an activist who was instrumental in helping the Jews of Rhodes from the very beginning of the blood libel crisis. Later, on May 29, 1840, he sent a letter to London aimed at attracting the attention of British officials to the conduct of the

English consul in Rhodes, who had initiated the libel, and urging them to discharge him.[14] During the investigation in the summer of 1840, he brought four members of the Rhodes community to Istanbul and helped them to produce and publicize an account of the tragic events (*Der Orient*, August 8, 1840, 245–248).

David Pincherle, Esq., as he was referred to in the Anglo-Jewish press, was both a merchant and a lawyer. Sometime before 1846, he co-founded Peter Miller & David Pincherle in Izmir. It was described as a joint stock company which had close relations with Venetian merchants but whose activities were directed toward the German market.[15] Judging by the notes in the *Jewish Chronicle*, the *Voice of Jacob*, and the latter's list of subscribers, sometime between 1843 and 1846 David Pincherle moved to London, where he opened an office right outside the city. According to the two periodicals, he contributed to many of Montefiore's charities and enthusiastically supported the idea of raising funds to pay for a portrait of the great philanthropist[16] (*Jewish Chronicle*, January 2, 1846, 55).

Settled in London, David Pincherle frequently traveled to Izmir. One of his missions on these trips was to deliver English periodicals and bring back the news of Ottoman Sephardim, which would later appear in the two Anglo-Jewish papers. It was David Pincherle who informed British Jews about the establishment and closure of Uziel's periodical and who often summarized its articles. Moreover, in February–March 1846, he published at least three advertisements in the *Jewish Chronicle* urging the public to subscribe to *Gates of the East*.

It is impossible to tell how the Pincherle brothers met Uziel but, given the small size of the local Jewish community and the occupation of the three Italians, this must have happened rather quickly. We do not know what brought Isaac and David Pincherle there, but Izmir, a port city on the western Anatolian coast of the Aegean Sea, began to attract European merchants in the seventeenth century, when the Francos' quarter was first established. From the beginning, the Ottomans' influence in Izmir was rather weak, and to a large degree the city was created by Europeans. Turkish was only one of the many languages spoken there, and all travel accounts and nineteenth-century European press reports state that most inhabitants spoke some form of French or English, which they learned from foreign sailors. The Levantine culture that developed in Izmir during the eighteenth and nineteenth centuries was culturally and ethnically Western European, Italian, Armenian, and Greek.

According to the Ottoman Census of 1831, there were 3,530 Jewish males in Izmir,[17] which means that the indigenous Jewish population numbered around 7,000. However, as is well known, foreign Jews residing in Ottoman cities preferred not to join the local communities so as to avoid paying communal taxes and, therefore, usually they were not counted. Yet Izmir and other port cities had significant numbers of European Jews who actively participated in the community's life. In 1841, the *Voice of Jacob* called the German-Jewish periodical Die Israelitische Annalen's estimate of Izmir's Jewish population at 10,000 "an understatement" (October 29, 21). On the basis of these estimates and some other data, it is safe to assume that in the early 1840s, Izmir's Jewish community numbered between 10,000 and 12,000, including the foreigners.

Before the Great Fire of July 29, 1841, which affected mainly the Turkish and Jewish quarters, the latter had nine synagogues, a hospital, a library, and a *talmud torah*.[18] The local French-language newspaper, *L'Écho de l'Orient* (July 31, August 7 and 14),[19] states that the fire reduced to ashes 500 large Jewish houses that used to be home to 1,500 families, the Jewish hospital, the library, and seven synagogues. As a result, 2,000 Jews had to be housed in the military barracks, lazarettos, and municipal buildings, while around 4,000 continued to be homeless; some 7,000 rations of bread were distributed daily among the starving victims. According to Uziel, 90 percent of Jewish houses were burned down (*Sha'arei mizrach*, no. 12, 89).

From the moment it was formed until at least 1844, Isaac Pincherle was on the committee for support of the fire victims, which regularly published its subscription lists in *L'Écho de l'Orient*. These lists show that Montefiore, Rothschild & Sons in London, I. Camondo & Co. in Istanbul, Aron Isaac Pariente and M. M. Morpurgo & Leon Tedeschi in Trieste, and many other merchants donated large sums to the victims, regardless of their religion, which were transferred to Izmir through I. Pincherle & Co. Many other European Jews sent money to the committee through other local companies. A few months after the fire, *L'Écho de l'Orient* published a letter signed by twelve local Jews expressing their profound gratitude to Montefiore and the Rothschilds for their great support of the victims (November 5, 1841). (Curiously, Uziel was not among them.)

Undoubtedly, the prompt and generous aid provided by European Jews to the victims of the Great Fire earned them the high respect not only of their coreligionists but also of the local authorities. According to David Pincherle's account in the *Voice of Jacob* (July 22, 1842, 175), the position of Izmir's Jews "in the estimation of the people at large has to some extent been benefited by the visit of Sir Moses Montefiore" (in the fall of 1840). However, it is evident that this was achieved not only thanks to his brief visit but perhaps more so by his generous donations to the city rather than only to his coreligionists. Thus, while the local Jews had been greatly impoverished by the fire, the influence of their European brethren had grown much stronger.

Such were the socioeconomic circumstances of Izmir's Jewish community in 1842, when Rafael Uziel undertook an audacious attempt to create the first Jewish periodical in the Ottoman Empire. However, *La Buena esperansa* (Good Hope) did not go beyond the prospectus that came out on May 22, 1842, despite immediately attracting great interest of the Jewish press in Europe. But the earliest reference to *La Buena esperansa* appeared in *L'Écho de l'Orient*. On June 9, without mentioning the publisher's name, it announced the forthcoming Hebrew periodical *La Bonne Espérance,* which was going to inform Ottoman Jews about international events. The editor wished the new publication luck and expressed the hope that it would be supported by Jews all over the world (a notion recently learned by Izmir's public).

A few weeks later, on July 8, the *Voice of Jacob* informed its readers of Uziel's prospectus, of which the editor had learned "by the politeness of Sir Moses Montefiore" (166). Expressing the post-1840 Anglo-Jewish ideology, the author anticipated that "*La Buena Speranza*" would become an "organ of mutual information among our brethren in the east" and an "important link to the great chain of communication which we hope soon to see established between Jews all over the world."

On July 23, the two Jewish periodicals published in Leipzig, *Der Orient* and *Die Allgemeine Zeitung des Judentums* (AZJ), also welcomed the first Ladino periodical. The most valuable evidence on the prospectus comes from a resident of Hamburg, who received it from "Dr. Loewe in London," that is, from Montefiore's secretary, Louis Loewe, and sent an account to Ludwig Philippson's *AZJ*. The author reports that, according to the prospectus, the forthcoming Judeo-Spanish weekly would contain "commercial news, exchange rates, port traffic updates, and advertisements of auctions and sales, as well as political news from all parts of the world, and finally, articles that aim at spreading light and knowledge among the Jews of the Turkish Empire" (39–40).

Fortunately for us, instead of simply quoting the prospectus in German translation, Philippson's correspondent accompanied the rendering of two Ladino sentences with direct quotations printed in Hebrew characters (see fig. 1.1). However, since the German printer did not know Ladino or even the Rashi script, the quotes were printed in square letters with many errors caused by his inability to identify some characters. Here are my translations of an approximate reconstruction of those two quotes, all that is left of Uziel's prospectus:

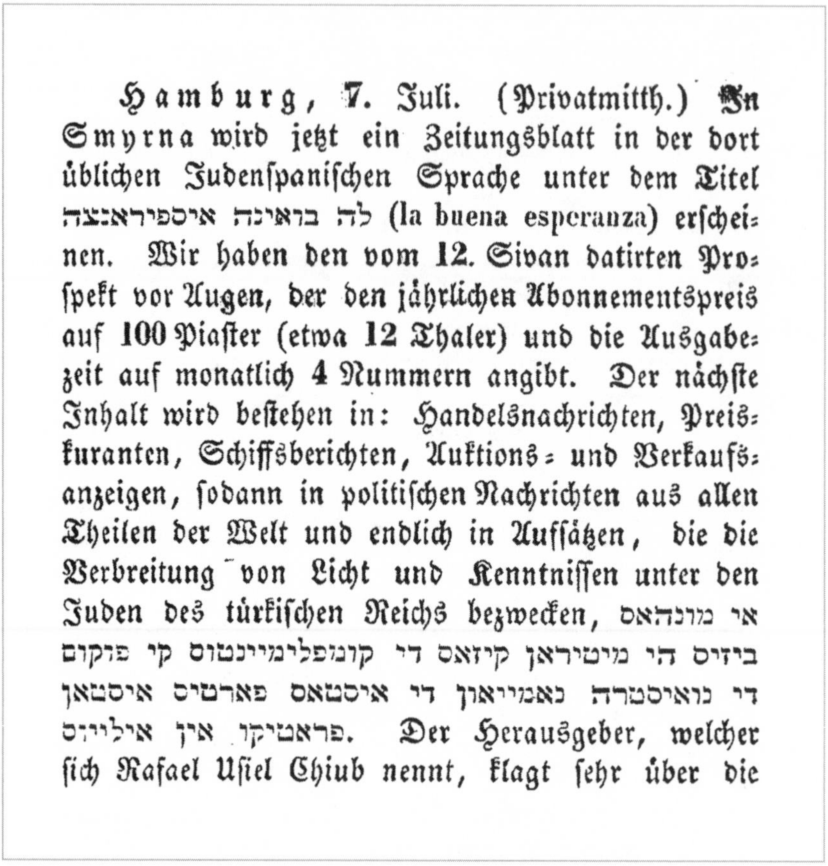

Hamburg, 7. Juli. (Privatmitth.) In Smyrna wird jetzt ein Zeitungsblatt in der dort üblichen Judenspanischen Sprache unter dem Titel לה בואינה איספיראנצה‎ (la buena esperanza) erschei= nen. Wir haben den vom 12. Sivan datirten Pro= spekt vor Augen, der den jährlichen Abonnementspreis auf 100 Piaster (etwa 12 Thaler) und die Ausgabe= zeit auf monatlich 4 Nummern angibt. Der nächste Inhalt wird bestehen in: Handelsnachrichten, Preis= kuranten, Schiffsberichten, Auktions = und Verkaufs= anzeigen, sodann in politischen Nachrichten aus allen Theilen der Welt und endlich in Aufsätzen, die die Verbreitung von Licht und Kenntnissen unter den Juden des türkischen Reichs bezwecken, אי מונהאס‎ ביזיס הי מיטיראן קיזאס די קונפלימיינטוס קי פוקום די נואיסטרה נאמייאון די איסטאס פארטיס איסטאן פראטיקו אין אילייוס‎. Der Herausgeber, welcher sich Rafael Usiel Chiub nennt, klagt sehr über die

Figure 1.1. From the prospectus of *La Buena esperansa* in *Die Allgemeine Zeitung des Judentums* (July 23, 1842).

And we will often publish additional things with which few people of our nation in these parts are familiar.

But the wise men in our parts of Turkey do not waste or employ their time on such things, nor do they study, and this is so because of the great poverty and a great lack of money in these parts.[20]

According to the *AZJ*, the prospectus said that it is ignorance that causes "general poverty and the contempt of the neighbors and makes it almost impossible for those who lost their property due to the current instability to recover" (40).

The penultimate sentence of the piece seems to have little to do with reality, but rather expresses Philippson's loathing of all rabbis as enemies of progress, formulated in his characteristic style. The article suggests that the new periodical will need a lot of strength "to resist those rabbis who, as far as we can judge, will not stop short of using their weapon: unlimited and feared *herem* [excommunication]." The available data, however, make it clear that it was not the alleged rabbinic persecution that caused the failure of Uziel's project. The article ends with a questionable quote from Montefiore's secretary, who presumably ascribed Uziel's intention to establish a newspaper to his acquaintance with Philippson's periodical, which is presented as an inspiration for all ignorant Jews of the East.

The July 23 issue of *Der Orient* opened with news borrowed from *L'Écho de l'Orient* about the emergence of *Die gute Hoffnung* (233). A week later, the paper announced that the new journal would come out in "corrupted Judeo-Spanish printed in Hebrew characters" (July 30, 241). This information was borrowed by *Les Archives Israélites*, appearing in its August issue (476), which was the last mention of *La Buena esperansa* in the press.

It must have been the word "continue" in the editorial of the first issue of *Sha'arei mizrach* that led some scholars to believe that *La Buena esperansa* did come out for a short time.[21] Uziel makes it clear that his first attempt at publishing a Ladino newspaper failed for financial reasons:

> On 13 Sivan 5602 [May 22, 1842], I published an announcement of a newspaper in the Spanish language entitled *La Buena esperansa*. The reason I could not continue the publication at that time was the terrible costs. And the subscriptions that I had the honor of receiving were so few that they would have covered less than half of the costs. (1)

An annual subscription to *La Buena esperansa* cost a hundred piastres, approximately two and a half times more than the European Jewish periodicals and more than *L'Écho de l'Orient*, also a weekly.[22] It is possible that Uziel would have had to pay a lot more for printing than his French colleague did.

The prospectus and *Sha'arei mizrach* were printed at a missionary press run by the Englishman G. Griffith,[23] who had the Rashi font because the missionaries published Ladino translations of the scriptures. This seems to have been Uziel's only option, at least in 1845–1846. Between 1841 and 1844, there was just one Jewish press in Izmir, which printed Hebrew books and thus may not have had a Rashi font. The next Jewish press was established in Izmir in 1852.[24] This is why Uziel resorted to a Christian printer—not in order to circumvent the hypothetical opposition of the rabbinic establishment, as suggested by Bunis.[25] There is no reason to believe that Uziel was ever persecuted by the rabbis. The chief rabbi of Izmir, Pinchas de Segura, was an educated man who, during Montefiore's visit in 1840, gave a strongly pro-western sermon glorifying him and other European Jews for rescuing their

Ottoman coreligionists.[26] A few months earlier, de Segura had published a letter in *L'Écho de l'Orient* calling for mutual understanding between Jews and Christians, who share the "Old Testament."[27]

It is evident that in the aftermath of the Great Fire, an expensive Ladino periodical which, according to all available secondary sources, was not going to have a specifically Jewish content had no chances of surviving in Izmir. If it was indeed going to contain only political and business news, it could not attract the well-off Sephardi merchants who read *L'Écho de l'Orient*, which often informed its readers of Jewish news. In fact, in 1840, its reports on the local community were frequently quoted in the German-Jewish press and thus are available today even though the paper itself is not.[28] Hence, those Jewish businessmen who knew French would have preferred to stay with the less expensive newspaper. The majority of Izmir's Jews, however, were extremely poor and thus unable to afford a subscription.[29] Besides, the literacy rate among Sephardim was quite low at the time. The failure of Uziel's first publishing enterprise made it clear that, in order to succeed, a Ladino periodical had to be affordable to many members of the community and had to publish materials on Jews and Judaism unavailable to them otherwise.

The first issue of the first Ladino periodical, *Sha'arei mizrach/Las Puertas del Oryente*, appeared on December 29, 1845. Though the establishment of censorship was still far away, Uziel announced that he would publish all materials sent to him in various languages if they did not offend the government or the religion (1). A few months later, readers were informed that the periodical had been officially licensed (no. 9, 65).

Each issue of *Sha'arei mizrach*, which was a bimonthly,[30] had eight pages that were divided into two parts. Initially, the first part would often start with a discussion of a biblical verse, which served as an editorial containing a moral lesson. It was followed by detailed accounts of Ottoman news (most likely translated from Francophone periodicals)[31] and a rather long article on natural history or sciences, usually based on the teachings of Aristotle and Ptolemy (or attributed to them).[32] Finally came international and local Jewish news, mainly borrowed from European periodicals and the local French press, respectively. At the end of the first part, there would often be a crime story, sometimes continued to the next issue, that was obviously meant to entertain readers. The second part of the periodical had commercial information, which included wholesale prices, exchange rates, and port traffic updates. It is notable that, despite the editor's efforts to encourage private advertisements, there are none in the newspaper.

As *Sha'arei mizrach* was a semi-religious publication largely inspired by the *Haskalah* (Jewish enlightenment), its pages were permeated with religious

Figure 1.2. *Sha'arei mizrach*, no. 12 (July 29, 1846). Ben Zvi Institute Library

references. Thus, on the masthead of numbers 1–13, the newspaper's title is followed by the biblical verse that serves as its motto: "For from the rising of the sun to its setting my name is great among the nations, and in every place incense is offered to my name, and a pure offering; for my name is great among the nations, says the Lord of hosts" (Mal. 1:11). This verse may be understood to mean that Jews can serve their God even in diaspora. To make sure his readers would interpret it in this sense, Uziel accompanied the Hebrew verse with its Aramaic translation from Targum Jonathan, which clearly states that the devotions of diaspora Jews are not inferior to the offerings made in Jerusalem,[33] that is, their good deeds are no less valuable.

Starting from number 14, the Ladino title—*Las Puertas del Oryente*—was added to the masthead and the first motto was replaced with a new one: "Your gates shall always be open; day and night they shall not be shut, so that nations shall bring you their wealth, with their kings led in procession" (Isa. 60:11). Here, the biblical writer suggests that the "nations" can also contribute to the rebuilding of the Temple.[34] These two mottos clearly affirm the periodical's universalist perspective and its publisher's faith in the important role of the Jews of the diaspora.[35]

The abundant use of biblical references and the function assigned to them in *Sha'arei mizrach* are consistent with Uziel's goal to transform Ottoman Sephardim into modern Jews not only by enlightening them on secular matters but also by providing them with religious education in the new spirit. This is not surprising, given that Montefiore's endeavor to build up modern Jewish philanthropy, to which the emergence of *Sha'arei mizrach* was directly related, had a marked religious dimension. The new "Jewish International," as Abigail Green called it,[36] required a network of Jewish newspapers in which, according to the *Voice of Jacob,* the first Sephardi periodical was going to be an "important link."

Obviously, the first Ladino periodical was meant only for a male audience, more precisely, for somewhat educated men able to read Hebrew. It contained rather long biblical passages and many Hebrew words in almost all of its articles, in some of which the proportion of Ladino and Hebrew was equal. For instance, the editorial in number 12, which is constructed around a comparison of the destruction of the Jerusalem Temple and the Great Fire in Izmir, is fifty-four lines long. It not only contains fourteen Hebrew phrases of three words or more but is full of Ladino renderings of scriptural passages, which the readers were expected to recognize.[37]

It is unlikely that men who had studied only at a *talmud torah* or a *meldar,* where the Torah was memorized and "much of the teaching and learning was done orally,"[38] would have been able to understand biblical passages taken out of context. For this reason, Uziel tried to make some of the material in his newspaper accessible to those who were illiterate in Hebrew or even Ladino. In his articles on natural history, for example, he employed few Hebrew words, always glossed in Ladino, and designed those texts to be read out loud.

Uziel's method of teaching Judaism differed from that of the vernacular rabbis, who focused on the proper Jewish lifestyle that presupposed Torah study in some form as well as certain social practices. Uziel, by contrast, emphasized the importance of faith and of text interpretation, the latter requiring the knowledge of Hebrew. *Sha'arei mizrach* persistently urged its readers to educate themselves in the sciences and to teach their sons more things than their fathers had taught them, because the world had changed since those times. In the spirit of the Italian Jewish emancipation, Uziel indefatigably promoted the "balance between an absolute faith in man's rational faculties and an equal trust in religion and faith in God."[39] He insisted that his "brothers" should have their sons learn not only the law of Moses but also the sciences and foreign languages, which would awaken them and make it possible for Sephardim to follow the way of other nations (no. 3, 17; no. 4, 25). Finally, the first Sephardi journalist was convinced that the press would allow Ottoman Jews to "become as knowledgeable in all sciences as the most civilized nations of Europe" (no. 9, 66 ).

I believe that the last extant issue of *Sha'arei mizrach*, dated November 4, 1846, was indeed the last one published, because on March 19, 1847, the *Jewish Chronicle* noted: "December 1st. Discontinuance of the 'Gates of the East.' Raphael Uzziel [*sic*] has, it appears, been obliged to give up publishing his Judeo-Spanish newspaper through want of support" (100).[40] In number 15, dated September 22, Uziel had warned his readers that, unless they continued to subscribe to it, the periodical would no longer come out (113). Evidently, he expected to receive more subscriptions by the beginning of the new Jewish year, but did not get enough. Number 16 appeared six weeks after number 15, whereas previously, with one exception, *Sha'arei mizrach* was indeed a bimonthly.

According to the editor, the journal's circulation was "below 100 copies" (no. 2, 16), yet it had distributors in Istanbul, Bucharest, Beirut, Salonica, Edirne (Adrianople), and a few other cities, though it is unlikely that many subscriptions were sold in those cities. It is noteworthy that Uziel's representative in the capital was the Italo-Jewish company Frases & Figli Kanuna, which had business or other relations with Isaac Pincherle and communicated with him in May–June 1840 regarding the blood libel in Rhodes.[41] This offers a window onto what the Pincherle brothers' role might have been in the production of the first Ladino periodical, aside from advertising it in London and delivering papers and Jewish news (especially on Montefiore's activities) to Izmir. It is also noteworthy that Uziel often published articles from the *Voice of Jacob* and *Les Archives Israélites*, whose lists indicate that in Izmir only David Pincherle subscribed to the former and only Isaac Pincherle to the latter. Among Uziel's sources were not only these two newspapers but also the *Jewish Chronicle* and *Chambers's Edinburgh Journal* (one of the most popular British periodicals in the 1840s).

It is impossible to tell whether Uziel knew English or whether Isaac or David Pincherle translated English articles for him into Italian, their common language, but it seems that they were at least partly responsible for the selection of the articles for publication. For instance, Uziel published a long excerpt from the *Voice of Jacob* that was taken from the testament of the deceased Isaac Cohen, Lady Montefiore's brother, who left some money to "the Portuguese congregation Bevis Marks" and a few charitable institutions (no. 9, 68). This choice of material for translation appears odd, especially since the editor does not explain who Isaac Cohen was or where Bevis Marks is located.

The confusion of Rafael Uziel and Isaac Pincherle by historians is explained by the fact that the early scholars of the Sephardi press did not have an opportunity to see *Sha'arei mizrach*, which was purchased in Palestine by Aaron Mallah, a well-known Salonican Zionist and a co-founder of *El Avenir,* and given to the Jewish National Library in Jerusalem sometime in the late 1920s.[42] Otherwise, they would have seen the name "Rafael Uziel" in every issue of his newspaper. Those scholars who have relied mainly on the Anglo-Jewish press were misled by it, since Uziel, unlike Pincherle, was barely mentioned there. The Pincherle brothers undoubtedly had a tendency to exaggerate their own importance in the community, for instance, by suggesting that, being "the only [sic] European Jews," they had "some weight" (*Voice of Jacob*, July 22, 1842, 175).

It is evident that Uziel produced his newspaper in collaboration with Isaac and David Pincherle and that, aside from specific information and personal contacts, Isaac Pincherle had a lot to offer, intellectually. Uziel's attempt at creating the first Sephardi periodical as a means of fighting ignorance and propagating modern ideas—like Crémieux's efforts to establish the first European-style schools in the Middle East in 1840[43]—was part of the larger European project of "regenerating" eastern Jews, which was brought to life by the Damascus Affair. In the eyes of western Jews, the emergence of the first Ladino newspaper was such an important event that almost all Jewish periodicals in Europe and even the *Occident* in the United States quoted, cited, discussed, or at least mentioned the prospective *La Buena esperansa* or *Sha'arei mizrach.*

Both Crémieux's and Uziel's endeavors were unsuccessful because they did not receive sufficient (if any) support from the indigenous Jews. There is, indeed, no evidence showing that in the 1840s–1860s, Izmir's Jewish community felt the need to have a newspaper of its own. the next Ladino periodical in this city, *La Buena esperansa* (1874–1917?), appeared twenty-eight years later and in its early stages encountered significant opposition.[44] Its editor, Aron de Yosef Hazan, was not aware of Uziel's attempt to publish a newspaper with the same title,[45] and even though he might have known about *Sha'arei mizrach*, there was no continuity between the two journals. Thus, the first Ladino newspaper was an isolated enterprise forgotten by or unknown to most later Sephardi journalists. In fact, the production of *Sha'arei mizrach* was much more an episode in the history of the European Jews than of Ottoman Sephardim. Finally, it is incorrect to say either that Rafael Uziel's cause was taken up by the literati of other Ottoman cities[46] or that Izmir was the cradle of the Ladino press.[47] The second and third Ladino newspapers were established in Istanbul and the fourth one in Salonica, and none of them had the educational agenda or the religious emphasis of *Sha'arei mizrach*.

## Other Beginnings

### Or Israel

The second Ladino periodical—*Or Israel* (Light to Israel)—was published in Istanbul in 1853–1855, but only two of its issues have survived. The Parisian *L'Univers Israélite* indicates that *Or Israel* first appeared in the fall of 1853 and was discontinued in August 1855.[48] But *L'Univers's* correspondent obviously did not see any issues of *Or Israel*, whose masthead always indicated the number and date.

The first extant issue is number 36, but only the first letter of the Hebrew date can be seen. All we have is "*shin* . . . Heshvan 5614," November . . . 1853. We also know that it was a Thursday. By correlating the dates of the events reported in this issue with the date of the second extant one (April 27, 1854) and analyzing the newspaper's schedule, I was able to establish the missing date (November 22) and the approximate time of *Or Israel's* first appearance. Its first issue came out sometime in late January 1853. As for the paper's last issue, such dates can rarely be established with certainty, because many Ladino periodicals (like *Sha'arei mizrach*) reappeared after a break. In any case, the second Ladino newspaper appeared for at least two and a half years, which is a long period even compared to some European Jewish journals of the time.

*Or Israel's* publisher, Leon Hayim de Castro, belonged to an influential Jewish family of Istanbul, whose other branches lived in Europe.[49] *Or Israel's* editor refers to himself and his readers as Francos: "Franco [European] Jews that we are" (no. 57, 3). However, as his writings demonstrate, Leon de Castro, regardless of what his citizenship might have been, was an Ottoman patriot. When he talks about the Crimean War, which is the main subject of the extant issues, he constantly praises the Turkish soldiers for being generous, honest, and good-natured people who immediately forget the harm done to them. De Castro indignantly condemns both Greece and Russia and enthusiastically commends France and Britain, especially after they enter the war (March 28, 1854). It is clear from de Castro's accounts that he had good connections and reliable sources and regularly read the French press. Judging by his quotes from Ottoman sources and the large number of Turkish terms he uses (mostly military ones), it seems likely that he knew Ottoman.

Though the paper defined itself as *Gazeta de Kushtandina* (Constantinople), it aspired to reach other parts of the empire and, like *Sha'arei mizrach*, had distributors in other cities. One of them, Aron Asher, used to represent the first Ladino periodical in Bucharest, while the distributor in Izmir, Avram Ganon, must have been related to Nathan Ganon, one of the twelve Jews who thanked the Rothschilds and Montefiore in the letter published in *L'Écho de l'Orient*. However, *Or Israel*'s language would have been hard to understand for readers in some places, such as Belgrade or Jerusalem, since de Castro never glossed any Turkish words. In fact, he explains the Italian *vitoriozo* by the Ottoman *gazi* (but then translates vitoria by the Ladino *ganansya*).

Language was only one of the factors limiting de Castro's audience. The second Ladino periodical was undoubtedly created only for educated male readers. Though, being a purely secular journal, it used little Hebrew, the editor expected his readers to understand a rather long Hebrew text unrelated to the Bible. Furthermore, *Or Israel* was published for those men who would be interested in detailed descriptions of every battle as well as in diplomatic communications between Russia, England, France, and the Ottoman Empire. The journal mentions dozens of foreign politicians, places, warships, and newspapers with very few explanations. (Curiously, quoting European diplomats, de Castro refers to the Ottoman Empire as "the *sick* man.") Finally, judging by the editor's concise instructions on earning interest from the bonds available as a result of the Rothschilds' loan to the Ottoman Empire, the paper was meant for well-off readers familiar with banking.

Since all we have is a few pages from two issues of *Or Israel*, it is impossible to tell what kind of information it published before the war, but those two issues look like war bulletins rather than a regular newspaper. Addressing his "esteemed subscribers" after the Passover break, de Castro assures them that the current issue will update them on every event that took place in the previous three weeks (no. 57, 1).

As for its Jewish component, the second Ladino journal also had a Hebrew title, but its meaning was transparent. Other than that, the extant issues contain only three Hebrew words: the editor refers to the Paris Consistory as *kolel de Pariz,* condemns the Russian government for making its impoverished population ask for *tzedaka* (charity), and uses *hayom* (today) to mark the news of the day. The only other Jewish element, though an important one, found in *Or Israel* is the information about the petition sent by the Central Consistory of France to Napoleon III on March 24, 1854 (no. 57, 3). But, instead of translating the petition into Ladino, de Castro published its Hebrew version (not extant), which he probably borrowed from another publication. Finally, the last page of the second issue (the only extant last page) concludes with two Hebrew lines serving as the editor's signature: "Constantinople. Today, 29 *Rosh Hodesh* Nisan of the current year, I who am writing this, Leon de Castro, may God watch over me and keep me alive."

At first glance, in terms of content and message, the two earliest Sephardi newspapers seem to have been produced in two different historical epochs, as if between 1846 and 1853 the Ottoman Jewish community had undergone tremendous social transformations and made great steps toward secularization. In reality, this profound disparity is accounted for by the papers' drastically different purposes and different target audiences. Among other things, in the capital, the Jews were more interested in Ottoman news than were the readers in the Europe-oriented Izmir. But, more important, Uziel's goal was to transform his coreligionists by means of the knowledge he deemed appropriate, while all de Castro aspired to achieve was to keep his readers up to date on politics and the current war. In this sense, *Or Israel* was closer to the non-Jewish European press, which undoubtedly served as its model.

## El Jurnal israelit

The third Ladino periodical, *El Jurnal israelit* (Istanbul, 1860–1873), first appeared, according to its masthead, on December 27 *ala franka,* December 15 *ala grega,* 1860: Tania 13, 1277: 14 Tevet 5621. This representation of the date immediately informed readers of the newspaper's multiple loyalties: while being a Jewish periodical, it demonstrated its allegiance to the Ottoman state as well as its connection to the European culture in general (hence, both Christian calendars are used). Later, many Ladino newspapers would adopt this format, at least partially. *El Jurnal* was the first long-lived Ladino periodical, the first one (as far as we know) to be banned by the rabbis, to have a supplement, and to coexist with another Ladino journal in a different city.

At various times, *El Jurnal* was a weekly and a triweekly, but it always came out on Thursdays to provide Sephardim with reading material for the Sabbath. At all times, it had four pages, and its subscription cost a hundred piastres. In many ways, *El Jurnal israelit* set the pattern for most Ladino newspapers that appeared after it. Yet it was unique in a few important aspects.

First, unlike all other Sephardi periodicals before 1908,[50] *El Jurnal* was not run by a private publisher but was the organ of a legal body, namely, the Mejlis Pekidim, the lay council of notables in charge of communal affairs.[51] This council was established by the liberal chief rabbi, Jacob Avigdor, in 1860 with the goal of reforming the community administration and enforcing the collection of taxes. It consisted of the leading figures of the Istanbul community, mainly Francos, and was headed by Abraham de Camondo, "the most important and well-placed Jew in the Levant in the mid-nineteenth century,"[52] a great supporter of westernization and of European-style schools in particular. When the council decided to publish its own periodical that would propagate its ideas and announce its reforms, it was decided to appoint as editor its secretary, Yehezkel Gabay (1825–1898).

Gabay was a grandson of his namesake, Baghdadli Yehezkel Gabay, who had served as banker to Mahmud II and was involved in the financial affairs of the Janissary corps.[53] The grandson, who, aside from Hebrew, French, and Italian, knew Ottoman and possibly Arabic, was an expert in Islamic law, which won him the respect of many Ottoman officials. In 1869, while being *El Jurnal*'s editor, Gabay served at the Ministry of Public Instruction and subsequently became president of the supreme criminal court.[54] Thus, the third Ladino newspaper was created and supported by members of the Sephardi pro-western intellectual elite, and a clear vision of its purpose was formulated in the editorial of its first issue. Gabay thanks the Mejlis Pekidim for creating the journal, "much needed and required by the people and, even more so, by the government, whose goal is to do everything possible in order for its people not to lack any knowledge." He promises that *El Jurnal israelit* will disseminate knowledge and promote progress among Jews.

Second, this newspaper was in a privileged position in terms of funding, because the council, no doubt, provided it with some resources. In addition, it is quite possible that Camondo, who from 1858 onward was the only financial supporter of Albert Cohen's school in Istanbul,[55] would have partly subsidized the periodical as well. Hence, unlike most of his colleagues, Gabay did not have to worry about getting enough funds for the next issue, but to some extent, he, too, depended on subscriptions. He informed his readers of this in the very first issue, urging them to welcome his newspaper by subscribing to it.

He was the first journalist to print books at his press and sell them to the public which, also for the first time, included women. Thus, aside from his own works and translations, Gabay sold a multivolume Ladino adaptation of *The Thousand and One Nights,* which he recommended to his readers of both sexes (*sinyores i sinyoras*). Later, *El Jurnal* began to publish commercial advertisements at a rather high rate.

For some time, the newspaper had a bimonthly supplement, *El Trezoro* (The Treasure), which, according to the advertisement in the first Ladino periodical in Salonica, *El Lunar* (Moonlight, 1864–1865), focused on politics (no. 2, 1).[56] Since many issues of *El Jurnal* are lost, we do not know if Gabay, in turn, advertised his Salonican counterpart, but he probably did. Furthermore, it is quite likely that the two editors, Yehezkel Gabay and Juda Nehama, both passionate supporters of the Alliance schools, met in Istanbul. It seems that they shared some information with each other. At least, one sometimes finds news from Salonica in *El Jurnal* . Of course, Gabay, through friendships and other connections with the council members, had access to the most recent and reliable information, which would not have been as easily available to Nehama. For instance, on May 26, 1864, *El Jurnal* not only informed its readers of Montefiore's return from his successful trip to Morocco, also covered by *El Lunar,* but even published his epistolary exchange with Camondo on the subject (2).

*El Jurnal israelit* served as a forum where like-minded people expressed their opinions in the form of letters, such as the one by Barukh Mitrani on teaching Hebrew, quoted in the introduction. In addition, the chief rabbi and the Mejlis Pekidim used *El Jurnal* to address Istanbul's Jews, to announce their new measures, and to explain the sultan's firmans (decrees). For instance, on December 31, 1860, readers were informed of the national assembly's order requiring all congregations to cover their dead with regular cloth rather than with traditional clothes and shawls during funerals, which attracted too much public attention and "in the last thirty years has become a calamity."[57] On the other hand, in 1866, the Karaite community used *El Jurnal* to convey its concerns to the chief rabbinate.

Every issue of *El Jurnal israelit* began with the official news followed by the news from Istanbul and the empire, information from other countries, and reports from the Jewish world. Sometimes, Gabay published short stories of quasi-ethnographic character meant to fight superstitions and ignorance in an entertaining form. He often included articles from the non-Jewish European (mainly Italian) press and used every opportunity to introduce his readers to new words and concepts, glossing them in parentheses. *El Jurnal israelit* was a highly informative periodical that aimed at enlightening its audience without being obviously didactic. In this sense, it is similar to *Or Israel*. In fact, given the size of the Istanbul community,[58] it is likely that Gabay would have known de Castro and read his paper. The same must have been true of some of his subscribers. It is, therefore, quite possible that Gabay had in mind *Or Israel* when in his first editorial he stated that "until now, many newspapers were established in the world and began to come out, but none of them could survive, because nobody was concerned about them except for the publisher."

*El Jurnal israelit* indefatigably decried its enemies, the conservative faction of the capital's Jewish community that fiercely opposed the reforms. At the same time, it constantly expressed the reformers' loyalty to the Ottoman authorities on whose protection from their own coreligionists they often relied. But after a few conflicts with the chief rabbinate, *El Jurnal* was banned, together with its editor. In the special issue of *La Buena esperansa* dedicated to its twenty-fifth anniversary, Aron de Yosef Hazan wrote that *El Jurnal israelit*'s powerful voice, its articles in support of reason and progress, and its editor's liberal ideas caused "the ire and persecution of backward people and led to serious and dramatic disagreements in the Jewish community of Constantinople" (1896, 58). In short, the first long-lasting Ladino periodical succeeded in becoming a potent political force.

After being closed in 1873, *El Jurnal israelit* soon reappeared, albeit directed by other journalists, as *El Nasyonal* (1873–1878), which was replaced by *El Telegrafo* (1878–1930). Among the editors of both periodicals was Gabay's son-in-law Moses Dal Mediko.[59] *El Telegrafo*'s director and editor in chief was his son Isaac Gabay, who published it until his death in 1930. In the mid-1890s, Gabay's other son, Yosef, became the newspaper's owner.[60] In short, Yehezkel Gabay founded not only the first full-fledged Ladino periodical but also the first dynasty of Sephardi journalists.[61]

*El Jurnal israelit* occupies a particular place in the history of Sephardi journalism. While in many ways it prefigured the later Ladino press, Gabay's newspaper significantly differed from most others in terms of its goals and agenda. Unlike the later periodicals and *Sha'arei mizrach*, *El Jurnal israelit* did not have an explicit pedagogical program, yet its unambiguous social stance and choice of materials were meant to compel its audience, consisting of educated males, to embrace a set of modern liberal values shared by the members of the Mejlis Pekidim and to support their program of reform.

Despite the fact that Camondo was the president of the regional Alliance committee in the Ottoman Empire, *El Jurnal israelit*, born a few months after the Parisian organization, did not fully embrace its program with its emphasis on moralizing and sometimes criticized its actions. In some ways, Gabay's newspaper had more in common with the other early Ladino journals—*Sha'arei mizrach*, *Or Israel*, and *El Lunar*—which placed knowledge above all values, hoping that it would enable Sephardim to catch up with Europe.

## The Birth of the New Ladino Press

In the 1870s, several new Ladino periodicals, all of them long-lived, emerged in the three major centers of Sephardi culture: *El Tyempo* (1872–1930) in Istanbul, *La Buena esperansa* (1874–1917?) in Izmir, and *La Epoka* (1875–1911) in Salonica. Their founders were not only familiar with *El Jurnal israelit* but personally knew and highly respected its editor. Nevertheless, while having a lot in common with each other, these new publications differed from *El Jurnal* in two major, interrelated aspects, which defined everything about them, including their physical appearance and their language. These three newspapers, as well as all those that appeared after them, targeted a new audience and had a new major goal.

Unlike the early periodicals, the new Sephardi press addressed all Ladino speakers of both sexes and different ages. Later, referring to *El Tyempo*, David Fresco thus defined its intended readership: the newspaper should appear in the hands of "the wise, the theologian, the artist, the worker, the businessman, the industrialist, the manager, the teacher, and the believer, the young, the old, men and women: everyone receives an indispensable lesson from the journal" (*El Tyempo*, March 7, 1892).[62] This statement takes for granted a notion of the press as a vehicle of education for the masses rather than a source of information for the few. Alexandre Benghiat, in the opening issue of his *El Meseret* (Izmir, 1897–1922), formulates this idea even more directly when he announces that his newspaper will serve as "a kind of school, where everybody—young and old—will be able to study" (January 15, 1897, 1).

Furthermore, the very concept of the education to be provided by a periodical had changed. The new Sephardi press saw its function not only in awakening readers' curiosity, offering information, or discussing new ideas but—no less important—in inculcating in their minds certain moral values. Now, Ladino periodicals combined—if not replaced—information with straightforward indoctrination. In his first editorial, *La Epoka*'s founder, Saadi Halevy, announced that his paper, "aside from enlightening the readers' minds by providing them with more progressive ideas, will update them on everything that happens and will instill in them the taste for good and the fear of bad" (November 1, 1875, 1).

What led to this new understanding of the press's mission? No doubt, it was the impact of Franco-Judaism promoted by the Alliance Israélite Universelle, which in the last third of the nineteenth century became the most influential western Jewish organization operating in the Ottoman Empire. Like all other European westernizers, the Alliance leaders saw the need to enlighten and inform their eastern coreligionists, but moral edification was considered equally important, as it was believed that by becoming "civilized" and "modern," Jews would eliminate grounds for antisemitism and thus would eventually eradicate it. The Alliance's understanding of moral edification is expounded in its Central Committee's circular of 1896. Beside the three main goals—"casting a ray of civilization" on the degenerated-by-oppression and ignorant Sephardim, preparing them for more respectable jobs, and destroying their superstitions—"the action of the Alliance principally aimed to give to . . . the Jewish population as a whole a moral education rather than a technical instruction, to create rather than semi-scholars tolerant good men, attached to their duties as citizens and as Jews."[63] In short, for the Alliance, a moral person was a tolerant one, a responsible Jew, and a conscientious citizen. The notion of morality was no longer a merely religious one but included new, bourgeois virtues, such as tolerance and patriotism.[64] And it is by no means coincidental that *La Epoka*'s program mirrors this agenda when it promises to enlighten, inform, and morally educate its readers, since its editor, like many Sephardi literati in other cities, was deeply involved in establishing the Alliance schools in Salonica.

Another of the Alliance's priorities was providing education for girls because, until its first girls school opened in Edirne in 1868, there was no formal schooling for women in the Ottoman Empire. Since the local literati agreed that laziness, gossiping, and superstitions were among the main causes of women's moral degeneration, they enthusiastically invited them to join the other readers of their periodicals, meant to serve as schools. Indeed, as Stein has shown in her study of *El Tyempo,* in the 1870s–1880s many editors eagerly set to the work of educating female readers.[65] It has been noted, however, that the formation of "the female reader of magazines is a contradictory process in which women's importance is both confirmed and strictly delimited."[66] Thus, in France and England women had their own magazines, which discussed recipes, fashions, and sensational news, keeping their audience away from more serious subjects.[67] In the Sephardi community, however, separate periodicals for women were not just unfeasible but were uncalled for, because women were not the only inexperienced readers: there were also poorly educated men, probably mainly of older age, who also lacked knowledge of the sciences and history or were not even interested in those subjects and were looking for something else. They, too, were encouraged to subscribe to Ladino periodicals that promised to satisfy everybody's taste.

It would be wrong to assume that educated Sephardim fluent in European languages did not read Ladino periodicals. While some foreign newspapers were available in the Ottoman Empire, for most Jews the Ladino press was the only source of local news. Aware of this, Dascopulos (whose full name is unknown), the "Director of the Salonican Press Agency," advertised in *La Epoka* the French and Italian periodicals, whose titles were printed both in Latin and Hebrew characters, available at his shop (August 2, 1895, 4). In other words, this category of readers also had to be taken into account by the editors.

Thus, starting in the 1870s, Sephardi journalists faced the challenge of attracting all groups of Ladino speakers, which was particularly difficult in Istanbul, Izmir, and Salonica, where by the end of the nineteenth century two or three Ladino publications appeared at the same time. One way to increase readership was to include a greater variety of materials, which required either expanding the newspaper or publishing more than one issue per week. In the 1870s–1890s, even a journal that started with four pages, such as *El Tyempo,* would often expand to six, eight, and even twelve. Both *La Epoka* and *El Nuvelista* (The Courier; Izmir, 1890–1922) first appeared as weeklies, then became biweeklies, and for some time after the Young Turk revolution (1908), they appeared five times a week. Their number of pages also doubled.

A good way of attracting readers with different interests was publishing a supplement that focused on particular topics, such as politics, poetry, or fiction. Often, they would be free for the newspaper's subscribers. As was mentioned above, *El Jurnal israelit* was the first to do this, and one of its successors, *El Telegrafo,* followed its example. Its supplement, whose slogan was "Reading is for the mind what nourishment is for the body,"[68] was advertised in *La Epoka*.

> [*El Telegrafo*] has expanded its edition by adding another publication that will appear every Tuesday. This new publication will respond to the desire of Jewish families, friends of progress, that want to spend their free time reading useful and entertaining things, by printing most interesting articles on various thrilling subjects, exciting travel accounts, novels

selected from among the most dramatic modern ones, various poems, songs, riddles, etc. (April 20, 1888, 5–6)

The publisher strongly encouraged his coreligionists to subscribe to this supplement, "whose price is so low and the value is so high" that, no doubt, a great number of people would hurry to support it by their subscriptions. One finds in this passage the three key concepts of the new discourse adopted by the Ladino press that it would always use in various combinations: useful, progressive, and entertaining.

Not all periodicals, however, especially in the beginning, could afford to print additional pages or supplements. A cheaper, albeit less effective, way of attracting readers with specific interests was adding a subtitle that defined the paper as commercial, political, literary, Jewish (Turkish-Jewish), historical, or scientific. Typically, a newspaper would combine two or three terms (a pattern borrowed from the French press), such as "political, commercial, and literary," suggesting that readers of both sexes would find something of interest there. (In comparison, *Sha'arei mizrach*, a male newspaper par excellence, defined itself as a "journal of news, commerce, and notices.") Men were expected to read the political and commercial news, whereas women were assigned the sections "devoted to faits divers and serialized fiction. The territory of the newspaper was thus thematically divided according to gender-based expectations."[69]

Most Ladino weeklies and biweeklies had a similar structure. They would begin with didactic editorials and then turn to local, Ottoman, and international events, which in later years, due to the use of the telegraph, would include the updates received the previous day by cable, which were printed in a separate column. Every periodical had a section covering events in other Jewish communities in the empire and abroad, presented in the form of news reports, letters, or travel accounts. However, those travelogues were often fantastic and entertaining rather than informative. Some papers gave more space to articles on science and history, while others favored household advice, theater reports, or serialized stories.

Among the new rubrics borrowed from the European press, one finds *diversos* and *variedades* (*faits divers* of the French periodicals) that contain all sorts of strange, funny, or informative materials. Furthermore, the Ladino press had a curious feature: in the midst of serious reports and discussions, one suddenly comes across absurd little stories whose only goal is to make newspaper reading, and thus the process of education, more attractive.[70] It is noteworthy that the bizarre mini stories found in Ladino periodicals never offer any lessons and always describe events that allegedly took place abroad. For example, one story informs readers about a microbe of laziness discovered in Puerto Rico, where the disease is treated surgically (*La Epoka*, July 18, 1905, 4). No doubt, these stories were usually meant as tongue-in-cheek in order to entertain the less naive readers as well.

These were some of the devices intended to make Ladino newspapers appealing to the Sephardi masses and thus to increase their circulation. Yet certain socioeconomic and ideological factors hindered the growth of the circulation of Ladino periodicals.

## Reading Practices and Literacy

It is generally accepted that the Ladino press, despite its low circulation, succeeded in reaching out to the masses and achieving great influence in the Sephardi community. In the absence of any reliable statistics, this belief is based mainly on the testimonies of Sephardi journalists and their admirers. While it is impossible to verify this fundamental assumption, it is useful to reassess certain related facts that should enable us to qualify it. Obviously, the main question to be considered is the availability of the Ladino press to the so-called masses, which depended on literacy rates, the circulation of Ladino newspapers, and their affordability.

There was another important factor affecting the circulation of Ladino periodicals and making them both accessible to the illiterate and affordable to the poor: the practice of collective reading, which in the Sephardi community, according to Lehmann, was largely shaped by the vernacular rabbis who encouraged Sephardim to read musar books in small groups of relatives and friends. If we are to believe the rabbinic sources, by the last third of the nineteenth century, a significant number of men and a smaller number of women were used to getting together on holidays or the Sabbath to read Ladino ethical literature or to listen to someone read it aloud. Though the rabbis urged their coreligionists to study, they did not directly encourage Ladino literacy, because from their vantage point, acquiring reading skills was not important as long as there were enough people able to read laloud to the rest. Besides, since musar literature was a purely reader-oriented (rather than market-oriented) genre, the rabbis did not pursue commercial goals and did not aim at increasing the sales of their works.[71] No doubt, the custom of collective reading slowed down the growth of individual literacy.

Sephardi westernizers, who always encouraged mass education and hoped that growing literacy would make their pedagogical endeavor more effective and allow them to sell more periodicals, were forced to admit that their readers preferred sharing newspaper subscriptions with friends and neighbors to getting one of their own. I suggest that, contrary to the commonly accepted view that attributes this practice merely to low literacy and general poverty, at the turn of the twentieth century the custom of collective reading still played a role in keeping press circulations low.

As Lehmann indicates, the vernacular rabbis urged Sephardim to get together to study on "long winter nights," which, as all scholars of Sephardi culture know, starting with *Me'am Lo'ez,* had become a common formula of Ladino rabbinic literature meaning "free time." The following recommendation in a nutshell describes the Sephardi reading practices that survived well into the twentieth century. Juda Papo encouraged his coreligionists to read his Ladino version of *Pele Yo'ets* (1870– 1872): "Everyone should read [this book] at home with his family on the Sabbaths and festivals and the long winter nights. The neighbours should gather and read it together. Those women who can read should assemble friends and relatives and should read it with them."[72]

Needless to say, collective reading on winter nights (as well as at other hours) was not unique to Ottoman Jews; this practice was known in Europe since the early modern period and in some countries persisted among the lower classes until the turn of the twentieth century. For example, in his study of collective reading in France, Jean Hebrard states that it was considered beneficial for factory workers and peasants to get together to hear someone read out loud, because "on long winter nights it allowed . . . the maximum number of people to gather at a minimal expense of light and heating, at the same time encouraging men and women to continue their handiwork, such as fixing tools and knitting."[73] Such gatherings, common in Europe in the nineteenth century and often organized by educational institutions or libraries for factory workers, differed from the Sephardi practice of collective reading in that they fulfilled additional social functions often unrelated to the content of the given text. At the same time, they were similar to the reading groups (*meldados*) recommended by the vernacular rabbis who encouraged Sephardim to study under the guidance of a more knowledgeable person.[74] However, in the last third of the nineteenth century, Sephardim began to get together spontaneously in order to read a newspaper or a thrilling serialized novel and continued to do so even in the 1920s.

This custom was so deeply rooted in the Sephardi reading culture that even when a subscription was affordable, which was not at all rare, purchasing one was not deemed necessary. Instead, one subscription would be shared by a few households, a practice constantly condemned by the publishers. Uziel had asked his readers not to share the newspapers (*Sha'arei mizrach,* no. 1, 5), but all admonitions and complaints remained in vain even in the twentieth century when the importance of the press was recognized by many

Sephardim. Moreover, even the audience of Sam Lévy's newspaper El Luzero (The Beacon; Zemun, summer of 1905), which was meant for intellectuals and certainly not needy readers, had to be warned against sharing the periodical. Its third issue ended with the following advice: "Read El Luzero. Show *El Luzero*. Recommend *El Luzero*. Do not share *El Luzero*" (June 30, 4).

At the time of low literacy and mass poverty, collective reading was the only way to ensure that everybody would get the recent news and learn an appropriate lesson from the periodical. Aware of this situation, the editors had to adjust to it. As I mentioned earlier, aside from the linguistically difficult articles meant for educated readers, *Sha'arei mizrach* published some didactic articles accessible to those who did not know Hebrew (all Hebrew terms were translated in parentheses) or were illiterate even in Ladino. Moreover, some pieces were obviously meant to be read out loud. For instance, an article from *Sha'arei mizrach* (no. 2, 2–3) introduces readers to the Aristotelian classification of plants and animals and, at the same time, emphasizes the greatness of God, who created so many species that one cannot hope to count them all. The passage that does not contain any information but simply reiterates this axiom is rhymed, yet it is printed in such a way that only reading it aloud reveals its rhythmic structure. Here, to make it obvious, I break the text into lines indicating the stressed vowels:

> . . . kansár te kansarás
> y náda no arás,
> y si tódos tus días lazarás
> fin no toparás.
> Días se trokarán,
> y ányos pasarán,
> y tódas tus lazerías kómo náda serán.
> Ke no ay ni kuenta ni mizura para las kriansas ke el Santo
>     Bendicho Él krió.[75]

A few other sections of this piece, albeit not rhymed, also end with *Él krió* (He created). This device was often used in rabbinic writings. Thus, every section of Huli's Hebrew introduction to Me'am Lo'ez ends with the word *gadol* (big). the passage above, however, is more similar to the *coplas* that were originally composed by rabbis to educate Sephardim who were unable to understand Hebrew, and it employs devices typical of coplas. This stanza consists of two quatrains using the so-called Mozarabic rhyme: A A A A B B B V, where V is the end rhyme that repeats and is common to all stanzas (sometimes in free verse).[76] I believe that this little poem, like the funny short stories inserted between the serious articles, was meant to make the lesson intended for collective reading more entertaining.

In order to discuss literacy rates among Ottoman Sephardim, it is, first of all, necessary to define what exactly literacy means in this case, since this term has a variety of meanings, including the ability to sign one's name (a criterion adopted by some censuses). In this book, I will understand *literacy* as the ability to read and comprehend a printed text. Second, in the context of diglos*sic* speech communities, some of whose members are bilingual, one must specify the language of *literacy*. Since this book deals with Ladino print culture, I am mainly concerned with Ladino literacy, though literacy in other languages, especially French, also has to be taken into account. As for Hebrew, in the era of westernization and secularization, its knowledge among Sephardim, together with traditional education in general, was in decline. Third, when speaking of the nineteenth century, one must examine male and female literacy separately. It is generally true that the gap between the two "had always been the widest at the lowest end of the social scale,"[77] but this discrepancy is even more extreme in traditional societies that consider female education not only unnecessary but even detrimental. Obviously, the Sephardi case is quite different from what one finds in the nineteenth-century European nation-states with compulsory education for both sexes in the official state language. In France and England by the end of the nineteenth century, the discrepancy between male and female literacy rates had disappeared because there, in the 1880s, primary education effectively became free, general, and compulsory.[78] By contrast, the available statistics on Jewish literacy indicate that in the Russian Empire the gap remained wide even at the turn of the twentieth century.[79] Furthermore, in Jewish communities that were always marked by diglossia, literacy in different languages was gender-related, which additionally complicates its assessment.

We have no real statistics on the Sephardim's literacy in Ladino, so I rely on contemporaneous testimonies, all of which indicate that it was quite low. Claims about its rapid growth are also speculative and are not corroborated by any evidence.[80] The only figure I was able to find appears in Sam Lévy's memoir. Saadi Halevy's youngest son, who later became the editor in chief both of *La Epoka* and its French counterpart, *Le Journal de Salonique,* states that, in 1898, 50 percent of Salonican Jews were illiterate.[81] It is clear from the context that by literacy, he means the ability to read Ladino periodicals. This figure cannot be taken at face value, but, based on other available information, it appears to be a rather accurate assessment.

Due to its low status, the Sephardi vernacular was never taught properly: in Uziel's words, neither the grammar nor the vocabulary was explained or learned (*Sha'arei mizrach*, no. 1, 1). Yet Sephardi boys used Ladino to translate the Torah, and those who went beyond the *meldar* also translated the Talmud. Some girls from middle-class families who had private Hebrew tutors learned it as well. Of course, both men and women acquired reading and writing skills in Ladino, which were increasingly important for professional activities and everyday needs, but this evidently happened in informal ways, which is one of the reasons we have no data. In the Alliance institutions, Ladino was banned under the threat of penalty, but it was used by the rabbis who did not speak French to teach Judaism.

As for foreign-language literacy, by the 1870s–1880s, it had undoubtedly risen, because in the 1860s–1870s the number of modern schools available even to the poor had significantly increased. The first Alliance school for boys was established in Edirne in 1868, followed by one for girls in 1870. In Izmir, a boys school opened in 1873 and a girls school in 1878; in Salonica, this happened in 1873 and 1874; and in Istanbul, both schools opened in 1878.[82] A number of communal and private institutions offering instruction in French and Italian appeared in Istanbul, Izmir, and Salonica. Another kind of European-type school available to Sephardi children, and especially attractive to the poor, was missionary institutions, whose number considerably increased in the 1860s–1870s. For instance, in 1855–1864, the London Society for Promoting Christianity amongst the Jews founded three institutions in Istanbul, among other cities.[83]

Thus, literacy in Italian and especially in French among Sephardim was indeed increasing, and among women excluded from traditional education it grew faster than among men. The Alliance alone established in the Ottoman Empire more than forty-five girls schools, including vocational institutions, all of which taught French.[84] Thanks to it, we have some reliable figures for French literacy, and even separate data for boys and girls. In 1873, the first Alliance school in Salonica had 200 students, all of them boys, but later six new institutions were added, four of them for girls. In 1908, the Alliance schools in the city had 2,132 students altogether, approximately half of whom were girls.[85]

Since the fiction and periodicals produced in European languages were meant for individual reading, French literacy did not have a noticeable impact on Sephardi reading practices. First of all, many students from poor families attended school only for a brief period. So, in many cases, students did not acquire the skills for reading complicated texts and would have still preferred Ladino fiction or periodicals. Second, French and Italian books were often unavailable or unaffordable, and students only had access to them through school libraries. In short, the fact that in the early twentieth century the number of Alliance students, both proportionally and numerically, was quite high, does not mean that all of them could or chose to read French periodicals. Though the importance of the Alliance schools for the education of Ottoman Jews cannot be overestimated, especially for women, the majority of adult Sephardim continued to read in Ladino, and thus in groups.

To sum up, in the 1870s–1890s, foreign-language literacy grew significantly among all Sephardim, especially among women, and Ladino literacy must have grown as well, but we have no statistics to evaluate it. One should also keep in mind that the intended audience of Ladino periodicals included a large number of Sephardim born in the 1820s–1850s who had little or no schooling, especially women. Hence, the proportion of illiterate consumers of Ladino periodicals remained rather high.

## Prices and Circulation

Since Ottoman press regulations did not stipulate any indication of the newspapers' circulations,[86] we have no precise figures for Ladino periodicals, and most of the available information comes from unreliable sources. All we know for certain is that the numbers were very low but were always exaggerated by the publishers and understated by their rivals. In 1908, Benghiat bragged about the circulation of El Meseret surpassing 1,000 copies, while El Nuvelista and El Komersyal, which were also published in Izmir, allegedly produced only 120 copies together. Benghiat must have forgotten that less than a year earlier he had announced that his paper's circulation had grown from 1,200 to 2,000 copies, thanks to the fact that Avram Galante, his former collaborator and now a rival, had stopped writing for El Meseret. In the same period, according to Benghiat, Galante's La Vara (The Stick; Cairo, 1905–1908) had lost half of its readers and printed less than a hundred copies.[87] Sam Lévy claimed in Le Journal de Salonique (July 30, 1900, 1) that its rival, Le Progrès de Salonique, did not print more than 50 copies, whereas Le Journal's circulation—he insisted—was 1,000.[88] While these claims cannot be taken at face value, they reveal the number of subscribers the editors would have liked to have, which was probably somewhat above the real maximum.

The demographic data correlated with the numbers for the Jewish press in Europe and for the publications of other Ottoman minorities suggest that the circulations of the most popular Ladino newspapers did not exceed hundreds of copies. Jonathan Frankel argues that in the middle of the nineteenth century, even the most influential western Jewish journals sold in the hundreds rather than the thousands. He cites the following figures: "the Archives Israélites had some four hundred subscribers in 1841; the Occident published by Isaac

Leeser in Philadelphia had five hundred in 1845; the *Allgemeine Zeitung des Judentums* in 1850 had seven hundred, the *Orient* five hundred and fifty; and the *Razsvet*, ten years later, six hundred and forty."[89]

The circulations of Greek and Armenian periodicals in the Ottoman Empire, correlated with the sizes of the respective communities, corroborate my assumption. According to the official Ottoman Census of 1910, the adult Armenian population of the capital had reached 83,000, while there were roughly 71,000 adult Greeks.[90] Each of these communities had no less than ten periodicals,[91] the circulation of each not exceeding 5,000 and 4,000 copies, respectively.[92] The Turkish journals sold 12,000–15,000 copies.[93] For comparison, the French-language journal *Le Moniteur Oriental*, published in the capital, had a circulation of 5,000 copies.[94]

In 1881–1893, the Jewish population of the city of Istanbul and Greater Istanbul numbered approximately 44,000[95] (around 20,000 adults), and the community always had at least two Ladino periodicals. Hence, to say, as Avner Levi does, that the circulation of *El Tyempo* reached 10,000[96] is to suggest that every second adult and every Sephardi family in the capital subscribed to it. And, as Stein rightly notes, it could not have had a large number of subscribers outside the city.[97] The figures quoted by Paul Fesch, on the contrary, seem quite realistic—900 for *El Tyempo* and 500 for *El Telegrafo*[98]—although we do not know what sources of information he used.

Given the scarcity of the available data on publishing in the Ottoman Empire, I was unable to find the prices and circulation numbers for all cited periodicals in the same year. My goal was to offer a general idea of how the numbers for the Sephardi press compared to those of the major newspapers of the three largest ethnic-religious communities and the European community in the empire.

As is well known, small circulations incur high costs for publishers, which means high prices for readers. This is demonstrated by table 1.1, which is based on the scarce available data for the Ottoman press. One can see that the least expensive journals were those with the largest circulations. However, all Turkish periodicals as well as most foreign-language ones published in the empire (the *Levant Herald* among them) were at least partly subsidized by the government, since Abdul Hamid needed to have a docile press that would follow his directives.[99] A few Ladino periodicals were subsidized by Zionist organizations, B'nai B'rith, or, rarely, the Alliance Israélite Universelle, while the majority fully depended on subscriptions, sales, and advertisements. Low circulations made newspaper publishing more than unprofitable, which is why many journalists were quite poor and, barely making ends meet, functioned as editors, publishers, translators, and distributors, often

Table 1.1

| Periodical (Language, City) | Year | Circulation | Price per Issue[1] |
|---|---|---|---|
| *Sabah* (Turkish, Istanbul) | 1900 | 12,000[2] | 10 paras |
| *Constantinoupolis* (Greek, Istanbul) | 1900 | 3,500[3] | 10 paras |
| *Sourhantag* (Armenian, Istanbul) | | 3,000[4] | 10 paras[5] |
| *Levant Herald* (French, English, Istanbul) | 1892 | | 10 paras |
| *Tyempo* (Ladino, Istanbul) | 1890 | 900[6] | 80 paras |
| *Progrès de Salonique* (French, Salonica) | 1900 | 700[7] | 30 paras |
| *Epoka* (Ladino, Salonica) | 1898 | 750[8] | 60 paras |
| *Avenir* (Ladino, Salonica) | 1897 | | 40 paras |
| *Meseret* (Ladino, Izmir) | 1904 | 1,000[9] | 1 metalik |
| *Luzero* (Ladino, Zemun) | 1905 | | 40 paras |
| Foreign French periodicals | | | 40 paras |

*Notes*: All periodicals in this table, except the Sephardi ones, were dailies. In 1900, El Tyempo was no longer a daily.

1. All information on the prices of the non-Jewish periodicals is from A. Djivé-léguian, *Le Régime de la presse en Turquie* (Paris, 1912), 64–65. The data on the Sephardi press are mine.

2. Ibid., 64.

3. Paul Fesch, Constantinople aux derniers jours d'Abdul-Hamid (New York, 1907), 64.

4. Ibid., 67.

5. Other Armenian dailies cost 20 paras.

6. According to Fesch.

7. According to G. Groc and I. Çaglar, La Presse française de Turquie de 1795 à nos jours: Histoire et catalogue (Istanbul, 1985).

8. Sam Lévy, Salonique à la fin du XIXe siècle: Mémoires (Istanbul, 2000), 101.

9. According to Benghiat.

producing their newspapers single-handedly and signing their articles with different pseudonyms. Fresco later described "his position at *El Tyempo* as that of 'director-administrator-accountant-secretary' and 'editor-in-chief.'"[100] Many Sephardi literati went through tremendous hardships to keep their newspapers afloat, but a great number of journals still closed, and some editors joined the staffs of other newspapers.

Before 1908, only a few Sephardi periodicals were available by the issue, and single copies cost as much as (or even more than) those of foreign publications. *La Epoka* was the first to start this practice in 1875. Evidently, most publishers were not sure how many copies they would be able to sell. To secure sufficient funds for the following year, they offered mostly annual subscriptions, though with time they became more flexible, selling six- or even three-month subscriptions and often making the annual one more advantageous. Thus, an annual subscription to *Le Journal de Salonique* cost ninety piastres, while a six-month one was fifty piastres. *El Avenir*'s rates were divided equally: fifty piastres per year, twenty-five piastres for six months, and twelve and a half piastres for three months.

Outside the city of publication, the rates were always higher. Thus, an annual subscription to *El Avenir* outside Salonica cost sixty piastres. Many newspapers, including *Sha'arei mizrach*, announced higher rates for subscriptions outside the empire. *Or Israel* had a particularly curious range of prices reflecting the costs of transportation: in Istanbul, its annual subscription cost 100 piastres, while in "port cities and Brusa [Bursa, Prusa]" it was 130 piastres and in inland cities 150 piastres. By the turn of the twentieth century, unlike in the 1840s–1860s, the "abroad" category made more sense, as it must have referred to the former Ottoman territories, such as Bulgaria and Serbia, but it is unclear how many subscriptions were sold in those places.

According to Saadi Halevy, before the Russo-Turkish war (1877–1878), which negatively affected the postal service, *La Epoka* had over fifty subscribers outside Salonica,[101] most of them in Istanbul, but also in other cities, including Monastir (Bitola, Bitolj), Alexandria, and Trieste (*La Epoka*, December 10, 1877, 4). Halevy bitterly scolded those readers who failed to pay on time, refused to cover the postage, or sent *kaime*[102] instead of mejidiye.[103] Obviously, subscribing to a second Ladino periodical, whether local or published in another city, was unfeasible for the majority of Sephardi readers.

It is difficult to assess how affordable the Ladino press was for its intended audience. As I suggested earlier, the fact that subscriptions were often split between a few families does not necessarily mean they were too expensive for all Sephardim. No doubt, a hundred piastres for the first prospective Ladino newspaper was indeed too much for the Jewish community of Izmir, which had recently been devastated by a fire. Twenty years later, a hundred piastres for *El Jurnal israelit* was still a lot for the poor, but the periodical was not meant for them. The key question is whether the Ladino popular press produced in the 1870s–1890s was still too expensive for the working classes it hoped to reach. Given how little data we have on the wages and food prices in the Ottoman Empire in the late nineteenth century, this question can be answered only tentatively. Still, table 1.2 offers a clearer picture by placing the prices of Ladino periodicals into the context of the overall

Table 1.2

| City | Istanbul | Izmir | Salonica |
|---|---|---|---|
| Year | 1901 | 1897 | 1891, 1893[1] |
| Daily wages (piastres) | craftsman 12 | factory worker 12[2] | factory worker approx. 9.5 |
| Bread/beef prices (piastres per oka)[3] | 1.42/6.82[4] | 1.42/6.82[4] | 0.5/1.8 |
| Periodical | *Tyempo* | *Meseret* | *Epoka* |
| Annual subscription (piastres) | 120 | 40 | 60 |
| Equivalent in work days | 10 | approx. 3.3 | approx. 6.5 |
| Equivalent in pounds of bread/beef | 232/48.3 | 77.4/16.1 | 330/91.7 |

*Notes:*

1. The year 1891 is used for the food prices, 1893 for the wages.
2. In 1896. No information is available for 1897.
3. An oka equals 2.75 pounds.
4. Since the food prices for Istanbul in 1901and Izmir in 1897 are not available, in both cases, I am using the average prices for the Ottoman Empire in 1900.

*Source:* Charles Issawi, The Economic History of Turkey: 1800–1914 (Chicago, 1980), 334–336.

Ottoman economy. I was unable to find data for the three cities in the same year, but the economic situation in the empire did not significantly change between 1891 and 1901. The subscription prices of most Ladino periodicals seldom changed.

This table demonstrates once again that the socioeconomic conditions in the three major centers of Sephardi life in the Ottoman Empire differed from each other more than is usually assumed, which makes generalizations tentative or even impossible. In 1901, in Istanbul, a craftsman (a common occupation among the capital's Jews) would have to work ten days in order to subscribe to *El Tyempo*. In other words, he would have to support his family while working ten days fewer each year.[104] Furthermore, food prices in the capital always tended to be higher than the average in the empire and, of course, everywhere kosher meat cost more than the regular kind.[105] Unfortunately, I have no data on the Sephardim's diet at the time that would allow me to assess how much bread and meat an average family consumed per year.[106] But, in any case, it was obviously difficult for many Sephardim to buy an annual subscription to Fresco's journal.

In 1897, in Izmir, whose Jewish population was considerably smaller,[107] the newly founded *El Meseret* had to compete with two well-established Ladino periodicals, *La Buena esperansa* and *El Nuvelista*. There, a factory worker would have to give away his pay for only 3.3 days in order to get a subscription to Benghiat's journal. Between 1897 and 1904, *El Meseret* was distributed only by subscription, at two mejidiye per year, whereas annual subscriptions to both *La Buena esperansa* and *El Nuvelista* cost approximately twice as much: twenty francs[108] for the former and four mejidiye for the latter, that is, about eighty piastres. In 1904, to make his paper competitive, Benghiat started selling *El Meseret* by the issue at one metalik[109] and even advocated this form of distribution in an article.[110] In 1908, he founded one of its literary supplements, *El Meseretpoeta*, which also cost one metalik and was sold only by the issue. Not surprisingly, *El Meseret* quickly became very popular, no doubt stealing many readers from its rivals, though probably more from *La Buena esperansa*, which also targeted the working classes, while *El Nuvelista* mostly catered to Francophile intellectuals.

It is impossible to tell whether in the early 1900s *El Meseret*'s circulation indeed got near 1,000 copies, as its editor claimed. However, given the size of the Jewish community in Izmir, this seems unlikely. Besides, after *El Komersyal* (1906–1908?) joined the other three newspapers, their respective circulations must have dropped. But in 1897, the emergence of Benghiat's newspaper had drastically changed the Ladino press market as compared to 1896, when it was similar to that of Istanbul. In other words, the affordability of Sephardi periodicals, aside from varying from city to city, could change within one community. As far as I can tell, in Izmir at the turn of the twentieth century, many Sephardim could afford a subscription of their own.

The case of Salonica is quite different and surprising. Though in the early 1890s this city had some 75,000 Jewish residents,[111] until December 1897, there was only one Ladino periodical, which had a small circulation. However, both the available statistics and Sam Lévy's memoir suggest that a certain part of the working class, which formed a large section of the city's Jewish population,[112] could afford their own subscriptions. A factory worker had to work about 6.5 days, or give away approximately five piastres per month, to get a subscription.

Sam Lévy recalls in his memoir that in 1890 he started a job at the Oriental Railroads office, where he had to convert and calculate various weights, measures, and currencies. He hated the job, and the only thing that reconciled him with it was what he perceived as a very high pay: ten piastres per day, evidently including days off. "Ten piastres! At the end of the first month, which was May, I received 310 piastres. To give the reader an idea of what 310 piastres was worth, it is enough to say that a family of 3–4 people lived comfortably on a hundred piastres per month."[113] If this was indeed so, then even a bigger working-class family would have been able to subscribe to La Epoka, since the daily wages of a factory worker varied from eight to eleven piastres. However, it must be kept in mind that the numbers found in this memoir, written half a century after the events, cannot be taken as true statistics but only as—most of the time—good estimates.

Elsewhere in the same memoir, Lévy states that in 1898 at least 10 percent of Jewish families in Salonica had enough means to pay for an annual subscription to La Epoka.[114] Since the community consisted of 20,000 families, according to his calculations, La Epoka's circulation could potentially have reached 2,000, yet it was only between 700 and 800. Lévy offers two explanations for this "mystery," each of them interesting in its own way.

One night, the journalist discovered that the printers had been fraudulently printing twice as many copies of La Epoka, about 1,500, and selling half of them secretly, cutting out the publishers and thus making a lot of money. In other words, according to Lévy, for some time, the newspaper had a much larger circulation than its owners assumed, though we do not really know how many copies were printed before and after the disclosure. What is important here is that this fraud, according to the author, had begun fifteen months earlier, when La Epoka started publishing serialized novels,[115] which is the only available evidence to show that printing fiction by installment was indeed an effective way of increasing the circulation of a Ladino periodical.

Lévy's discovery alone, however, did not explain why *La Epoka* had so few subscribers, even if there were as many as 1,500 of them. The true reason, of which the journalist learned with great amazement, was the practice of collective reading. Having returned to his native city from Paris, he saw *La Epoka* in many hands and heard many people of different classes discuss it, which made him conclude that all of them subscribed to it. Therefore, he was immensely surprised to find out that the newspaper had only a few hundred subscribers. It was explained to him that families passed a copy of the periodical to one another and that it circulated this way for a whole week. Neighbors would get together to read the paper collectively, and thus one subscription sufficed for eight to ten readers or listeners.[116]

In this connection, I would like to clarify a certain misleading assumption shared by scholars of the Jewish press. Reflecting on the role of Jewish periodicals in Eastern Europe in the middle of the nineteenth century, Frankel notes that "a single copy of *Hamagid, Hameliz, Hakarmel* or *Kol Mevaser* would often be passed from hand to hand during the course of the week, thus multiplying the real, as opposed to the formal, circulation many times over."[117] But what exactly is meant by "many times over"? Stein explains *El Tyempo*'s influence, among other things, by its "real" circulation being many times higher than the number of printed copies.[118] I suggest that "many" is less than scholars tend to think, and we should be more specific in our assessments.

Lévy states that one subscription sufficed for eight to ten readers or listeners, not for ten families, which means that in Salonica the practice of collective reading multiplied the formal circulation only three or four times. For example, in 1898, Lévy's own family consisted of at least five adults living in the same house, and they would only have needed one newspaper subscription. But if eight or ten people read or listened to one issue of a newspaper, the only Ladino periodical in Salonica reached no more than 7,000 members of the community, that is., approximately every fifth adult.[119] This number is surprisingly low, especially compared to Izmir, whose Jewish population was about three times smaller. Yet, after 1897, there were three and, after 1906, four Ladino journals whose combined circulation could have indeed reached 1,000. To some extent, this can be accounted for by the existence of another Sephardi newspaper, *Le Journal de Salonique,* but between 1895 and 1900 it was essentially a non-communitary publication. In any event, as I will show in chapter 2, for some time before 1898, *La Epoka* was not very successful, and we do not even know when its circulation rose from the alleged 200 to 750.

The case of Salonica's Jewish community, where around 75,000 persons, of whom arguably 50 percent were literate and 10 percent could afford a subscription to the only available Ladino periodical, were satisfied with a few hundred copies, convincingly demonstrates that low literacy, poverty, and the practice of collective reading were not the only factors responsible for the low circulation of the Sephardi press. I suggest that another important factor affecting the demand was the unevenness of the impact that westernization had on different social strata. The paradox of *La Epoka*'s low circulation is largely explained by the extreme social and cultural polarization of the Salonican Jewish community, a fact repeatedly emphasized in Minna Rozen's work.[120]

## Mechanisms of Press Control

The paralyzing effect of censorship on the Sephardi press was brought into sharp relief by the enormous boom the press experienced within a few months after the Young Turk revolution, when the freedoms of expression and association made possible the emergence of dozens of new periodicals in Ladino and French, representing a variety of ideological trends. Among them were Ottomanist, Alliancist, Zionist, and socialist publications, as well as a great number of humor newspapers satirizing all orientations.

Ottoman press regulations had no special provisions for minorities, but Sephardi literati were often subject to the control of yet another repressive mechanism, usually referred to as rabbinic censorship and taken to be some kind of institution. Robyn Loewenthal states: "Before the [Young Turk] revolution, governmental and rabbinical censorship had exerted a profound influence upon all [*sic*] writers and journalists of the Ottoman Empire, including those of the Jewish community."[121] According to this view, which is shared by some other scholars, the revolution liberated Ottoman Jews from both kinds of censorship. In reality, however, the so-called rabbinic censorship was merely a practice whose purpose was to preserve the weakening rabbinic power, and thus no revolution could lift it.

Indeed, the rabbis often persecuted the journalists who were critical of their handling of communal affairs and sometimes banned newspapers together with their publishers. Yet, at the time of advancing secularization, the *herem* was no longer as effective a measure as it used to be. In addition, due to the legal status of the *millets*, the rabbis could not close periodicals licensed by the state, which is why, in order to achieve this goal, they had to resort to the Ottoman authorities. In other words, they served as informers denouncing their coreligionists to the state, a conduct highly disapproved of by their predecessors in previous centuries. Now, the actual power of the rabbis depended both on the role and authority of religion in the community and on the willingness of the state to support them.

Here, I will examine the mechanism and dynamics of the rabbinic press control as well as its relation to state censorship. However, I will begin with a brief overview of the latter's history, focusing on its aspects relevant to the Sephardi press.

Ipek K. Yosmaoglu believes that the first press regulation in the Ottoman Empire was the communiqué issued on June 11, 1849, by the Ministry of Foreign Affairs that required every embassy to notify it before publishing books or periodicals. She states that only in 1857 did the regulations assume a more formal character, obliging all Ottoman citizens to apply to the Council of Education and the Ministry of Police for a publishing license.[122] Yet, as will be remembered, *Sha'arei mizrach* was licensed as early as 1846. Indeed, Siren Bora indicates that the first decree requiring all publishers to obtain permission was issued in 1841.[123] Unfortunately, she does not provide any further details, but "The Memorandum on Printing Presses in the Ottoman Empire," published in *L'Écho de l'Orient* on July 8, 1842, confirms the existence of an earlier press regulation.[124]

In the introduction to this document, which was issued on July 6, the editor explains that, concerned about the potential negative consequences of the operation of unlicensed printing presses, the Ottoman government has addressed a communiqué on this subject to the ambassadors of those states whose citizens are involved in publishing without prior authorization. In addition, the memorandum reconfirms an earlier stipulation (unknown to us) limiting the publishing activities of minorities to the presses belonging to the Greek and Armenian patriarchates. Curiously, the Jewish presses are not mentioned. It is not surprising that in the 1840s the Ottoman government was mainly concerned about foreigners founding printing presses in the empire, as until 1860 there were only two Turkish periodicals in the country. Yet there was another, increasingly more important factor that affected most press regulations and censorship laws in the empire through 1913: Europe was always seen as a source of dangerous ideas and undesirable influences that threatened the regime.

In 1864, in response to criticism of the government voiced by the private Turkish periodicals, a new press regulation was adopted. It was an adaptation of the 1852 press law of Louis Napoleon, described as one of the "most ingenious punitive censorship laws of nineteenth-century Europe."[125] The new regulation required that all Ottoman subjects obtain a license from the Council of Education, while all foreigners were to apply to the Ministry of Foreign Affairs. These licenses could be suspended or revoked if the publication was believed to have committed a "press offense." The press law also required all publishers to send a copy of each issue of their periodical to the Administration of Press Affairs in Istanbul or to the governor in the provinces.[126]

Arguably, the first victim of this law was Juda Nehama's *El Lunar,* shut down in 1865.[127] In 1864, Nehama had started printing his monthly at Saadi Halevy's press but later established one of his own without obtaining a license. When Hefzi Pasha, the governor of Macedonia, learned about this, he ordered the confiscation of Nehama's property and was going to imprison him. Only the intercession of the British consul in Salonica and some other prominent figures saved Nehama from jail.[128]

In April 1876, another state decree tightened control over the "smuggled" (i.e., foreign) press and introduced a stamp tax of two paras on every copy of a newspaper (repealed only in 1901).[129] However, it seems that due to the low circulation of Ladino periodicals, the tax was not a big burden for the publishers and had no negative effect on the Sephardi press.

Censorship proper—preliminary and punitive—was first established in the Ottoman Empire on May 11, 1876; it was lifted two days later but was soon reestablished.[130] On December 23, 1876, a few months after Abdul Hamid's ascension to the throne, the first Ottoman Constitution was promulgated. Article 12 stated that the "press is free within the limits of law,"[131] the law being the press regulation of 1864. However, on February 13, 1878, at the end of the Russo-Turkish war, Abdul Hamid dissolved the parliament. The constitution was abrogated, and years of absolutism and reaction followed.

Though during this period only two press regulations were passed, various communiqués and arbitrary directives were constantly issued by Yildiz Palace. Ottoman periodicals that barely contained any news would be suspended or closed for the smallest breach, including "subversive" typos. The lists of forbidden words published in those years include constitution, revolution, liberty, anarchism, socialism, tyranny, dynamite, massacre, Armenia, reform, and many others.[132] Yet, as Yosmaoglu has suggested, these lists, which appear in every work on Ottoman censorship, were to a great extent a result of the journalists' self-censorship, which quickly reached "preposterous levels" and which, together with informing, was a major component of the control mechanism generated by the political culture of the period.[133] Reports on all sorts of breaches were sent to Yildiz Palace by thousands of official spies and regular citizens. Among the open informers were some Sephardi rabbis. In fact, it appears from the scarce evidence available that Ottoman authorities rarely persecuted Sephardi literati without being asked to do so by the rabbis. In a few cases, like that of *El Lunar,* it is unclear who initiated the persecution. Another case is the suspension of *El Meseret* in the winter of 1899–1900, which was a busy time for Ottoman censorship. In the same period, a few journals were suspended in the capital. For instance, *Le Journal de Salonique* reported two such suspensions during one week: "An official note issued by the Press Administration has announced that *El Tiempo* of Constantinople is suspended for an indefinite period. As of February 27, the Turkish journal *Malumat* is suspended by 'a higher order'" (February 26, 1900, 2).

On January 7, 1900, *Le Journal de Salonique* announced that the "ex-editor-in-chief" of *El Meseret*, "our new collaborator," was going to travel in Asia Minor and send dispatches to both *Le Journal de Salonique* and *La Epoka* (1). On May 11, the latter informed its readers about the new development:

> The journal *El Meseret* of Izmirna that was suspended a few months ago has received authorization to resume publication, and this week we had the pleasure of reading its first issue.
>
> From now on, *El Meseret*, whose director is going to be [lit. "which was put under the direction of"] our friend Si[nyor] Aleksandro b. Ghiat, will appear on Tuesdays, half in Turkish and half in Spanish.[134]
>
> We are sure that Si. Aleksandro b. Ghiat, who has always shown great desire to see peace return to the Jewish community of Izmirna, is going to work with all his energy to support those who, inspired by noble feelings, serve the sacred interests of the nation with all their heart.
>
> We wish our colleague a long life and success in his mission. (2–3)

Lévy's ardent assurance that Benghiat would do his best for the restoration of peace in his community and serve its welfare makes it clear that *El Meseret*'s suspension was related to the ongoing strife in Izmir's Jewish community. The statement that the paper "was put under" Benghiat's direction may be simply a poorly constructed sentence, but it could also mean that its previous director and owner, a Muslim, Mehmet Hulussi, was removed. Benghiat's decision to add to his newspaper a page in Turkish, among other things, was probably meant to reaffirm his loyalty to the empire. In any case, he was able to obtain authorization to reopen *El Meseret*. It is not entirely clear why Sam Lévy decided to dedicate such a long note to this event. Perhaps he did so merely out of friendship and journalistic solidarity, though he might have had other reasons that are unknown to us. What is important for my analysis is that Lévy did not hesitate to hire Benghiat and that he was able to express solidarity with him both in his Ladino and French periodicals without being censored himself.

Among other evidence, this suggests that censorship was not equally strict in all parts of the empire and that a lot depended on the local bureaucrats. In the capital, journalists had to be particularly cautious, which is why *El Tyempo* avoided reporting not only on international but also on local news, while *La Epoka*, most of the time, was more at ease. The latter covered, or at least mentioned, political events that were entirely omitted in its French counterpart, which means that either the Ladino press received less attention from Ottoman censorship or that the local censor in charge of the Ladino press was less strict than his Francophone colleague. Available evidence indicates that the censor's attitude sometimes depended on his personality or a journalist's relationship with him. For instance, in 1901, Sam Lévy, already *La Epoka*'s editor in chief, announced in one of its issues that the following week the paper would publish his interview with Theodor Herzl on his unsuccessful negotiations with Abdul Hamid on a charter for Jews in Palestine. As Sam Lévy's brother, Daout, was the personal secretary of the provincial governor, the latter informed the brothers that he had received a secret missive from the capital instructing him to close the periodical if the interview appeared. Of course, it never did.[135]

An even closer relationship between the Greek journalists of Izmir and their Jewish censor is described in a note published in *La Epoka*'s section titled "Jewish News" on November 17, 1905 (4). It proudly reports that the Greek periodicals of Izmir and even Istanbul were praising Yakov Efendi de Vidas, who had served as a censor of the Greek press in Izmir for twenty years. We also learn that "Si. Solomonides, director of the newspaper *Amalthea,* proposed to organize a banquet in honor of the amiable censor and to open a subscription with the purpose of giving him a memorable present. Both proposals were accepted with great enthusiasm." This note shows that Yakov Efendi's friendly attitude toward the local Greek journalists was not a secret from anybody and could be openly discussed even in the fall of 1905, a period of very tight press control. Obviously, the Administration of Press Affairs was not concerned about this situation, which once again exposes the arbitrariness of Ottoman censorship. Indeed, between 1885 and 1905, the Greek community of Izmir, the single largest ethnic-religious group in the city, had an amiable censor whom the journalists did not hesitate to praise and even to bribe. This case as well as the analysis of Ladino periodicals seems to suggest that Hamidian censorship was less interested in the press of the minorities (with the obvious exception of Armenians), especially outside the capital. The interview with Herzl was a different matter, because the Zionist project threatened the empire's territorial integrity.

As far as I can tell, neither *La Epoka* nor *Le Journal de Salonique* was ever closed, which should be explained mainly by the editors' strict self-censorship combined with assurances of their allegiance to the "glorious Padichah." The first issue of *Le Journal de Salonique* (November 7, 1895) opens with a formulaic expression of profound gratitude to the magnanimous monarch for giving the director authorization to found the periodical. But on the same page, one finds a most unusual thing—a humorous poem dedicated to the "newborn," warning it against Ottoman censorship, presented as an old woman named Anastasie:

> First, know that Anastasie
> Gets mad about nothing
> And, at a smallest whim
> —Bang!—will leave you speechless.
> Very often, by holding your tongue,
> You will avoid suspicions
> Of this austere old lady
> Who knows how to make you obey.

The author recommends that the "baby" be prudent and, among other things, remember that excessive interest in politics leads to Charenton (i.e., to insanity), so it is better to focus on everyday things.

"Anastasie" (and "les ciseaux [scissors] d'Anastasie") was the code word used by French literati to refer to censorship.[136] Evidently, this term was familiar only to those readers of *Le Journal de Salonique* who also read the French press, whereas the rest had to wait for the explanation until the subject could be discussed openly. Years later, one week after the censorship was lifted, the newspaper published a song titled "Complainte d'Anastasie,"[137] which talked about an old woman named Anastasie and explained that her last name was Censorship. At the end of the song, the people overthrow her, singing the "Marseillaise."

No doubt, the joke in the first issue of *Le Journal de Salonique* was transparent for the censor and probably would have been impossible in some other periods, for instance, in 1905 or 1908, when only caution and rigorous self-control allowed Sam Lévy to avoid conflicts with "Anastasie." Even a brief analysis of the news coverage offered by *La Epoka* and *Le Journal de Salonique* in October–November 1905, at the time of the first Russian Revolution, reveals his strategy.

In those weeks, the European press thoroughly covered the events in Russia, namely, the strikes and pogroms in different parts of the empire, the general strike in Moscow, and the proclamation of the October Manifesto (the first Russian Constitution) on October 17 (October 31 in the Gregorian calendar), which was immediately followed by the establishment of the Cabinet of Ministers headed by Sergei Witte. As for the Ottoman news, in October there were reports on the repression of Armenians following the attempt on the sultan's life on July 21, arrests of Greek "rebels," conflicts between Bulgarians and Muslims, and the resistance of the Arab tribes in Yemen to the Ottoman army. Most of these subjects could not be discussed in the Ottoman press, as the sublime porte "absolutely prohibited . . . mentioning any insurgencies that might have taken place in other countries, because it is not good for our loyal and peaceful populations to learn about such things."[138] In addition, according to Le Temps, Ottoman censorship proscribed any mention of the Russian Constitution, because this news "might fuel the Young Turks propaganda" (November 4, 3).

*Le Journal de Salonique* left out most of these events and talked about Russia only in the context of international relations, vaguely mentioning some cabinet changes. However, the editor found it necessary to inform readers about the death of the famous British actor Henry Irving (October 19, 2). In late October, the periodical mentioned some violence and robberies around Salonica, but it dedicated most of its space to reports on theater shows, the local society for the protection of animals, the new hospital, and a local orchestra. Among other favorite topics that month were earthquakes, insects carrying infectious diseases, hygiene tips, and the lack of Cailler, a Swiss chocolate, in Salonica. Obviously, following the advice given at its birth, *Le Journal* focused on minor local issues rather than discussing politics. Consequently, in the fall of 1905, its readers, presumably unaware of the violence and revolutions, were expected to continue enjoying the city's rich cultural life, concerned only about the shortage of Cailler chocolate. Yet French newspapers remained available in the Ottoman Empire through the French post offices, which used their status to distribute European publications banned by the porte.[139] This absurd situation is described by Frederick Moore in the account of his trips to Istanbul in the early 1900s: "Persons who are interested in the provinces subscribe to European papers, and have them brought in by the foreign posts."[140]

Though *La Epoka*'s audience did not receive much more information than did the readers of *Le Journal de Salonique*, it was offered a somewhat different and less idyllic picture of the world. On October 6, *La Epoka* reported that imperial troops had clashed with thirteen Bulgarian bandits (10) and quoted a Turkish periodical writing about fifteen bombs discovered in Istanbul (9). but it condemned the Viennese press for "pulling out of thin air" stories about Albanians sacking Serbian villages (November 24, 2). *La Epoka*'s Jewish news from St. Petersburg was positive: a special committee had set up a monument in honor of the famous Jewish sculptor Mark Antokolsky (October 6, 4). On October 27, its readers were informed that it had been decided to make some changes in the Russian government, presumably only with the purpose of introducing "the European model" (2). The paper never mentioned the promulgation of the first Russian Constitution, but its editor was apparently concerned about the first snow in Sofia, a cyclone in Mardin, and storms in Baghdad (November 3, 11). In general, in October–November, the periodical gave a lot of space to reports on natural disasters and train crashes in all parts of the world. Though *La Epoka* announced a subscription for "the unfortunate Russian Jews" (December 1, 4), it did not explain what exactly had happened to them.

Thus, while *La Epoka* never mentioned the political news from Russia or Yemen, preferring endless natural disasters to all other topics, a shrewd reader could figure out that there were constant conflicts in Serbia and Macedonia (of which Salonicans would have probably learned anyway by word of mouth). It seems that Ottoman censorship considered a Ladino periodical with a small circulation less dangerous than its Francophone counterpart. But at certain moments, such as the summer of 1908, newspapers did not serve as a source of information even on local events, which, however, received a lot of attention from the international press.

As is well known, Salonica and the nearby Macedonian towns where the Third Army was garrisoned were in the very center of the July 1908 events. On July 3, Ahmed Niyazi of the Third Army Corps led a revolt against the provincial authorities in Resna, and his example was soon followed by other conspirators. On July 24, the capital of Macedonia was the first city to announce the reinstatement of the constitution and to celebrate it in the city squares.[141] Yet until that moment, Salonicans were not supposed to know about this development around their own city.

In June–July, the only signs of political tension found in *Le Journal de Salonique* were the notes on the temporary suspension of two Salonican newspapers, the Jewish *Le Progrès de Salonique* (June 29, 4) and the Turkish *Asr* (July 9, 1), which had allegedly published false information, thus violating the censorship law. Another, albeit less obvious, symptom was the absence of political news. In those weeks, Sam Lévy dutifully updated his readers on the ongoing restoration of Saint Sophia and the archaeological discoveries made on the site, as well as on the new theater shows and the construction of sewers. But most of all, Le Journal's editor in chief was concerned about the local harvest, a topic recommended for the press by the Yildiz Palace: "Give preference to the news on . . . the harvest, the development of trade and industry in Turkey."[142] The international news was limited mainly to a note on the Fourth Esperanto Congress in Dresden (July 9, 3), a detailed discussion of the scandal around the Parisian newspaper Le Matin (July 9, 2; July 13, 3), and a few other miscellaneous events. On July 20, *Le Journal de Salonique* gave a lot of space on its front page to a poem about the stray dogs in the city, but just four days later, on July 24, it was among the first to publish the text of the 1876 constitution. In its next issue, July 26, the paper added to the masthead the words "Constitutional Organ." Whether Sam Lévy indeed followed some instructions or acted intuitively, he proved to be more prudent than his enemies and rivals, the editors of the Ladino *El Avenir*, the Greek Alithia, and the Francophone *Le Progrès de Salonique*, all of whom—after the latter resumed publication—were warned against speaking about politics "in an inappropriate manner."[143]

All of the evidence discussed above and analysis of the available newspaper materials indicate that before mid-1908 the Sephardi press shared the fate of all Ottoman publications, though the control of Ladino periodicals might have been less stringent. Yet the Ottoman press enjoyed only a brief period of freedom. The coup attempt of April 13, 1909, gave the Committee of Union and Progress a pretext to tighten control, which included limiting the freedom of the press. When the constitution was revised in the spring of 1909, Article 12 still remained in effect, but "the limits of law," within which the press was free, were soon defined by new legislation, the press law of July 29, 1909.[144]

In this period, newspapers continued to be suspended and licenses were revoked, which is why some editors would often get a few licenses to be used in case their periodicals were shut down.[145] But, as far as we know, the Sephardi press, including the Zionist periodicals, was not persecuted by censorship during the second constitutional period (1908–1913). In fact, in the Hamidian period, Zionism as such was never banned, but the 1876 constitution did not guarantee freedom of association, so in view of their plans for a Jewish state and the failure of Herzl's negotiations with the sultan, Zionists had to be cautious and act clandestinely.

The modifications to the constitution adopted after the Young Turk revolution guaranteed the freedom of association to all Ottoman subjects, though with some restrictions: certain nationalist organizations and "separatist" movements whose goals jeopardized the integrity of the Ottoman Empire were banned.[146] The Young Turks were somewhat suspicious of Zionism, but Jabotinsky, who was in charge of Zionist press activities in Istanbul, made every effort to convince the authorities that the movement did not aim at the partition of the empire and would not challenge its unity.[147]

Zionist organizations had to work under various covers and until World War I appeared to focus only on the revival of Hebrew.

The change of regime per se would not have affected the power of rabbinical press control if the rabbis had not relied on state censorship for its realization. In the Hamidian period, both repressive mechanisms aimed at safeguarding the status quo and eradicating all anti-establishment forces. The Young Turks, on the contrary, wanted to create a new order, and their nationalist aspirations had nothing to do with the internal problems of the Ottoman minorities. As a result, the rabbis lost state support, which in the last third of the nineteenth century had allowed them to maintain power in the community despite the encroachment of secularization.

When in 1862, a local rabbi excommunicated Camondo for his reformist activities and the chief rabbinate of Istanbul punished *El Jurnal israelit* for promoting the reforms, the Ottoman authorities happened to be on the westernizers' side and demanded Camondo's exoneration.[148] Nonetheless, in 1873 the newspaper and its editor were banned. The same year, *El Tyempo* published the budget of the chief rabbinate accompanied by an editorial which accused it of mismanaging communal funds and of being "abusive of the poor."[149] This article was written by David Fresco, who continued to condemn the corrupt administration of the chief rabbi, Moshe Levy, and demanded transparency in communal financial affairs, for which the rabbinate banned *El Tyempo* multiple times, and in 1885 excommunicated Fresco himself. A week later, a sultan's decree solicited by the rabbis[150] ordered him to quit his position as editor of *El Telegrafo*.[151] However, he continued working for other newspapers and soon established one of his own. Recounting Fresco's controversy with the chief rabbinate, Galante states that *El Tyempo*, to which Fresco contributed at the time, was closed numerous times by Ottoman censors on the rabbis' demand.[152] According to Galante, after his excommunication, Fresco had no relations with the rabbinical establishment until 1908, when a new chief rabbi was elected.

In Izmir, the chief rabbi, Hayim Palachi, known for his reactionary policies, attacked *La Buena esperansa* and *El Nuvelista*. The latter closed a few times, and in 1896 was banned, but it continued to come out until 1922.[153] In 1903, Avram Galante and his colleague Joseph Romano left the city, presumably under pressure from the chief rabbinate. Some sources indicate that their exile was demanded by the rabbis under a false pretext: their eating in public on Yom Kippur.[154] However, Galante's biographer, Albert Kalderon, claims that his decision to leave Izmir was prompted by more complex factors, namely, his "frustrations derived from communal rejections of his ideas and his inability to write freely."[155] In a letter to Narcisse Leven, Galante explained that he moved to Egypt "in order to live in a free country and give a free course to my intellectual and moral aptitudes."[156] This explanation, however, does not entirely contradict the other one. No doubt, the critical stance taken by the two journalists vis-à-vis the rabbinic establishment—labeled by Galante *la bande noire* (the black band)[157]—caused them serious trouble, but in 1903 the rabbis could no longer easily force their critics to leave the city.

Saadi Halevy was excommunicated in 1874, even before he founded *La Epoka*, for his critique of the rabbinate, but the following year he was able to establish his first periodical. The fact that a Jewish publisher, while being excommunicated by a rabbinic court, was granted permission to start a periodical by Ottoman officials reflects the new legal situation and "the new conception of Ottoman citizenship, which included all the subjects of the Sultan irrespective of their religion, with rights and obligations now in theory flowing mutually between the state and the individual without any mediating bodies, such as religious organizations, in between."[158] Furthermore, despite being excommunicated for thirty-one years, Halevy continued to enjoy the respect of his liberal-minded coreligionists in various cities and, in 1903, was buried with great pomp.

At the turn of the twentieth century, there were more signs of the weakening of the rabbinic influence, at least on the educated classes. For example, in Sofia in 1896, some anti-Zionist Jewish notables wanted to have the Zionist periodical *La Boz de Israel* (Voice of Israel) closed. Apparently, they were also under pressure from the leadership of the Istanbul and Izmir communities. At the demand of the Bulgarian anti-Zionists, the chief rabbi, Moshe Levy, put the *herem* on the newspaper, together with its readers, and probably requested the assistance of local authorities. Yet these measures did not prevent the editor from continuing to publish his newspaper.[159]

The reluctance of the new Ottoman government to get involved in intracommunal Jewish affairs became apparent soon after the appointment in 1908 of Haim Nahum. It turned out that this enlightened friend of the Alliance did not enjoy being mocked, and he, too, tried to get help from the Ottoman administration, but this time in vain. In 1908, the famous humor periodical *El Djugeton* (The Joker; Istanbul, 1908–931) made ironic comments about the rabbinic establishment of Istanbul. In response, the chief rabbi sued the journal. As Elia Carmona, its permanent editor in chief, later recalled, this affair brought *El Djugeton* more fame in the first four months of its existence than it enjoyed in the next twenty years.[160] *La Boz del puevlo* (Voice of the People; Izmir, 1908–1919?), run by Joseph Romano, reprimanded rabbi Nahum, who then appealed to the Ministry of Justice, demanding Romano's exile. But the tribunal of Izmir found Romano, who was defended by his colleague Gad Franco, not guilty.[161] The new regime obviously had other concerns.

The story of the so-called rabbinic censorship is, in fact, a history of the secularization of the Sephardi community accompanied by a growing dependence of the rabbinic establishment on the Ottoman state. As the role of religion was diminishing and excommunication could no longer isolate reprobates from other members of the community, rabbinic persecution made its victims even more famous among their colleagues and readers.

## The New Discourse

Despite the economic hardships and censorship, Sephardi journalists succeeded in producing effective periodicals. In addition to serving as a means of westernization, the Ladino press was also its mirror, which today, in the absence of other data, can be used to assess the transformation undergone by the Sephardi reading public in terms of its cultural and ideological orientation as well as its social structure. The early periodicals, designed to enlighten men, in the 1870s were succeeded by mass-oriented newspapers written in a simple language intended to edify and entertain men and women of all ages. The following analysis exposes the gradual replacement of one set of cultural references with another, which happened between 1846 and 1898.

In the three pieces under examination, the editors express gratitude to the sultan for licensing their newspapers. Uziel thanks the sultan for allowing him to publish *Sha'arei mizrach* in number 9 (June 11, 1846, 65), which opens with *Ha-noten teshu'ah*, a Hebrew prayer for a non-Jewish monarch. In the Ladino passage following the prayer, Uziel extols Abdul Mejid, who "wants us, as well as the other nations, subjects of His Majesty, to be informed and developed in all things, because he is sure that the benefits of the press are so great that we can become as knowledgeable in all sciences as the most civilized nations of Europe."[162] The publisher states that the press is a perfect means of instruction which will serve the public good and make Ottoman Jews equal to Europeans. He encourages his readers to make every effort to instruct their "sons and relatives" in every field of knowledge. He speaks only to fathers and husbands, who read or listen to his periodical and who are expected to know some Hebrew or at least the prayers.

Fourteen years later, in the opening issue of *El Jurnal israelit* (December 27, 1860, 1), its editor partially relates *Ha-noten teshu'ah* in Ladino,[163] combining it with the title of Ottoman sultans introduced by Mehmed II.[164] He asks "the Almighty God on High to give a long and brilliant life to our ruler, our king, the source of our life, king of the earth and master of the seas." In this short piece, Gabay manages to demonstrate his loyalty to the Mejlis Pekidim (i.e., the reforms), the sultan, and Judaism. His editorial is full of biblical and liturgical allusions, messianic references, and syntactic Hebraisms. The two words most frequently used in the two editorials are "knowledge" and "science" (and their derivates), which are not found in the piece published on the front page of *El Meseret* on July 1, 1898, to mark the paper's first anniversary. Benghiat, too, thanks the sultan for licensing his journal, but he does this in the form of a poem. Evidently, he no longer needs to prove the benefits of the press and knowledge and, instead, explains why it is better for Jews to be in the Ottoman Empire than anywhere else in the world. He describes Turkey as a "place of peace and quiet," a land of love and friendship governed by a "God-sent king seeking justice," who is also "a friend of arts and education." He likens Abdul Hamid to King Solomon, but his biblical references, while being precise,[165] are self-explanatory and do not require a special knowledge of the Bible. The poem is quite elegant and even contains a pun on the newspaper's name ("joy" in Ottoman). Even its obsequious ending is playful, as it rhymes the sultan's name with "God": "demandare syempre a Dyos / kon mi flaka vos / vida i glorya para Sultan Hamid 2 [dos]."[166]

Benghiat's pragmatic flattery is of an entirely secular nature, and his poem, unlike the one from *Sha'arei mizrach* discussed above, is modeled after European poetry rather than the semi-religious *coplas*. Moreover, it has a new function, namely, to entertain the readers. But who are Benghiat's intended readers? First of all, they are lovers of literature, able to appreciate the form rather than simply the idea. Second, they are educated modern Jews, possibly—like the editor—alumni of the Alliance schools, well informed about the situation of their coreligionists in other countries. They know from the papers about the Dreyfus Affair, the persecution of Romanian Jews, the pogroms in Russia, and the misery of their non-European coreligionists. All those Jews are suffering.

> in France and Paris, land of freedom,
> in Italy and Rome, land of Christianity . . .
> In Rumania, which is called little France,
> where our brethren live in fear,
> in Persia, Morocco, as well as in Russia.

It is hardly coincidental that Benghiat rhymes *Fransya* with *ansya* (anxiety, fear). Nevertheless, the mention of France as a country where freedom does not guarantee safety to Jews does not mean that the "myth of the West" was shattered in his mind, but rather indicates that the Dreyfus Affair had become a crucial point of reference for all Sephardi intellectuals. What is important for us here is that instead of lecturing his readers—undoubtedly of both sexes—on the causes of antisemitism, Benghiat merely alludes to the event in a sophisticated and noncommittal way without insisting on a single interpretation of the Affair.

These three texts do not tell us how many people these periodicals reached and, therefore, what influence the press had on the community as a whole. What they do show is how much the social composition of the reading audience and its cultural baggage had transformed. Most important, this change of discourse is an indicator of the pace of secularization.

## Conclusions

> I have already made great sacrifices for my compatriots with the intention of gradually leading them out of their ignorance.
>
> I have twice created a newspaper not with the purpose of gaining profit, but with a nobler goal, and twice I had to give it up as I was unable to bear the costs alone. From my second attempt, I have 1,000 francs' debt which I certainly do not regret, but my means do not allow me to continue the publication. I have abandoned it for the moment in the hope that better times will come. (*Les Archives Israélites*, May 27, 1847, 549–550)

In this letter, one of the most poignant documents in the history of Ladino print culture, Rafael Uziel briefly relates the story of the first attempt to westernize Ottoman Jews. He explains that the goal of his publishing endeavor was to help his coreligionists to emerge from their "ignorance," which in the *Haskalah* parlance stood for religious fanaticism and a lack of secular knowledge that could be received only from Europe. In other words, Uziel aimed at leading Ottoman Sephardim out of the darkness of ignorance to the light of European civilization. He does not see himself as a hero, nor does he resent his coreligionists for not supporting his enterprise. In fact, he obviously does not expect any action on their part, perceiving them as passive recipients of education, but instead hopes that, one day, he will have more resources to continue his noble work.

However, we know that lack of funds was only one reason for Uziel's failure, and later some Sephardi journalists who had no personal resources, such as Elia Carmona, managed to create long-lived periodicals. It appears obvious that Uziel's isolated endeavor was doomed from the start, and it required an organized effort of like-minded reformers in the capital to establish and sustain *El Jurnal israelit*, which served as a school for a few journalists who worked there, like David Fresco, or read it, like Saadi Halevy.

Better times for the Ladino press came with the advancement of a new project of westernization of Ottoman Jews, which differed from the earlier spontaneous attempts in that it had a coherent agenda, was secular in nature, and aimed at mass education of both sexes. The Alliance's activities inspired a new generation of journalists who enthusiastically adopted its program and created a new Sephardi press for mass audiences which, despite the many obstacles in its way, soon gained significant influence in the community. And even though a Ladino newspaper did not appear in everybody's hands, as Fresco had hoped, by mid-1908 the readers of Sephardi periodicals were ready to form different movements and associations and participate in local political life. Thus, in terms of its functions, the Sephardi press had essentially caught up with Europe.

However, the success of the Ladino press, whose reach was limited by the poverty and low literacy of the Sephardi masses, would not have been so overwhelming without the impact of the two other genres of modern Ladino culture. While being closely related to the press the belles lettres and theater had a different scope and promoted westernization in other ways. I will discuss their methods and role in chapters 3–6.

# ▯▯▯ 2

# The Press in Salonica:
# A Case Study

The case of Salonica is unique in that, from the end of the 1520s through the early twentieth century, Jews formed a majority, or at least half, of the city's population. Already in 1519, more than 53 percent of the households (i.e., roughly 15,000 people) in Salonica were Jewish.[1] Another crucial factor in the history of the Salonican Jewish community in the Ottoman period was its demographics. Earlier, as part of Mehmed the Conqueror's plan of repopulating the Ottoman capital,[2] Salonica's Greek-speaking (Romaniot) community was deported to Istanbul, so that by 1478 there were no Jews in the city. A new community was established in the 1490s by Jewish immigrants fleeing from persecution in Europe. In 1530–1531, almost 60 percent of Salonica's permanent inhabitants were Jews,[3] forming a community that consisted of twenty Sephardi congregations "comprising 2,548 households and one Ashkenazi congregation made up of 97 households."[4] Only 4.98 percent of the "Sephardic" immigrants were Italian Jews.[5] These statistics suggest that the overwhelming majority of Salonican Jews spoke Ibero-Romance languages (mutually understandable, at least in writing)[6] and that, forming the majority of the city's population, they had to use Greek and Turkish much less than their coreligionists in other Ottoman cities. These circumstances contributed to the preservation and dominance of the Ibero-Romance vernacular and to the linguistic homogeneity of the Jewish community, which at the time was the largest in the empire. It is, therefore, not coincidental that the first original works in Ladino, Moses Almosnino's *Regimiento de la vida* and *Crónica de los reyes otomanos,* were produced in the 1560s in Salonica. Following the establishment of the first printing press in the city in 1512,

*Regimiento de la vida* and *Crónica de los reyes otomanos,* were produced in the 1560s in Salonica. As is well known, it was also famous for its Talmud Torah (founded in 1520), which attracted numerous students from abroad.

In the mid-sixteenth century, Salonica, the empire's second maritime center (after Istanbul), was a flourishing Aegean port city that exported grain, cotton, wool, silk, and textiles. By the end of the century, however, Salonica's economy began to show signs of decline, which increased in the seventeenth century due to the monetary crisis in the empire. The fall of the city's textile industry and the demise of its commercial activities, together with numerous plagues and fires, led to the mass emigration of Salonican Jews to more prosperous Ottoman cities, causing the community's further impoverishment.

In the nineteenth century, the financial situation of Salonican Jews worsened again. This had to do with the most rapid debasement and inflation in Ottoman history, which, as it has recently been shown, happened in the first decades of the century, before the *Tanzimat,* which was "a period of wars, internal rebellions, and reform."[7] As a consequence of the dissolution of the Janissary corps in 1826, Salonica's old tax arrangements, which had been advantageous for the Jewish community, were revoked. At this time, the city's economy deteriorated to an unprecedented level, and Salonica was "in debt to the Ottoman administration, a debt carried over from year to year."[8] In the 1850s, the economic penetration by the Great Powers into Macedonia, the restrictions imposed on the transit trade at the end of the Crimean War, and the Civil War in America turned Salonica into a "European warehouse."[9] The U.S. Civil War made Macedonia the largest producer of tobacco in the world and an important exporter of cotton. The city also experienced a boom in international trade, leading to a period of extraordinary economic prosperity and subsequent rapid industrialization and urban development.

In 1859, in preparation for sultan Abdul Mejid's visit, Salonica underwent some urban renovations, and its connection to Western Europe was facilitated by a railroad built in 1873 and the inauguration, in 1887, of the Salonica-Marseille maritime line. Two years later, the city saw the construction of a new port. "External connectivity contributed to new internal linkages and intersections for the people of Salonica: the construction of the modern port stimulated the proliferation of new places of social exchange in offices, cafés, bars, hotels, and, later, cinemas along the waterfront promenade."[10] In 1890, a few streets were furnished with gas lights. Three years later, the first tramway line in the city was established.

The economic revival of the 1850s had encouraged a few wealthy Franco families—the Allatinis, the Fernandez, the Morpurgos, and the Modianos—to get more actively involved in communal affairs. In 1856, supported by other Francos, Moïse Allatini initiated a series of reforms aimed at improving the education system and medical services in the city. He spearheaded the establishment of Hessed Olam (World's Justice), a foundation whose first goal was opening a modern school in Salonica.[11] In 1856, Allatini indeed managed to establish the first European-style school open to Jews and non-Jews alike. However, it was closed under pressure from the rabbis five years later, and Allatini resigned his post on the community council.[12] In 1873, the Alliance Israélite Universelle established in Salonica its first school for boys, which a year later was followed by a girls school.[13] During the period of the Alliance schools' existence in the city, some 10,000 Salonican students attended those institutions.[14]

The first practical result of modern schooling was the creation of the Cercle des Intimes. This social club was founded in 1873 by westernized Jewish tradesmen and graduates of the modern schools with the purpose of protecting the interests of Jewish professionals. In 1880, it began to push for the actual implementation of the Organic Statute of the Jewish Nation in Turkey, which had been authorized by the imperial edict of 1867 for all Jewish communities in the empire. A related goal of the Cercle was to weaken the position of the chief rabbi.[15]

It must be emphasized that, even at the beginning of the twentieth century, the majority of Salonican Jews lived in poverty. While the wealthy Salonicans—members of the Jewish elite among them—"congregated day and night in spacious cafés or luxury hotel restaurants where they sat on Viennese chairs at round marble tables" reading foreign newspapers,[16] 90 percent of Salonican Jews, all the reforms notwithstanding, did not make enough money to be eligible to vote in 1912.[17] that year, the city was captured by the Greek army, and the following year it was ceded to the Greek kingdom by the Treaty of Bucharest, which marked the end of the Ottoman period in the history of Salonican Jews.

The richness of the Jewish press of Salonica allows me to examine phenomena not found in the press of other communities. The unique feature of the Salonican Jewish press is the coexistence of periodicals in two languages and, even before 1908, of two conflicting ideological orientations. It is quite remarkable that out of the forty Jewish journals published in the city between 1865 and 1918, seven came out in French and the rest appeared in Ladino.[18] As for the existence of periodicals expressing opposing ideological viewpoints, one of which cautiously conveyed the perspective of a clandestine movement, this had to do with the size of the Salonican Jewish community (70,000—85,000, depending on the source), the city's peripheral location in the empire, and a certain leniency of the local censorship.[25]

## Juda Nehama, Activist and Intellectual

The second half of the eighteenth century witnessed the beginning of a new era of printing in Salonica, which lasted until World War II. Between 1814 and 1941, the city had eight printing presses[19] that published books and periodicals in Hebrew, Ladino, and French. Among the oldest printing presses in Salonica was the one established by Bezalel Saadi Halevy Ashkenazi, the great-grandfather and namesake of La Epoka's founder, who had come from Amsterdam in 1731.[20] It is symbolic that the first Ladino periodical—in fact, the first periodical in any language to appear in Salonica—Juda Nehama's El Lunar, was initially printed at that press.

Juda Nehama (1826–1899), according to his obituary in El Avenir (February 1, 1899, 1), was meant by his father, "a rich Jew of the good old days," for a rabbinic career. In his adolescence, Nehama studied "only the Torah, the Talmud, and the rabbinic commentaries, which he knew in depth." Nevertheless, as a "dedicated partisan of modern civilization" and a man of "extraordinary power of will," he succeeded in getting a good basic education in various fields of secular knowledge. He knew French, English, and probably Italian. Like his father, Nehama was a merchant, and even served as a representative of some European trade companies.[21] As an active proponent of the reform of the Sephardi community, in 1875, he was elected to the Salonican Community Council, later becoming the president of Bikur Cholim (Society for Visiting the Sick).

Nehama married into an influential Franco family, the Modianos,[22] and with them, Moïse Allatini, and some others actively participated in the establishment of modern elementary schools; in 1864, Nehama founded his Colegio de Padre de Familia.[23] The following year, he wrote to the Alliance leaders in Paris asking them to institute a local committee in Salonica, which happened a few months later.[24] Around the same time, Nehama informed the Jewish community of Volos about the Alliance schools and thus encouraged the launching of the Alliance's first institution in the Ottoman Empire (1865).[25] With Saadi Halevy, Nehama was instrumental in establishing Alliance schools in his own city in the 1870s.[26] In addition, in 1861, he translated from English a history book which appeared under the title Istorya universal (reprinted in 1878) and was used for teaching at his own and other modern schools.[27] This chapter exposes the continuities and ruptures between two generations of journalists and the polemics between different camps within one generation. Yet, Juda Nehama, nicknamed the Turkish Mendelssohn,[28] not only actively participated in communal affairs, but also produced a number of texts in Hebrew and Ladino, including his Hebrew poems and essays, as well as correspondence with Samuel David Luzzatto, Leopold Zunz, and other European Jewish intellectuals (published in 1893).[29] Nehama's history of the Jews of Salonica perished in the fire of 1890, together with his famous library of Hebrew books (*El Avenir*, February 1, 1899, 1).

*El Lunar*, which strictly speaking had little to do with journalism as it is understood today, reflects all three facets of Nehama's public persona: he reveals himself as a passionate social activist, an inquisitive intellectual, and, most notably, an indefatigable educator. Indeed, as the editor of a Ladino periodical, he saw his primary goal in enlightening his readers in various fields of knowledge without moralizing or directly advocating a particular lifestyle. But, although *El Lunar* did not discuss current news, it left no doubts about its publisher's liberal views. Starting on October 1, 1864, Nehama's encyclopedic almanac appeared every month until sometime in 1865, when it was shut down by the local authorities. That Nehama, a liberal rabbi with pro-western views, was rescued by influential Europeans (not a rare instance in Salonica) suggests that he might have been denounced by the local rabbis known for their conservatism.

The first Salonican serial contained various kinds of information on natural sciences and history, translations of travel accounts, explanations of Jewish holidays, and contemporaneous documents. The selection of texts for publication clearly indicates that *El Lunar* was intended for a rather educated male audience engaged in trade and financial activities, similar to the readership of *El Jurnal israelit* and *Or Israel*. Thus, one finds in its pages full translations of the commercial Franco-Turkish treaty of 1861 and the Napoleonic Code, the latter published in installments. Other serialized publications included chapters on Chinese Jewry from a travel book by Israel Joseph Benjamin (known as "Benjamin II") and a history of Columbus's voyage to America. Nehama evidently wanted to make his lessons balanced in terms of their subject matter, which is why every issue discusses a great variety of topics, as indicated in the table of contents. For instance, number 2 starts with a Hebrew poem on science; offers a categorization of literary genres, arts, and sciences; explains the reasons for economic crises; provides the historical context of Hanukkah; informs readers about Montefiore's trip to Morocco; and updates them on some recent astronomical findings.

While *El Lunar* uses much less Hebrew than *Sha'arei mizrach,* it often contains biblical quotes, and it, too, has a biblical verse as its motto, though translated into Ladino: "The fear of the Lord is the beginning of knowledge" (Prov. 1:7). Yet, Nehama's perspective on science significantly differs from that of Uziel. At first glance, the latter's views appear to be more progressive, because, in discussing this verse in one of his articles, he concludes that the fear of God alone is not enough: one needs to study the sciences (*Sha'arei mizrach,* no. 3, 17). Nevertheless, Giselle Elbaz's[30] analysis of Uziel's earlier article on the "wisdom of nature" (no. 2, 9), the rhymed excerpt of which was discussed in chapter 1, demonstrates that this is not so. Uziel's piece, based on Aristotelian classification, presents nature as divided into four categories: the silent, the growing, the living that do not speak, and the living that do. Elbaz points out that, instead of introducing new scientific knowledge, the article merely restates what was accepted by the rabbis centuries earlier, because the author's true purpose is to promote the study of science as a means of reaching "an understanding of the wondrous works of God." Indeed, Uziel declares that the study of nature "is very useful for the young men of our nation, so that they will know the greatness of the One who created them."

Around the same time, in 1843, two vernacular rabbis, Isaac Bekhor Amarachi and Joseph ben Meir Sason, published in Salonica *Musar Haskel,* chapter 10 of which deals with geography and astronomy.[31] Although, as Lehmann indicates, this work is atypical of mid-nineteenth-century Ladino *musar* in that its authors' educational project includes secular knowledge,[32] one of its goals is to reaffirm that "there is nothing which is not written or hinted at in our holy Law,"[33] and, therefore, science cannot contradict rabbinic teachings. According to Uziel, the purpose of science is not to make new discoveries but to make the previously received knowledge clearer. Thus, even though "things are much clearer to us than they were for those [who lived] two hundred years ago," the ancient sages—he explains in parentheses—already knew it all.

Nehama's article on astronomy (*El Lunar,* no. 2, 2), written about twenty years later, significantly differs from the works of his predecessors in the field of mass education. He is evidently familiar with contemporaneous astronomical research from the European press and, albeit very cautiously, introduces his audience to this information. His piece reports on an astronomical study carried out in England that predicted the date of the next transit of Venus and attempted to use this observation to measure the distance between Earth and the sun. However, this information is put in a long footnote, which suggests that the emphasis of this essay is not on the new data but on explaining to readers that the world is full of God's glory and that the purpose of science is to testify to this. It is only "in this push for the study of science for the purpose of creating sensitivity to the wonders of God," argues Elbaz, that Nehama's and Uziel's articles are similar. The former, she notes, goes on to ask, "how does it come to be that every morning God creates new stars? Or are they the same stars that orbit . . . above our heads?" No doubt, Nehama was aware of the view that disagreed with the Ptolemaic, geocentric notion of the sphere of "fixed stars" and invites his readers to think of possible answers to these questions. Furthermore, Elbaz indicates that the author becomes even bolder in the last paragraph, where he states that the Earth, "like the rest of the stars, is held without anything in the air and is flying in space." This claim is particularly important for two reasons: first, it contradicts the previously accepted notion that the planets and other celestial bodies are held up in space by a physical medium. Second, it acknowledges that "the Earth moves, even though the type of motion is not specified."

However, Nehama adds a footnote in which he cites both the Bible and a rabbinic commentary to support his claim that the study of science serves to reinforce faith by instilling the awe of God in people's minds. It seems that this footnote as well as Uziel's parenthetical comment were meant to appease the rabbis and the more pious readers, but they could have also expressed the authors' true beliefs or, at least, their fear that young people might question the validity of *all* religious assumptions. In any case, it is clear that the early Ladino press as a medium of mass education had not yet parted ways with the contemporaneous *musar* literature and, regardless of the westernizers' own beliefs, the latter continued to be its cultural referent.

Change did not come until the early 1870s, when the press openly proclaimed the power of science, which "liberates the people from the darkness, illuminates them by sending out the rays of its light and makes them feel the weight of their cloak of ignorance and the pleasure of throwing it off."[34] (This declaration, among many others, demonstrates that for a great number of Sephardi westernizers, science had become a new religion.) Since *El Jurnal israelit*'s editor did not show particular interest in promoting scientific knowledge, it is legitimate to say that Juda Nehama was the first Sephardi westernizer to encourage—albeit with caution—his coreligionists to go beyond the confines of the rabbinic teachings and pursue scientific knowledge.

## Bezalel Saadi Halevy Ashkenazi in Service to His Community and the Jewish Nation

We have a lot more information about Saadi Halevy (1820–1903), the oldest known Sephardi journalist except Uziel, than about Juda Nehama not only because he was the publisher of two major Sephardi periodicals, but also because his sons—not without his help—made every effort to glorify him. His sons—Sam Lévy in particular—did their best to inculcate in the minds of their contemporaries and posterity an image of their father as a victim of fanaticism, a martyr for progress, and an intrepid fighter for the enlightenment of his nation and humanity. After his death, Saadi Halevy was compared to Jacob, King David, as well as to ancient philosophers and heroes, and his widow, Esther, correspondingly was likened to a biblical heroine. Halevy himself contributed to the construction of this image with his memoir which, though finished some time before his death, was meant to be published only in 1905, when his excommunication term would be over, and was to serve as the dowry of his orphaned granddaughter. Indeed, in 1905, Sam Lévy announced its serialized publication in El Luzero (August 3, 1905, 1), but a few weeks later the newspaper was shut down; some chapters of the memoir appeared in La Epoka in 1907. As Rodrigue and Stein indicate, this version as well as the one that appeared in 1931–1932 in the Salonican periodical La Aksyon were significantly rewritten and embellished by Sam Lévy.[35] His own memoir is written in the same mode with the difference that, in addition to extolling his father, he presents himself as his father's spiritual heir.

But even when Halevy was alive, his sons made sure he would be duly appreciated and did not hesitate to chastise those who, in their opinion, failed to do so. For example, having published a laudatory letter sent to Halevy on the occasion of his eightieth birthday by El Amigo del puevlo (Friend of the People; Sofia, 1890–1902), his son Bezalel, then La Epoka's director, added with irritation: "These lines reminded us that there are in the East other colleagues . . .[36] or, rather, other journalists. Should not they, if only in the news section, sacrifice two lines to the birthday of La Epoka's founder? . . . isn't this required by elementary politeness?" (La Epoka, December 29, 1899, 1).

Because of the efforts of Halevy's sons to craft and maintain a particular image of their father, we have plenty of material on his life, but the hagiographic mode adopted by his family renders it unreliable. In addition, Halevy's memoir, far from being an objective account, is best described as an "apologia and polemic as much as memoir, the rant of a man shaped by a trauma long since past but still intensely vivid."[37] In order to reconstruct Halevy's life, if only in general terms, I had to compare and analyze the evidence found in different sources, though this still cannot guarantee reliable results. I used the memoirs of both father and son, two of Halevy's obituaries (La Epoka, January 16, 1903, 1–4; Le Journal de Salonique, January 19, 1903, 1), and some of La Epoka's articles.

Unlike Juda Nehama, who was born into a well-off family and received a good education, Saadi Halevy was an autodidact, a fact emphasized in all available sources. By the age of thirteen, he was an orphan in charge of his five siblings and a dilapidated printing press operated by three old printers. Having left the *meldar* after a few weeks of frustrating studies, he was barely literate. We are told that later, with the help of a young printer, a former seminary student from Livorno who had converted to Judaism,[38] Halevy educated himself in Hebrew, the Bible, and rabbinic writings. He was fluent in Turkish, but there is no evidence that he knew French or was familiar with European literatures. Nevertheless, not only did he establish *Le Journal de Salonique*, the first Francophone newspaper in the city, but he was also among the first to send his daughters to the Alliance school.

In 1877, Fortuné Halevy was selected by the Alliance committee to study in Paris at its teacher training college, the École Normale Israélite Orientale.[39] Her sister Rachel Halevy (c. 1864–1947) entered this institution the following year, later serving as an Alliance teacher. Together with her husband, Elie H. Carmona,[40] she was sent to various cities, from Plovdiv to Tetuan, to run Alliance schools. In 1909, she received a medal from the Alliance Française.[41] However, all we learn about the nine Halevy sisters from their father's obituaries is that in 1877 he sent one of them to Paris and between 1874 and 1902 he married off seven of them,[42] but none of his daughters is mentioned by name.

Not surprisingly, there is much more information about Saadi Halevy's four sons, especially the youngest one. The eldest was Hayim, whose allegedly inappropriate conduct was used by Halevy's enemies to start the excommunication affair. Hayim was excommunicated together with his father, which might account for his decision to volunteer to serve in a civil guard unit in September 1876. Later, Hayim operated *La Epoka*'s printing press,[43] but, for unclear reasons, his name is never mentioned in published sources.[44]

When Saadi's second son, David (1863–1943), was about to graduate from the Alliance school, its director wanted to send him to study in Paris. However, the father refused to let him go, because at the age of fifteen the young man was already fluent in a few languages and worked as *La Epoka*'s translator.[45] In 1879, having studied with a Turkish lawyer,[46] he started a job at the Passport Bureau and from that moment on was always referred to as Daout Efendi. In January 1900, Daout replaced his father as director of *Le Journal de Salonique,* though apparently he wrote very little himself. In addition, he continued to serve as the personal secretary of the provincial governor. Between the two world wars, Daout Efendi was the head of the Jewish community of Salonica; in 1943, together with most of its members and his own relatives, he was deported to Auschwitz.[47]

Almost nothing is known about Saadi's third son, his full namesake, who, starting in 1897 or 1898 served as *La Epoka*'s director and sometimes wrote for it.[48] Bezalel must have been about a year older than the youngest one, Shemuel, and also graduated from an Alliance school. Shemuel Saadi Halevy, as he signed his Ladino articles, was probably better known as Sam Lévy. His life and work will be discussed in the next section.

When in 1874 Saadi Halevy was excommunicated, the local chief rabbinate sentenced him to a very severe punishment, *herem gadol,* which was meant to be valid through 1905 and was intended to isolate him from the community by not allowing anybody to visit him or commission any work from him. In the words of one journalist, Halevy's persecutors "tried to take away his bread" (*La Epoka,* December 29, 1899, 1), but this worked only partially and only for a short time. As both Saadi and his son Sam indicate, the family was supported by the Cercle des Intimes of which Saadi was the administrator.[49] Therefore, while the Halevy press, which earlier had printed mainly religious literature, lost its old clients, the Cercle's committee, as well as Allatini and his business partners began to commission its owner to print all their materials. Saadi published all sorts of translations of European literature, from history books to fiction, which not only compensated for his financial losses but even proved to be more profitable.[50] Because the workers had been forced by the excommunication of their employer to leave their jobs at the press, the members of the big Halevy family served as composers, editors, and binders.

Aside from the young westernizers, the family was visited by some neighbors and by Saadi's father-in-law, rabbi David Florentin, and his cousin rabbiBekhor Florentin,[51] who took turns calling on their relatives when the head of the family and his eldest son were gone.[52] They continued to do so despite being reprimanded by the chief rabbinate. While Saadi Halevy was banned from attending synagogue, the family celebrated the Sabbath at home, singing the hymns he had composed. In fact, he was famous for his songs of all genres, from the Hebrew *piyutim* to Ladino romances, which were sung by many Salonican Jews at weddings and religious holidays. In addition, Halevy was often invited to sing at rich Turkish and Christian homes and at consular receptions, as there were no European musicians in the city.[53] He was particularly proud of having conducted a choir of forty men that performed in front of sultan Abdul Mejid during his visit to Salonica in 1859.[54]

A few months after "the catastrophe," as the excommunication ordeal was referred to in the family, encouraged by Moïse Allatini, whom he always considered *La Epoka*'s co-founder, Halevy traveled to Vienna to buy a new set of Rashi characters and a Latin font for his press, as he was planning to start a periodical. *El Koreo de Vyena* (The Viennese Messenger; 1869–1884), a Ladino newspaper mainly targeting Ottoman Sephardim, had already informed its readers about his excommunication, which ensured him a warm reception among his coreligionists in the Balkan provinces. It is noteworthy that during this trip Halevy not only attended Sabbath services but was called to read the Torah.[55] In 1875, he received a license for publishing a Ladino periodical, and in 1890 another one, this time to establish its French counterpart.

However, the most striking and emblematic event in the story of Halevy's excommunication is his funeral which, as we learn from a note in *Le Journal de Salonique,* was attended by the rabbinical corps, thus hardly differing from any other Jewish funeral (January 19, 1903, 2). Having acknowledged various people and entities for their support on that day, the family of the deceased expressed gratitude to the community council and the chief rabbi. The same note indicates that Halevy's will was read to his family by rabbi Shaul Amariyo. In other words, not only the lay leadership of the community and the enlightened rabbiAmariyo, a member of the French Astronomical Society and the local committee on Jewish education,[56] but even the chief rabbi of Salonica recognized Halevy's services and chose to ignore the *herem.* It is notable that Saadi's sons were clearly not surprised by this circumstance. Indeed, chief rabbiYakov Kovo (1887–1907) was quite different from Shaul Molho (1835–1849), who used the *herem* against his coreligionists for the smallest transgression,[57] and even from the more liberal Asher Kovo (1849–1874), who had excommunicated Halevy. Yakov Kovo, a supporter of modern education and community reforms, closely collaborated with the local westernizers and in many cases represented their interests.[58]

According to Sam Lévy's estimate, in the 1880s, three-quarters of Salonican Jews were "backward" and only 15,000 or 20,000 embraced liberal views.[59] Therefore, regardless of how accurate this assessment is, I am convinced that it is Halevy's partial isolation from the community, caused by his recent excommunication, and the conservatism of Salonican Jews that are responsible for *La Epoka*'s low circulation in 1877. This explanation is confirmed by the fact that it grew in the 1890s when alumni of the Alliance schools joined the newspaper's readership.

Of course, there were other factors that also had a negative impact on *La Epoka*'s circulation of which we learn from Saadi Halevy himself (*La Epoka,* December 10, 1877, 4). The Russo-Turkish war, as we already know from this article was one of them. Another circumstance that cost the newspaper at least a temporary loss of readers was Halevy's "somewhat thoughtless" article against rabbi Avram Gatenyo, who was generally known to be progressive on the issue of education. Apparently, the journal's attacks on the rabbi were so imprudent that many of its editor's allies and friends withdrew their support, which, uncharacteristically, forced him to recognize his "mistake."

Still, given the size of Salonica's Jewish community, the circulation of the only Ladino newspaper in the city even at the end of the nineteenth century remained disproportionately small, as it did not go beyond 750 copies or so. For comparison, in 1870 the Greek community numbered 18,000[60] while the first Greek periodical in Salonica, which started in 1875 as *Ermis* and ceased publication in 1912 as *Pharos tis Thessalonikis,* claimed a circulation of 400 in 1881.[61] Although the latter figure cannot be taken at face value, these numbers certainly reflect the general situation. Therefore, I would argue that, at least in the first fifteen to twenty years of its existence, *La Epoka* was essentially preaching to the converted, that is, talking to those who did not take its editor's *herem* seriously and who shared his faith in modern education.

The first issue of *La Epoka* came out on November 1, 1875, and the last one appeared on November 22, 1911.[62] It was intended for all Sephardim of the city and nearby Macedonian towns, most of whom in 1875 did not read any other language. Retrospectively, Sam Lévy ascribed to the paper mainly didactic functions, claiming that it was "an organ of the enlightened class of the Jewish community of Salonica . . . that greatly contributed to the awakening of the masses from their lethargy."[63] Sam Lévy's other newspaper, *El Luzero,* advertised *La Epoka* as "the most popular, best written, most liberal, and best informed of all Jewish periodicals in Turkey" (July 4, 1905, 4). The journal's program declared, among other things: "We Jews are very backward. . . . It is our obligation as Jewish journalists to take upon ourselves the duty of propagating the noble ideas in all classes of our nation." Halevy went on to state that a city half of whose population is Jewish ought to have a Jewish periodical.

*La Epoka,* which defined itself as a political, economic, and literary newspaper, started as a weekly, later became a biweekly, and eventually appeared five times per week, ranging from four to eight (and sometimes even ten) pages in different periods. Until the fall of 1900, when its format and print became larger, it used a small font with the subheadings barely distinguishable from the rest of the text. On November 30, 1879, Halevy announced that, as the letters *yod* and *vav* were hard to distinguish, *La Epoka* would try to use Latin script. This note was printed in both fonts, but the experiment lasted only a few weeks,[64] since at the time not many Sephardim were familiar with the Latin alphabet. In 1907–1908, the journal had a weekly supplement, *La Epoka literarya,* edited by Shem Tov Arditi, of which very little is known.

Like most Ladino periodicals, *La Epoka* usually dedicated its first column to editorials and then turned to local news, international events, Jewish news, stock market rates, and port traffic. In the early 1880s, it started publishing commercial advertisements and letters from readers. In the 1890s, the journal began to use graphics and, at the turn of the twentieth century, even occasional photographs, including Saadi Halevy's picture (fig. 2.1), which was printed with his obituary. For most of its history, *La Epoka* promoted cultural assimilation and championed Ladino as the legitimate vernacular of Sephardi Jewry.

Fifteen years after its first appearance, *La Epoka* announced that the Ministry of the Interior had communicated to the provincial governor that the Sublime Porte had given Saadi Halevy permission to add to his Ladino newspaper a French one that would appear twice a week (December 19, 1890, 6). The newspaper's director expressed great joy on the occasion, interpreting this decision as a reward for his special services because many other journalists were denied such permission. The French version of *La Epoka* promised to pursue the same program: it was going to "defend the sacred interests of our fatherland, the beloved Turkey, denounce false allegations and phony information found in foreign periodicals, and protect the interests of our nation." Aside from this, the new journal would cover political and commercial news and talk about all sorts of things. At the end of the note, however, Halevy informed his readers that the French edition would not appear right away, as the press did not yet have the required equipment.

It took another five years for *La Epoka*'s French counterpart, *Le Journal de Salonique,* to appear on November 7, 1895. Aside from expressing its loyalty to the empire, the new periodical promised to provide readers with "intellectual nourishment" and reliable information on foreign politics, commerce, and social life in the city, which would include updates on salons and clubs as well as theater reviews. *Le Journal de Salonique* was the longest-lived French-language Sephardi periodical in the Ottoman Empire. Although its last extant issue is dated November 20, 1910, it is cited by other Salonican newspapers at least through the summer of 1911.[65] Until mid-1908, *Le Journal* was a biweekly and had four pages.

*Le Journal*'s first editor in chief was Vitalis Cohen (known as Sheridan), the son of Barukh Cohen, founder of the Masonic lodge Macedonia Resorta. Sheridan was Daout's classmate and had continued his education in Paris, where he later collaborated at boulevard periodicals.[66] In 1895, after twenty years of Parisian life, he returned to Salonica, but even during his tenure as editor in chief of *Le Journal de Salonique,* Sheridan continued to write for *Le Figaro* and *La Gazette de Toulouse.* In 1898, to everybody's regret, he decided to go back to Paris and was replaced by Lucien Sciuto (1868–1947), also an Alliance school graduate and a talented journalist who soon left *Le Journal* to work for *Le Moniteur Oriental* in Istanbul (and later became editor in chief of the Zionist *L'Aurore*). Sciuto's "betrayal" forced Sam Lévy to assume the position of editor in chief in 1898.[67] Unlike *La Epoka, Le Journal* was not a didactic publication, but rather an informative, entertaining, and literary one. It also published serialized novels.[68]

Outside his hometown, Saadi Halevy was best known as the founder of *La Epoka,* one of the major Jewish periodicals in the Ottoman Empire. His life was closely connected to the history of Salonican Jewry in the second half of the nineteenth century, but he was respected not only by his coreligionists. Among the people his sons thanked for their condolences and assistance on the day of the funeral, one finds the governor-general; the heads of the police, gendarmerie, and city guards; journalists from three Salonican newspapers, *El Avenir,* the Turkish *Asr,* and the Greek *Pharos tis Thessalonikis*; the leaders of other religious communities, including the Orthodox metropolitan, who ordered the churches to ring their bells along the route of the funeral procession.

Saadi Halevy's story illustrates the important changes that took place in the last third of the nineteenth century in the life of the Ottoman Sephardi community in general and that of Salonica in particular. To begin with, it shows that by the mid-1870s, due to the emergence of modern schools which accelerated the encroachment of secularization, the Salonican community was no longer homogeneous in its attitude toward religion. Consequently, the rabbis' influence was limited to the conservative segments of the community, who were referred to by the Halevy family as "religious fanatics." Furthermore, unlike in previous centuries, decisions of a local rabbinic court were no longer valid in neighboring provinces and were ignored even by some local rabbis. By the turn of the twentieth century, the chief rabbi of Salonica obviously considered the *herem* an obsolete punitive measure and felt free to disregard Halevy's excommunication. Finally, the new status of the *millets* ensured a direct relationship between the Ottoman government and its individual subjects.

The French obituary signed by Halevy's children depicts him as an ancient philosopher and a biblical hero, because he was never afraid of death and ten years earlier had bought a tombstone, composed his own epitaph, and left detailed instructions on what materials to use for his grave. This obituary is followed by another, shorter one, presumably penned by one of *La Epoka*'s young readers, which allegedly conveys the general mood in Salonica's Jewish community. The author begins by relating Genesis 50:15–21, where Joseph forgives his brothers and promises to guide and nourish them. The author continues in a solemn, quasi-biblical tone:

> Like our Father Jacob and King David, like all great men who rise above the ordinary, Saadi Halevy called his children to his deathbed, blessed them, counseled them, and advised them not to abandon their duties. . . . Let others enumerate his merits and talk about his services to our city and the Jewish nation. All I will say is that Saadi Halevy's life, work, and example are enough to immortalize him. Our community owes him a monument.

## Sam Lévy, Apostle of Sephardism

Sam Lévy (1870–1959) was half a century younger than his father and, despite the proclaimed and real continuity between them, was very much a man of his time. Though the difference between father and son as they appear in photos (figs. 2.1 and 2.2) seems self-explanatory, its full interpretation would require a more comprehensive analysis than can be undertaken here. The two pictures were taken no more than a few years apart. Judging by his look, Saadi must have been around eighty at the time.[69] Sam's picture can be dated more precisely, as it appeared in the preface to his rewriting of a French novel published in February 1905 but could not have been taken before 1904.[70] No doubt, both men dressed up for the occasion, presenting themselves in the way they wanted to be seen by the world. In his only extant (and, most likely, only) photo,[71] Saadi is wearing the traditional garb of Turkish Jews which, in terms of cut and quality of materials, follows the rules set by the Ottoman government in the sixteenth century.[72] The sultans' decrees prohibited *zimmis* (non-Muslims) from dressing sumptuously, wearing green or white, and using expensive furs, such as sable or ermine. These regulations ensured that they would not have more luxurious attire than the Muslims and would be easily identifiable. In the nineteenth century, the reforms aimed at the westernization of the empire abolished clothing restrictions, thus allowing Jews and Christians to wear Turkish fezes and European clothes or anything else they chose. In Salonica, "the Greeks were the first to adopt the European costume. The Jews lost no time following their example. The Dönmes and then the others imitated the Jews."[73]

In his photo, Halevy is wearing a lynx-fur scarf and an *entari*, a sort of robe with a loose, open front and a high, tight collar, and his facial hair is traditional. He would have dressed the same way for the Jewish and non-

Figure 2.1.
Saadi Halevy
in *La Epoka*
(January 16, 1903)

Jewish celebrations where he was invited to sing. Given that the clothing restrictions had been lifted and that he was a passionate westernizer, one might expect Halevy to wear European garb. However, for a man of his age, social background, and occupation, dressing in a European way or shaving off his beard was an unlikely choice and might have meant a conscious rejection of his culture. In his only extant picture, Yehezkel Gabay, just five years younger than his Salonican friend, has a trimmed beard and moustache and is wearing some kind of uniform and a fez.[74] But, as will be remembered, aside from editing *El Jurnal israelit*, Gabay served as an Ottoman judge and therefore had to follow the dress requirements for civil servants. In other words, Saadi Halevy did not actually have many options in his choice of dress, and therefore how Halevy looks in his picture cannot be viewed as a personal statement.

Sam Lévy's photo presents a man from a different world, an impression enhanced by the lack of familial resemblance between father and son. He has an upturned moustache and the short hair en vogue at the time and is

Figure 2.2.
Sam Lévy, 1905,
in *El Giro del mundo
kon sinkometelikes*
(Salonica, 1905).
Ben Zvi Institute Library

wearing a soft hat and a dress shirt with a wing collar. On the whole, he looks like a member of the European bourgeoisie, whether Jewish or not. In an earlier picture, he is hatless, which was common among westernized Sephardim of his generation and had little to do with their attitude toward religion. According to his memoir, Lévy was first dressed *à la franque* at the age of ten, when he entered the Alliance school,[75] which encouraged students to wear European clothes. As Ottoman state institutions had also adopted the European way of dressing, an inspector from the capital visiting the Imperial Turkish Lycée, which Lévy attended in the late 1880s, could not determine his religious affiliation and asked if he was a Muslim.[76] Later, Lévy noted that, while the Turks called his brother "Daout Efendi" because he was a civil servant, they referred to him as "Monsieur Lévy" because he "wore a European hat and a small curled moustache in the French style."[77] Like all Ottoman officials, Daout would have worn European-style clothes and a fez. Sam Lévy's observation, therefore, shows that the abolition of distinctive clothing for different *millets* allowed Turks to identify the social status and cultural affiliation of individual Jews (whom they already knew as such) instead of seeing them as one homogeneous group.

In the process of westernization, an old dichotomy, Muslim versus non-Muslim clothes, was replaced with a new one, European versus non-European clothes. In other words, the point of reference shifted from Istanbul to Paris, allowing Ottoman subjects to express and affirm their cultural allegiance, occupation, and even personal taste instead of exposing their religious affiliation.[78] As a result, collective identities became much less prominent than individual ones, which means that by wearing European garb, westernized Jews by no means intended to hide or deny their Jewishness, but simply expressed their belonging to the European rather than the Ottoman world. This also means that in the case of Sephardim of Saadi Halevy's generation, traditional apparel cannot be interpreted as a sign of conservatism. Rather, it was an unselfconscious expression of their cultural integrity. Indeed, Juda Nehama, Yehezkel Gabay, and Saadi Halevy, while propagating European ideas, did not see themselves as Europeans, but as Ottoman Jews whose mission was to civilize their backward coreligionists.

At the age of six, Sam Lévy (or, more precisely, Shemuel Saadi Halevy) entered a private elementary school where he studied the Bible and the prayers. According to him, however, during those four years of religious instruction, he gained a lot more from listening to his brothers and sisters reading aloud the translations of foreign-language books printed at the family press.[79] In 1880, he was admitted to the Alliance school, where he spent six years. He was mostly interested in the sciences and languages and learned French, Italian, Greek, Turkish, and Hebrew. His Greek was good enough at least for oral communication, and his knowledge of Turkish was apparently quite thorough. As the Halevy family had no means to send the young man to study in Paris, he continued his education at the newly opened Imperial Turkish Lycée, where he learned the Ottoman language and literature. However, as a result of a conflict with his classmates and teachers, he was forced to leave the *lycée*[80] and finished his education at a secondary Dönme institution, the Terakki (Progress) School of Commerce.[81]

In 1890, Lévy started a job at the Oriental Railroads office, which he bitterly hated. In the fall of 1893, he had finally managed to save enough for a two-month visit to Paris, where he was welcomed by his friends from the Alliance school and where he established new connections. This trip made such a profound impression on the young man that he returned to Salonica and his much-hated job with a clear plan for his future career. He formulated it in his diary on May 30, 1894: "I will calmly study here for three or four years. In the meantime, I will work and try to save some money. When I decide I am ready for serious things, I will go to Paris and study there for another three or four years. Only then will I be able to dedicate myself to my coreligionists."[82]

Also in 1894, Lévy became concerned about the future of *La Epoka* which, he believed, was somewhat "out of breath" and needed to be revived, or else other publishers would push the Halevy family out of the market. According to Hélène Guillon, he was looking for ways of increasing its circulation, repeatedly insisted on implementing new European technologies and adopted a more aggressive subscription policy. He suggested that *La Epoka* should celebrate its twentieth anniversary by enlarging its format and adding a supplement.[83] However, he found an "insurmountable obstacle" in his father, who "was born at the beginning of the century" and therefore was unwilling to reform the periodical.[84] Furthermore, Sam was critical of his brothers for being incompetent: "My brothers . . . are not extremely educated. They have the most noble intentions, but feelings are not enough for journalism. . . . I am not better educated than my brothers. . . . Yet, I have an advantage over them. I always keep track of the development of journalism in Paris. As I follow it, I retain many things that I will imitate and put into practice later."[85]

Lévy's 1894 diary is the only published document where he complains about his family being conservative and not understanding him. For instance, he blames his relatives for putting obstacles in his way and not letting him stay in Paris longer. His criticism of his father's lack of flexibility must have had some grounds, but overall this disapproval of his relatives and their conduct reflects Lévy's romantic self-image as a daring and lonely intellectual isolated from the hostile world by his unique qualities. As Guillon observes, he turns himself into a protagonist of French Romantic literature, which he was avidly reading at the time.[86] He even talks about killing himself by contracting pneumonia. In this diary, for the first time, we see Sam Lévy in all his complexity, which will later reveal itself in his journalistic work. The young man's profound dedication to the enlightenment of his coreligionists, an immense sense of duty, and a practical approach to publishing coexist with his rather unrealistic view of himself as an unappreciated European intellectual.

Lévy's second trip to Paris (1896–1898) was quite productive. He took a number of classes at the Sorbonne, met well-known people, did a lot of reading, and at the same time regularly contributed to *La Epoka* and *Le Journal de Salonique,* particularly during the Dreyfus Affair. This period of Lévy's life is described only in his memoir and, given his penchant for self-aggrandizement and exaggeration, requires additional research. He talks at length about his encounters with great French intellectuals and famous politicians with some of whom he was, allegedly, on friendly terms.

In 1898, following his father's retirement, Sam Lévy had to interrupt his studies and return to Salonica to help his brothers run *La Epoka*, whose existence, they feared, was endangered by the success of *Le Journal de Salonique*. Though he did not share these fears, Shemuel Saadi Halevy soon became *La Epoka*'s permanent editor in chief[87] and a few months later—as Sam Lévy—assumed the same position at *Le Journal*. But two papers were obviously not enough for the indefatigable journalist: already in his father's obituary, he mentions that soon they will be joined by a third one. Indeed, two years later, *Le Journal de Salonique* announced the appearance of *Le Rayon* (The Ray), a second Francophone biweekly to be edited by Sam Lévy, which was scheduled to appear in early May in Zemun, then a town in Austria-Hungary. The new journal, "especially intended for the Orient" and "inspired by the purest idealism," aimed at providing "quick information (a day earlier than the Viennese press) and at propagating economic ideas and progress" (*Le Journal de Salonique*, February 23, 1905, 1). But that was not all. On March 10, *La Epoka*'s readers saw exactly the same announcement, except instead of *Le Rayon*, it talked about its Ladino counterpart, *El Luzero*. The only other difference in the announcements was the replacement of "the purest idealism" with "the purest truthfulness" (4).

At the turn of the twentieth century, Zemun, now a suburban part of Belgrade on the Sava River, had a small Jewish community consisting of Hungarian Ashkenazim and Serbian Sephardim.[88] No doubt, Sam Lévy decided to establish his new periodicals in Zemun because it was beyond the reach of Ottoman censorship and because he had relatives there: a cousin named Reuven Kadmon Halevy, who was the *shammash* at the Sephardi synagogue,[89] and his son Shemuel Halevy (Samuel X. Löwy). When it turned out that a new Croatian law required the directors of local newspapers to be Austro-Hungarian subjects, Sam Lévy assigned this function to his young namesake (*La Epoka*, June 16, 1905, 3). Both periodicals were printed at the local press but were mainly intended for Salonica, where they were distributed by subscription or sold by the issue.[90]

It is evident that Lévy hoped that his new journals would have a long life, as he "definitively moved to Zemun" and decided to rent out his Salonican house (*La Epoka*, June 21, 12). The next day, *Le Journal de Salonique* congratulated its editor in chief and his wife on the birth of their first daughter (June 22, 1).[91] However, things in Zemun did not work out as planned. Neither of the two newspapers had appeared on the first projected date,

May 1, nor on the new one, May 15. On June 4, the first issue of *El Luzero* had come out but was stopped by the prefect of Mitrovica under the pretext that its editor was not an Austrian subject. On June 22, the problem solved, *Le Journal de Salonique* announced that *Le Rayon* would appear that same day. The second issue of *El Luzero* came out the next day, Friday, June 23. Yet, two weeks later, *Le Journal de Salonique* informed its readers that, due to Sam Lévy's disease, the next issues of his two new periodicals would be delayed and wished him courage in his "moral and patriotic enterprise" (July 6, 1). Indeed, Lévy's "disease" had little to do with his health: sometime around July 4, the police presented *El Luzero*'s director with a document in Croatian saying that the paper would be shut down because it was written "in the characters of a dead language and in a non-recognized tongue" (*El Luzero,* July 19, 1). We do not know whether this was the final pretext for closing the two periodicals, but the last extant issue of the Ladino one appeared on August 19, and there is no mention of later issues.

Although Sam Lévy had a lot of experience avoiding conflicts with Ottoman censorship, he proved to be helpless in the face of its Habsburg counterpart, which effectively continued to exist after 1848. "Censored were disloyal expressions aimed at the chief of state; attempts to undermine love of fatherland, peace, and order; the incitement of hatred between peoples and religions; the insulting of moral or religious feelings."[92] Though the two Sephardi periodicals did not do any of these things, given the general situation in Austria-Hungary in 1905, they must have been found to be suspicious and were shut down.

Immediately after the Young Turk revolution, Lévy announced that he would make ample use of the freedom of speech granted to the press by the constitution (*Le Journal de Salonique,* July 28, 1908, 1). Both *La Epoka* and *Le Journal* started coming out three times a week, Saturday being the only day when neither of them appeared. Later, at different times and for short periods, both were dailies. For many months, *Le Journal de Salonique* had a free supplement in a smaller format that discussed political events.

Not surprisingly, Lévy passionately plunged into heated political discussions on many fronts; ending up in a serious conflict with some local members of the Committee of Union and Progress that eventually led to his emigration.[93] On June 6, 1911, Sam Lévy left Salonica and went to Belgrade, later moving to Bern and then Paris, where he died in 1959. He visited Salonica sometime between 1916 and 1918 to give a series of lectures,[94] and it seems that in this period Lévy seriously considered going back permanently and even made some practical steps to ensure the safety of his return or, at least, the financing of his projected periodicals. The following excerpts from

Foreign Office correspondence expose Lévy's attempts at establishing secret relations with the Allies who, in 1915–1918, used Salonica as the base for their operations in the Turkish straits.

On September 5, 1916, Sir Francis Elliot, a British diplomat in Athens, reported to the Foreign Office in London: "Your letter of July 27 enclosing one from Mr. Sam Levy to Lamb suggesting the subsidising of his Salonica press, reached me by bag on August 27th. Our intelligence service here have reported that Sam Levy is a well-known pro-German, and he has already been reported to the F.O. by the Legation at Berne as a suspect." Citing another report, the diplomat concluded that, since "no local newspaper now dares print anything hostile to the allied cause," the Foreign Office "can let Mr. Sam Levy's suggestion drop."[95] The intelligence report must have referred to a missive from the French embassy in Istanbul stating that, in 1909, *Le Journal de Salonique* was receiving funding from the German consulate and publishing pro-German articles.[96] Lévy was certainly not "pro-German," but he was always ready to accept money from all kinds of sources as long as it allowed him to keep his periodicals going.

Although Sam Lévy spent more than half of his life in other places, he always identified himself as a Salonican and as a Sephardi journalist. he gave talks on the Salonican Ladino press in various countries, including Palestine, and continued contributing to it. And, no matter where his articles appeared, he signed them, "Formerly, editor of *Le Journal de Salonique*" (or *La Epoka*, depending on the language). In the 1930s, he wrote for the Salonican *La Aksyon*. In 1933, he published in his hometown *Les Juifs de Salonique: Quelques considerations sur les origines et le passé des Juifs de Salonique,* which was accompanied by a most complimentary preface and the author's photographs (fig. 2.3 is one of them). During the Holocaust, Lévy tried to intercede on behalf of Salonican Sephardim. After World War II, in 1947, he founded in Paris *Les Cahiers séfardis,* which was dedicated to the history of different Sephardi communities, including some that had been wiped out by the Nazis. It ceased to exist in 1949. Lévy's last work was his memoir (1956).

Sam Lévy was admired and revered by many Sephardim, both readers and publishers of Ladino periodicals in Europe and America, who often referred to him as the doyen of the Sephardi press. In 1947, a new Greek-Jewish journal in Salonica, *Israelitikon vima,* invited him as a collaborator for its Ladino section, and its bulletin, *La Tribuna djudia,* happily informed readers that, despite being very busy with his "Sephardi encyclopedia" (*Les Cahiers séfardis*), "the doyen of the worldwide Jewish press" had accepted the invitation under the condition that the new periodical would "faithfully serve the highest moral interests of Sephardism" (March 26, 1947).[97] Summarizing his long journalistic career, the newspaper used Lévy's own words to describe him as a courageous fighter who was always ready to encounter " 10, 100, or even 1,000 enemies, Jewish and non-Jewish," afraid of harsh truths, which he never hesitated to proclaim. If he had lowered his head before his numerous enemies—the article claimed—he might have become a rich financier, but he "always preferred to be Sam Lévy and nothing else," that is, a writer, historian, and "apostle of Sephardism." Like his ancestors, the "immortal Allatini" and "his glorious father"—continued the panegyric—Sam Lévy "contributed to the development of civilization" in Salonica. Though *La Tribuna djudia* announced that he was alive and well, Sam Lévy could not have wished for a better epitaph.

## David Isaak Florentin, Alias David Palestina

When the validity of the universalist ideas promoted in the Ottoman Empire by the Alliance Israélite Universelle was challenged by a new set of circumstances which gave rise to the ideology of Jewish nationalism, some Sephardi intellectuals, many graduates of the Alliance schools among them, opted for Zionism.[98] Some of them, like Lucien Sciuto—who began as editor in chief of *Le Journal de Salonique,* then worked for the non-Jewish *Le Moniteur Oriental,* and ended up directing the Zionist paper *L'Aurore*— hesitated for a long time before converting to Zionism or even went back and forth between the two movements.[99] Sam Lévy became an even more enthusiastic proponent of French universalism, whereas his schoolmate and a prolific rewriter of French novels, David Florentin, was one of the first Sephardim to espouse Jewish nationalism. The former died in Paris, the latter spent his last days in Palestine.

Photographs of the two Salonican journalists (figs. 2.3 and 2.4) taken long after they had left their hometown illustrate the differences between both their personalities and their later careers. In his photo, taken in 1920 probably in Paris, Lévy is no longer the fashionable young bourgeois we saw earlier, but a casually dressed, aging European intellectual. He has a meditative expression and is holding a manuscript he was, presumably, working on. No earlier photos of Florentin have survived, but he too must have changed a great deal between 1905 and the mid-1930s, when his picture was taken in Tel Aviv. Though it has been retouched, one can still see that Florentin's double-breasted suit jacket with its wide 1930s lapels is rumpled. The intense look on his face, enhanced by the wrinkled brow, makes it clear

Figure 2.3. Sam Lévy, 1920, in *Les Juifs de Salonique* (Salonica, 1933)

that the man in the picture is less interested in the impression he may give than in what he sees in front of himself. Moreover, it is immediately clear that he is a man of action rather than an introspective intellectual.

Little is known about the life of David Isaak Florentin (1874–1941) before the time he became a political activist.[100] Like Lévy and Sciuto, Florentin studied at the Allatini school (the first Alliance school in Salonica). Like Juda Nehama, he received a rabbinic education at a *yeshiva* but did not serve as a rabbi. We do not know what jobs he had between graduation and the establishment of *El Avenir*, but he continued learning European languages and probably made his living by producing translations and adaptations of foreign novels for serialized publication. In chapter 4, I will examine Florentin's rewriting of Dumas's *La Dame aux Camélias*, which testifies to his literary gift that was revealed in its entirety in his journalistic work. In this respect, he was similar to the founders of Zionism, many of whom were talented literati embracing European aesthetic norms and cultural values.

Soon after the First Zionist Congress (1897), Florentin became a co-founder of the Salonican pro-Zionist association Kadima (1899), which later became an influential political club or even a movement with its own publications. Before 1908, Kadima offered Hebrew classes and evening lectures on Jewish culture and put on educational theater shows. It also had a library with a reading room.[101] In December 1897, together with Moshe Aaron Mallah (whose name later disappeared from the masthead), Florentin founded one of the major Ladino periodicals, *El Avenir* (The Future), which continued to appear through 1916. It started as a weekly but after the Young Turk revolution became a daily. It had a weekly supplement, which was at first called *El Nuevo Avenir* but, starting from number 6, changed its name to *La Revista popular* (1909–1918?).[102] In 1909, after Victor Jacobson's

Figure 2.4.
David Florentin.
Courtesy of David
Florentin's grandson
and namesake

consultation with the chief rabbi of Salonica, Yakov Meir, *El Avenir* began to receive funding from the Zionist Organization (ZO).[103]

David Florentin was an astonishingly energetic and productive person. Starting in 1909, he combined his indefatigable journalistic work with political activities on behalf of Salonican and, later, Greek Jews. He edited numerous periodicals, including *La Tribuna libera, La Aksyon zyonista, La Renasensya djudia, La Boz del puevlo, La Vara,*[104] *El Punchon,* and *L'Oriental,* and he contributed to all of the other Zionist publications in the city. During the same period, Florentin served as vice president of the Makabi Club, gave numerous lectures on Zionism to Salonican youth, and headed a nationalist organization, the Education Committee of Salonica. He was convinced that even Salonican Jews who were relatively safe should go to Palestine and participate in the building of a Jewish state. After visiting Palestine three times, he became an even more passionate proponent of this idea, which earned him the nickname David Palestina.

Between 1909 and 1919, Florentin participated in eleven Zionist congresses representing Greece and was a member of the Central Executive Committee of the ZO. He spent almost three years (1918–1920) in London where he served as secretary of the eastern division of ZO's council. In June 1918, together with David Matalon and others, David Florentin founded the Greek Zionist Federation of which he was the head from 1921 until 1933, when he emigrated to Palestine.[105] During his previous visits there, he had supported the idea of creating agricultural settlements for Greek Jews and helped to raise funds for establishing one of those, Moshav Tsur Moshe, commemorating the work of the Greek Zionist Moshe Kofina. During the last years of his life, Florentin continued to support this settlement, co-founded the Kadima club in Tel Aviv, and was engaged in various other activities. David Florentin died on July 27, 1941, and was buried in Tel Aviv, where a street was named after him.[106]

*El Avenir* targeted a rather educated audience which included the more advanced readers of *La Epoka* and those Sephardi readers of *Le Journal de Salonique* who were interested in Jewish matters. Hence, its language and materials are more sophisticated than those of its Ladino rival, and only a small number of words are followed by glosses. Furthermore, it has very few of the short funny stories common to most other Ladino periodicals, so that the note on jewelry for dogs allegedly popular in France and America seems rather out of place in this newspaper (August 2, 1905, 4). The entertainment offered to *El Avenir*'s readers appears in the form of serialized novels, many of them of educational character, as well as historical accounts, didactic stories on Jewish culture, and updates on the progress of the sciences. The issue of November 21, 1900, for example, has chapters from three different serials: "A la Americana," "Justice to the Jews," and "A Hundred Years Ago and Today: The Greatest Miracle of the 19th Century: Anesthesia."

On January 14, 1908, *El Avenir* printed the first installment of the instructive story "The Grandfather's Tree: A Novella for Tu B'shvat Written for *El Avenir*" (5–6). On a snowy winter day, a grandfather is telling his grandchildren a story for Tu B'shvat (New Year of the Trees), which is what he did for Purim, Shavuot, and Hanukkah. One of the children seems to confuse Tu B'shvat with Ashura (a Muslim holy day), for which he is rebuked by the other one. Then the grandfather talks about his marriage to the grandmother and the blossoming of their family tree. This novella is similar to the Zionist play *Purim Eve* (1909; see chapter 6), which presents ignorant Jewish children from a westernized family who confuse Purim with Hanukkah and Passover, which gives their Zionist uncle a chance to educate them. *El Avenir*'s story is not as straightforward, but its purpose is the same.

Though *El Avenir* called itself a political, commercial, and literary newspaper, political and commercial news did not occupy much of its space. The only two news topics it reported rather thoroughly—within the limits stipulated by the censorship laws—concerned the Dreyfus Affair and Russian Jewry, the treatment of which was consistent with the Zionist agenda. The manner of presenting news in *La Epoka* and its Ladino counterpart, *El Avenir,* differed a great deal, pointing to the differences between the two readerships. Thus, the Dreyfus Affair was presented by the former in slogan-like terms that conveyed the general mood of the moment as perceived by the editor rather than focusing on the facts. *El Avenir,* which dedicated its first issue to the Affair, continued to discuss it in detail even in the 1900s. For instance, on September 5, 1900 (5), the periodical raised arguments against the bill calling for amnesty concerning all matters related to the Affair, which had been introduced by the French senate earlier that year. While *La Epoka* tended to refer to Dreyfus's enemies as scoundrels and prophesied their imminent defeat, its rival apparently translated articles from serious European newspapers and relied on readers' familiarity with the events. For example, the *El Avenir* article informing readers of Joseph Reinach's libel trial at Madame Henry's request, which took place on January 27, 1899, is entitled "The Lawsuit of Henry vs. Reinach" and begins: "Everybody knew that the trial of Henry-Reinach would be an occasion for a great battle" (February 1, 1899, 2).

Reports on Jewish communities in various parts of the world always took a few columns in *El Avenir*'s issues, even though those accounts were not equally valuable. Some of them put into relief the inherent Eurocentric character of the Sephardi press. Indeed, all Ladino periodicals, regardless of their ideological stance, adopted the Orientalist view of their non-European counterparts, who were perceived as backward and deserving of pity. For instance, one finds in *El Avenir* a translation of an Italian Jew's travel account entitled "The Customs and Traditions of Moroccan Jews" that describes their despondent condition (January 31 and February 7, 1900). Its description of a Moroccan Jew whose "physiognomy is characteristic of the whole race" and whose eyes are "lively and intelligent" barely differs from those published by the anti-Zionist *Les Archives Israélites*. *El Avenir*'s correspondent is horrified by the *mellah* (Jewish quarter) where the traveler "observing this small and unknown Jewish world" will have "to cover his nose passing through the streets where garbage of all sorts has collected and is rotting" (January 31, 1900, 51). *Les Archives Israélites* (May 24, 1900, 162–163), for its part, reports that, aware of the "material and moral situation" of Moroccan Jews, the Alliance decided to put an end to it by opening schools in Marrakesh in order to bring a sense of dignity to those populations who were "bent under brutalizing slavery."

Yet, the situation of Ottoman Jews was discussed in Florentin's periodical with true compassion although often in a pessimistic tone. For example, an article with the disturbing title "A Letter from Sheres: What Is Going to Happen?" (January 9, 1901, 2) talks about the poor Jews in the Macedonian town of Sheres (Sérrai, Serres, Siris), who are suffering from the cold, and asks readers to contribute at least a metalik to support them. Characteristically, the piece is signed "A Jew." The news from Palestine, often borrowed from Ben Yehuda's newspapers *Ha-Zvi* and *Ha-Hashkafa,* by contrast, is always positive and uplifting, and the materials translated from Hebrew are more informative. One article taken from *Ha-Hashkafa,* "Female Journalists in Jerusalem" (December 27, 1897), talks about women writers who not only know the "new language" but contribute to the development of Hebrew literature. Among them is Hemda Ben Yehuda, who is helping her husband to edit this periodical.

It must be remembered that *El Avenir* had to be cautious about its true agenda both because of the censorship restrictions and because it wanted to cater to all westernized Jews of Salonica, most of whom at that time were Alliance supporters. Hence, its critique of this organization was mostly indirect and its discussion of certain subjects, such as religion, was couched in generally acceptable terms. *El Avenir* cited the Alliance's thesis about the need to distinguish between religion and superstitions and to purge the latter from the former, and on May 2, 1900 (184), Florentin published a speech on teaching Judaism delivered by the Alliance's secretary-general, Jacques Bigart, on February 6.[107] Bigart declared that the goal of the Alliance schools is to "strengthen and purify" the religious feelings of their students in the Orient and Africa and stated that "some backward or too advanced minds confuse religion with superstitions (false beliefs)[108] and accuse us of destroying religious feelings in our students," which is contrary to the organization's purpose. Obviously, this pronouncement was as dear to David Florentin as it was to Sam Lévy.

However, responding to the second issue of Avram Galante's *La Vara*, defined by its editor as a "revolutionary organ" and enthusiastically supported by *El Luzero*, Florentin reprimands it for its disrespectful way of referring to the "religious leader of the Oriental Jewry" (August 9, 1905, 10). Lévy, for his part, did not hesitate to make irreverent jokes about his opponents. He made fun of Fresco, for example, who promised to respond to his earlier article "if God allows," but, Lévy concluded, "it seems, God never did" (*La Epoka*, July 12, 1901, 1). Overall, *El Avenir* was a lot more courteous and subtle than Lévy's Ladino papers, which makes its attacks harder to decipher. Nonetheless, when it comes to what the editor perceives as a threat of assimilation, the paper's tone becomes very harsh. For instance, a note in *El Avenir* (January 31, 1900, 48) indignantly describes the balls organized at some Jewish schools that invited many non-Jewish men who, apparently, courted the female students. The anonymous journalist condemns this practice as a "sacrilege" that must never happen again.

Before the Young Turk revolution, the only fundamental disagreement between Zionists and Alliancists that was openly discussed in *El Avenir* was the teaching of languages in Jewish schools. The Paris inspectors who visited Salonican Alliance schools during the first week of 1909 concluded that the language of instruction there should remain French, that Turkish should also be taught and used especially in science and history classes, and that Hebrew should be taught up to a level that would allow the students to improve it later if they wished (*Le Journal de Salonique*, January 13, 1909, 2). As an Alliance graduate and a translator of French novels, Florentin certainly did not object to French instruction. between July 1908 and May 1909, he even published a Francophone Zionist daily, *L'Oriental*,[109] and his illustrated magazine *La Renasensya djudia* (1919–1927) initially came out in Ladino and French.[110] However, Florentin always expressed great concern about the inadequate place given to Hebrew in the curricula of all Jewish schools in Salonica, which he attributed to its low prestige. A note in *El Avenir* (July 26, 1905, 7) mentions a new prize for the study of Turkish, set up by the Alliance's Association des Anciens Élèves, and asks why there is no prize for excellence in Hebrew. The author finds this situation disgraceful, particularly in view of the fact that there is also a Hirsch Prize for French and a Ferrara Award for Italian.

A programmatic article (February 1, 1899, 39), signed by "Israel" and written in the form of a dialogue between two teachers, talks at length about the practice of teaching Jewish children at least three languages—Hebrew, French, and Turkish—at the same time. One of the teachers notes that Alliance institutions also teach Italian, English, and German, as well as Serbian, which is offered after the regular classes. The other one says that the same is done in Europe, to which the first responds that it is easy for Europeans to learn three Romance languages because they speak one themselves, while Sephardi children are forced to learn three unrelated tongues. Obviously, the Europeans whose mother language is a Romance one are the French, that is, the Alliance functionaries in charge of the schools. What is striking about this argument is that Ladino is obviously not considered a valid language (let alone a Romance one) and is not even mentioned, except as the derivate *ladinar,* meaning to translate from Hebrew to Ladino. one teacher insists that Hebrew should be taught first until the children are able to read the Bible, which should happen when they reach the age of eight or nine. Only then should other languages be added.

According to the article, all teachers agree on this point and call for a reform of school curricula. Yet, the reason that Hebrew is the most important of all languages is not given. An indirect explanation is found, among other places, in the conclusions of the Alliance commission which, following the discussion of language instruction, states: the organization is not responsible for the decline of "Jewish sentiment," which it regards merely as a sign of the times. Furthermore, the Alliance does not engage in propaganda "in the Zionist understanding," as its goal is to contribute to the moral and material welfare of all Jews "wherever they are suffering as such." In other words, Zionists, Florentin among them, considered Hebrew to be an indispensable element of Jewishness and blamed the decline of Jewish feelings on its inadequate teaching. This was only one point of disagreement between *El Avenir* and its ideological opponents in Salonica.

## The First Boom of the Salonican Press: 1895–1905

"The Dreyfus Affair awoke in Salonicans a passion for reading and led to a rapid development of the local press. Before 1895, aside from the official Turkish periodical, there was only one weekly. After the first debates around the famous Affair had started, periodicals began to mushroom."[111]

Although this statement from Joseph Nehama's brief history of Salonica gives a good idea of the general situation and the first boom of the city's press, it is imprecise in terms of facts. By "weekly," he must have meant *La Epoka* (then a biweekly, however), and "the official Turkish periodical" most probably referred to the multilingual monthly *Selanik* (1869–1874). But, there was also a Greek biweekly, which in 1895 was entitled *Pharos tis Thessalonikis* (Lighthouse of Thessaloniki); the Ottoman *Mutalaa* (Debate), which spoke of science and culture; and the short-lived Dönme *Gonca-i Edeb* (Rosebud of Literature), founded in the early 1880s, which, in terms of its goals and subject matter, was similar to *El Lunar*.[112] The Serbian and Bulgarian communities had no local press, receiving all their news from Istanbul, Belgrade, and Skopje.[113] In addition, unlike in Izmir and Istanbul, foreign residents and guests did not have a printed source of information on the city's life in a European language.

Aware of the vacuum, Saadi Halevy obtained authorization to publish a Francophone newspaper as early as 1890, but *Le Journal de Salonique* began to come out only in 1895.[114] After the appearance of the bilingual *El Nuvelista* of Izmir (1890), the use of French in a Jewish periodical was not astonishing. What was indeed striking about Halevy's new journal was the absence of the words "Jews" or "Jewish" not only in its program but also in the issue and the paper's masthead. Moreover, in a short note on the front page, under the rubric "Local News," one can read that the new periodical was born on the day of St. Ernest, St. Florint, and St. Thessalonica. The director's message was unambiguous: *Le Journal de Salonique* was a non-communitarian periodical meant for *all* "our populations." Indeed, on December 7, 1895, *Le Journal* published an article on antisemitism in Austria written in a detached tone (1), and a month later it recommended a non-kosher "remedy" for sea sickness: champagne with oysters (January 9, 1896, 4). Thus, for the first time, a Jewish-run periodical attempted to address the residents and guests of a whole city and did so in a language that was not native to any of them (except for a few Frenchmen).

The bilingual newspapers, such as *El Nuvelista* and *La Renasensya djudia*, and the French-language *L'Aurore* (Dawn; Istanbul; 1908–1922) were meant only for a Jewish audience, and thus the use of French was a matter of the publishers' choice. In the case of *Le Journal*, however, Halevy's decision to address all Salonica's residents, that is, individuals from all communities rather than one community as such, left him only one linguistic option. French was the idiom of intracommunal communication in the multilingual city.[115] In fact, it was adopted as the official language of the Cercle de Salonique, a club created in 1873 by members of the Jewish elite and their counterparts from other ethnic groups with the purpose of strengthening social and economic contacts between the communities.[116] Thus, *Le Journal de Salonique*'s intended readers were educated people united by sociocultural allegiances rooted in the European civilization.

Already in the 1850s–1860s, long before the arrival of the Alliance institutions, French was taught to Jewish children at Allatini's school as well as at Juda Nehama's Colegio de Padre de Familia and its successor, run by his student Hayim Asher Shalem.[117] According to *El Avenir* (February 1, 1899, 39), by that time, all Jewish communal schools provided French instruction: "At the end of the nineteenth century Jewish educational establishments in Salonica had imposed French culture to such a degree that the French considered them to be the most perfect centers of their propaganda."[118] In a letter to the Alliance's Central Committee dated January 3, 1909, Moise Benghiat (in this article spelled "Benguiat"), interim director of its first school in Salonica, stated that "approximately 12 percent of the Jewish population over the age of twenty had benefited from the action of the Alliance."[119]

A contemporaneous source indicates that, in 1908, Salonica had thirty-two Turkish schools,[120] twenty Greek ones, seven French ones, and a number of Italian, Bulgarian, Serbian, and Romanian institutions, most of which provided French instruction. Together with the Alliance schools (seven by that time), they taught French to approximately 6,000 students of both sexes.[121] Though we do not have any statistics for the 1890s, it is evident that even then there was a considerable number of Salonicans literate in French as well as foreigners who had learned this language in Europe. This audience was big enough to ensure the financial success of Halevy's new journal.

As will be remembered, Sam Lévy indicated in his memoir that, in the late 1890s, *Le Journal*'s circulation reached 1,000 whereas that of *La Epoka* did not go beyond 750. The only conclusion one can safely make from these statements is that Halevy's first periodical was less popular than the second one. This is also confirmed by the fact that the publisher's sons were concerned that *Le Journal* might overshadow *La Epoka*. In fact, their fears were more grounded than Sam Lévy wanted to admit in his memoir, which does not mention any of the family's competitors in the publishing market (or even the existence of *El Avenir*). While he states that the reports on the Dreyfus Affair he provided from Paris in 1897–1898 contributed to the growth of popularity of both periodicals,[122] he never talks about the indirect negative consequences of this political development for the family business. Meanwhile, on December 15, 1897, the first issue of a new Ladino journal, *El Avenir,* offered its own detailed coverage of the Affair which, together with the First Zionist Congress and certain local events,[123] had hastened the newspaper's emergence. As a result of *El Avenir*'s appearance, the Halevy family lost its monopoly on the Jewish press in Salonica and acquired a commercial and ideological rival.

Since *El Avenir*'s intellectual level and linguistic quality were superior to those of *La Epoka,* it would have attracted many readers of the latter. Besides, its subscription rate (fifty piastres per year) was lower than that of *La Epoka* (sixty piastres). Ironically, the emergence of a Ladino newspaper for an advanced audience was the best evidence of its predecessor's educational achievement: *El Avenir* could not have appeared without the work of the Halevy family. Yet, by the late 1890s, *La Epoka*'s didactic emphasis could no longer satisfy some of its better educated readers who, on the other hand, did not find enough Jewish content in its French counterpart and therefore welcomed the appearance of a new Ladino journal.[124] Besides, for the first time, Salonican Jews had an opportunity to choose between two different ideologies. The success of *Le Journal de Salonique* and the emergence of *El Avenir* were the main factors that, as of the late 1890s, kept *La Epoka*'s circulation low.

*Le Journal* must have also lost some of its readers, albeit not as many, to *El Avenir.* In any case, their audiences overlapped, which is indirectly confirmed by the fact that Lévy informed his Francophone readers about the following incident. His article "My Affair" (January 4, 1900, 2) recounts the defamation suit filed against him because "Mochon Efendi, son of Aaron Mallah of *El Avenir,* and even a rabbi, did not find it to his liking that I discussed in *La Epoka* the procedure of tax collection in the Jewish community." Lévy had already appeared in court on January 2 and was supposed to reappear there on January 16. A week after the first article, on January 11, *Le Journal* published its editor's retort to *El Avenir*'s response, but then the subject was dropped.

Needless to say, the real disagreement between Sam Lévy, a staunch supporter of Franco-Judaism, and David Florentin, a lifelong proponent of Jewish nationalism, was a lot more profound and lay on the ideological level. But, since out of fear of censorship Sephardi periodicals could not embrace or even reject Zionism openly, the two journalists had to find discreet ways of disagreeing in the pages of their periodicals, camouflaging their polemics under various guises. As for Saadi Halevy, he regarded Florentin's journal as an evil meant to harm him personally. "But," he wrote in his memoir, intended for posterity, "I hope to God it will not last long."[125]

However, another open war was still ahead, and it had little to do with Lévy's political views. The most convincing evidence of *Le Journal de Salonique*'s commercial success was the birth of its Francophone competitor,

*Le Progrès de Salonique* (1900–1913?), which also started as a non-communitarian biweekly and later turned into a Jewish daily. Though only one of *Le Progrès*'s issues published before 1910 has survived, we have some information about it thanks to the relentless war between the two rivals.

A comparison of the numbers dutifully cited by *Le Journal de Salonique* with those indicated in *Le Progrès*'s 1910 issues shows that *Le Progrès* came out regularly, possibly with the exception of only one week in late June 1908, when it was suspended by censorship. Its permanent owner was Elie Jacob Cohen, and its first publishers were Salvatore Muratori, an Italian citizen and a "staunch philhellene,"[126] and N. A. Xenophontides, the owner of a press and a bookstore in the Greek quarter. Its first editor in chief, one learns from *Le Journal de Salonique,* was the latter's frequent contributor Alfred Combarnous, a Frenchman who called himself a "Marseillais" and signed his articles as "Protis."[127]

On February 26, 1900, *Le Journal de Salonique* announced *Le Progrès*'s appearance—perhaps insincerely—in a friendly tone (2). But a month later, Sam Lévy wrote a long article in the form of a dialogue on the benefits of competition that clearly reflected his growing concern (March 29, 2). A skeptical young man doubts that Salonica's small Francophone elite needs two periodicals, but a wise old man, "a lover of paradoxes," hopes that a "gracious rivalry" will be beneficial both for the public and for the newspapers that will find their own audiences. If there is only one newspaper, he concludes, it is likely to stagnate. The others laugh at the old man's prophecies.

In mid-April, for unknown reasons, Combarnous was fired and announced his return to *Le Journal* (April 16, 1). Lévy immediately declared war on *Le Progrès.* After weeks of virulent polemics, Lévy, without mentioning his rival, proclaimed that competition contributes to economic progress and the common good and that there is enough space for everyone. But, he continued, when it is a matter of personal ambition and self-interest, such competition becomes destructive for all (June 18, 2). Six weeks later, one of *Le Journal*'s contributors, also recently fired from *Le Progrès,* called it an "Italo-Judeo-Gallo-Greek rag pompously named 'Progress'" (July 30, 1). In September, for purely personal reasons, Lucien Sciuto joined the war on *Le Progrès*'s side. Until early October 1900, the two periodicals kept attacking each other, engaging in bitter personal insults in almost every issue. In the following years, the same kind of futile polemic, albeit not as vitriolic, would often spark between the editors of the two papers, even though during that time *Le Progrès* had a few different ones.

Obviously, the two newspapers had high stakes in this war: one tried to acquire as many subscribers as possible, while the other did its best to lose as few as possible. As was mentioned earlier, according to Groc and Çaglar's catalog, which does not cite its sources or dates, *Le Progrès* had a circulation of 700 copies while that of *Le Journal* was 1,000. Both figures appear exaggerated, but at least we know that the latter number, borrowed from Lévy's memoir, refers to the late 1890s, the time of *Le Journal*'s highest popularity. Not surprisingly, during the first weeks of the periodicals war, Lévy claimed that his rival printed no more than fifty copies. In any case, one thing is certain: the total circulation of 1,700 copies of local Francophone periodicals is a highly unrealistic figure. And since few people would have subscribed to both newspapers, in 1900 *Le Journal*'s circulation must have dropped. Though it addressed all Salonicans, it spoke about Jews more than about the other communities, which is why readers uninterested in Jewish matters would have preferred *Le Progrès,* whose annual subscription rate was lower (seventy-six piastres Versus ninety piastres). *Le Journal* must have experienced its first loss of readers already in July 1900, as both periodicals offered six-month subscriptions. Under these circumstances, Sam Lévy promised that, around October 15, his newspaper would start coming out in a larger format and would have an Italian supplement, its own telegraphic news service, and another supplement that would contain serialized novels by "the greatest modern authors," who so far had not been published in Salonica (September 6, 2).

Only some of these plans were realized, but Lévy had evidently decided that *Le Journal*'s survival would be facilitated if it became a French-language newspaper for educated Jews open to non-Jewish topics. Indeed, by the fall of 1900, its Jewish agenda became highly prominent and, judging by the materials it published and the treatment of Jewish topics, its target audience had become primarily Jewish. Not only did its content and perspective change, but it now frequently used the same materials as *La Epoka,* though presenting them differently and often even in different newspaper genres. The readerships of Lévy's two periodicals now overlapped more than they had earlier, which is clear from the references in *Le Journal* suggesting that its readers look for a certain article in *La Epoka* (but not vice versa).

Though initially *Le Progrès de Salonique* pushed its rival away from the center of the Salonican publishing market, in a few years, it moved in the same direction, also becoming a Jewish periodical. Unfortunately, the information we have on this development is scarce and indirect. *Le Progrès*'s issue of May 16, 1900, came out during the newspaper war, and at least one of its Pieces—a joke about the dumb inhabitants of Marseille—was definitely meant to offend its fired editor in chief. However, this issue also has a philosemitic article whose true meaning cannot be adequately construed for

lack of context. It might have been a response to accusations of antisemitism
(though not from Lévy) or a means of protecting the newspaper from such
accusations in the future. In any case, the piece, which is entitled "Jew!!!" (2)
and signed by Victor Salaha (spelled in French "Salacha"), the periodical's
new editor in chief, is hardly flattering to Jews. Written in a patronizing tone
and from a liberal Christian perspective, the article begins, "Some people are
born with defects! And some families have both noble brothers and pariahs!"
Nevertheless, continues the author, instead of cutting them from the stock,
one should abandon medieval ignorance and follow the biblical injunction
to love each other. It is time to reconcile with everybody, Salaha concludes.

This piece is particularly interesting in view of Le Progrès's subsequent
transformation. Apparently, in 1903, the journal's staff split, and its publisher
and one of the editors quit. On June 12, 1903, Muratori published the
first issue of his Greek triweekly newspaper, Verita/Alithia (The Truth),
covering political, commercial, and philological topics.[128] In May 1909,
this periodical, now called Nea Alithia, was accused of antisemitism by the
editors of Le Progrès and Le Journal de Salonique, who complained to the
local authorities. As a result, the prefect of Salonica ordered them to stop the
publication of the antisemitic Greek novel The Devil in Turkey, published in
serialized form by Nea Alithia and Pharos tis Thessalonikis.[129] In addition,
around the same time, Lévy accused these newspapers of antisemitism for
their inappropriate attacks on the Club des Intimes (Le Journal de Salonique,
May 30, 1909, 1).

In 1903, sometime after the split, Le Progrès became a Jewish periodical.[130]
In May 1908, a well-known Salonican journalist and Alliancist,[131] Alberto
Matarasso, joined the newspaper's editorial staff,[132] later serving as its editor
in chief and director. After the Young Turk revolution, Menahem Molho
took charge of Le Progrès as its manager.[133] Between 1909 and 1915, it even
had a Ladino counterpart, El Imparsyal, directed by Matarasso, Molho, and
M. Ben-Sandji.[134]

Thus, when Sam Lévy decided to establish in Zemun two new journals
intended for Salonica, there were already four Jewish ones in the city. Since
not a single issue of Le Rayon has survived, it is impossible to tell whether the
two newspapers differed only in their language, but it is unlikely that in 1905
Lévy would have attempted to create a non-communitarian Francophone
newspaper again. The fact that the two journals were advertised in the
same words suggests that El Luzero's French self-definition, printed on its
masthead after the Ladino one, did not differ from that of Le Rayon. It
said: "Organ of the moral and economic interests of the Orient and the

Judeo-Spanish [speaking] Jews." All we know about *Le Rayon*'s content is that the issue scheduled to appear after August 19 was going to have a big article dedicated to Franz Joseph's seventy-fifth birthday accompanied by his portrait, while *El Luzero* promised readers a picture of Abdul Hamid II and a special article to mark the twenty-ninth anniversary of his ascension. The choice of the monarch to be praised in combination with the language suggests that *Le Rayon,* at least partly, targeted the local Ashkenazi Jews who did not know Ladino. Besides, the decision to publish a special issue dedicated to Franz Joseph in a "recognized" language no doubt was aimed at pleasing the local authorities. Since Ottoman censors were much more concerned about Lévy's Francophone periodical than about its Ladino counterpart, one can assume that *Le Rayon* was intended to provide uncensored coverage of international news for *Le Journal*'s audience, as well as for that of *Le Progrès.* However, this would not have attracted foreigners who had easy access to the international press.

As for *El Luzero,* twelve of its issues, numbers 3–14, have survived, albeit in poor condition and with some articles cut out. It had six large-format pages and an eight-page supplement (*foyeton*) that contained serialized novels. It is noteworthy that *El Luzero* barely mentioned Ottoman news, and in the rare cases when it did, Lévy was careful about not saying anything he could not have said in *La Epoka.* The only substantial difference in the news coverage between Lévy's three extant periodicals concerns the treatment of the political situation in Russia. This difference is illustrated by the following example. On July 4, the first two items in *El Luzero*—"The Russian Question" and "Notes on Odessa and Kronstadt"—cover in detail the "bloody disorders," and the fourth one informs readers about the revolutionary committee organized onboard the battleship *Potiomkin* (1). *La Epoka* states that, according to the official data, "the number of victims of the recent unrest in Odessa came up to 6,000" and goes on to discuss the situation of Russian Jews (July 7, 3). *Le Journal de Salonique* discusses at length various international news, dedicating to the situation in Russia only the following update: "*Odessa.* Calm has been restored in the city" (July 6, 3). Since *El Luzero* did not use its freedom to criticize the Ottoman government, it is evident that Lévy's main motivation for establishing a periodical outside the empire was to create a forum for his anti-Zionist views. Five of the twelve extant issues of *El Luzero* include his serialized article "I Am an Anti-Zionist" (July 29—August 12), and every issue criticizes and ridicules the Zionist movement.

Unlike *La Epoka, El Luzero* was not an educational newspaper for the masses but, rather, an intellectual journal for their educators, which is why it often discussed pedagogical issues concerning Alliance schools in the Ottoman Empire. One of its most frequent contributors was Elie Carmona, Lévy's brother-in-law, who at that time ran the Alliance school in Yanina (Janina, Ionina). Aside from that school, *El Luzero* talked about the schools in Deregach (Dedeagac, Alexandroupolis) (August 2) and Bosnia (June 30); discussed in detail the method of teaching languages used in Demotica (Dimetoka, Didimoteikhon)[135] (July 26); and covered religious education in Alliance institutions in general (August 2).

*El Luzero* addressed Sephardi intellectuals who shared Lévy's cultural values, including an appreciation of Ladino, though most of them could read French or, at least, Castilian Spanish. The journal often uses Latin characters and, sometimes, French words. One even finds there a popular French maxim without a Ladino translation: *La bêtise humaine est insondable. La vanité donne une idée de l'infini* (Human stupidity is unfathomable. Vanity is infinite). *El Luzero* even published, in Latin characters, the chapters on Hungarian Jews from Angel Pulido's famous book *Españoles sin patria y la raza sefardí* (Madrid, 1905), to which both Lévy and Carmona had contributed.[136]

Following Pulido, who tried to emphasize the Spanish roots of Ottoman Sephardim, *El Luzero*'s editor, in a non-extant issue, referred to Carmona as "Enriquez" instead of "Elie" or "Eliyahu." Annoyed by this, Carmona joined an ongoing debate on names between Lucien Sciuto and Shelomo Shalem. Shalem, a Ladino poet, criticized Sciuto for using the French "Lucien" instead of his real one, "Levi" (July 19, 1). In its next issue (July 22, 1), the journal published an article entitled "My Name," whose author, "Eliyahu, not Enriquez," gave reasons why Jews should not change their names. He wants them to be proud of their ancestors, their nation, and their race and jokingly suggests that one may as well use a Japanese name, since "Japan is now en vogue." He mildly reproaches Lévy for preferring the European "Sam" to "Shemuel" and, in a friendly way, warns him to be careful with his steel weapon (the pen), lest he cut his ties with the past. On August 2 (1), the exchange concludes with the article "Rodrigo and Lucien," signed "Spectateur" (in Latin characters), which suggests that, instead of reprimanding each other for using European names, people should try to be good Jews. The author closes by asking a rhetorical question: would Lazare have been a better Jew or a better supporter of Dreyfus if he had been Barukh rather than Bernard? Judging by the author's style and the example he used, I suspect that Spectateur was Sam Lévy himself.

This discussion about the limits of westernization is a most valuable document on Sephardi intellectual history. Its four participants—an Alliance teacher, a Ladino poet covering Salonican cultural life for *La Epoka,* a former editor of *Le Journal de Salonique* soon to become editor of the Zionist *L'Aurore,* and an anti-Zionist editor in chief of two French and two Ladino periodicals—are like-minded intellectuals devotedly working toward westernization and the enlightenment of their coreligionists who disagree on minor issues. The first two worry that westernization may turn into de-Judaization, whereas their opponents assure them (and later indeed prove with their work) that these fears are groundless and that external cultural manifestations do not matter as long as one is a good Jew. Of course, there is nothing new about these ideas per se, but the tone of the conversation is quite unusual for the Ladino press. Unlike most Sephardi journalists, *El Luzero*'s contributors usually expressed disagreement with their opponents from other periodicals in a polite manner.

For example, on July 22, having warned Lévy against cutting his ties with the past, Carmona responds to the latter's note in the previous issue, where Lévy indirectly compared himself to Don Quixote. The teacher from Yanina encourages *El Luzero*'s editor in chief to continue fighting with windmills but, at the same time, use Sancho's good judgment. If he succeeds in this, promises Carmona, Sam Lévy will become "a new hero famous from the banks of the Danube . . . to the . . . docks of the Bosphorus." This prophecy is an ironic paraphrase (the effect of which is enhanced by the ellipses) of Fresco's characterization in Moïse Franco's *Essai sur l'histoire des Israélites de l'Empire Ottoman depuis les origines jusqu'à nos jours* (Paris, 1897). The author, a well-known Alliance teacher in Edirne and Demotica and a frequent contributor to *El Luzero* and *Le Journal de Salonique,* claims that David Fresco was the most famous Jew in the Orient, "from the docks of the Bosphorus to the banks of the Danube" (218). Carmona's advice to Lévy in a rather subtle way expresses his dislike for *El Tyempo*'s editor who, presumably, would be surpassed by his rival in Salonica. Since most Ottoman Jews were not familiar with Castilian literature, *El Luzero*'s allusions to Cervantes' novel served as a kind of cultural shibboleth, understood and accepted by those westernizers who, at the turn of the twentieth century, were rediscovering the Sephardim's Spanish roots and their belonging to European civilization.[137] Furthermore, I suggest that it was this new ideology that informed Sam Lévy's passionate defense of Ladino as a Romance idiom which, allegedly, made Sephardi Jews closer to Europeans than to Hebrew speakers.[138]

Lévy was aware of the ongoing heated discussion about race, language, and religion among French intellectuals, including Alliance leaders, which in the late 1890s had assumed a political dimension.[139] A superficial familiarity with this polemic, combined with his political agenda, prompted him to understand race as a language community. He enthusiastically concluded that, "despite everything, we are of the Latin race," in fact even more so than Spaniards themselves, because Sephardim retained Spanish in its uncontaminated form (*La Epoka*, May 10, 1901, 1). A few weeks later, during a visit to Izmir, he referred to Ladino speakers as Latins and called for unity among *izmirnyotes latinos* (June 28, 1901, 1). Years later, he revealed the anti-Zionist motivation for his language-race claim by openly accusing Zionists of trying to make Jews "a separate race of Hebrew speakers," that is, "Semites" (*Le Journal de Salonique*, June 29, 1909, 1).

In 1941–1942, Sam Lévy, perhaps halfheartedly, reverted to his old theory, adopting the original meaning of the "Aryan race" in an attempt to alleviate the situation of his Sephardi coreligionists in German-occupied Salonica. Together with Léon Rousseau, on behalf of the Association Culturelle Séphardite de Paris, he wrote to the French Office of Jewish Affairs and the German embassy in Paris requesting that the Sephardim in France and their relatives in Salonica be exempt from the treatment intended for Jews, because in view of their Spanish descent, they should be regarded as a separate race, namely, as "Ario-Latins of the Mosaic faith."[140] These documents were written a few months after Florentin's death in Palestine. Needless to say, nothing could have been further away from the Zionist ideology he had espoused from the moment of its emergence. The old argument between the two Salonican journalists, graduates of the same Alliance school, was over.

## Jews of Three Colors

Since Franco-Judaism was the only modern Jewish ideology available to Sephardim until the late 1890s, Juda Nehama and Saadi Halevy, as westernizers fighting religious fanaticism and backwardness, were in the same camp. Although the journalists who started their professional careers in the mid-1890s never gave up the war on ignorance, the rise of the Zionist movement forced them to choose between the two modern ideologies and the two models of emancipation advocated by their European coreligionists. This schism in the westernizers' camp, which had long-term consequences for Sam Lévy's whole generation, played the same role in his intellectual life as the excommunication did in his father's. The ignorant rabbis of Saadi's battle for Jewish emancipation were replaced with the educated proponents of Zionism, seen as a flawed form of emancipation. The following examples expose some of Lévy's veiled attacks on this new foe.

### European Jews

For the first time in my life I felt proud of being a Jew. To avoid traveling on Yom Kippur and especially in order not to exhaust the young girl whom I was accompanying to her school in Paris, we decided to spend 2–3 days in Vienna.

The day of our arrival was the Sabbath. I was assured that the number of Jews who feel obliged to say the morning and evening prayers is incalculable. The majority of them even close their banks.

But that is not what made me feel proud. Far from it. Everybody knows that at some point the city of Vienna was the center of Austrian antisemitism. The episodes of anti-Jewish actions that took place in the Austrian capital were extremely upsetting. And on Monday, 10 Tishrei, Yom Kippur, the best streets and the most fashionable boulevards of the city, which had seen so many scandalous incidents, seemed to be in mourning. The most important shops, the main commercial companies, the big banks, and even the treasury were closed. And why? Because the Jews could not work that day.

How can one not feel proud seeing the important place the Jews occupy in one of the world's most active centers! On the contrary, the temples were full of people, and how they all prayed! What peace! What serenity! One could hear a fly buzz. And the cantor's voice accompanied by the choir produced a very profound impression on all listeners without exception.

Such sights should be seen by everyone in the world, even by nonbelievers and non-Jews.

—Shemuel Saadi Halevy, "Impressions," *La Epoka* (October 11, 1901)

This description of the Yom Kippur observance in Vienna is an excerpt from a rather long essay about Lévy's trip from Salonica to Paris via Belgrade and Vienna. The dispatch conveys in a nutshell the attitude toward European Jewry shared by all westernized Sephardim before the late 1890s but, in the face of rising antisemitism in France and in the German-speaking countries, no longer unanimously embraced by them. The purpose of this text was to offer readers an example of the Jewish lifestyle deserving emulation and thus to advocate assimilation. Hence, on one level, it functions as the medieval exemplum, a short didactic narrative intended to inspire model behavior, and, on another, it polemicizes with the proponents of Jewish nationalism.

To achieve these goals, Lévy employs one of his favorite rhetorical devices: pretending to adopt the viewpoint of an opponent in order to challenge it. In this case, the assumption espoused by his ideological adversaries is that westernized Sephardim are not proud to be Jews. Hence, the author announces that the Yom Kippur observance in Vienna made him feel proud of being Jewish for the first time in his life, and he goes on to explain that what has impressed him so much is the prominent positions of the Jews in one of the most important financial centers of the world; their faithfulness to Judaism, expressed in a civilized way; and the defeat of antisemitism, achieved by their socioeconomic accomplishments. The importance of gaining economic prominence is reiterated in most of Lévy's dispatches from Ottoman cities. He always vehemently criticizes the local Jews for not making enough effort to become useful members of society, and he offers concrete recommendations as to what they should do. For instance, in a letter from Edirne (*La Epoka,* August 17, 1900, 5–6), he insists that the local Jewish "capitalists" should invest in wool factories, which will allow them to export local fabrics and thus revive the city's economy. By doing so, they will play an important role in Edirne. "So, get to work, coreligionists!" he urges.

It seems that Lévy felt proud of being a Jew earlier on that trip, even during his visit to Belgrade, where he learned that Serbian Jews are as much Serbs as Serbian Christians are. They speak the same language as everyone else, they have the same customs as the rest of the population, and some even hold positions in the state administration. Yet, they maintain their religious particularity. "Is this an advantage or a disadvantage?" asks the author. His answer is positive: it is not only an advantage but also an "excellent response to those who claim that Jews cannot assimilate to the ways of those peoples among which they live."

In his Ladino newspapers, Lévy used every opportunity to profess the commendable Jewish living he found in Europe. The publication of a brief history of Hungarian Jews, borrowed from Pulido's book, concludes with the following lines, concisely formulating Lévy's ideal: "Hungarian Jews no longer see themselves as a separate race and even indignantly refute this idea, but they continue to exist as a *religious community.* They are good Hungarian patriots and nothing else" (*El Luzero,* July 19, 2–3). And in Zemun, "there are no Jews and non-Jews. All respect the same laws, all have the same rights" (*El Luzero,* July 26, 3).

It is clear from the account of the Vienna trip that its author is not observant, because he travels on the Sabbath and seems to be more concerned about the health of his companion than about Yom Kippur. Yet he praises the piety of Viennese Jews who pray twice a day and whose synagogues are places of intense prayer and admirable calm. Although the author does not mention which synagogue he attended, one can be almost certain that it was the neologist Stadttempel in Seitenstettengasse, built in 1826,[141] whose first rabbi was Isaac Mannheimer. Thus, it was one of those "civilized" neologist services that so much impressed the Sephardi journalist. It is unlikely, however, that Sam Lévy was particularly interested in Reform Judaism, let alone tried to advertise it to his Orthodox coreligionists. Rather, like most other westernized Sephardi literati, he would have liked to see religious ceremonies conducted in a civilized way that would ensure Sephardim the respect of non-Jews, by which he means potentially antisemitic Europeans. Moreover, he concludes the passage on Vienna by declaring that the local Yom Kippur services are worthy of being seen by non-Jews and even nonbelievers. It is noteworthy that he does not recommend that non-Jews learn from Judaism but wants to demonstrate to them that Austrian Jews, like their French coreligionists, are able to pray twice a day and conduct their ceremonies like true Europeans. Lévy obviously saw Judaism as a religion that could be separated from the everyday life of Jews, which would allow them to be like their compatriots of other faiths, differing from them only on the Sabbath and religious holidays.

What makes Lévy's Vienna account particularly remarkable is his belief in the defeat of Austrian antisemitism despite the dramatic events covered by one of his own newspapers only a few months prior to this publication. In fact, this firm belief was expressed in those very accounts. Reporting on the antisemitic violence in Vienna that followed a heated discussion in the municipal council (*La Epoka*, April 26, 1901, 2), the journalist presented it as an unsuccessful attempt of twenty-five "ignorant donkeys" to rob a few Jewish houses that was averted by just one Jew with a hammer in his hand. On May 3, *La Epoka* reported that the supreme court had rejected Leopold Hilsner's appeal and confirmed his earlier death sentences on ritual murder charges (2). (In 1899, in Bohemia, Hilsner was condemned to death for murdering a Christian woman for ritual purposes. In 1900, he was accused of another ritual murder and again condemned to death by hanging.) The author of the note was obviously less shocked by the court's decision than by the fact that this could have happened in "such a civilized country as Austria." Furthermore, on July 12, 1901, the periodical proclaimed that antisemitism in Austria was approaching its end every day (2). According to *La Epoka*, this had been demonstrated during the Reichsrat elections when the "antisemitic candidate" promoted by Karl Lueger, the "head of Austrian antisemite," lost to a Jew, Victor Adler.

All of these articles express not only profound faith that progress and education will put an end to antisemitism but also the conviction that this is already happening in Europe, which is perceived as an almost perfect world. Although one can still find there some remnants of the dark past, they are the exceptions proving the rule and usually can be rectified. This unwavering faith in Europe is especially evident in Lévy's response to the

Dreyfus Affair. As far as one can tell from his contemporaneous publications and the memoir, the crisis of French universalism had little effect on his worldview. His memoir presents the events of late 1894–1895 in dark colors, but then the author skips directly to the end of 1897 and moves on to the uplifting events of 1898. In an exultant tone, he compares the effect of "J'accuse . . . !" to the explosion of the atomic bomb over Nagasaki[142] and describes Émile Zola's trial as a great victory.

This steadfast faith in France even during the Dreyfus Affair is particularly evident in Lévy's triumphant article "The Honorable Captain Dreyfus" (*La Epoka*, March 9, 1898, 1). He is happy to inform his audience that "international and even the French press" is on Dreyfus's side and now refers to him as "captain" rather than "traitor." Lévy is confident that it will soon call him the "honorable Captain Dreyfus." This change presumably proves that Truth and Justice are on the march. According to *La Epoka*'s editor, all big newspapers "condemn the conduct of the judges in the Zola, Esterhazy, and Dreyfus trials" and are demanding a revision of the Dreyfus case. Clearly, this article misrepresents reality by ignoring the gloomy events that took place in France during the first two months of 1898. As is well known, on January 11, Ferdinand Esterhazy was unanimously acquitted at his court-martial, whereas Colonel Georges Picquart was indicted for revealing military secrets and arrested. On February 23, Zola was convicted, sentenced to one year in jail, and fined 3,000 francs. The support of the French intellectuals notwithstanding, Lévy still had little reason to celebrate victory and tell the anti-Dreyfusards, "Wait, yellers, bums, scoundrels, and rascals, you can scream and curse like crazy, but nobody is going to pay attention to these wild screams and will continue to work hard." However, it should be remembered that this piece was written during the first months of *La Epoka*'s rivalry with *El Avenir* and is, therefore, intentionally polemical.

### Eastern Jews

[I]n China, there are around 40 . . .[143] million Jews whose lives are as good as anyone can hope for, and nobody mistreats them because of their religion or anything else. Some of them—the poor—perhaps suffer as much as all the other poor in China. There are whole cities of 80–90 thousand souls, even whole regions, inhabited by Jews. There are more than 600 synagogues, which were established 500 years ago or even earlier. Chinese Jews practice all kinds of professions. Some of them chose liberal professions; they are journalists, doctors, professors, lawyers, and so forth.

In Peking, there is a newspaper that has existed for 2,000 years. This newspaper employs a great number of Jewish journalists. There are Jews who are professors at the Peking University, there are Jews who are advisors of high-ranking officials. There is a very high number of Jewish soldiers, officers, and even generals.

There is no distinction based on race or religion. All are Chinese, all are equal but have different beliefs. That is all. Religious tolerance in China is great, which proves that today's war was caused by the missionaries who provoked the masses with their conduct.

The Jews of China settled there more than 2,000 years ago. Some claim that they are the descendants of the tribes that disappeared after the second *Churban beit ha-mikdash.*

If there are indeed 40 million Jews in China, what will say those who want the people of Israel to be separate from the other nations? Are they going to invite Chinese Jews to join them, or are they going to make distinctions even between Jews, so that there will be Israelites of two colors?

And if Chinese Jewry is so advanced, it is good for Jews to become Chinese.

—Shemuel Saadi Halevy, "The Jews of China," *La Epoka* (August 31, 1900)

For 3,000 years, Jews have been ruling, governing, and controlling Abyssinia as its masters and lords. The greatest notables, great officers, and the most aristocratic ladies—all descend from the noble race of Israel. And this is official: this is what Abyssinian history says. The Ethiopians (*habeshes*) come from the 12 tribes of the ancient people of God. Around 400,000 descendants of Jews, pure Jews, formed the caste of priests that governed 14 million people of different colors.

—"Israel in Abyssinia: Black Jerusalem," *La Epoka* (January 3, 1908)

These two texts from *La Epoka*—a passage from a series on Falashas and an excerpt from an essay on Chinese Jews—at first glance seem to be drastically different from the Vienna dispatch. Yet the three pieces have a great deal in common both on the functional level and in terms of genre.

Lengthy, sometimes serialized stories about eastern Jews, regularly published in Ladino newspapers, including the nationalist *El Avenir,* were presumably meant to serve didactic purposes, namely, to inform Sephardim about the history and the present situation of their less privileged coreligionists and to evoke their empathy. Yet these accounts more often than not were used to provide entertainment and, later, to promote certain ideologies. This can be explained by the fact that, though in terms of their values Sephardi intellectuals increasingly identified with European Jews, unlike their emancipated counterparts, they did not feel any responsibility for other non-European Jews (whom they hardly ever met). Consequently, the distortion of facts became the norm in the pseudo-ethnographic accounts in Ladino newspapers, which were usually adapted from already inaccurate foreign-language sources, a practice allowing journalists to misrepresent reality at will to suit their goals.

The second excerpt is from the Falasha history series published in *La Epoka* in January–February 1908. Although the announcement of the series on December 31, 1907, promises to present a translation of a French study, this can be only partly true, because the series is obviously a compilation of various sources ranging from pseudo-historical accounts to the legends about the Queen of Sheba and King Solomon. The proclaimed goal of the series is to serve as "a preface to Rvd. Nahum's notes" from Abyssinia, where the future chief rabbi had been sent by the Alliance to establish schools that would provide education and thus alleviate the plight of the local Jews.[144] In early 1908, articles on Falashas appeared in *Le Journal de Salonique, El Meseret, El Telegrafo,* and other Sephardi periodicals publicizing the Alliance's mission.

*La Epoka* begins its series by introducing readers to the "history" of Ethiopian Jews and later offers a description of religious tolerance in Abyssinia, where, unlike in Europe, Jews and Christians did not fight but for a long time lived in such harmony that they shared many customs and used the same names. This remarkable coexistence is presumably epitomized by the imperial crest of Negus, which "has a cross on one side and on the other the lion of Judah that holds in its right paw a globe around which is written the name of Negus and below which appear the words 'King of Israel'" (January 21, 3). (This crest is the official coat of arms and seal of the Ethiopian monarchy, and the words are "Conquering Lion of the Tribe of Judah.")

An additional article on Falashas (July 3, 1908, 2) was meant to correct some errors in the previous account and promised to tell the true story of the Ethiopian Jews, who, according to the author, "remained fully Jewish" and "played a great political role in the country." This essay was signed "M.B." (Moïse Benghiat) and had a provocative title: "Jewish History: The Jewish State in Abyssinia." Curiously, this optimistic outlook contradicted the Alliance's view as formulated by Jacques Bigart, who described the condition of Ethiopian Jews as "most grievous and distressing" (*Le Journal de Salonique,* January 23, 1908, 2).

In Lévy's "Jews of China," one finds the same elements: the Chinese Jews come from the lost tribes of Israel; their numbers are even more fantastic; and they too live in harmony with the rest of the population, enjoying religious tolerance that allows them to become generals, professors, and lawyers. In other words, both eastern communities have seen the Golden Age and enjoy an idyllic coexistence with their compatriots of other faiths. Obviously, these stories are variations on the old Jewish myth, which is found in Ladino press accounts of non-European Jews discovered in the most improbable places. For example, in the pro-Zionist *El Avenir* (August 9, 1905, 9), we read about the "black Jews" in New Guinea discovered by a British scholar, who identified them as such because their noses were long and wide, they were beautiful, they fasted a few days a year, and they were persecuted by their neighbors. Based on this evidence, the scholar concluded that they were descendants of the lost tribes of ancient Israel.

Another common feature of most reports on the Jews of Japan, Yemen, Ethiopia, and Morocco is that they were not signed. Their validity was affirmed by brief introductions presenting them as translations from German, Italian, or French. This is true, for example, of another article on Chinese Jews, which appeared in *La Epoka* (September 21, 1900) as a clarification of Lévy's essay. It was presumably translated from German and is a typical report on eastern Jews that laments their abandonment of Judaism and their becoming "pagans" as a result of intermarriage and the loss of Hebrew. The appearance of Lévy's "The Jews of China" three weeks earlier was timely, because in the summer and fall of 1900 the Jewish press throughout Europe and the Ottoman Empire published articles on Chinese Jews in connection with the Boxer Rebellion. For instance, a note in *Les Archives Israélites* (August 9, 1900, 862) spoke about the situation of the Kaifeng community and attempts to establish relations with them. The author concluded that it was necessary to find another Joseph Halévy, who would go to the Celestial Empire and find out whether the local Jews, like the Falashas, are the descendants of the ten lost tribes. *El Meseret* enthusiastically summarized Lévy's story in its news section under the title "40 Million Jews of China" (September 7, 1900, 6).

Thus, at first glance, "The Jews of China" does not differ from other texts of this genre, and, though it is signed by Lévy, the actual story is attributed to a Chinese doctor visiting Argentina. It contains implausible facts, and it claims that Chinese Jews are descended from the lost tribes. The author is obviously confused about dates, because he suggests that the ten tribes of Israel disappeared after the destruction of the Second Temple (70 CE) rather than in 722 BCE after the fall of the northern kingdom of Israel, but incorrect dates are typical for all publications of this kind. What makes this piece different from other accounts of eastern Jews is that, though it has all the requisite elements of the genre, it does not use any information from European sources on Chinese Jews that was available at this time of great fascination with the Kaifeng Jews. Moreover, its thesis that, despite complete assimilation, Chinese Jews have maintained their faith contradicts the general consensus of the time: they lost their religion and needed to be reeducated by their European brethren. Apparently, Lévy intentionally ignored the information that did not fit his construction and did not expect this to attract too much attention. His disregard of facts is manifest in the editor's (that is, his own) introduction to the later China essay (September 21, 1900, 3), which was advertised in Le Journal de Salonique the previous day. This is quite unusual and may mean that he felt the need to provide a quick response to his puzzled readers, who wanted to make sure there were indeed 40 million Jews in China, or to protect himself from possible attacks. The newspaper explains that the editor in chief "certainly did not invent the numbers." He had presumably heard or seen it in some newspaper, which must have borrowed the information from another source, and, since "there is no smoke without fire, it is quite possible that a Jewry unknown to Europeans does exist in China."

It is obvious that "The Jews of China" was fully invented by an author who needed the kind of material that would allow him to fabricate anything he wanted and make his argument clear without getting in trouble with the censor. Lévy managed to construct his essay from existing building blocks and clichés, which he held together with his favorite idea, formulated in the Vienna piece and more subtly and less coherently expressed in the Falasha series. Here, again, he insists that the most practical course of action to ensure a happy future for all Jews is full integration into society. Although his dispatch from Europe offers a concrete plan of "nationalization which, while preserving Judaism, will put an end to antisemitism," "The Jews of China" is also a critique of Zionism on the grounds of its impracticality. Lévy needs the 40 million Chinese Jews in order to expose the perceived absurdity of the Zionist project of bringing all of world Jewry to one place. "If there are indeed 40 million Jews in China, what will say those who want the people of Israel to be separate from the other nations?" he asks. Or will the founders of a new Jewish home "make distinctions even between Jews, so that there will be Israelites of two colors?" Yet, if the Jews of China successfully assimilated a few hundred years ago and are so "advanced," all other Jews should "become Chinese" (that is, assimilate), in which case they will be happy where they are and will not need another homeland.

It is likely that "The Jews of China" was Lévy's response to Theodor Herzl's opening address at the Fourth Zionist Congress on August 13, 1900.[145] In his inflammatory speech, Herzl denounced official Jewish leaders, the Alliance Israélite Universelle, the Hilfsverein der Deutschen Juden, and "other assimilationists" for not providing help to Romanian Jews, many thousands of whom had been forced to leave the country, and those who stayed were subject to persecution. Yet Herzl notably failed to offer a concrete plan for solving the problem. Lévy evidently found his own program more useful and realistic than the Zionist solution, though it was based on the experience of a fictional Jewish community residing in an imagined empire of "many mysteries and many wonders."[146] Furthermore, the Falasha account demonstrates that he did not give up on the assimilation project even in 1908, which a few weeks later, after the Young Turk revolution, he was able to announce openly and did not need the continuation of M.B.'s story. Clearly, Lévy had no interest in Chinese or Ethiopian Jews but simply used them as convenient material for a political discussion. He was able to do this because the Ladino press, except for the occasional news reports, presented Jews from distant countries as one-dimensional cardboard figures rather than real people, which made them perfect puppets to play any role assigned to them by Sephardi journalists. Thus, in *La Epoka*, they were no longer the backward and suffering eastern Jews of earlier press accounts but, instead, embodied the ideal type of Jew who could not be associated with any particular place, the model Jew of the Alliance's ideology.

### Russian Jews

As we said in one of the previous issues of *El Luzero*, Russian Jews have organized themselves to prepare for the attacks of antisemitic criminals as well as the cruelties and atrocities from which they suffer every day. They founded a society called the Bund, which exists in all Jewish ghettos of the Russian Empire. They decided to defend themselves at all costs and will fight for their lives and property with all their might. Finally, they asked all their coreligionists around the world to help them by sending either money or weapons. [NB. A few lines are missing in the original.]

Since the pogroms in Homel, a Jewish union has been in existence. The Jewish workers have organized a strong opposition to the murderers by arming themselves and sacrificing their lives. They made it impossible for the bloody scenes of Kishinev to be repeated.

We must *also* add that, since this organization has emerged, all attacks of criminals and reserve soldiers who want to strip and rob our coreligionists have encountered strong resistance from the young Jews who refuse to be slaughtered like sheep.

This organization attracted interest not only among our European coreligionists but *also* among prominent non-Jewish figures. This is how committees in support of the Bund were formed in London under the presidency of our coreligionist Lucien Wolf, a renowned publicist, and another under the presidency of the Countess of Warwick.

—"With Arms," *El Luzero* (July 19, 1905)

This piece is one of the news reports on Russian Jews that appeared in every issue of *El Luzero*. The East-West dichotomy of the Jewish world, adopted by European Jews, placed Russian Jewry, together with Moroccan and Ethiopian Jews, in the category of "eastern" Jews as victims of a cruel regime. Yet the opening sentence shows that—unlike the idealized Viennese Jews who had presumably become respected members of society thanks to their own efforts, or the imaginary Jews of China who had reached their blissful condition due to some unclear historical development—Russian Jews still had to fight for the very right to exist. According to Lévy, while European and eastern Jews demonstrated an enviable ability to assimilate to the ways of their compatriots, their disenfranchised Russian coreligionists did not have an opportunity to become full-fledged members of Russian society or even simply to move out of their ghettos. The difference is explained by the fact that the advanced European Jews and their uncivilized but potentially happy eastern brethren existed in a fictional world where everything was defined in terms of the progress-backwardness dichotomy, whereas their Russian coreligionists lived and died in a real world divided into Jews and antisemites.

In the early 1890s, Ottoman Sephardim had an opportunity to meet Russian Jews when the latter, fleeing from the pogroms, spent some time among them en route to Palestine. In his memoir, Lévy writes that more than 120 Jewish families from Bessarabia found temporary refuge in Salonica, where the local Jewish community received them "with brotherly love."[147] Yet only a few of the "unfortunate refugees from the barbarity of Moscow" managed to learn Ladino and adjust to the new place. Most of them either left for Palestine or went back home. At that time, all Ladino periodicals wrote about Russian refugees, portraying them as victims of persecution. However, in 1904–1905, this discourse began to change, and Russian Jews were more often described by the international Jewish press as brave young men ready to defend themselves and their neighbors from antisemites.[148] The Ladino press also changed its attitude toward Russian Jews and, instead of describing them as victims of violence or as passive recipients of help, started to emphasize their ability to organize self-defense and to find new supporters in Europe. For the first time, Sephardi journalists wrote about real eastern Jews with admiration, albeit still mixed with pity.

Of course, Lévy did not have his own correspondent in Russia and borrowed information from the European Jewish press. But so did the editors of other Ladino newspapers, which is why a few of those periodicals often published the same story with only slight variations. Usually, they differed in length and hence in the amount of information as well as in tone. Our text from *El Luzero*, for example, was preceded by a publication in *El Avenir* (July 11, 1905, 10), which offered its version of the story about the self-defense groups. It begins by announcing that the news from Russia is "sadder and sadder every day." The journalist goes on to cite all the tragic events that took place there and all the accusations against Jews and concludes that the situation is desperate. The article only briefly mentions the self-defense movement and states its goals without going into details.

In contrast, *El Luzero* skips the bad news and focuses on the program of the self-defense groups, emphasizing the good morale of Russian Jews rather than their suffering. It ends on an optimistic note, leaving the reader with the hope that European supporters of Russian Jews will join forces with those of the Bund, which promises a positive outcome. Lévy evidently admires the decision of Russian Jews to defend their lives and property with their own hands, since he recognizes that their situation is different from that of their Austrian counterparts and that one person with a hammer cannot put an end to persecutions organized by the government. Hence, he does not recommend this formula for a perfect Jewish life to those who do not have an opportunity to obtain important positions or even practice the professions of their choice. All Lévy can do is formulate his position as a statement of faith, which is what we find in his article "A Week in Russia" (*El Luzero*, June 30, 3). He declares that the eyes of the whole world are fixed on the events in Russia because of the fight going on there, the fight between "darkness and light, civilization and ignorance, fanaticism and liberal ideas." "Who is going to win?" he asks, and immediately responds, "Of course, progress. The government will introduce reforms as soon as it understands that progress and civilization are inseparable from civic rights. So, it is only a question of time."

We have seen that in the early 1900s, Lévy's periodicals continued to propagate the Franco-Jewish project of emancipation. In response to his Zionist opponents, *La Epoka*'s editor claimed that his travel experiences confirmed his prior conviction that assimilation was the best option for Jews, both in independent states and in various parts of the Austro-Hungarian Empire. If Sephardim chose to take this route, which is the only viable path to modernity, they would have to learn the national language, achieve economic prominence, receive secular education, conduct religious ceremonies in an inconspicuous way, and obey the same laws as everybody else. Until antisemitism was fully eliminated, the state would defend its citizens of Jewish faith. The Russian situation, however, demonstrated that antisemitic regimes did not favor this strategy, which is why Russian Jews had to rely on each other and on their coreligionists abroad. Hence, in 1905, Jewish solidarity became another important issue on Sam Lévy's agenda; and its perceived absence among Sephardim is discussed in the pages of *El Luzero* in dramatic terms. For instance, the well-known journalist from Edirne, Jacques Danon declares, as if it were an established fact, that unlike Ashkenazim, 93 percent of Sephardim are not united (August 2, 3).

The main purpose of Lévy's programmatic article "Ashkenazim and Sephardim: A Confessed Sin Is Half-Absolved" (*El Luzero,* July 26, 2) is to give Sephardim a lesson on solidarity. Its other goal is to show solidarity with Ashkenazim by defending them from antisemites, which is clear from the article's dedication: "To Dr. J. Frank of Agram [Zagreb]." Josip Frank (1844–1911) was a convert from Judaism and the ideological leader of the radical nationalist movement Frankovci, a precursor of the pro-Nazi Croat party, Ustasha.[149] Once again employing his favorite rhetorical device, Sam Lévy pretends to share a negative opinion of Ashkenazim, presumably common among Sephardim. He confesses having seen in Ashkenazim the cause of antisemitism and having believed that they deserve persecution because of being dirty, mean, and stingy. But during his travels, he has learned that they are good people, and it was the suffering and misery that made some of them unpleasant and dishonest. Lévy contends that, even so, Ashkenazim are superior to Sephardim because of their great sense of solidarity: they are always ready to sacrifice their lives for others and often die defending their coreligionists. The journalist interprets this as the solidarity invoked by the Talmudic injunction *Kol Yisrael arevim zeh bazeh,* adopted by the Alliance as its motto and understood to mean that all Israelites are in solidarity with one another.[150]

This alleged change of heart might suggest that Sam Lévy's attitude toward Zionism, which greatly valued Jewish solidarity, also changed. In fact, in the same article, he speaks about Herzl with admiration. However, a few weeks after the Young Turk revolution, he used the freedom of speech to announce publicly, "I am an anti-Zionist. I was always one under the previous regime, and there is even more reason for this now" (*Le Journal de Salonique,* September 17, 1908, 2). But a few weeks later, Victor Jacobson offered to subsidize *Le Journal* and *La Epoka* in exchange for their support of the Zionist cause. In a letter to Nahum Sokolow (October 22, 1908), Lévy agreed to put his periodicals at the service of Zionism under the condition that he would not be required to challenge the territorial integrity of the Ottoman Empire nor to campaign against Ladino.[151]

Consequently, he toned down his critique of Zionism, opened his newspapers' pages to the letters and speeches of Zionist leaders, such as Max Nordau, Jabotinsky, Sokolow, and others, and advertised *Die Welt,* the official organ of the movement (*Le Journal de Salonique,* January 26, 1909). Yet, despite speaking with respect about its ultimate goal, Lévy never authored an article fully supporting Zionism. Furthermore, on June 29, 1909, *Le Journal* published a long, unsigned article titled "Jewish Solidarity and Zionism" that juxtaposes Zionism and the Alliance in favor of the latter, stating that Jewish solidarity existed long before the former was founded (1). The author, undoubtedly close to the editor in chief if not Lévy himself, warned readers that Zionism could jeopardize Jewish unity. Lévy responded with a signed article explaining Zionism's impracticality ("Nationalism or Zionism?" July 1, 2) and, as his "impartiality required," published a critical letter from David Florentin called "Jewish Solidarity or Zionism?" (July 4, 2). Obviously, Lévy's strategy did not deceive Jacobson and others, who concluded that he was unreliable and in early 1911 stopped funding his newspapers.[152]

## Between Ladino and French

An important idiosyncratic feature of the Sephardi press, particularly in Salonica, is the use of two languages—Ladino and French—in one periodical or in different ones directed by the same editor. Even though French largely replaced Hebrew as the language of high culture, its use by the press did not become an ideologically divisive factor. This is accounted for by the distinctive role of French in the Ottoman Sephardi world, as described by Rodrigue: "Acquisition of French, far from weakening Judeo-Spanish ethnicity, simply marked it even more. . . . Speaking French on a daily basis became yet another ethnic marker in the local context."[153] The fact that even Zionists (Sciuto and Florentin among them) published Francophone newspapers and that Saadi Halevy founded one despite not being able to read French shows that the choice of language was entirely determined by the target audience.

The use of the two languages in the same paper for different materials was also intended to attract more readers by creating a certain atmosphere of cultural exclusivity, which made readers feel like members of an elite club. They did not even have to be fluent in French to participate in this sociolinguistic game, because the French texts often took very little space in the bilingual periodicals and, rather than offering substantive information, served as a kind of cultural dessert for a bourgeois audience. For instance, in 1897, El Nuvelista had only a small French section on the last page, which included a few aphorisms and jokes. On March 12, under the pretentious title "A Bouquet of Thoughts," one could read the following maxim: "A woman who does not have anybody to absolve her transgressions sins less." Perhaps it is this dessert function of the French materials that eventually led the publishers of El Nuvelista and La Renasensya djudia to give up on these sections and use only Ladino.

Most Francophone Sephardi newspapers lasted only a few months. For example, Les Annales, published by Alexandre Benghiat's wife, Graziella, in Izmir appeared for just six months in 1914. Only three French-language periodicals survived for more than a year: *Le Journal de Salonique, Le Progrès de Salonique,* and *L'Aurore.* I have already discussed the socioeconomic factors that brought into existence the two Salonican periodicals, but the sociocultural functions they fulfilled for both their editors and readers require special examination. For this purpose, I will analyze Sam Lévy's account of the Ninth of Av commemoration in Edirne, written for *Le Journal de Salonique,* and compare it with the Vienna account of Yom Kippur observance in *La Epoka.*[154]

In August–September 1900, Sam Lévy took a trip "toward the Danube" (*vers le Danube,* as he called it, which included a visit to Edirne. He spent the first half of August there and wrote two dispatches for *Le Journal de Salonique* (August 13, 2; August 16, 2) and one for *La Epoka* (August 17, 5–6). The following is taken from his second French account:

> Every year, on the Ninth of Av, Jews observe the anniversary of the destruction of the Jerusalem Temple. On that day, crowds of believers go to the synagogue, sit on the ground as a sign of mourning, and read the Book of Lamentations, so gripping and sad that it rends the heart. In Adrianople, these rituals take on a particular form. Usually, the streets are almost empty in the evening. At nightfall, everybody goes home, and after one o'clock Turkish time,[155] one rarely hears the harried steps of a late passerby.
>
> On the eve of the anniversary of the destruction of the Temple, the Jews do not light their lamps, but remain in utter darkness. Unaccustomed to going to bed early, they sit before their houses or walk in the street in wool slippers. These shadows moving in the dark, talking in low voices, gesticulating, give a strange appearance to the whole Jewish quarter. From time to time, there rises a plaintive voice bitterly chanting a chapter from Lamentations.
>
> This causes quite an impression. A stranger passing through these darkened streets full of people would be frightened, imagining himself surrounded by ghosts and nocturnal apparitions, and would flee in bewilderment.
>
> It so happened that the first time I came to Adrianople *also* fell around this gloomy commemoration. It made a powerful impression on me. That year, too, I experienced an intense sensation walking alone through a colorful crowd in large dark coats, their gestures evoking Kabbalistic signs worthy of Victor Hugo's pen.
>
> Oh! What an immense role is played in life by such religious rituals born of absurd imaginations and mysticism! What influence they have on the mind of a credulous and impressionable crowd! One almost wishes to see

all these customs disappear. Yet, one dares not wish for this openly, not out of fear of fanatics, but lest sensitive souls be deprived of the mysticism that has such appeal for them. (S. Lévy, "Toward the Danube: Adrianople," *Le Journal de Salonique,* August 16, 1900, 2)

It is immediately clear that this piece differs from Lévy's Vienna dispatch on several levels. In terms of its narrative structure, the latter presents a simple account in the first person, the author of which explicitly identifies himself with his Ottoman coreligionists. While the Yom Kippur observance is presented only from the narrator's point of view, the subject structure of the French passage is complex. The author begins by producing an objective report of what happens in Adrianople every year on the eve of the "gloomy commemoration." But then he tries to defamiliarize the city by making it look mysterious and even frightening. To achieve this effect, he introduces an external point of view by suggesting that a stranger—if there were one— would find the Jews so scary that he would take them for ghosts or nocturnal apparitions and would flee in terror. In the next paragraph, however, we learn that the hypothetical stranger frightened by those bizarre shadows was the author himself during his earlier visit to Edirne. The journalist enhances the sinister mood by switching the narration from his internal point of view to the external one of a stranger and back to the internal one. This transposition of viewpoints, according to Boris Uspensky, is often achieved by the use of modal expressions, such as "he seemed to think," "it was as if he wanted," etc. "These modal expressions function as special 'operators' to translate the description of an internal state into an objective description."[156] In this case, the function of the operator is assigned to the "stranger who would . . . ," which allows the author to convert a newspaper dispatch, presumably reporting on real events rather than on the journalist's mood, into a higher literary genre, the travelogue.

Yet the most striking discrepancy between these two texts is that they seem to be written by different people. The author of the Ladino report is a Jewish educator whose goal is to indoctrinate his readers about proper Jewish living, whereas the French essay appears to belong to a European traveler who, in this particular excerpt, does not even seem to be Jewish. Indeed, the Ninth of Av observance honored by Ottoman Sephardim, as well as by all other Orthodox Jews, is presented as a strange practice and is referred to by the author as "this gloomy commemoration" and "religious rituals born of absurd imaginations." Furthermore, the writer refers to the Jews observing the Ninth of Av as "Jews," "believers," "a colorful crowd," "a credulous and impressionable crowd," etc. These referring expressions indicate that the author does not include himself in this religious community or chooses to detach himself from it, which is why he never uses inclusive pronominal elements, such as *nous* or *notre* ("we/us," "our"). This assumption is corroborated by his comparison of the gestures made by Jews on the Ninth of Av to Kabbalistic signs "worthy of Victor Hugo's pen." A Jew would hardly use this expression to refer to his coreligionists, especially because at the turn of the twentieth century the words *cabalistique* and *cabale*, originally used by Christians to express their hostility toward Jews, still had pejorative connotations.[157] Thus, the narrator describes the Jewish observance not only from the point of view of an outsider but even in terms of a potentially hostile culture. Indeed, the author of the essay appears to be a non-Jew with a rather vague knowledge of Judaism, who regards the Ninth of Av mourning as one of those obsolete religious practices that should have already disappeared alongside all other mystic rites. Yet, as a tolerant European and a sophisticated traveler, he does not wish to deprive the naive "sensitive souls" of the mysticism so important in their lives. Thus, these two descriptions of Jewish observances seem to express different if not opposite attitudes toward religion. Yet, this disparity is only apparent.

As we already know, Lévy does not show any interest in religion per se, but only in the way it is practiced. In fact, always eager to imitate the new ways of European Jews—in the spirit of the discussions of Jewish burials in France—he used Chopin's and Beethoven's funeral marches at his father's funeral. When asked about this by an astonished fellow citizen, he explained that it is not prohibited by religion and that in Europe this is done "every day" (*Le Journal de Salonique,* January 22, 1903, 3). In fact, one might wonder whether, being a "progressive" Jew, Lévy presents the Ninth of Av commemoration as obsolete, replicating the perspective of Reform Judaism which, in the nineteenth century, did not observe this ritual. However, although most French Jews favored reforms, the majority of the innovations adopted by the consistory were of a ceremonial nature.[158] The Alliance, whose position on religion was mirrored in Lévy's writings, tried to introduce some of those changes by means of education, but it never criticized the Sephardi Orthodox liturgy or rites. Furthermore, although Sam Lévy almost never mentioned Jewish holidays, *El Luzero* published an article entitled "Tisha B'Av and Russian Jews," signed "A Pole" (August 16, 1). Having summarized the terrible recent events in the lives of Russian Jews, the author concludes that all days are like Tisha B'Av for them. It follows from the article that only Russian Jews do not have to observe the Ninth of Av, while everybody else should. It is clear from this publication that the Ninth of Av was a meaningful day for Lévy and his peers regardless of how strictly they might have observed it. Nonetheless, Lévy finds it socially permissible to ridicule the archaic aspects of the ritual in his French travelogue. The author of the "Toward the Danube" series evidently resents religion because it was born at the time of absurd beliefs incompatible with the modern age.

This attitude is expressed in Lévy's other texts, most strikingly in a letter to Angel Pulido. Perhaps overstating his true views in order to impress his European addressee, Lévy wrote, "I do not practice religion, quite the contrary. My socialist and even somewhat evolutionist-idealistic views keep me far away from all religious practices to which I am opposed. That is why I am very happy to see religious boundaries, which divided peoples like the Chinese wall, collapse."[159] On the other hand, aware of the role of religion in the public sphere and the importance of teaching Judaism to children, Lévy supported the Alliance's educational project as formulated in its circular, quoted in *El Avenir*. This document states that the organization has always wanted "to strengthen and purify the religious sentiment among the Jewish populations of the Orient and North Africa."[160] In fact, the author of the article "Schools in the Orient and Religion" (*El Luzero*, August 2, 3), a frequent contributor to Lévy's periodicals, complains about the lack of religiosity in the Alliance schools. He suggests that the teachers should incorporate religion not only in teaching but also in everyday life. While he does not maintain that the teachers have to believe in God, he insists that they should not speak negatively about religion in order not to pass on their doubts to children, because for Jews religion and nationhood are inseparable.

Lévy is convinced that children and the masses require religion in order to remain Jewish but also because it satisfies their need for mysticism. However, as a devoted Alliancist and Saadi Halevy's faithful son, he would like to see religion purged of superstitions and practiced "in serenity." Thus, the narrators of the Vienna and Edirne accounts essentially agree about the functions of religion and the ways of practicing it. In fact, on his way from Vienna to Paris, Lévy sees a Polish Jew who boards the train, takes out of a small bag "imagine! . . . guess what! . . . a pair of *tefillin*," and starts praying. Like the Jews of Vienna, he prompts the journalist's admiration by praying on time in spite of being on a train and probably traveling on business.

As for Sephardi intellectuals, according to Sam Lévy, they can refute religion in their private lives because they have other ways of being faithful to their nation. In other words, as an educator of the Sephardi masses, he supports religion in the public sphere, while as the author of French travel accounts, he is free to express the personal views of a European intellectual. However, the limits of his self-expression are largely set by the rules of this genre, adopted by many Sephardi literati writing in French.

It is evident that the Vienna account was written mainly for educational purposes, though it also had obvious polemical overtones. But why did Lévy produce the Adrianople essay for his French periodical? In order to answer this question, I will place this piece in the context of contemporaneous literary production in French. Here is a description of the service in a mosque in Istanbul attended by the imperial army:

> Just below me, the superb army, ever immobile and meditative, silently follows the prayers being sung in the shining mosque before them. It seems as though the soul of Islam were at this moment concentrated within this white sanctuary. Oh, those chants vibrating beneath the dome, as monotonous as magical incantations and possessed of such rare sonorous beauty! Are they the voices of children? Of angels? One cannot say. There is *also* something very Oriental: the tones, exceedingly high, are held onto tirelessly, with the inalterable freshness of oboes. They go on and on, ever renewed; they are sweet, they lull you, and yet they express with infinite sadness human nothingness. One feels dizzy, as before a great abyss.[161]

This is a fragment of Pierre Loti's travelogue in the Ottoman Empire (1890). The narrator, a European, describes a Muslim service in terms that would not be used by an insider. He perceives the prayers as magical incantations and finds in them the "soul of Islam." The similarities between Loti's piece and Lévy's French essay are obvious, and the main difference between the two descriptions of a religious ceremony is that the Jewish one is represented in negative tones and appears quite somber while the Muslim liturgy is seen as luminous and blissful.

The next excerpt belongs to Moïse Franco. In a letter to the Alliance's Central Committee sent from Edirne, he describes the local customs:

> Finally, there is another custom here, as curious as it is moving. Nowhere in the East would any Jewish woman dare set foot in a cemetery. This is not the case in Adrianople. On the first two Sundays of the month, young Jewish widows, either alone or accompanied by their daughters, go in throngs to the cemetery, some in carriages, others on foot. There, not only do they grieve at the tombs of their deceased husbands and give alms to the beggars and poor rabbis, but they *also* confide touchingly and naively in their departed relatives.[162]

Franco creates distance between himself and the local Jews by adopting the point of view of a European ethnographer and, as such, perceives local customs as "curious," "naive," or "touching." He has internalized the European view of his own culture and, by means of defamiliarization, produces a text belonging to the French genre of travelogue in the Orient.

This genre is characterized by quasi-ethnographic representation of local peoples and by interpretation in European terms of their culture as undeveloped or moribund. This is particularly evident in the descriptions of local religions, which are always seen from the Christian perspective. Sam Lévy's representation of the Ninth of Av observance belongs to the same genre. In the essay from which it is excerpted, the outsider whose perspective dominates the account is a European traveler, if only because the narrator's cultural references are those of a European. For instance, he states that some monuments in the city make the trip worthwhile, compares Jews to Hugo's images, and even declares, "in the Orient, work is not valued." Furthermore, he describes the Jewish ritual and dress from an ethnographic perspective and sees the mourning Jews as shadows and specters belonging to the half-dead world of an obsolete religion. As a result, Lévy creates a dark picture of Judaism similar to that found in Loti's travelogue of Morocco. Having described the dirty and smelly streets of Meknes, inhabited by gloomy Jews, the French writer concludes: "For a moment, I . . . am horrified by what may be the lives of these Jews, confined to observe the Law of Moses in fear, buried in their narrow quarter, in the middle of this mummified city cut off from the whole world."[163] The striking similarity between these two representations of Jewish religious life is a result of Lévy's uncritical adoption of the French Orientalist discourse which, among other things, is a product of Christian triumphalism. Consequently, instead of the intended ironic description of a Jewish ritual, the Sephardi journalist produces a rather xenophobic portrayal of his coreligionists.

Obviously, this was a literary exercise rather than an attempt to ridicule Judaism, but it reveals Lévy's eagerness to identify himself with Europeans even though this sometimes implies identification with European Christian culture as such. The same is true for J. Kohn, one of *Le Journal*'s contributors, who suggests that in Salonica many Jewish women, "their delicate faces marked by a certain melancholy, could serve as a lovely model for the Madonna" (May 28, 1900, 2).

Speaking about the first generation of Alliance schools graduates, Guillon notes, "like the provincial bourgeoisie in France, it tries to recreate in its mores and cultural references an idealized Parisian ambience."[164] This observation is certainly correct and is even confirmed by Sam Lévy, who proudly refers to *Le Journal de Salonique* as the "most Parisian publication in Turkey and the Balkans."[165] Indeed, both social groups wanted to distance themselves from their environment, but the westernizers' self-identification with French intellectuals served yet another purpose. Producing a French-language travelogue in the Orient was for Lévy a means of social (rather than literary) self-expression that allowed him to see himself as a European intellectual, culturally superior to his Oriental coreligionists. This legitimized the pedagogical distance between author and readers, presupposed by all didactic literature and therefore necessary for his educational work. This, he obviously felt, justified his speaking to *La Epoka*'s audience in an imperative mode.

In his Ladino dispatch from Edirne (August 17, 1900, 5–6), Lévy does not mention the Ninth of Av but instead presents a detailed account of all the expenses of the local Alliance school, describes the state of local industry, and discusses a few similar matters. Then, he calls upon Edirne Jews to work harder in order to achieve the progress of their community. From the very first sentence, it is clear that the journalist is displeased by the local Jews for not organizing their communal life as he sees fit. Having related to them his socioeconomic program, Lévy impatiently exclaims, "Enough sleeping. . . . So, get to work, coreligionists!"

As we see, both the Edirne report and the Vienna dispatch published in *La Epoka* were intended to serve as lessons on appropriate Jewish living. In fact, the genre repertoire of the Ladino press was quite limited, not leaving the journalist many other options. One of the most common ones was "A Letter from . . . X," which would be written either by a local correspondent or by a journalist whom the periodical would send to an Ottoman city with a Jewish community. Like Lévy's Ladino account from Edirne, these articles never included any descriptions of the place and presented everything from the "Jewish point of view," like, for example "A Letter from Sheres" found in *El Avenir.*

Lévy traveled quite a lot and described in *La Epoka* what he had seen with a didactic purpose in mind, offering his readers a moral lesson whenever possible. He would go to a place that had a Jewish community, even if a tiny one, and report on its life in *La Epoka,* most of the time also producing an essay for *Le Journal de Salonique.* One can take a travel account from either periodical and almost always find its counterpart in the other one, differing the two pieces invariably differed on the ideological level. Since enlightening the Sephardi masses by means of his Ladino writings was undoubtedly Lévy's greatest passion, one can conclude that his French travelogues were a by-product of his work for *La Epoka.*

As a bilingual writer, Sam Lévy appeared before the Sephardi public in two different guises, that of an Ottoman educator and that of a European intellectual whose interlocutors were Bernard Lazare, Theodor Herzl, or even Édouard Drumont. The fact that his audiences partly overlapped and thus many readers of *Le Journal de Salonique* read both versions of the same story suggests that they not only accepted the rules of what I termed a sociolinguistic game but actually participated in it by changing their own guises attached to the respective languages, as they opened each paper. Indeed, the comparison of Jewish gesticulation to Kabbalistic signs was not offensive only because the readers understood that it was a sociocultural convention and that the author was one of them. Otherwise, *Le Journal de Salonique* would not have been a successful Jewish paper.

To conclude, I suggest that Lévy's two accounts of Jewish observances, rather than contradicting each other, expose two facets of the author's social identity, characteristic of Sephardi westernizers of his generation. These two perspectives, which would have been incompatible within one text or even one periodical, did not clash when they appeared in the two newspapers directed by the same journalist because of the two languages coexisting in a quasi-diglossic relationship.

## Conclusions

Between 1875 and 1895, there was only one Jewish periodical in Salonica, but by the summer of 1905 there were six, including the two published in Zemun. Thus, it is evident that, until the late 1890s, the role of the press in the westernization of the Salonican Jewish community was quite limited. *El Lunar*'s circulation was, undoubtedly, very small, and it existed only for about a year. As for *La Epoka*, if we are to believe its editors, in twenty years, its circulation grew from some 200 to around 750 copies. Even if these figures are accurate, given the size of the Salonican community, and Halevy's partial isolation, as well as *La Epoka*'s belligerent tone, this paper evidently addressed only those readers who, at least to some extent, already shared its outlook. This means that, despite the goals stated in its program, most of its subscribers were not the "ignorant masses" but, rather, the alumni of the European-style Jewish schools and those who, understanding the importance of modern education, sent their children to those institutions. Therefore, I suggest that, aside from various sociocultural and ideological factors, the rise of the Jewish press in the city was made possible by the educational endeavors of the Alliance, whose influence extended beyond its own schools to the Talmud Torah.

Although this issue requires additional research, it appears that in this sense Salonica was quite different from Istanbul, where the emergence of the Sephardi press by far predated the establishment of Alliance institutions. The case of Izmir is more similar to that of Salonica, yet the permanent split of the

Jewish community generated almost constant opposition to the press. In any case, by 1905, the Jewish press of Salonica had surpassed that of Istanbul and Izmir in terms of numbers, languages, and ideological orientations. Istanbul and Izmir had two and three Jewish periodicals, respectively, all of them in Ladino and essentially representing only the ideas of Franco-Judaism.

In this chapter, I made the first attempt to study the Jewish press in one city as a unity both on synchronic and diachronic levels, which enabled me to interpret a number of articles in the light of the discussions and polemics between different newspapers and camps. I have uncovered certain facts and topics that until now were hidden from us in their pages. These preliminary results clearly point to the need to expand this research for Salonica, which should also include a thorough study of Jewish schools and the non-Jewish, especially Greek, press. The same kind of investigation will allow us to learn more about the Sephardi press in other Jewish communities in the Ottoman Empire.

*Part 2*　Belles Lettres

# 3

## The Serialized Novel as Rewriting

Sarah Stein's insightful analysis of the advertisements for fashions and cosmetics, as well as dietary recommendations and the pictures found in Ladino periodicals reveals the immense role of indirect means of westernization, which functioned as such regardless of the journalists' intentions. Here, I will examine an even more effective instrument of westernization, which, although initially not intended for this purpose, succeeded in introducing new cultural patterns for imitation in all strata of the Sephardi community. Unlike news reports and history lessons, which frequently used new terms and figures, Ladino novels, which appeared in the pages of newspapers, as separate feuilletons, and, later, depending on the demand, as chapbooks, were well suited for being read aloud. For the same reason, Sephardi Theater, which was specifically created for educational purposes, could also have been effective, but we know too little about its actual audience before 1908 to assess its real impact. In any case, it is clear that, due to economic and spatial constraints, the theater could not reach nearly as many Sephardim as the belles lettres.

In Europe, Jews had been familiar with the novel since the Middle Ages,[1] and among the books printed at the Soncino press one finds an abridged Hebrew version of *Amadís de Gaula* (Istanbul, c. 1540).[2] In the eighteenth century, however, Huli, Assa, and many other rabbis harshly censured those who bought "perverse books written by liars, invented by non-Jews," and those who "wasted time on vanities and jokes."[3] As entertaining secular literature was now seen by Sephardi moral authorities as a new "calamity," such books were not printed. Hence, it is almost a miracle that a significant fragment of a chivalric novel produced in Ladino in the eighteenth century has survived until our day. Paleographic analysis of this unique manuscript demonstrates that it was produced by a professional scribe for a well-off patron.[4] The Ladino belles lettres created by Sephardi westernizers differed from the earlier fiction in the vernacular in that it was published in serialized form and intended for mass consumption which, for the first time, made literary entertainment socially significant.

In the 1870s, Ladino periodicals began to publish serialized belles lettres in order to expand their readership and increase circulation. This new genre, referred to as *romanso,* soon earned a leading position in the Sephardi literary market. By 1939, a few hundred of such works had been published in the Ottoman Empire and its former territories.[5] The length of Ladino novels varied from 16 to a few hundred pages, though most of them did not go beyond 150 pages.

This genre emerged as the adaptation of foreign fiction, most often produced in French, but later also in Hebrew and some other languages. Consequently, not only the so-called faithful translations and adaptations of various kinds, but *all* Ladino novels—including those that claim to be original works—borrowed elements from foreign-language texts and thus depended on them to varying degrees. Since this dependence cannot be quantified and the borderlines between the types of literary production are blurred, I describe all Ladino novels as "rewritings" and refer to their creators as "rewriters."[6] The use of this term is suggested by descriptive translation theories that regard translation as a transfer from one literary system to another.[7] From this vantage point, there is no fundamental difference between calque translations, paraphrases, and summaries, all of which may be called rewritings whether they are produced in the same language or another one as long as they use different semantic codes. So far, my approach to Ladino belles lettres[8] has proven to be the most productive one and has been adopted by some other scholars.[9]

Before my publications on the subject, the Ladino novel had not been interpreted as a genre in its own right. There are quite a few studies of Ladino fiction, published primarily by Spanish scholars whose works, though usually valuable in terms of the information they provide, are descriptive rather than analytical and often make a value judgment on the object of their study. The two leading scholars in this field are Elena Romero, who has produced the most comprehensive synthesis of Ladino narrative fiction,[10] and Amelia Barquín, whose doctoral dissertation and articles contain specific text studies.[11] However, both scholars treat Ladino novels as inadequate translations of European works rather than as a domestic genre. Researchers of Jewish history, for their part, have not attempted to explore Ladino literature as such and have limited their work to cataloging Ladino novels and adding brief descriptions of them.[12] Here, I will develop some aspects of my previous work on this subject, namely, the question of the audience, reconsider and revise certain claims I made concerning the role of translation, and raise new questions, such as the genealogy and functions of the subcategories of the Ladino novel.

Ladino novels often appeared without any indication of the rewriter's name, which is why our knowledge about the creators of this genre is limited and imprecise. In some cases, when scholars are unfamiliar with the foreign-language sources, they attribute the texts in question to the Sephardi literati whose names appear on the title page, which is sometimes erroneous. In addition, many rewriters signed their works with various pseudonyms, which often makes it difficult or even impossible to identify the real person behind a pen name. To make things even harder, some novels were published a few times under different titles.

## Rewriters of Serialized Novels

At least since Huli's time, Ladino literature was produced by members of one social group, the learned class, for another, usually referred to as the ignorant masses. But in the last third of the nineteenth century, as a result of the Alliance's efforts to make education available to everybody by providing free or almost free instruction for poor students, the borders between these two groups became more permeable. Despite the fact that poor students usually could not stay at school for a long time, as they had to help their families to earn a living,[13] even a few years of schooling allowed alumni to become prominent and make an impact on the intellectual life of their communities. As Carmona's story shows, journalists' professionalism depended on their experience rather than on formal education and usually required only some knowledge of French. He spent four years at an Alliance school, which in the early 1880s was far above the average,[14] but because of his family's financial losses he did not finish school, let alone receive a secondary education. Carmona started as a private tutor of French, later worked as a printer at *El Telegrafo* and *El Tyempo,* and ended up publishing his own periodical, the famous and long-lived *Djugeton.*

The majority of Sephardi rewriters were alumni of or teachers at the Alliance schools. Among them were well-known journalists, such as David Florentin and Victor Levy (between 1885 and 1933, the latter published six Ladino periodicals in Istanbul), as well as an Alliance teacher, Jacques

Loria. But arguably the most prolific creator of Ladino novels and a paradigmatic figure of the time was Benghiat whose life is rather well documented.[15]

Alexandre (Bekhor) Benghiat (c. 1862–1924) was not only a journalist and editor but also an amateur actor, inexhaustible author, and translator. He was born and educated in Izmir, first at a *meldar* (which he described in his memoir) and later at an Alliance school. His wife, Graziella, must have been an Alliance alumna as well, because she edited a Francophone Sephardi newspaper. His younger brother Moise was a journalist and an Alliance teacher. At some point in his career, Benghiat changed his Hebrew name, Bekhor, to the European Alexandre, which provoked criticism from some of his colleagues.[16] In 1922, after Greek-Turkish fighting devastated Izmir, he fled to Salonica.

In 1884, Benghiat (still using the name Bekhor) co-founded the Ladino periodical *La Verdad* (The Truth), which closed in a few months for lack of funds. Also around this time, he collaborated with *La Buena esperansa* and *El Telegrafo*. In the early 1900s, the journalist contributed articles to *La Epoka* and *Le Journal de Salonique* and, later, to his brother's newspaper *La Luz* (The Light; Cairo, 1907–?) and to Graziella's *Les Annales*. However, Benghiat was known and remembered primarily as the editor in chief of *El Meseret*. From the outset, the newspaper promised to be more literary and entertaining than political (a wise decision for the time) and declared its intention to provide instruction rather than make a profit. *El Meseret* dedicated a great deal of space to poetry and serialized novels and even had literary contests for its readers. At different times, it had four supplements: *El Kismet poeta/El Meseret poeta* (The Poet's Fate), *El Kismet de martes* (the Tuesday supplement), *El Mazalozo* (The Lucky One), and *El Soytari* (The Clown).

Seeing adaptations of foreign literature as an effective means of westernization, Benghiat produced dozens of skillful rewritings of European classics, which he published first in serialized form and later as chapbooks sold at a very low price. Among his adaptations are works by Jonathan Swift, Harriet Beecher Stowe, Daniel Defoe, Abbé Prévost, Victor Hugo, and Dumas père, but also light contemporaneous stories. It is believed that between 1902 and 1914 his publisher, Shelomo Yisrael Sherezli, printed about fifty of his rewritings.[17] Galante, testifying to Benghiat's orientation toward the poor and uneducated masses, notes that *El Meseret* "greatly contributed to spreading the taste for reading among the backward groups of the population. Written in a simple language, this newspaper was very popular. Benghiat published a great number of popular adaptations in the form of chapbooks, "accessible to everybody and always sold for one metalik."[18]

Benghiat, undoubtedly, saw himself as an educator par excellence whose work, as he put it, was motivated by a love of progress and the wish to educate Jews in Jewish matters, which is why he was willing to make financial sacrifices. However, not all Sephardi literati were willing or able to sell their literary production at such a low price and, as in the case of the periodicals, they urged their readers to stop sharing serialized novels, which Sam Lévy described as the cause of all ills (*El Luzero*, August 3, 1). We find the following indignant admonition against borrowing books in Shelomo Eliezer Ben-Sandji's preface to a collection of novels that he published: "So, you understand, dear readers, that I did this not just because I wanted to please the public, but also because I wanted to please my stomach and those of my family members. By lending this book to one another, you are going to cause damage: neither I will get profit, nor you will have in your libraries such great entertainment."[19]

To be sure, the economic reason that brought the Ladino serialized novel into existence affected the choice of texts for translation and the quality of the rewriters' work. An important source on the writing and publishing business of the time is Elia Carmona's "Autobiography," even though it should be taken with a grain of salt, since the author—a humorous journalist—had a taste for exaggeration. Carmona (1870–1931) writes that, after a few years at an Alliance school, he tried several odd jobs until, encouraged by his mother, he decided to become a writer. His mother suggested that she would tell him short stories (*konsejikas*), and he would print and sell them at a low price. Surprised, Elia asked her, "But can I write?" "If you cannot, you will learn," she responded. "Nobody is born knowledgeable."[20] Carmona then explains that when his Turkish censor prohibited him from using the words "murder," "rob," and "love," he felt that there was nothing he could do as a writer in Istanbul and decided to leave for Alexandria.[21] Even if this is an exaggeration meant to satirize Ladino belles lettres, it aptly captures the situation of the literary market, which was flooded with thrillers, crime stories, and formulaic love novels.

## Readers of Ladino Serialized Novels

In her elucidating essay on the Yiddish-reading public in Eastern Europe, Alyssa Quint challenges the generally accepted notion of two stages in the development of modern Yiddish literature and suggests that in reality it had two discrete beginnings.[22] The first one initiated "highbrow" Yiddish

literature, which was generated throughout the first three-quarters of
the nineteenth century. The second, beginning in the early 1880s, marked
the rapid growth of the "lowbrow" modern Yiddish book industry.[23] Based
on this assumption, she posits the existence of two different audiences
and argues that many *maskilim* wrote for themselves and their educated
contemporaries, even if some of them claimed they wanted to be useful to
the masses.[24]

In the Sephardi community, the situation was drastically different. While
in the first three decades of the Ladino press Sephardi journalists targeted a
small audience consisting of somewhat educated male readers, in the 1870s
they began to address a mass audience of both sexes. At any given time,
there was only one Ladino-reading public, which was offered one set of
secular texts. As I demonstrated, the gradual transformation of the Ladino
press came with the expansion of the audience, which now included the
intended male readers of the earlier periodicals as well as illiterate women.

As an author of mass fiction par excellence, Carmona emphasized that
it was the new readers, previously not exposed to mass secular literature,
who brought him his first financial success: "Having noticed that those who
read in Spanish [Ladino] are those who know neither Turkish nor French,
I started writing in the popular language understood even by children and
old women, and that way my little stories began to have true success."[25]

Carmona's characterization of his readership should be understood in
the sense that, for commercial purposes, he had to make sure that even the
least educated readers would be able to follow his stories. His statement
certainly cannot be taken literally,[26] if only because very few Sephardi Jews—
and only men—were able to read Turkish. On the other hand, among the
readers of Ladino fiction there were many people fluent in French, simply
because educated Sephardim also read Ladino periodicals and thus would
have seen the stories published there. Even *El Luzero* depended on the sales
of serialized Ladino novels, though the majority of its readers would have
known French. Thus, the claim that Ladino belles lettres was produced for
uneducated Sephardim does not imply that Sephardim who were literate in
French did not read it but, rather, that it was primarily *intended* for those
who did not know any other language.

As for children being the intended or at least potential readers of Ladino
fiction, this question has not been dealt with so far, but there is no evidence
showing that Sephardi literati produced anything specifically for children.
Nevertheless, in the next chapter, I will argue that Benghiat's version of
*Gulliver's Travels* was intended for children no less than for adults. It is
possible that Sephardi westernizers did not really target young readers,

leaving their education to schools, and, like Carmona, used the words "children and old women" simply as a merism to emphasize that their production was accessible to everybody. Besides, we do not even know what age group was referred to by the word "child" (*kriatura*) in this context. For instance, *El Meseret poeta* had a rhymed subtitle that described it as "a political and literary periodical comprehensible even for a child."[27] Did Benghiat really believe that children would appreciate his political accounts, or did he use the word *kriatura* because it rhymed with *literatura*?

We know for certain that, since women and children were expected to be present during family readings, there was always concern for propriety (which was also guarded by censorship). Thus, introducing a new serialized novel, Sam Lévy declares that, in choosing appropriate fiction for publication, one has to be careful not to offend the sensibilities of the family or to harm women's morals and children's innocence. "In *La Epoka's Library*," Lévy continues, "we always make sure not to publish immoral works, which could not be read in the presence of the whole family seated around the table" (*La Epoka*, June 27, 1911, 5). The emphasis on family reading is also evident in the following advertisement: "On long winter nights, seated around a lamp, you will spend pleasant hours avidly reading the novel *The Lady of the Camellias*."[28]

All available evidence suggests that all literate speakers of Ladino at least sometimes read Ladino fiction. This assumption is supported by Sam Lévy's article, even though it cannot be taken at face value either, since, as we know, this author also had a penchant for exaggeration and wishful thinking. The article claims that reading has indeed become an absolute necessity for all Sephardim, who need it as much as food and sleep, but each group has its own particular interests: "Men read things that are important for their business and that relate to them as members of human society; women read things that satisfy their curiosity and that talk about household issues and fashions; young lads and girls enjoy reading poetry, essays, literary expressions of new ideas, etc." (*La Epoka*, June 27, 1911, 5). But, the journalist concludes, all members of the family of every age love reading novels.

## Goals of Rewriting and Selection of Source Texts

Though, initially, serialized Ladino fiction was a commercial product, very soon Sephardi literati realized that it could also be used as an instrument of education and would allow them to reach out to new, especially female, audiences. In other words, the Ladino novel was both a market- and reader-oriented literary genre. It had two educational objectives: to encourage Sephardim to read and to expose them to new secular knowledge often different from that found in the press. Obviously, the proliferation of serialized mass fiction automatically expands readerships and thus spreads literacy. As for enlightening Sephardim about other countries and acquainting them with the authors of the foreign novels translated into Ladino, this endeavor undoubtedly had some positive effect, though the new information and the source texts were mediated in such a way that the foreign writers and their works often became almost unrecognizable.

In many cases, Sephardi publishers, such as Shelomo Yisrael Sherezli, saw themselves as educators and, hence, aimed at both making money and enlightening their coreligionists. As most of the printed production was adaptations of foreign novels, the selection of sources had to satisfy both purposes. But since this was usually unfeasible, the rewriters or editors picked the novels that promised commercial success and had them reworked in order to make them acceptable and even instructive, which sometimes required their Judaization.

At first, newspaper publishers would print books at their presses and sell them to their readers as separate editions. The first to do so was *El Jurnal israelit*, which saw its mission as promoting reading among men and women. This goal is directly stated in the advertisement of its three-volume edition of *The Thousand and One Nights*: "We ask you, sinyores and sinyoras, who understand the value of translation, to take notice of our great efforts to encourage the taste for reading in our nation" (February 29, 1864, 1). It is notable that, about sixty years later, the publisher's preface to *Romeo and Juliet*, rewritten by Josef Karaso in the form of a novel, also presents translation as an educational endeavor and a mission: "There is an immense work of education to be done, the education that so far has not been undertaken by anybody seriously and methodically."[29] The publisher, writing under the pen name "Julien," goes on to explain that only good fiction should be translated, because the reading of cheap novels is detrimental to the public's taste and has no educational value. He complains about a "real attack of translations of mediocre works that will increase the number of worthless books translated into Judeo-Spanish."[30]

David Fresco voices the same concern and aspires to counter this flood of trashy fiction with his "free translation" of *Captain Grant's Children* which, he argues, belongs to a genre almost nonexistent in Ladino literature. According to Fresco, it differs from most Ladino novels in that it does not contain love scenes, murders, police investigations, or secret exchanges of babies. Unlike the majority of Ladino novels which, in Fresco's opinion, do not offer any moral lesson or useful knowledge, his rewriting of Jules Verne's novel is instructive and allows the reader to learn many new things, for instance, what the globe is. Finally, "there is nothing indecent in it, and it suits men and women, children and adults" (*El Tyempo*, June 4, 1897, 4). Having formulated his concept of good fiction, on the next page Fresco starts the publication of a new serialized novel, which tells the story of a man from a Jewish family who, it turns out, is not his parents' biological son but that of a non-Jewish maid, who sold him to the childless Jewish woman without the husband's knowledge. The young man murders his adoptive mother and is arrested, while his father loses his mind.[31] This novel demonstrates that Ladino periodicals did not have enough "appropriate" fiction and published works for financial reasons that the editors themselves found objectionable. (One can safely assume that the original story had nothing to do with Jews, but was Judaized by the rewriter.)

Sam Lévy disagrees with the view expressed by Fresco and some other literati, arguing that *all* reading is useful and has some educational merit, since all fiction has some moral value. Even the least sophisticated pieces "serve as educators for those who did not have the privilege of receiving good basic education." Little by little, Lévy contends, the public will develop better taste and will eventually prefer "more refined and instructive" works (*La Epoka*, May 30, 1901, 1). Four years later, in the preface to one of his rewritings, *La Epoka*'s editor in chief, "all modesty aside, congratulated himself on the success of his newspaper's efforts to promote reading among his coreligionists.[32] Responding to Fresco's prediction of Ladino's imminent disappearance, Lévy claims that its funeral is not going to happen soon, because his own work of translation, among other things, has succeeded in awakening in the public the love of reading in the vernacular. The number of readers has significantly increased, and they have become more demanding, he insists. Lévy even attempts to represent this growing interest statistically: "A few years ago, only . . .[33] a tiny percentage of Jews read in Judeo-Spanish. Today, about the same percentage does not read in our language and is not interested in it."

Lévy's educational program was by no means an empty declaration, and he was indeed confident that his audience was becoming more knowledgeable and experienced. *La Epoka* was gradually publishing more sophisticated fiction. When *El Luzero* was closed in August 1905 and its prospective publication of the Ladino rewriting of Jacques Loria's *Les mystères de Pera*—a sensational and elaborate novel—had to be suspended, Lévy did not transfer it to his Salonican paper. But six years later, he must have decided that *La Epoka*'s audience was ready to read the novel and announced its publication there. (However, the summer of 1911 was not an easy time for him, and the novel failed to appear once again.)

Though most Sephardi literati justified their choices of particular foreign texts for rewriting by attributing educational and moral values to them, they would often add another powerful argument: these texts have been translated into all other languages. We find this kind of reasoning already in *El Nasyonal* in 1873. Announcing a Ladino rewriting of Christoph von Schmid's *Genoveva,* published as a chapbook, the newspaper describes it as a story that is "known to everybody" and that contains a "moral example for everybody."[34] Introducing his rewriting of Jules Verne's *Captain Grant's Children,* Fresco writes that this book has been translated into almost every language (*El Tyempo,* June 4, 1897, 4). The preface to the rewriting of *The Count of Monte Cristo* published in *La Epoka* claims that it was "translated into all languages," except Ladino (June 29, 1900, 1). The same preface announces that this rewriting will be followed by *The Thousand and One Nights, The Three Musketeers, Les Misérables,* and *The Thousand and One Days* (tales allegedly translated from the Persian original into French in the 1700s).

It seems that of all Sephardi literati, Benghiat put together the most comprehensive program of what had to be rewritten in Ladino. In 1914, in the Passover issue of *El Meseret,* he printed a list of twenty-two foreign works he considered necessary to translate, most of which had already become part of the canon of serialized fiction. This canon included the novels by Dumas père and Dumas fils, Sue's *Les mystères de Paris,* Hugo's *Les Misérables,* Defoe's *Robinson Crusoe,* Swift's *Gulliver's Travels,* Bernardin's *Paul et Virginie,* Fénelon's *Les aventures de Télémaque,* and many other texts, which were published in serialized form in Turkish, Armenian, Russian, Spanish, or Yiddish. In other words, Benghiat (as well as other rewriters) did not make a selection of his own, but adopted the existing repertoire[35] that came to the westernizers through French periodicals, which were full of *roman-feuilletons,* and through the reading lists and libraries of Alliance schools.[36]

The fact that the same novels were adapted in many languages spoken in the Ottoman Empire suggests to Johann Strauss that, instead of talking about various national literatures, scholars should regard them as components of one Ottoman literature produced by one "reading nation" that included not only Turks, but "also Bulgarians, Armenians, Jews and Arabs, 'Franks' and Levantines."[37] Furthermore, Strauss argues that, despite all of the linguistic differences and the fact that many Ottoman subjects knew only one language, "there were many channels of transmission and works which attracted a readership within all communities," thus making it possible for them to borrow literary texts from one another rather than translating them from the original language.[38]

However, in the nineteenth century, the same texts were also translated in other countries, such as Russia and India. Moreover, while most literati in the Ottoman Empire were unable to read in co-territorial languages even if they spoke them, all westernizers knew French. Hence, it seems more logical to conclude that, in the majority of cases, the novels were translated from French. In fact, Strauss's study demonstrates that, despite the immense differences between them, all local literatures were going through a process of westernization and were adopting the same canon of serialized fiction, which came to them from France. Therefore, rather than focusing on the intercommunal connections, one should turn to the canon of serialized novels to explain why its export to a great number of countries was so successful. However, since this question is beyond the scope of my book, I will only suggest that this cultural phenomenon cannot be understood without a sociological study of mass culture in the context of westernization.

## The Ladino Novel as a Genre

The serialized novel as a genre emerged in France in the 1830s and soon made its way to many European and non-European countries, where it became known as the *dime novel, roman-feuilleton, roman de quat'sous, romanzo d'apendice, novela por entregas,* and *tefrika roman.*[39] Later, it also had counterparts in some Jewish literatures.[40] By keeping mass audiences in suspense for months, serialized fiction brought the rapidly expanding periodical press great profits. Publication by installment drastically increased newspapers' circulations, which was aided by the new printing technologies. For instance, thanks to Eugène Sue's serialized bestseller *Le Juif errant* (1844), in a few months, subscriptions to *Le Constitutionnel,* the paper that published the novel, rose from 3,600 to over 40,000.[41] It must be emphasized that, in general terms, Ladino belles lettres did not significantly differ from mass fiction in other languages. For this reason, my analysis will focus mainly on its idiosyncratic features, determined by its particular purposes and constraints.

On their title pages, the majority of Ladino novels were labeled *romanso,* which apparently meant an invented story. In Florentin's rewriting of Dumas's *La Dame aux Camélias,* entitled *The Lady of the Camellias; or, Angel of Love,* we find direct proof of this. Dumas claims that the story of Marguerite Gautier is a true one, and Florentin relates this idea in the following way: "What I am going to tell you is not at all a novel [*romanso*] but a true event, which happened in the city of Paris a few years ago" (3).[42] The rewriter of *The Stepmother*,[43] introducing his heroine's false story, says that she "made up a moving novel [*romanso ezmuvyente*]" (15). But quite often, for marketing purposes, Sephardi literati would give their piece a subtitle that contained the word *fato* (fact, real event), for example, *A Terrible Woman: A Real Event* (i.e., true story, *fato akontesido*). Thus, the Ladino novel was understood to be an invented story, described by Sam Lévy as a work of imagination.

Ladino novels can be roughly divided into two categories: love stories and adventure stories. This division, which at first glance appears superficial, is essential, as it takes into account crucial differences between the two subgenres, reflecting the dilemmas of Sephardi culture in the era of westernization. While sharing the basic genre characteristics, they differ in their genesis and relation to the preexisting literary canon, which tends to affect their functions and methods of production.

Until the emergence of serialized Ladino fiction, Sephardim found love stories only in the ballads (*el romancero*) which, despite being rather complex, spoke primarily of the sufferings caused by betrayal or the death of the loved one and used traditional folklore tropes[44] to describe love, pain, or jealousy. In other words, ballads were not specific and did not tell recent or "real" stories. Biblical literature, in spite of having many female protagonists, had little interest in romantic love. Therefore, since western love stories had no counterparts in the domestic canon, the Sephardi literati who created the love story as a subgenre of Ladino belles lettres fully relied on the European model. However, after a certain number of Ladino novels had been produced, later adaptations assimilated to this corpus, and as a result, by the turn of the twentieth century a high level of genre uniformity made adaptations of eighteenth-century classics indistinguishable from rewritings of short-lived contemporaneous novels.

The emergence of the Ladino love novel in the last third of the nineteenth century was, at various levels, a revolutionary event in domestic literature. Under the new circumstances, Sephardi literati both faced the challenges never dealt with by their predecessors and enjoyed the freedom of being innovative, as long as they respected the rules of propriety set by the tradition and local customs and monitored by the censors. The new genre called for linguistic innovations that would allow Sephardi rewriters, who did not have at their disposal the literary means available to European authors, to name or relate in the vernacular their characters' rather complex emotions and mental operations. Existing terms, usually of Hebrew or Turkish origin, were replaced either with French calques or with made-up words constructed on the basis of productive Spanish models. Because Ladino novels spoke about a variety of topics not discussed in periodicals, they contributed to the Gallicization of the vernacular no less than the press did. Sometimes, faced with the need to convey a character's mood, rewriters would represent it by descriptions of action. For instance, in his rewriting of *La Dame aux Camélias,* in order to render Alfred's rapture at receiving a letter from his beloved, Florentin adds a new episode in which the young man joyfully lifts in his arms the bewildered maid who delivered it.

Undoubtedly, the most revolutionary feature of Ladino novels was that a great number of them had women as their protagonists who, rather than mourning their lost loves, participated in events no less than men did. This is reflected in the novels' titles, such as *Manon Lescaut, Ana Maria; or, A Woman's Heart, A Woman Brigand, Donna Flor,* and many others. Telling stories of women's lives gave the rewriters additional opportunities to contribute to female education, which included advocating modesty. Thus, despite significantly abridging Bernardin's *Paul et Virginie,* Benghiat makes a rather long addition to laud Virginie's extraordinary chastity. Despite this, the contents of love novels sometimes made them a target of Ottoman censorship, which was concerned with protecting public morality. The communiqué from Yildiz Palace cited in chapter 1 instructed journalists "not to publish any feuilleton that was not approved from the point of view of morality by His Excellency, the Minister of Education, guardian of good mores."[45] Barquín quotes Sam Lévy complaining that some episodes of his novel *The Martyr* were taken out against his will, because a censor found them offensive. He protests, insisting that his descriptions of the characters' love relationship were simply "realistic" and he only related "true facts."[46] Barquín believes that the fact that Lévy did not specify whether it was a state censor or a rabbi means that this was obvious to his readers, while today we can merely speculate about it. However, only state censorship, which was both preliminary and punitive, obliged journalists to submit their materials prior to publication. The author of the play *Han Benyamin,* which was printed by *La Epoka* press in 1884, indicates on the title page that it was approved for publication by the local Council for Public Education, that is, a state censor.

It is obvious that some modifications of the translated novels were prompted by the rewriters' self-censorship and their genuine faith in the educational benefits of family reading. For this reason, "fallen women" had to be turned into singers or even into married women. But when the subject of extramarital relationships could not be avoided, the rewriters would use this opportunity for educational purposes, for instance, by adding to the original story a pious Jewish woman who would defy the promiscuity of her gentile counterpart. In Benghiat's rewriting of Hugo's *Le Roi s'amuse* (*The King's Fool*) and Piave's libretto of Verdi's *Rigoletto*, entitled in Ladino *The Curse of the Jew*, the immoral behavior of Rigoletto and his daughter is contrasted with the righteous conduct of the invented Sephardi Jew Isak Pinto and his daughter Rachel. Thus, while Sephardim were introduced to a wide range of new subjects, the "innocence of women and children" was duly protected.

In the case of adventure, in particular, travel stories, Sephardi rewriters were in every way in a better position from the very start, because the travelogue as a genre had existed in all Jewish literatures since the Middle Ages. Some of those semi-religious medieval travelogues in far-away countries were translated into Ladino and were familiar to many Sephardim. We have no evidence showing that Benjamin of Tudela's work was ever translated, but educated men would have read it in Hebrew. Yet, we do know that *Sefer Eldad ha-Dani* (*The Book of Eldad the Danite*),[47] popular not only among Jews, had at least two Ladino versions and was published in the Ottoman Empire at least six times: twice in Istanbul (1766, 1863) and four times in Salonica (1812, 1840, 1849, 1891), which means it was the second most popular Ladino text after Huli's volumes of *Me'am Lo'ez.*[48] Hence, we can assume that most Sephardim were familiar with it. But, unlike *Me'am Lo'ez, The Book of Eldad* is not a religious text, but rather a fantastic travel account that required from the audience only some familiarity with the legend of the ten lost tribes. Also unlike most of the tales in *Me'am Lo'ez,* it did not offer any moral lesson and was intended only to entertain the audience. Eldad is believed to have been a ninth-century traveler, supposedly from the tribe of Dan, who made a trip to Mesopotamia, Egypt, North Africa, and Spain and allegedly discovered the ten lost tribes of Israel. Like many adventure stories, Eldad's account begins with a shipwreck. In Ladino, *The Book of Eldad* was sometimes printed in collections of medieval stories (*ma'asiyyot*), including the one used below along with the rabbinic thriller *The Miracle in Spain.*

Since the travelogue as a literary form already existed in the Ladino canon, Sephardi literati were mainly concerned with finding appropriate foreign sources that would interest their audience. The Ladino press from its early days published fantastic accounts of Oriental countries and real travelogues, such as the second volume of Israel Joseph Benjamin's diary, which appeared in *El Lunar* in serialized form as early as 1865. About a year earlier, Gabay published a Ladino translation of *The*

*Thousand and One Nights,* which was later reprinted by other presses. Among the foreign books adapted in Ladino were Alfred Assolant's *Les Aventures merveilleuses mais authentiques du Capitaine Corcoran (The Marvelous but True Adventures of Captain Corcoran),* Ponson du Terrail's *Rocambole,* J. B. Henri Savigny and Alexandre Corréard's *Naufrage de la frégate la Méduse (Wreck of the Medusa),* Jules Verne's *Captain Grant's Children,* and the French novel by Paul Dubois that Sam Lévy translated under the title *The Voyage around the World with Five Metaliks.*[49] Benghiat also produced many adventure stories that involved shipwrecks and other maritime disasters, among which one finds *Perished at Sea, A Disaster at Sea,* and *Gulliver's Travels.*

The invention of the Ladino love novel played an innovatory role in the development of domestic belles lettres by introducing new literary patterns, by raising questions about human relationships never discussed before, and by expanding the Ladino vocabulary. Therefore, it undoubtedly furthered the westernization of Sephardi culture in general. The role of adventure stories is more complex. Generally speaking, Ladino adventure stories and travel accounts tend to be enlightening, though in many cases the information they offer is incorrect due to the rewriter's own ignorance or is intentionally distorted for ideological purposes. For instance, *Hasan-pasha* (discussed in chapter 4), on the one hand, provides a lot of data on the history of Tunisia, Algeria, and Morocco (albeit oversimplified) and, on the other, it significantly misrepresents Ottoman history to suit the author's political agenda.

However, the Ladino rewritings of travel stories present a more serious problem at the genre level. It is well known that, in order for a foreign-language work to be accepted by the target literature, it has to adhere to at least some of its norms. Since the genre of semi-religious travelogues and shipwreck stories already existed in Ladino literature and was authoritative, some rewriters tended to fit the modern foreign fiction into the old domestic form. Yet, the more authoritative the genre, the more conservative it is, which is why not all adaptations of European fiction contributed to the westernization of Ladino literature. This is not to say that all Ladino travelogues had religious overtones, but some of them indeed acquired a didactic character, especially when the rewriters aimed at edifying their readers. For example, Benghiat's rewriting of *Gulliver's Travels* not only distorts its message but reverses it by turning Swift's novel into a semi-religious story meant to teach children and adults not to be like the stubborn Jonah but to obey God immediately. The rewriter of Molière's *Miser,* at the end of the comedy, creates a mini adventure story where the righteous characters are saved by God from a shipwreck for which they praise him in a mini psalm. The rewriter does not make up this scene but brings out and enhances religious elements that are barely noticeable in the French text.

Having exposed the differences between the two subgenres, I must emphasize, first, that many Ladino novels combine elements of both categories, and, second, that they are subgenres of *one* genre, which emerged and developed within sixty-five years. Consequently, the differences notwithstanding, all Ladino novels adopted the same literary conventions, had similar goals, and targeted the same audience. As a result, the majority of Ladino rewritings have more in common with each other than with their respective foreign-language sources, which belonged to different genres and were created in different countries in different epochs.

Since the primary goal of all Sephardi literati was to create thrilling stories, they followed what may be a universal strategy of producing a bestseller, while taking into account the local circumstances that allowed them to incorporate into their novels some didactic elements:

> [O]n the one hand, if the text is to speak to current issues, the novelist must create a world the reader recognizes. On the other, the escapist nature of the fiction demands a certain degree of fantasy. Simplicity of language, reliance on stereotypical and trite images, the absence of psychological subtlety, and readily identifiable characters permit the reader easy access to the imaginative world because the values these characters represent are obvious and well known.[50]

Ladino fiction never discussed current issues but instead intended to attract readers by its escapist nature. Nevertheless, Sephardi literati managed—without even realizing it—to make their characters recognizable and easy to relate to by presenting them in similar terms. Once readers learned to sympathize with one unhappy European girl, all other unfortunate heroines were perceived as her literary sisters.

Exoticism was undoubtedly one of the crucial factors in attracting readers to serialized Ladino novels, whether travel stories or love novels whose action took place in faraway countries where people's lives did not resemble the tedious reality of the readers' own world. As for psychological subtleties and character development, Juan Ferreras argues that, in serialized fiction, "the make-up of the novel's characters is determined from the very beginning, i.e., it cannot change in the course of complex and unexpected events."[51] Furthermore, he suggests that "the length of the theme of the story and the plot are determined by the editor's wish."[52] Thus, Florentin did not expect his unsophisticated audience to follow Marguerite Gautier's inner evolution, which is why at the very start of his version of Dumas's novel, the heroine is directly declared to be an angel of love and apparently remains one until the end. As to the length of the plot, the advancement of this Ladino novel is rapid: after all of the major events have been described and there is no more action left, the heroine quickly dies, and the novel is over.

In general, if the foreign source had anything in it besides action, that part would be deleted without any second thoughts. An example of such editing is Benghiat's rewriting of *Paul et Virginie*, which he reduced to twenty-one pages. The Ladino version of *Manon Lescaut* is not only significantly abridged, but in the preface the rewriter directly assures his readers that he will leave out its "less important passages" (2). One inconsistency typical of all serialized fiction has a particular manifestation in Ladino literature: the new words introduced by Sephardi rewriters in one installment might be reintroduced five more times or might be abandoned and never used again.

## Authorship and Anonymity

The next question to consider is why such treatment of foreign-language sources was socially acceptable even in the twentieth century. I suggest that it is accounted for by the general perception of a given text as collective property rather than that of its individual creator. One of the distinctive characteristics of Ladino belles lettres is its virtual anonymity. Here, the term *anonymity* refers to two interrelated features: the arbitrariness of the designations on title pages and the treatment of source texts as common property rather than that of its individual creator. This was possibly due to the premodern state of Ladino literature, characterized by an essential lack of interest in the authorial voice, which it never surpassed, and the low cultural status of the Ladino novel, defined by its purpose and intended readership.

Before the emergence of Ladino fiction, the concept of authorship was familiar to Sephardi readers from religious literature. But the main function of the rabbi's name on a *musar* book was to enhance the authority of a given text rather than to protect the author's intellectual property.[53] As for the Bible commentaries, the rabbis did not claim authorship, presenting themselves only as mediators of the biblical message. Thus, in both cases, the rabbi's name was associated with religious authority, which had little to do with the notion of authorship introduced by modernity. The semi-religious stories, such as Talmudic tales or even *The Book of Eldad the*

*Danite,* had been created centuries earlier and had become part of the tradition and, therefore, belonged to all Jews. The same was true for the folklore. The ballads, anonymous by definition, also belonged to all Ladino speakers in the sense that every singer could freely change their words, thus contributing to their reproduction and survival. While some Sephardi playwrights began to copyright their works already in the nineteenth century, the creators of mass fiction often did not even sign theirs. This circumstance is explained by the status of the two genres. The playwrights using copyright were mainly those who were commissioned to produce works for didactic purposes. Ladino belles lettres, by contrast, was created by literati who were motivated mainly by financial interests and who were always in a hurry to prepare a new portion of the novel for the next installment. As a result, these authors often had no time to consult the previous installments, relying solely on their memory. Besides, serialized fiction was intended for unsophisticated readers who were not expected to criticize the rewriters for their errors nor challenge their authorship. Not considering their adaptations to be serious literary work, the Sephardi literati were not particularly concerned about signing their rewritings and usually cared even less about the names of the foreign authors. When a novel was published in installments in a periodical, the rewriter's name usually appeared after the last segment, while the previous parts were rarely signed. Only a small number of Ladino novels published as chapbooks indicate on the title page both names: the author of the foreign source and the rewriter. A rare case of a title page that has both names and the language of the original is *Nantas* by Émile Zola, which is described as "translated from the French by M. Menashe." In the majority of publications, however, we find one of four variations: only the name of the foreign author (the third edition of *The Twins* [*The Comedy of Errors*], "One of the most beautiful comedies by the famous sage Shakespeare"); only the name of the rewriter (*Manon Lescaut,* "A very moving novel translated by Alexandre Benghiat"); no names at all (*The Lady of the Camellias*); or the designation varies from one edition to another. Thus, *Leonidas the Swimmer* appeared in *El Meseret* in 1908 without any names, but Shelomo Yisrael Sherezli's reprint of the same year says "by Aleksandr Benghiat."[54]

Yet, the prestige of the foreign authors was an important factor determining the choice of texts for adaptation. Some of the rewritings were preceded by brief introductions that contained a little information about the original author. A preface might say that the author is an English writer (in Swift's case), but quite often it would speak of the author without mentioning his or her name. For example, in the introduction to *The Stepmother*, Carolina Invernizio, a prolific fiction writer, is several times referred to simply as "a famous Italian [female] writer." More frequently, the introductions to the novels would provide no information at all about the author of the source, as in the case of *La Dam o kamelyas*.

Despite the fact that Sephardi rewriters did not hesitate to abridge and modify the original text to the point of making it unrecognizable, they did not realize they were, in fact, creating new works of Ladino literature. They believed that all they did was translate, summarize, or adapt preexisting foreign novels. Ladino novels indeed appeared with such indications as *trezladado* (translated), *rezumido* (summarized), *imitado* (imitated), *adaptado* (adapted), *aranjado* (arranged), *reeskrito* (rewritten), and *por* (by), but there is no correlation between these terms and any particular methods of adaptation. In fact, these terms were, most likely, added by the newspaper editors who, in their turn, had a free hand in abridging and changing serialized novels in a way they found more suitable for their audience. Galante thus describes what he did as a newspaper editor when he was given someone's text for publication: "Our role consisted *only* of putting the storyline in a better order and in using an easy language."[55]

Effectively, the rewriters' work differed from that of the editor only quantitatively rather than in essence. It is not surprising that the serialized novels which appeared anonymously in periodicals or were signed only at the end of the last installment became associated with the name of the newspaper's editor. If later these novels were reprinted as chapbooks, the publishers mentioned their original form of publication as *felieton,* adapting the French term *roman-feuilleton,* and indicated the title of the periodical where it first appeared. For instance, the Ladino version of *Manon Lescaut* is described as "feuilleton, published in *El Meseret* of Smyrna, translated by Alexandre Benghiat." It is quite possible, therefore, that Sherezli put Benghiat's name on the title page of his reprint of *Leonidas the Swimmer* because this rewriting first saw light in *El Meseret*.[56] This principle of attribution reflects the perception of any given text as collective property, if only of a small group.

Some rewriters believed (and often rightly so) that they played a more important role in creating a new literary piece than the author of the original text. They unselfconsciously expressed this understanding not only by omitting the latter's name, but also in other ways. For example, Sam Lévy's translation of a French adventure story, *The Voyage around the World with Five Metaliks,* was accompanied by a photograph of the translator rather than one of the author, who was not even mentioned in the introduction (*La Epoka's Library,* February 5, 1905). However, the Sephardi literati felt no obligations not only toward the foreign authors of their sources: they also used the fiction produced by their local colleagues without acknowledging them. Romero was able to establish some cases of rewritings of other Ladino rewritings, which were published earlier under different titles and names or anonymously.[57] Yet, the notion of plagiarism that she uses to describe this practice is not applicable here,[58] because at the time the concept of individual intellectual property and, consequently, of authorship had not yet emerged in the Sephardi community.

Elia Carmona's "Autobiography" offers an example that expresses in a nutshell the understanding of originality shared by Sephardi literati. He candidly tells his readers that some of his novels (such as *The Milkman* and *Little Jak*) were based on combinations of the French plays he saw in the theater, when he was unable to invent anything on his own.[59] In other words, in Carmona's view, it is the end product—the text submitted for publication—that should be considered original, that is, one's own. But where is the borderline between constructing a novel from borrowed foreign components and rewriting a foreign source in accordance with domestic conventions? Obviously, it is impossible to find any quantitative criteria for such a distinction, and this question has not been answered (or, in fact, even asked) by any scholar of Ladino literature in a satisfactory way, that is, applicable to all cases rather than ad hoc. Nevertheless, all researchers claim that most Ladino novels are not "original," thus implying the opposition "translated versus original text," though none of them offers a definition of "translation" or explains what he or she understands by "originality." Romero divides all of the novels into two groups— translations and original works—and dedicates a separate section to each category without explaining her principle of distinction. Paloma Díaz-Mas simply states that, between 1900 and 1930, the number of original works did not reach 50 percent,[60] a claim striking in its arbitrariness.

Barquín's approach to the study of Ladino fiction is no less surprising in its bias, which is particularly evident in the conclusions she draws from a thorough analysis of Sam Lévy's novel *The Martyr*: "Hopefully, with time, further investigations will add new titles to the list of novels recognized today as original, and the dates will be established more precisely, but, no doubt, our contention that the novel under examination was among the first original ones in Judeo-Spanish will not have to be reconsidered."[61] In other words, instead of suggesting any criteria or trying to identify the novel's possible foreign sources, this scholar hopes that no new information about it will ever be discovered and thus her conclusion about its originality will not be challenged. One of Barquín's arguments in favor of the novel's originality is a competent description of the construction work of a railway, because this subject was familiar to the author from his own work experience at the Oriental Railroads office.[62] Yet, what she says about *The Martyr* suggests that Lévy must have combined elements of at least two foreign novels, probably adding something of his own—the same way Carmona did.

Thus, we see that all scholars discuss—usually in pejorative terms—the dependence of Ladino fiction on foreign sources, the only disagreement between them being the proportion of "original" novels in its corpus. What are, then, the criteria of originality? Earlier in this book, I suggested that Almosnino's *Crónica de los reyes otomanos* is an original work, that is, created independently of any other text. If we apply the same criterion to Ladino belles lettres, we may not be able to find even three texts that all scholars would describe as original. Yet, it is impossible to deny that Ladino belles lettres *as a whole* was an entirely new genre. Therefore, I suggest that we approach the question of the originality of Ladino fiction from a different standpoint: instead of using anachronistic notions (such as plagiarism), making unverifiable claims, or looking for formal criteria and definitions, I will postulate that dependence on foreign-language sources is an essential characteristic of Ladino belles lettres. Nevertheless, as I proposed above, Ladino novels have more in common with each other than with their respective sources and often seem to be written by the same person. To be more precise, the rewriters always ignored the author's voice replacing it with what appears to be their own but is in fact the *collective* voice of Sephardi westernizers. Therefore, I suggest that, if a given literature contains a considerable number of texts, each of which to some degree depends on a foreign-language source but has more common features with the other texts in the group than with its source, it is legitimate to describe this corpus as a separate domestic genre.

Since dependence on foreign sources is a constitutive feature of this genre, the term *originality*—depending on one's perspective—either acquires a new meaning or becomes meaningless and is no longer a useful analytical tool. Thus, one might consider "original" every new text produced in Ladino regardless of its relation to the foreign source it uses. But what, then, is the opposite of "original"? I find it more productive to talk about different types of relations between Ladino novels and the foreign-language texts that in some way triggered their emergence. In the next chapter, without attempting to offer a clear-cut typology, I will describe various kinds of relationships between Ladino novels and their sources.

## The Functions of Translation in Ladino Belles Lettres

From what has been said about Ladino narrative fiction, it is evident that translation played a crucial role in its emergence and formation. Here, I will explain why it was unable to prevent its death. Since every literature going through a process of westernization depends on the European counterpart it wants to emulate, translation as a literary activity plays a prominent or even central role in the domestic literature in its search for new texts, forms, and patterns. An Armenian writer, referring to the state of his native literature in the Ottoman Empire in the last third of the nineteenth century, formulates the problem in a straightforward way: "Where must one begin when writing a novel among a people which has not one single example of this type of literature? No matter where one begins, one must copy foreigners, or more exactly, one must translate them."[63] While this recipe appears self-evident, it is less obvious what happens in the domestic literature after it adopts this strategy. Will it always be dominated by translations and thus depend on the foreign literatures from which the new genres were borrowed, or, once their domestic counterparts are established, will it become independent?

In 1925, Carles Riba, a major Catalan writer and translator, gave a definitive answer to this question when he declared that the only option for his literature, which was missing the novel as a genre, was "taking a branch of novelistic tradition from abroad and planting it in Catalan soil until it becomes independent."[64] In other words, Riba takes it for granted that literatures that once depended on the import of certain genres, with time, will no longer require translations and will become independent from foreign sources. But is this always true? Itamar Even-Zohar's hypothesis, based on his polysystem theory, offers a comprehensive model of the role and functions of translation in a receiving literature.[65] Though his hypothesis is not directly concerned with this literature's future, it implicitly offers an answer to our question which, in turn, elucidates the intrinsic reasons leading to the death of Ladino literature.

According to Even-Zohar, translated literature as a co-system of the domestic literary polysystem can occupy the central position or a peripheral one. This theory suggests that the central position of translated literature testifies to its innovatory function because it actively participates in the major events of the literary history of the target literature. Typically, when leading writers actively participate in translation—whether they formulate it or not—they recognize that there is some gap in the domestic literature.

Furthermore, Even-Zohar claims, under such circumstances, the distinction between "author" and "translator" is obscured. He argues that the position of translated literature is central in three cases: when the domestic literature is young and in the process of crystallization; when it is peripheral or "weak" or both; and when the culture is at a turning point, experiencing crises, because established models are no longer tenable for a younger generation and the literature discovers vacuums that need to be filled.[66]

The first case, undoubtedly, describes the state of Ladino secular literature, which was indeed young, "in the process of being established." As suggested by Even-Zohar, translation performed an innovatory function in its history by providing it with the genres it did not have before, namely, the novel and the play. The second case, however, does not fully apply to Ladino literature, because by the term "weak" Even-Zohar means "relatively established literatures,"[67] a stage it never reached. The third case is not applicable to Ladino narrative fiction either, even though at first glance it seems to be an accurate description of its development. The situation of crises and vacuums referred to by Even-Zohar results from an internal dynamic within the domestic polysystem and thus is a *literary* phenomenon rather than an *ideological* one. It presupposes the existence of at least two sets of literary models that are found in more advanced literatures, whereas secular Ladino literature produced only one type of narrative fiction, the serialized novel. At the turn of the twentieth century, such Sephardi literati as Sam Lévy, Alexandre Benghiat, and David Fresco were quite aware of a gap in Ladino literature and purposely contributed to bridging it by translating what they perceived as European masterpieces. Yet none of them complained about, for example, *Me'am Lo'ez* being an outdated literary model for their purposes. Religious texts were not part of the equation simply because their ideology did not suit the westernizers. In other words, there was no clash between the two literary co-systems as such and, therefore, no literary crisis. It is true that Sephardi rewriters barely turned to the "indigenous stock," but that was because it was inadequate for the new ideological agendas. In other words, the vacuums were more ideological than literary and were perceived by the westernizers as a sign of backwardness of the Sephardi community in general. This means that, aside from introducing new models and genres, translation served as a source of progressive ideas and secular knowledge and, therefore, also performed a vital extraliterary function.

It follows from Even-Zohar's theory that, unlike strong literatures that can borrow from their peripheral co-systems, young literatures have to rely on translation until a certain point in their development when they become independent. But this is precisely what did *not* happen in our case: Ladino literature never became independent of foreign sources in the sense that European works were required in order for the local literati to produce new Ladino texts, even if those were far removed from their foreign counterparts. This is why dependence on foreign literature should be understood as a constitutive feature of Ladino novels as a genre.

Yet, many other non-European literatures that experienced westernization eventually became independent of translation. The difference is that, unlike Ladino literature, they had a long tradition of high medieval fiction, usually consisting of epic narratives and romances with elements of both adventure and love stories. Pavel Grintser observes that, in the nineteenth century, Turkish, Bengali, Persian, Hindi, and other Asian print cultures produced new belles lettres based both on the works of Dumas, Defoe, Walter Scott, and a few other western writers and on the domestic medieval fiction.[68] In other words, the local literati succeeded in grafting European models and repertoires onto the preexisting domestic sources. Their Sephardi colleagues, however, did not have this option, because no secular fiction had been created in Ladino before, and the vernacular mass fiction had no highbrow counterpart. As a result, the belles lettres produced in the 1920s imitated the rewritings published twenty-five years earlier, thus never going beyond the confines of translated literature.

Under certain circumstances, even massive translation, no matter how revolutionary, does not suffice to render a nascent literature resilient and independent. To use Even-Zohar's terms, this is the case when the domestic polysystem is deficient and has no internal resources, for example, when the preexisting canon consists only of religious texts and there are no other contemporaneous secular genres to borrow from. It is often said that Ladino literature was stifled by translations, which evidently implies that without them it would have flourished and produced "original" works. Yet, my study demonstrates (as many others do) that translation not only brought Ladino secular literature into existence but remained indispensable for it through the sixty-five years of its life. It is evident that, the sociopolitical circumstances aside, it is not translation that led to the stagnation and death of Ladino literature but rather the lack of internal resources.

There is one more question to be asked in this connection: did the Sephardi literati themselves believe that one day their literature would become independent and would no longer require translation? Or, more precisely, did they ever think about this at all? As far as I can tell, they discussed only specific issues, in particular what needed to be translated into Ladino rather than what should be created in this language. As late as

1922, "Julien" urged his colleagues to translate instructive texts without even mentioning the possibility of producing original works.

Sam Lévy, the most vocal and the most successful advocate of the vernacular, seems to have been the only one to make a connection (albeit a vague one) between translation and the production of a new Ladino literature. He understood the functions of translation as follows:

> Beginning the translation of great works of imagination, we have two goals in mind:
> First, to introduce our readers who do not know other languages to the masterpieces of great writers. Second, to supply our language with [illegible word] translations, so that later we could produce works [*komponer ovras*] ourselves or give the pleasure of doing so to those who have a gift for writing. (*La Epoka*, June 29, 1900, 1)

There is no doubt that the lack of interest in Ladino literature per se and its future among Sephardi journalists and publishers resulted from their seeing Ladino fiction as a tool to achieve specific goals rather than as, at least potentially, an item of aesthetic value. This perception, in turn, was predicated on their perception of Ladino as a language of low culture inherently unsuitable for high purposes. Even Sam Lévy, who constantly spoke about the need to revitalize Ladino, saw this task primarily as a *moral* duty of Sephardi literati. For instance, in 1905, he declared that, in the previous five years, he had made great efforts to "serve the moral and material interests of our poor jargon, Judeo-Spanish, and had contributed to its development."[69]

Kenneth Moss's insightful study[70] of the goals and projects of translation into Yiddish and Hebrew put forward in Eastern Europe around 1917 provides a lens that allows us to look at Ladino literature from a new angle. Having analyzed the debates on the role of and need for systematic translation between Hebraists and Yiddishists across political and aesthetic lines, Moss observes the prevalence of a new "strategy of culture-building, namely, systematic, massive, immediate, and non-adaptive literary translation of a posited unitary, universal canon of Western literature into Hebrew or Yiddish."[71] Moss maintains that, despite their differences, most Eastern European Jewish writers and publishers agreed that translation was necessary for revitalizing Yiddish and Hebrew literatures. Their programs of translation—to be sure, very different from one another—were intended to deparochialize these literatures and "not merely to reshape the literature itself or to properly educate Jews as moderns, but to prevent the defection of the Hebraist (and *mutatis mutandis*, Yiddishist) intelligentsia from Jewish cultural engagement."[72]

The proposed way of deparochializing the two Jewish literatures was to transform them by means of *non-adaptive* translation, which would make them a part of the modern and universal literature. Sephardi westernizers, in contrast, believed that their backward culture could be deparochialized by means of *adaptations,* systematic only in that they followed the accepted canon of serialized fiction, which would allow it to catch up with those cultures that had already translated this canon. To be more precise, rather than aspiring to transform Ladino literature, they used it as a direct means of transforming their coreligionists, that is, making them equal to "other nations." Thus, while Sephardi literati had the same extraliterary objective as their Ashkenazi colleagues, namely, reshaping readers' identity in order to make them Jews and moderns at the same time (or, rather, modern Jews), their programs and proposed methods were different.

As for the danger of cultural defection, this issue constitutes, perhaps, the major difference between Yiddish and Ladino cultures. Whereas Yiddishists tried to prevent the intelligentsia from getting too engaged with Russian or Polish literatures, the Sephardi literati were themselves engaged with the French culture, which was not perceived as defection but as the only way of participating in a high culture (or, at least, in what they saw as such).

## Conclusions

The Ladino novel as a genre was not only a product of westernization, but also its powerful medium. Indeed, while the idea of publishing serialized novels was borrowed by Sephardi journalists from Europe to help periodicals survive, very soon, irrespective of their intentions, these novels became a most effective instrument of westernization. This was not only due to their content, but because they reached a larger audience than the newspapers did. No doubt, this was true even for those works that were not reprinted, because even the segment of the public that had no interest in history or politics would have been carried away by melodramatic novels and serialized thrillers. We even have material evidence of their popularity: many extant Ladino newspapers have holes where the novels were cut out to be kept separately and read more than once.

The creators of Ladino belles lettres reworked foreign-language novels as they chose, in order to make their own production appealing, edifying, and appropriate for the Sephardi mass readership. Even-Zohar suggests that, in the situation when translated literature "takes a primary position, the borderlines are diffuse, so that the very category of 'translated works' must be extended to semi- and quasi-translations as well."[73] I would argue, however, that, in the case of Ladino fiction, Even-Zohar's proposition should be reversed: it is the category of *original* works that has to be expanded to include adaptations. Since dependence on foreign sources is a constitutive feature of the Ladino novel as a genre, one can regard as original either the whole genre or each new Ladino text—or simply abandon the term.

Having limited internal resources, Ladino literature borrowed from Europe the very notion of belles lettres, as well as the new modes of publishing and a whole canon of texts, producing on this basis a new domestic genre. Its emergence represented a radical break from the preexisting Ladino literature with its religious and semi-religious repertoire. In the sixty-five years of its existence, Ladino secular literature made a gigantic step toward becoming a modern one, but, for the reasons examined above, it was unable to go beyond adaptations and imitations.

# ▌▌▌ 4

# Ladino Fiction:
# Case Studies

In this chapter, I will examine by means of close reading seven Ladino novels produced by four Sephardi literati in the first quarter of the twentieth century, by which time the genre had been fully developed and was blooming. We know the names of three of these rewriters: *Nantas* was rewritten by M. Menashe, about whom there is no further information; one of the two versions of Dumas's *La Dame aux Camélias* belongs to David Florentin, whereas the second version is anonymous; and the other four texts were produced by Alexandre Benghiat. All of the novels have foreign sources, while one—*Hasan-pasha*—though signed by Benghiat, is a rewriting of an unidentified French text. The topics of these seven novels rather accurately represent Ladino fiction: four of them are love stories, two can be classified as adventure stories (one of which is a travel account), and *Nantas,* despite not being typical of Ladino belles lettres, is a thriller with elements of a love story.

## Two Versions of Dumas's La Dame aux Camélias
## (The Lady of the Camellias)

*La Dam o kamelyas.*[1]
Adaptado por *El Jurnal* La Verdad
Istanbul: n.p., 192?, 8 volumes, 128 pages
Romanized Ladino.

The novel *La Dame aux Camélias* (1848) brought Dumas fils his first success and was translated into many languages, soon becoming part of the generally accepted canon of serialized fiction.[2] It was rewritten in Ladino

# LA DAM O
# KAMELYA

EDITADO POR
JURNAL LA VERDAD

1

Presyo 15 gr.

Figure 4.1. Title page of *La Dam o kamelyas* (Istanbul, 192?)

at least twice. This later and fuller version (hereafter *La Dam*) is, for the most part, a rather close—sometimes even literal—translation and relates the events quite accurately. Moreover, despite the changes he makes, the anonymous translator manages to convey the author's message. Dumas insists that "fallen women" may be morally superior to well-respected members of society, and therefore society, rather than despise and punish them, should educate them in the "science of good and evil." He goes through a list of famous French authors who rehabilitated some courtesans, describing them with great compassion. The first book on Dumas's list is *Manon Lescaut*, which plays a special role in *La Dame aux Camélias*, as Manon's life is a constant point of reference for Dumas's characters. The translator keeps most of the references to *Manon*, evidently expecting his readers to be familiar with Abbé Prévost's work.

*La Dam* is the first extant Ladino novel printed in Latin characters, which suggests that it was published in the late 1920s, around the time of Atatürk's language reform (implemented in 1928), when many Turkish Jews also decided to switch to the Latin alphabet, thus demonstrating their loyalty to the Turkish republic. Evidently, this rewriting was meant for rather educated readers who could manage a long text in Romanized Ladino and whose vocabulary was quite large, since not a single word in the text is glossed. The intended audience was obviously expected to be somewhat familiar with the names of the French authors cited by Dumas, as well as with Christian ways of life, since the anonymous translator kept, albeit abridged, the descriptions of certain Christian rites.

The Ladino adaptation has a lengthy preface, where the rewriter explains to the readers what they should expect from the book: "This very interesting novel becomes passionate and the action starts only in the second volume" (3). This somewhat apologetic phrase reveals the translator's attitude toward his work. He is aware of readers' interest in action and wants to keep them in suspense, but, unlike most of his predecessors, he does not feel entitled to skip all "unnecessary" parts. Nevertheless, in volume 8, he unexpectedly abridges the text, most likely due to space limitations. He starts the abridgement not at a random place, but from the episode of the lovers' last rendezvous, the psychological climax of the French novel, which is followed by a rapid denouement.

In *La Dame aux Camélias*, the love scene, presented as an encounter of two bodies and two hearts, is summarized in the following way: "A month of such love would leave merely the corpse of heart and body."[3] The translator replaces the whole episode with a single sentence of his own: "She covered me with kisses" (122). Thus, Dumas's compressed sentence is substituted with an equally short one which, however, describes an action rather than conveying the intensity of the characters' feelings. As was mentioned above, Sephardi rewriters, in search of ways to talk about human feelings, most often rendered characters' emotional states analytically. Their other great concern was propriety. Yet, in the 1920s, the censors apparently were not interested in readers' morality, which explains why we find in *La Dam* the Hebrew word *zonah* (prostitute). In other words, the anonymous rewriter voluntarily edited the original in the same protective manner as his predecessors were required to. This and a few other attempts at presenting the characters' feelings demonstrate that, even by the 1920s, Ladino fiction had not gone beyond its earlier methods.

The translator closes his version of the novel with a few sentences of his own. While in the source the narrator and Armand simply brought flowers to Marguerite's grave, in *La Dam* they "put there the flowers and cried bitterly with big tears" (128). Thus, the rewriter lets his readers know in a straightforward way that Armand is mourning Marguerite's death and then, in the final sentence, very much in Dumas's spirit, summarizes the essence of the story: "There are few souls as pure, beautiful, and noble as that of Margerita Gotye"[4] (128).

Thus, *La Dam* can be described as a slightly adapted translation intended for a rather educated audience. Although the rewriter treats his source with respect, he assumes a paternalistic stance toward his audience and feels compelled to make sure they will be patient at the beginning of the novel and grasp its emotional thrust at the end.

> *The Lady of the Camellias; or, Angel of Love.*
> *La Dama alas kamelyas; o, Anjelina del Amor*
> Izmir: Libreria i Emprimeria Efraim Melamed, n.d., 64 pages.[5]

This earlier Ladino rewriting of Dumas's novel (hereafter *Anjelina*) exemplifies another way in which a foreign text enters a target literature and is incorporated into it. Florentin's vision of his task and his method of work are made clear by the modification of the title, which is the key to this rewriting. Its first part—*La Dama alas kamelyas*—acknowledges, as it were, the text's connection to Dumas's novel. The second part—*Anjelina del Amor*—introduces the heroine's new name (formerly Marguerite) and gives the reader some idea of the novel's subject. It sounds like a typical Ladino love story, similar, for instance, to the one signed by Benghiat: *Ana Maria; or, A Woman's Heart: A Very Moving Novel.*[6] Florentin's title is

לה

דאמה אלאס קאמילייאם

אדאפטאדו פור איזאק דוד פ"לורינטין

Figure 4.2. Title page of *La Dama alas kamelyas*, 2nd ed. (Salonica, 1922).
Jewish National and University Library in Jerusalem

a literary declaration, which in a nutshell conveys the twofold nature of Ladino belles lettres in general and this text in particular: it is both inspired by a foreign author's work and is a Ladino novel in its own right.

The rewriter changes not only the heroine's name but also her occupation: "the girl, who used to be a singer, . . . was called 'Anjelina,' and everybody called her 'Angel of Love'" (4). Referring to the book Anjelina used to own, Florentin does not mention its title—*Manon Lescaut*—but calls it simply "a moving novel" (5).[7] This modification, along with the omission of Dumas's passionate defense of courtesans, leaves nothing of the original's message.

Through numerous deletions and additions, Florentin changes the characters' personalities in accordance with his readers' taste for melodramatic love stories. Thus, strong and intelligent Marguerite is transformed into a banal and docile girl. Unlike Marguerite, who never seemed to be concerned about religion and made very specific plans for her earthly life with Armand, Anjelina readily accepts her coming death and rejoices in dreams of love in heaven: "If there is another world, after this false one, you will see how in that world our two souls will love each other" (24). Ironically, it is here in her weakness that Marguerite's Sephardi counterpart resembles Manon before the latter's death.

In this rewriting, rather than describe his characters' emotional state, Florentin tends to illustrate it by actions, even if it takes adding made-up episodes. Thus, as was already mentioned, when Alfred (Dumas's Armand)[8] reads an "angelic note" from Anjelina, brought by her maid, he expresses his joy by lifting the woman in his arms and almost strangling her. Having explained the misunderstanding, Alfred watches the maid's disappointed face as she leaves. The only referent for this scene in the source is the fact that the young man receives a note from his beloved (though not through her maid), yet in the Ladino version it takes a whole page. Florentin's goal is to render Alfred's joy and make the readers laugh, although Dumas's character is going through a crisis.

Among the few linguistic innovations introduced in *Anjelina,* one finds *serkolyo* (coffin), which is translated by the Turkish *tabut* and explained as "a box for the dead, in which Christians put their dead inside the grave" (13). This gloss, as well as some changes introduced by the rewriter, make it clear that he does not expect his readers to be acquainted with Christian rites and customs.

No doubt, unlike the later version of *La Dame aux Camélias, Anjelina* has every right to be regarded as a domestic Ladino novel. It presents a perfect case of the amalgamation of local and imported components, which become inseparable. The rewriter borrowed from Dumas's novel parts of its plot and some other elements and constructed on this basis his own characters and their relationships, which are quite different from those in the source. Having obliterated the original's social message, Florentin reduced the novel to the level of popular entertainment for an unsophisticated audience.

*Manon Lesko*

A very moving novel
Translated by Alexandre Benghiat
*Manon Lesko*
Romanso muy ezmuvyenteTrezladado por Aleksandr Benghiat
Felyeton de *El Meseret* de Izmir
Cairo: Estamparia Karmona i Zara, 5665 [1904 or 1905], 82 pages

In the nineteenth century, Abbé Prévost's *Story of the Chevalier des Grieux and of Manon Lescaut* (1731), an eighteenth-century novel of feeling, became a classic of mass literature and appeared in serialized form in many languages, and it is found on Benghiat's list of foreign literary works to be translated into Ladino. Since *Manon Lesko* is longer than most of Benghiat's other rewritings, he seems to have felt the need to justify its length in a preface, where he both praises the novel and promises to keep only the important passages: "*Manon Lesko* is a story about two young people, passionately in love with each other, both made to be loved. . . . This is the story, which we are going to tell and from which we are going to remove the least important passages" (2).

As we follow the chain of events in Benghiat's rendering, it may seem that almost nothing is missing. Nevertheless, *Manon Lescaut* is more than two and a half times longer than its Ladino version.[9] This discrepancy can be explained by Benghiat's strategy in this rewriting, which is based on his interpretation of *Manon* as a "simple love story" (2). Prévost's goal, however, was not just to tell his readers an entertaining story but to evoke in them compassion that would foster their moral development, which is why each episode is accompanied by a detailed description of the characters' mood. The story is told in the first person by the Chevalier, who always registers Manon's tone of voice, her mood, and her expression as well as his inner response to it. This material is what Benghiat typically takes out, without having to change the plot.

The Chevalier des Grieux, a seventeen-year-old from a good family, ready for an ecclesiastical career, meets Manon, who is on her way to a convent. The young people fall in love and run away to Paris, where for a few weeks they enjoy idyllic happiness. However, when their money runs out, Manon starts a relationship with their rich neighbor, who notifies des Grieux's father of the young man's whereabouts. On the same day that his father's lackeys are going to abduct the Chevalier, he coincidentally begins to suspect Manon of being unfaithful, but, loving and credulous, he expects that at dinner she will offer an explanation, proving her innocence. Manon, disturbed as well, waits for the dramatic events planned for the evening. This is how Abbé Prévost describes the tension:

> Supper was served. Assuming an air of gaiety, I took my seat at table; but by the light of the candles which were between us, I fancied I perceived an air of melancholy about the eyes and countenance of my beloved mistress. The very thought soon damped my gaiety. I remarked that her looks wore an unusual expression, and although nothing could be more soft or languishing, I was at a loss to discover whether they conveyed more of love than compassion. I gazed at her with equal earnestness, and she perhaps had no less difficulty in comprehending from my countenance what was passing in my heart. We neither spoke nor ate. At length I saw tears starting from her beauteous eyes,—perfidious tears! O heavens! I cried, my dearest Manon, why allow your sorrows to afflict you to this degree without imparting their cause to me? She answered me only with sighs, which increased my misery. I arose trembling from my seat; I conjured her, with all the urgent earnestness of love, to let me know the cause of her grief: I wept in endeavoring to soothe her sorrows: I was more dead than alive. A barbarian would have pitied my sufferings as I stood trembling with grief and apprehension.[10]

Here is the same scene, rewritten by Benghiat: "We prepared to sit down at the table. I saw that she suddenly began to cry and get desperate. Baffled, I threw myself in her arms and asked her about the reason for her tears. But she was only pulling out her hair without answering me" (20).

Benghiat takes out whole sentences and briefly summarizes others. In addition, he removes the narrator's comments that reflect the Chevalier's later perspective. For example, having said, "I saw tears starting from her beauteous eyes," des Grieux responds to himself: "perfidious tears!"[11] Thus, in Benghiat's novel, the Chevalier relates events only from one temporal perspective. Like all other rewriters, he often substitutes subtle descriptions of the characters' emotional states with descriptions of actions meant to convey the respective feelings in a straightforward way. For instance, his Manon expresses her grief by pulling out her hair.

Aside from the modifications called for by the process of abridgment, Benghiat made a major change in order to render his rewriting morally acceptable. In the French original, soon after Manon and des Grieux meet, they decide to get married, but they forget about their plans quickly: "We defrauded the Church of her rights and found ourselves united as man and wife without reflecting on the consequences."[12] In fact, des Grieux calls Manon "my mistress." The Sephardi rewriter, however, could not allow this to happen. If Marguerite Gautier could be transformed into a singer, Manon could become a married woman. Hence, in the Ladino version, the young couple gets married, and thereafter the Chevalier refers to Manon as "my wife." Benghiat reminds his readers more than once that this relationship is legal.

In the original, the question of their marriage becomes crucial for the story when Manon is deported to America and des Grieux follows her there. The young people repent of their sinful past, start a new life, and decide to get married. When the local governor learns that Manon is not really the Chevalier's wife, he wants to give her as a mistress to his vicious nephew. Manon and des Grieux become victims of his persecution, and eventually the young woman dies. Evidently, by making the lovers a married couple, Benghiat could have ruined the story. Since at this point it was impossible to modify the plot, he made des Grieux offer a long and vague explanation about the need to openly celebrate his marriage to Manon. Even a short excerpt shows that this former seminary student is entirely confused:

> We thought of giving to our marriage a sacred form. We had gotten married completely without accomplishing the religious prescriptions. . . . Since now there were no obstacles in our way, we were obliged to crown our happiness by getting married now in front of God. . . . Otherwise, our conscience would not permit us to freely call each other by the sweet names "husband" and "wife." (69–70)

These puzzling explanations, repeated several times, must have satisfied the Sephardi audience. In any case, the story continued to be engaging.

The ten lexical innovations introduced in *Manon Lesko* fall into two categories: terms related to the Christian religion and abstract nouns designating a psychological state. The first category shows that Benghiat insists on using Gallicisms, even when domestic equivalents (two of them of Greek origin) already exist:

| | |
|---|---|
| *prete*[13] (papaz/papas) | priest (appears nine times) |
| *relijyoza* (monaka) | nun |
| *seminaryo* (eskola de papazes) | seminary |
| *preskripsyones relijyozas* (enkomendansas de la ley) | religious prescriptions |

The second category includes six Romance substitutes of Ladino lexemes, four of which are of Turkish origin. Five of these new terms designate feelings or mental acts:

| | |
|---|---|
| *kortezania, kortezia* (terbiyelik)[14] | good manners, education |
| *desizyon* (karar) | decision |
| *egzilo* (surgun), *estado de igzilo* (surgunluk) | exile (appears three times) |
| *insistir* (meter inat)[15] | insist |
| *kon inosensya* (kon mala idea) | innocently |
| *kompasyon* (akchedyamyento) | compassion |

In terms of its relation to the original, *Manon Lesko* differs from the two versions of *La Dame aux Camélias* while sharing similarities with each of them. Though Benghiat uses the original title, Prévost is not mentioned on the title page, and in the preface the rewriter refers to him just as "the priest" (*el prete*). The text is abridged, but the names of the characters are not changed. Almost all the events of the original are found in the rewriting, and the plot is not modified (with the one exception discussed above). Nevertheless, the emotional climate of the French original is gone and the message is lost. Abbé Prévost's novel portrays two worlds: one world is ruled by money and everyday needs and inhabited by financiers, card sharps, prostitutes, and policemen, whereas the other is a realm of feelings in which only the two main characters exist. Benghiat represents the first world in detail but disregards the other one. As a result, the "internal story of passion is replaced with an external love story,"[16] and a sentimentalist novel, loaded with analyses of emotions, turns into a piece of sentimental mass literature.

Although *Anjelina* and *Manon Lesko* were composed by different rewriters, they are literary twins and, theoretically speaking, could belong to the same pen. Both are first-person narratives relating dramatic love stories; both center around beautiful but somewhat immoral women who repent of their past lives and die, leaving their lovers heartbroken. If Dumas's Armand found similarity between Marguerite and Manon, in the Ladino adaptations there is hardly any difference between Armand/Alfred and the Chevalier des Grieux, whose feelings are represented in the same words.

Finally, *Anjelina* and *Manon Lesko* use the same local components, and the borrowed foreign elements are adapted according to the same pattern. The two Ladino rewritings, whose French originals were created more than a hundred years apart, belong to the same literary genre.

*Pavlo and Virginia*[17]
Novel by Bernardin de Saint-Pierre
Translated from French by Alexandre Benghiat
*Pavlo i Virjinya*
Romanso por Bernardin de San Pyer
Imitado del franses por Aleksandr Benghiat
Jerusalem: Estamparia de Shelomo Yisrael Sherezli, 5672
   [1911 or 1912], 21 pages
Originally published in *El Meseret,* 1905 or 1906

Bernardin de Saint-Pierre's novel *Paul et Virginie* is also included in Benghiat's list of the important works of world literature that have been translated into a great number of languages. In Ladino, it was rewritten twice, the other version belonging to Sara Siman-tov (Istanbul, 1901, 166 pages).[18]

*Paul et Virginie* appeared in 1788 as a supplement to the third edition of Bernardin's *Studies of Nature,* which was significantly influenced by Rousseau, and can be considered a manifesto of cultural primitivism and a precursor of the dawning Romanticism. It is a story of two island children, whose innocent love for each other begins in their infancy, develops in unspoiled natural surroundings, and ends tragically when civilization interferes. The girl, invited by her wealthy and heartless aunt, goes to France, but cannot adjust to the immoral life of the rich and decides to return home. As her ship approaches the island, a violent gale breaks out, and Virginie drowns. Heartbroken, Paul becomes ill and soon dies as well.

The action takes place far away from the metropolis, in what was then a French colony called Ile-de-France. The story is related by an old man, a witness to the events, and a significant part of it belongs to the narrator's monologues on history, morality, and religion. The old man directly expounds Bernardin's worldview, illustrated by the story of Paul and Virginie. For Benghiat's audience, the attractive aspect of the novel was the sad love story; the long monologues of the old man could not interest Sephardi readers and were deleted. Consequently, they received a twenty-one-page moving story about the love of two young people separated by implacable circumstances that cause their tragic deaths.

Alongside innumerable deletions, *Pavlo i Virjinya* contains some additions, most of which were called for by the abridgment and the change of the narrative structure. A few of them are significant for this study, because they make *Pavlo i Virjinya* a perfect example of a Ladino novel that successfully combines elements of instruction and entertainment. The first of these additions is meant to offer readers useful information on Ile-de-France, and thus the story opens with what should have been a footnote, not a rare thing in Ladino novels. Benghiat explains that the events take place in "Port Louis, a city by the Indian sea, now belonging to the British and sometime ago to the French" (3).

The second addition directly contradicts Bernardin's message, since it presents instruction as a fundamental element of the children's lives. In the Ladino version, the old man states that "every day they had a little time set apart to learn reading and writing" (5). Bernardin, however, emphasizes the children's illiteracy: "they were as ignorant as the Creoles and could not read or write."[19] Later in the novel, he stresses that Paul had to acquire these skills only because the hostile European civilization separated him from his beloved with whom he wanted to correspond.[20]

In the third case, the addition emphasizes one of Bernardin's ideas to suit the rewriter's own message. The immediate cause of the young girl's death in both the original and the rewriting is her chastity. When the last sailor on the sinking ship asks Virginie to take off her dress, so that he can help her to swim, she refuses out of modesty.[21] The same scene appears in the Ladino rewriting, but Benghiat dramatizes it even more by having Virjinya refuse three times to take off her clothes: "A sailor approached her and advised her to get undressed and jump into the water, so that he could save her. She refused. The captain of the ship advised her the same, she refused again. And those who were still able to save her advised her the same" (20). The scene has become more intense, yet this was hardly Benghiat's only goal. The rewriters of La Dame aux Camélias and Manon Lescaut had no choice but to delete everything that could present their heroines in a bad light, or the novels would have been unacceptable both for the female audience and the censors. For the same reason, Benghiat omits Bernardin's description of the girl's awakening sexuality, which she cannot explain to herself, but which makes her mother worry and confirms her decision to send Virginie away from Paul. However, in the scene of the girl's death, the rewriter makes the elaborate addition, reinforcing Bernardin's message, which suggests that the topic of female modesty was high on his pedagogical agenda, reflecting the Alliance concern with female moral education. Its 1903 instructions for teachers explain: "To the qualities we hope to develop in all our children . . . must be added in girls a few special qualities: gentleness, modesty, simplicity of dress, the wish to shine other than through a ridiculous display of jewels and petticoats, a sense of the equality between rich and poor, etc."[22] Sexual education was another Alliance concern.[23] Benghiat's Virjinya—gentle, modest, and loved by her mother's slaves—perfectly meets the standards set by the organization for its female students.

The language of *Pavlo i Virjinya* is interesting in that it illustrates the arbitrariness of Benghiat's linguistic endeavor. Here, he is not only less eager to introduce new words (there are just two), but he is notably inconsistent with his previous work. Thus, in *Manon Lesko* (1904 or 1905), he persistently replaces *papas* (priest) with *prete*, yet in this rewriting, which first appeared in *El Meseret* in 1905 or 1906, he goes back to the Greek term.

Alongside specific changes, *Paul et Virginie* underwent a fundamental genre shift, performed by the rewriter in accordance with the generally adopted pattern, which is why the new text has more in common with other Ladino adaptations than with the French source. Once again, the rewriter achieved this by using some imported elements (plot and setting), by removing others (philosophical discourses and characterization of the protagonists through descriptions of nature), and by making a few additions. As a result, *Pavlo i Virjinya* is more didactic and even more suitable for reading around the family table than the novels discussed above. (And it is certainly not the same novel that made such a profound impression on Emma Bovary.)

> *The Two Voyages of Gulliver: To the Lilliputs and to the Giants*[24]
> Translated by Alexandre Benghiat
> *Los dos vyajes de Guliver: Onde los lilipusyanos i onde los djigantes*
> Trezladado por Aleksandr Benghiat
> Jerusalem: Estamparia de Shelomo Yisrael Sherezli, 5672 [1911 or
>     1912], 20 pages Originally published in *El Meseret*, 1903 or 1904

Benghiat's *Two Voyages of Gulliver* is one of the most skillful adaptations of a piece of modern fiction matching the domestic production without differing from it in terms of ideology, genre, or poetics (i.e., symbols and imagery). Finally, it reveals an aspect of Benghiat's educational agenda that we do not find elsewhere in my corpus. In addition, this novel is of special interest for the scholar of Ladino literature, because it distinctly exposes the rewriter's strategy, which here is uncharacteristically consistent and transparent, making it easier to compare Ladino rewritings with other types of adaptations. As Swift's novel was retold multiple times for children, one has an opportunity to observe the affinity between a cultural adaptation for adults in a foreign language and children's versions of the same text in the original language.

Soon after its first publication in England (1726), *Gulliver's Travels* was translated into other languages and adapted for children. Given Benghiat's background and some indirect evidence, one can assume that he did not know English[25] and thus probably used a French version produced either for children or adults, possibly serialized.[26] All adaptations for children of Swift's work contain only the first part or the first and second parts. The same is true for the first translations for adults into Yiddish, Ladino, Turkish, and Armenian. All rewriters, including Benghiat, treated Swift's work as a collection of randomly assembled stories, some of which could be left out, and did not translate the third and fourth parts. Evidently, only the first two parts of the book easily lend themselves to the required genre modifications. They could become fairy tales or adventure stories, or they could combine elements of both, but could not remain satire on the specific political situation in England or on the human condition in general.

In order to transfer *Gulliver's Travels* to another genre, namely, a fairy tale or adventure story, Benghiat eliminated from Swift's text everything that required background knowledge, while the limited reading experience of his audience did not leave room for inadequate genre expectations. One of the tools that Swift uses to create satiric effect is stressing the similarities between Lilliputians and his compatriots. This does not suit Benghiat, whose goal is to enhance the contrast between the two worlds in order to render the setting more exotic.[27] Thus, in the original, Gulliver sees "a *human*[28] creature not six inches high,"[29] whereas in the Ladino text Lilliputians are first described as "small creatures, much smaller than dolls" (4) and later they are referred to as little animals who make little cries (5). While Swift's Lilliputians differ from humans only in size, otherwise also being greedy, disputatious, and spiteful, which makes them an object of criticism, Benghiat's little animals, albeit bizarre, are nice and helpless. The image of these strange creatures, resembling both humans and animals, would not have surprised Sephardi readers familiar with similar ones at least from Huli's *Me'am Lo'ez*. In a few instances, for example in Genesis 1:10, Huli, obviously wishing to entertain the audience, offers descriptions of fantastic worlds populated with strange creatures.

Another fairy-tale element found both in Benghiat's rewriting and in the children's adaptations is exaggeration. For example, in *The Two Voyages*, Swift's five hundred carpenters and engineers, who make the cart for Gulliver, become five thousand, and he is raised onto it by a thousand Lilliputians rather than by nine hundred, the latter number being too precise for a fantasy. Besides, as we have seen in the case of the press, Sephardi readers were fascinated with big numbers, which appeared in fantastic stories about non-European countries where everything was bizarre.

The compositional frame of the Ladino rewriting is rather close to the original. Yet, by means of intentional modifications, Benghiat turns

*Gulliver's Travels* into a story of a man who—as a result of shipwrecks—gets to two strange countries where, thanks to his ingenuity, he manages to survive and in the end is miraculously saved. Zohar Shavit suggests that, in children's literature, such manipulations are allowed if the rewriter adheres to two goals: "an adjustment of the text to make it appropriate and useful to the child, in accordance with what the society regards as educationally 'good for the child'; and an adjustment of plot, characterization, and language to prevailing society's perceptions of the child's ability to read and comprehend."[30] This is also true for cultural adaptations, due to the same underlying assumption of the addressees' inability to read a lengthy text. In both cases, rewriters tend to abridge and simplify the original by deleting the scenes they consider unimportant, unacceptable, or difficult to understand. "Unimportant" in both types of texts means insignificant for the development of the plot. Hence, most rewritings of *Gulliver's Travels* leave out the descriptions of the absurd ways of raising children in Lilliput. Benghiat also omits some funny incidents of Gulliver's life in Brobdingnag that do not advance the plot. "Unacceptable" means morally or educationally inappropriate. Though, in general, moral norms for children's literature differ from those acceptable for adults, in traditional societies some taboos are often the same. Thus, Benghiat and the rewriters for children delete the scene where Gulliver is accused of having a love affair with the High Treasurer's wife. Another episode deleted in Benghiat's version and in adaptations for young children (e.g., the Ladybird Classics version, retold by Marie Stuart, 1995) is Gulliver's extinguishing the fire in the palace by urinating. Both episodes are crucial for the plot because the decision to kill or blind Gulliver is based mainly on these events. Hence, Benghiat changes the plot entirely: Lilliput's parliament decides to punish Gulliver because the admiral of the newly acquired fleet tells the prince that Gulliver wants to join the enemy.

Benghiat's story of Gulliver's second voyage begins in a more dramatic way than in the original. In Swift's novel, Gulliver joins the sailors sent by the captain of the ship to look for drinking water but then leaves the boat to explore the unknown land. When he decides to return, he sees that a giant is trying to snatch the boat, which is rapidly moving away from the shore. In the Ladino version, the ship is struck by a whale, which results in a big leak, and everybody has to leave the sinking ship on boats. All of Gulliver's comrades, except for two, die of starvation and exhaustion. When the three survivors reach the shore, Gulliver alone goes to explore the new land and meets a giant. At this point, Benghiat returns to the general line of Swift's narrative and offers readers an abridged record of Gulliver's adventures in the land of giants, followed by a fascinating story of his salvation.

In the second part, the elements of an adventure story prevail over those of a fairy tale, but it is a lot more didactic than the first one. Furthermore, the end of the story is striking in its religious thrust, which goes against the grain of Swift's rationalism and faith in common sense. This transformation is achieved by means of a significant addition matched by a small adjustment earlier in the book. In the original, when an eagle picks up Gulliver's box, he realizes that it could be dashed to pieces at any moment, but he does not lose his calm. As the box falls four feet deep into the water, he immediately tries to adjust the crannies in order to stop the leakage. In the Ladino version, however, as soon as Gulliver sees that he has become a prisoner, having over his head the sky, underneath the sea, and around him emptiness, he becomes desperate. He confesses that, trembling, he entrusted himself to "the power of God, asking him to save me. I fell on my knees, crying from the depth of my heart and swearing that if I were saved and returned to my homeland, I would never leave my house. And since I was begging the heavens from the depths of my heart, God heard my prayer and, it seems, took pity on me" (19). When the box falls into the sea, Gulliver experiences another moment of panic, and "this time again, the heavens take pity" on him (19). And, on arriving home, in keeping with his vow, he decides not to travel again.

Gulliver's account of praying in a wooden box on the way to the depths of the sea is more than an obvious allusion to the book of Jonah; it is a paraphrase of Jonah's thanksgiving psalm praising God for his deliverance from the fish's belly:

> I called to the Lord out of my distress, and he answered me;
> out of the belly of Sheol I cried, and you heard my voice.
> You cast me into the deep, into the heart of the seas,
> and the flood surrounded me; all your waves and your billows passed
>     over me.
> . . . I, with the voice of thanksgiving, will sacrifice to you;
> what I have vowed I will pay. (Jonah 2:2–3, 9)

Benghiat's readers were prepared for the Jonah-like finale by the opening scene of the story of Gulliver's second voyage. It describes the shipwreck as being caused by a whale, glossed in parentheses as "the biggest fish" (8).[31] The whale's appearance in the story can be accounted for only by the need to bring up Jonah's lesson. The *Me'am Lo'ez* corpus does not include a commentary on the book of Jonah, but all Sephardim were familiar with it, if only because it is read at the Yom Kippur afternoon service. Furthermore, we have convincing evidence that, at the turn of the twentieth century, Jonah's story was quite alive in the minds of Ottoman Jews. Three years prior to the first appearance of *Two Voyages,* Benghiat published a story about some fishermen who caught a giant fish that vomited out many smaller fishes (*El Meseret,* December 12, 1900, 3). This reminded the journalist about the story of "a modern Jonah"—a man swallowed by a giant fish after it had struck with its tail and overturned his ship in the vicinity of the Falkland Islands. The article claimed that the "new Jonah" was later rescued by his comrades.[32]

Another text that would have come to the minds of Benghiat's readers is the opening of *The Book of Eldad the Danite,* which was reprinted in Ladino many times. This is how Eldad begins his story:

> I and a Jew from the tribe of Asher got on a small ship with other sailors, and in the middle of the night God caused a great and strong wind to blow, and it was so strong that the ship broke, but God provided a board. I got hold of it, and so did the Jew who was with me on the ship, and we floated until the sea cast us to [the land of] the people which is called Rom Domiom.[33]

These tall people eat Eldad's comrade who, in the Ladino version, tastes so good that they lick their fingers and want to eat Eldad next, but find him too thin and decide first to feed him "like a chicken." However, the ingenious traveler outsmarts the giants by spitting out the food they give him, and he survives until they are conquered by the fire worshippers.

In both referent stories, the storm is caused by God, who then sends a big fish to swallow Jonah and a piece of board to save Eldad. Gulliver suffers two shipwrecks, one of them caused by a whale, and finds himself in strange and dangerous lands, but when his wooden box is ready to crash, he asks God to save him, and God takes pity on him.

The opening sentence of *The Two Voyages* speaks of Gulliver's mother, and we learn that he was punished more than once because someone (his mother?) wanted him to give up the idea of travel. One cannot tell for sure whether the story of a disobedient son, who did not listen to his mother and would have perished had it not been for God's mercy, was meant to serve as a reminder of Jonah's disobedience to God. But if Benghiat indeed had this goal in mind, the didactic beginning of his novel and the replacement of Gulliver's wife with his mother suggests that it was intended specifically for children. This would also explain the particular simplicity of the novel's language whose vocabulary is strikingly poor even in comparison with Benghiat's other rewritings. Curiously, there is no textual evidence suggesting that Gulliver is not Jewish: all we know about him is that he has a mother and four siblings who live in England. In other words, *The Two Voyages* could have been understood by readers as a Jewish story.[34] In any case, the novel provides both children and adults with entertainment and offers a lesson in divine mercy and obedience suitable for a Jewish audience.

Although on some level Benghiat's novel is a summary of the first two parts of *Gulliver's Travels* (most likely based on a French version, possibly one adapted for children), the rewriter turned Swift's novel—the highest expression of eighteenth-century English rationalism—into a medieval semi-religious travelogue about faraway countries populated with outlandish humanoids. This transformation is achieved by the additions, deletions, and other modifications aimed at making the story comprehensible and amusing for Sephardim of all ages, but—no less important—bringing up what Benghiat saw as the message of the book of Jonah, which suited his educational purpose. As a result, *The Two Voyages* is transferred to the universe of discourse largely created in Ladino by traditional texts. This is not to say that this transfer was the rewriter's intentional choice, but his decision to bring a religious lesson into a travel account automatically placed his work in the category of premodern literature, where *Me'am Lo'ez* and *The Book of Eldad the Danite* were the only available sources of literary and linguistic borrowing. Finally, *The Two Voyages of Gulliver* hardly furthered the westernization of Ladino literature because, rather than imitating modern European fiction, it turned to authoritative domestic texts, which are always the most conservative in terms of ideology and literary form.

*Hasan-pasha the Terrible*[35]
Historical novel
by Alexandre Benghiat
*Hasan-pasha el terivle*[36]
Romanso istoriko
por Aleksandr Benghiat
Jerusalem: Estamparia de Shelomo Yisrael Sherezli, 5671 [1910
or religious prescriptions 1911], 20 pages

*Hasan-pasha* is generally considered to be Benghiat's original work. This assumption, I believe, is implicitly based on three circumstances: the title page indicates *por* (by) Benghiat, no foreign-language text is known to be its source, and the action takes place in the Ottoman Empire. I will argue, nevertheless, that it is a rewriting of a French text so far unknown to us.

*Hasan-pasha* is described on the title page as a historical novel, and it is indeed the story of a real figure, Cezayirli Gazi (Celebizade Serif) Hasan Pasha (1713–1790). The novel tells us how Hasan—a former slave of

Persian origin—started his free life as a pirate, became a navy hero, and died as grand vizier. This text contains elements of various genres, such as the fairy tale, the adventure story, and the history textbook. Although the narration opens like a fairy tale, there is a precise indication of the time when the first events in the story happened ("One hundred and fifty years ago") and the place: "the small city of Rodosto (Tekirdag) situated between the Dardanelles and Kostan [Constantinople]" (3). We learn that, once upon a time, there lived a hard-working man who had a slave named Hasan. When death approached, the good Muslim summoned his slave and promised to set him free, because in his dreams he had seen him as a great man, dressed in gold, walking in the sultan's palace. In return, the master asked the slave to take care of his widow. But Hasan did not keep his word, abandoned the widow, went off in search of adventures, and became a cruel pirate. Such is the *intrigue* (onset of action) of the story that makes the reader anticipate a series of exciting events, a climax, and a happy ending. But chapter 1 ends in a different genre: it seems to be the beginning of an adventure story about pirates.

Chapter 2, however, interrupts the narration with textbook-like passages on privateering in the Mediterranean in the eighteenth century. Then the story returns to Hasan, who participates in the war among various Berber tribes in Algeria, and the Algerian dey[37] becomes his enemy. Hasan flees to Europe and gets letters of recommendation from European monarchs, meant to ensure him a safe return to Turkey. But he is betrayed, thrown into prison, and awaits execution.[38] The sultan, who is thrilled to meet the famous prisoner, visits him in a guard's disguise, is impressed by his courage, and saves his life. Although the climax of *Hasan-pasha* is a fairy-tale cliché, the narrator offers concrete information: the sultan is identified as Mustafa III, and he talks with the prisoner about Turkey's losses in its war with Russia. Thus we learn that the events take place during the Russo-Turkish war of 1768–1774.

At this point, the story assumes a hagiographic character. The sultan releases Hasan, who manages to destroy the Russian fleet in the Black Sea in a battle that allegedly brings Turkey a maritime victory over Russia and is consequently appointed a navy commander, then minister of the navy, governor of Istanbul, and eventually grand vizier. The reader is offered an anecdote intended to demonstrate Hasan's extraordinary strength: he rescues a French diplomat attacked by a lion. This is followed by a story proving Hasan's wisdom in bringing about justice in a conflict between Turkish and French youths. For all of this, we are told, Hasan was not only feared as a navy hero but also respected as a wise and fair politician.

He died on March 29, 1790, during the next Russo-Turkish war, yet not gloriously in combat: an exact medical diagnosis (typhus) is cited.

Benghiat's novel contains a lot of facts, dates, and names, some of them completely unrelated to the story. For example, we learn that Abdul Hamid I died of gout and are provided with the exact date of his death.[39] Some of the events mentioned in the story, such as France's colonization of Morocco, took place long after Hasan's death. This abundance of superfluous information on Ottoman and French history is at first perplexing for the researcher and seems to suggest the presence in *Hasan-pasha* of another text, possibly an insufficiently abridged reference source. Yet I am convinced that these ostensibly unnecessary data are not a result of poor editing of the Ladino novel but were an essential part of its French source, which was produced for a French audience and was intended to serve propagandistic goals. Benghiat did not have to make drastic changes to the original, because it suited both his educational program and the tastes of his Francophile readers.

My assumption that *Hasan-pasha* has a French original is based, first of all, on linguistic evidence, both on the lexical and syntactic levels. The novel's vocabulary is quite rich compared to that of most other Ladino novels and contains a significant number of bookish words without glosses, such as *lisensya* (permission), *karakter* (character), and many others. One also finds in this text a few semantic calques that clearly reveal a French source, such as *remeter* ("deliver," from the French *remettre*). At the same time, *Hasan-pasha* has surprisingly few words of Arabic or Turkish origin, and only those that are necessary for writing about Ottoman history and that appear in many languages and are understood by everyone: *sultan, pasha, vizier, divan*.[40] The syntax of *Hasan-pasha* is extremely Gallicized in comparison with other contemporaneous Ladino texts.[41]

Aside from the linguistic evidence suggesting that Benghiat's source was produced by a Francophone writer, there is evidence confirming that it targeted a French audience, which would be interested in certain facts that were irrelevant for all other readers. In Benghiat's novel, France is mentioned more often than any other western country. The term *fransia/franses* appears in the text ten times, and only *turkiya/turko* is mentioned more often, fifteen times. In chapter 2, the readers are told that France suffered from the predations of pirates more than any other state did and finally decided to put an end to this by sending a military fleet to the region. At another point, without any connection to the story, the author informs us about the French colonies in North Africa. Benghiat mentions the French again when Hasan has to resolve a problem brought to his attention by the

French consul, and he punishes two Turks for harassing two Frenchmen. Hasan once again proves to be useful to France when his lion nearly kills the country's ambassador.[42]

The story of Hasan was meant to glorify the Ottoman past and to demonstrate that, even at times of downfall and crisis, Turkey had at its service great military heroes and wise politicians who, despite their obscure origins, were ready to come to its rescue and bring triumph. In order to convey this message, the author omits some facts, misrepresents certain events of the Ottoman past largely unfamiliar to the average French (and Sephardi) reader, and thus creates a portrait of an ideal Ottoman leader. According to the novel, sometime in 1769 or 1770, Hasan was let out of prison, appointed fleet commander, and, with twenty ships, attacked a Russian fleet in the Black Sea, fully destroying it. This victory allegedly made Russia sign a lasting peace treaty with Turkey. As a reward, Hasan was appointed minister of the navy and successfully reformed it. Yet, in reality, Hasan was a fleet commander during the Battle of Cheshme (July 6–7, 1770) in the Aegean Sea, which was lost by the Ottoman Empire and led to the complete devastation of the Ottoman navy. Upon his arrival in Istanbul, the historical Hasan was promoted to chief of staff and in the following years indeed managed to modernize the Ottoman navy.

I cannot tell whether the author of Hasan's biography made up the story of his maritime victory himself or based it on an existing Ottoman source, since the official version of the Russo-Turkish wars is not available to me. But, given how much the Turkish press distorted the present in the Hamidian period, there is reason to suspect that the past would have also been misrepresented. At any rate, after 1876, the representation of Ottoman history and even geography in state schools was fully controlled and marked by a strong political bias.[43] Yet, the nationalist critics of Hamidian rule in exile also distorted their country's history to promote their political programs.

There are a few different versions of Hasan's death. Among other sources, the *Nuttall Encyclopedia* (1907) states that, having been defeated by Russians, the grand vizier was "dismissed and put to death."[44] But this ending would not have suited the author's patriotic agenda, as it would not have allowed him to conclude his piece by saying, "Such was the great Hasan Pasha whose memory is cherished by Ottoman history" (20).

It is impossible to establish when *Hasan-pasha*'s French source was published. All we learn from the text is that it was produced 150 years after the death of Hasan's master, which could have happened any time in the 1740s–1750s. Indeed, the most likely time for a story of this kind to have appeared was between the mid-1890s and 1908, when the Young Turk press in Paris was trying to win the sympathies of French society. Benghiat's source could have been produced by a Turkish émigré fluent in French to appear in serialized form in one of the Young Turks' periodicals, namely, *La Jeune Turquie, Turkiya al-fatat,* or *Mechveret,* which came out in Ottoman or Arabic but had French versions and regularly published similar stories.

Benghiat's choice of this text for rewriting not only fits the general assimilationist project embraced by many Sephardi westernizers[45] but also reflects the new Ottomanist agenda that emerged in the period immediately following the Young Turk revolution.[46] In those years, Sephardi literati published numerous texts on Turkish literature[47] and history, the latter category including such works as *Los primeros sultanes* (*The First Sultans*) by Moïse Fresco (Istanbul, 1910) and *Mehmet-pasha: Su vida i su ovra* (*Mehmet-pasha: His Life and Activities*), translated from the French by Farhi (Istanbul, 1908).[48] *Hasan-pasha* suited Benghiat's purposes because, while being entertaining and providing readers with information on Ottoman history, it demonstrated that one did not have to be Turkish in order to make an extraordinary career and be appreciated in the Ottoman Empire. Until *Hasan-pasha*'s source is identified, we cannot evaluate the amount of editing and abridging Benghiat had to do in order to produce this Ladino novel. Given Sephardim's interest in France, it appears logical that he would have kept at least some of the digressions into French history.

*Hasan-pasha,* although in many ways differing from the majority of Ladino novels, puts into relief one of the idiosyncratic aspects of this genre, which was often used as a powerful ideological tool alongside direct indoctrination through the press. Furthermore, this novel offers a window on the perception of the Young Turks' propaganda by Ottoman Jews, who absorbed it with significant aberrations. It demonstrates that the ideological perspective of westernized Ottoman Jews was in many ways similar to that of the educated French readers interested in the story of an Ottoman hero. Consequently, this rewriting, unlike the love stories, hardly required significant adjustments.

*Nantas*
By Émile Zola
Translated from French by M. Menashe
*Nantas*
Por Emil Zola
Trezladado del franses por M. Menashe
Felyeton del *Nuvelista* de Izmir
Cairo: Estamparia Karmona i Zara, 5664 [1904], 53 pages

Menashe's version of *Nantas* is a rare case of a Ladino rewriting that meets even today's strictest definitions of translation. In addition, in my corpus of Ladino rewritings, this novella is the only text that has a known, non-canonized foreign source and the only one that cannot be considered a piece of mass literature. It is precisely *Nantas*'s marginal place in Ladino belles lettres that makes its analysis useful.

Due to Zola's role in the Dreyfus Affair, Jewish literati were eager to translate his works, and almost all of them, including *Nantas,* appeared in Yiddish. Yet only this story and *Thérèse Raquin*[49] were rewritten in Ladino. Evidently, Zola's monumental novels could not be adapted for the Sephardi readership, though not so much because of their length (which would not have been an insurmountable impediment), but primarily because they were in every sense alien to the domestic production and contradicted the optimistic view of France upheld by the Alliance. In any case, these novels could not be turned into thrillers or formulaic love stories and thus would not sell. Thus, *El Nuvelista*'s editors or the translator made a wise choice by picking *Nantas,* a short and rather engaging piece which, though much less famous, was likely to appeal to the periodical's audience.

In France, *Nantas* was first published in *Le Message de l'Europe* (October 1878) under the title *La Vie contemporaine* (*Contemporary Life*), which reveals the purpose of this rather odd story: it was meant to be a sketch of the Parisian business world and its mores in the 1870s. The plot of Zola's novella is uncharacteristically complicated and implausible. Nantas, a poor but extremely ambitious young man from a provincial town, comes to Paris determined to conquer it. One night, after he has decided that he will never achieve this goal, an unknown woman visits him and asks him to marry a beautiful and wealthy girl from a noble family who urgently needs to cover her pregnancy. The young man gladly sells himself to Flavie, whose only conditions are that their marriage always remain nominal and that their lives continue to be separate. The reader meets the spouses again ten years later, when Nantas, who has accumulated a lot of wealth and made an extraordinary career, is going to be appointed minister of finance. Now, he is madly in love with Flavie, but the arrogant woman contemptuously rejects him. A year and a half later, already a minister, Nantas gets desperate and hires the woman who once arranged his marriage to spy on Flavie. The greedy woman decides to get money from both Flavie's husband and her former lover and lets the latter into Flavie's bedroom. When Nantas finds a man hiding in his wife's room, he decides to kill himself, but only after he has finished an important memorandum for the emperor. Flavie is watching her noble husband through the keyhole and, when he lifts the revolver to his forehead, runs into the room crying: "I love you because you are strong!"[50] These are the last words of Zola's story.

Thus, the fifty-three-page Ladino novel contains enough action to keep the reader in suspense until the denouement, which happens at the very last moment. This far-fetched story in a different setting and somewhat abridged would have been attractive to the Sephardi mass readership, but the circumstances of Parisian business life, the knowledge of which is taken for granted, must have made it unsuitable for the majority. The protagonist's unromantic motivation to marry a beautiful young woman most likely would have been perplexing to the readers of Ladino fiction, and his social and financial success resulting from this union would not have been appreciated. No doubt, a Sephardi rewriter interested in commercial success would have deleted the first, naturalist part of the story, which describes Nantas's childhood, his father's death, and his wanderings in the busy streets of Paris. He would have also turned the long dialogues into a straightforward account of the events relevant to the love story. But this might have been impossible, given the author's name. In any case, Menashe chose to keep the extensive descriptions, the minute details of Nantas's everyday life, and the complicated psychological situations related through long dialogues, which could not have placed his translation further away from the domestic Ladino repertoire.

However, it is not just the literary form or subject matter that makes this text so alien to Ladino belles lettres. Another aspect of Menashe's version of *Nantas* that would have rendered it problematic for the mass readership is its linguistic makeup, namely, its vocabulary and syntax. A linguistic analysis of *Nantas,* which is marked by a great number of lexical and syntactic Gallicisms, reveals the rewriter's position vis-à-vis Ladino. I cannot tell whether Menashe supported the idea of replacing the Sephardi vernacular with French, but he definitely tried to "purify" and Gallicize it. Like some of his colleagues and in the spirit of *El Nuvelista*'s Francophile project, the translator of *Nantas* introduces many bookish words which, even if not indispensable for the story, served to enrich readers' vocabulary. But a much larger number of the lexical innovations are not dictated by the necessity to convey new meanings. The translator suggests forty-six replacements, the largest group of which comprises Romance substitutes of Turkish loans, though the Hebrew *mazal* (luck) is also replaced (with *destino*):

| | |
|---|---|
| *invalido* (sakat) | invalid |
| *eskambyador* (saraf) | money-changer |
| *ponte* (kyopri) | bridge |
| *jaula* (kafes) | cage |
| *departamyento* (velayet) | a province in France |
| *aryenda* (chiflik) | farm |
| *file* (sira) | line |
| *pavilyon* (kiosk) | pavilion |

Another linguistic feature of this text is an abundance of semantic calques. For example, *sufrir* (to suffer) is replaced with *sangrarse* (from the French *saigner*), despite the fact that the word *sangrar* already existed in Ladino and meant "to bleed." There are numerous lexical calques, such as *una chika muy grande* (a very tall girl), where *grande* is used instead of *alta,* that is, it has the meaning of the French *grand(e)*, which might have been confusing for the reader. Menashe's version is also full of idiomatic calques, few of which are explained in parentheses. For instance, *son orgueil restait debout* ("he kept his pride") is translated literally as *su orgulyo restaba en pyes* ("his pride remained on its feet"), which is incomprehensible in Ladino. Menashe's method of translation is illustrated by a comparison of the following excerpt and its French original:

> Esta manyana, Nantas estava akablado de echos. En los vastos (muy anchos) buros ke el avia instalado en el primer piso de la kaza reynava una aktividad prodijyoza. Era un mundo de empleados; los unos immobiles (kedos) en el buro de kasha, los otros yendo i vinyendo sin parar azyendo batir las puertas; era un ruido de oro kontinuado; sakos avyertos i koryendo sovre las mezas, la muzika syempre sonante de moneda donde la ola paresia dever undir las kalyejas. (26)

> Ce matin-là, Nantas était accablé d'affaires. Dans les vastes bureaux qu'il avait installés au rez-de-chaussée de l'hôtel, régnait une activité prodigieuse. C'était un monde d'employés, les uns immobiles derrière des guichets, les autres allant et venant sans cesse, faisant battre les portes; c'était un bruit d'or continu; des sacs ouverts et coulants sur les tables, la musique toujours sonnante d'une caisse dont le flot semblait devoir noyer les rues[51]

The similarities between these texts at all levels are striking. Even in terms of spelling, the Ladino excerpt has some peculiarities revealing the French influence. Thus, the new word *immobile,* meant to replace *kedo,* is spelled with two *mems* (mm) as in French, although there is no consonantal gemination in Ladino. There are two lexical innovations—*vasto* (wide) and *immobile* (still)—neither of them indispensable. There is a lexical calque (*akablado de echos* [overwhelmed with things to do]) and a lexical-syntactic calque (*donde* [where] for *dont* [of which]). As for the syntax, the whole passage is a calque. The translator copies Zola's syntax even when it is confusing: "era un ruido de oro kontinuado; sakos avyertos i koryendo sovre las mezas" (there was a continuous sound of gold; open bags and running on the tables). Curiously, even the number of words in the two excerpts is the same: seventy-seven.[52]

Menashe's work, undoubtedly intended to be progressive and innovative, is—paradoxically—similar to the stiff calque translations produced by Sephardi rabbis before Huli. While Huli chose a low stylistic register in order to make rabbinic writings accessible to the masses, Menashe aspired to create a high version of Ladino by enriching and "purifying" it, and in so doing he produced a text for the educated class. Like all proponents of Gallicization, he apparently is suggesting that the way for Ladino out of its "degeneration" is to become as close as possible to French and, hence, as far as possible from the spoken vernacular. Perhaps Menashe's translation of *Nantas* should be seen as an attempt to turn Ladino into an idiom of highbrow literature, yet there were no domestic genres that required a refined language.

## Conclusions

The analysis of the seven Ladino novels largely representing the two subcategories of this genre—love stories and adventure stories—allowed me to explore the correlation between their topics and the nature and amount of the innovations required to produce them. I also tried to establish the types of relationships between Ladino rewritings and their foreign-language originals. Finally, I exposed the similarities between the four love stories to demonstrate that they have more in common with each other than with their respective sources.

*Nantas* and *Hasan-pasha* to a large degree owe their appearance in Ladino to their creators' ideological agendas and aim at rather advanced audiences. *Nantas* is almost a literal translation, and *Hasan-pasha,* as far as I can tell, also significantly depends on its unidentified French source. The anonymous rewriting of *La Dame aux Camélias* is similar to both of them in that it is an unquestionable translation, but it is a slightly abridged and adapted one. Nonetheless, since Dumas's novel belonged to the canon of serialized fiction, its Ladino version, albeit rather faithful to the original, is a lot more congenial to the domestic belles lettres than the other two.

*The Two Voyages of Gulliver* is further from its source than any other text in my corpus and is the closest to the preexisting literary tradition. This novel demonstrates that the act of adaptation of European literature per se does not necessarily further westernization. Moreover, the complete conformity of adaptations to the preexisting domestic canon, that is, the reduction of the new to the familiar, contributes to the preservation of the old literary system rather than to its renewal. Indeed, Benghiat managed to produce this rewriting without any obvious literary or linguistic innovations.

In the case of the love stories, however, both Benghiat and Florentin had no choice but to introduce innovations borrowed from the respective French originals, and thus they created new methods of adaptation. Regardless of the rewriters' intentions, any assimilation of *Manon Lescaut* or *La Dame aux Camélias* to the preexisting Ladino narrative fiction was impossible, because they spoke about subjects never discussed by it. It is evident that even in the case of *Paul et Virginie,* which has no love scenes and which Benghiat reduced to twenty-one pages, completely distorting its message, he could not have told the story of joy and sorrow in the language available to Ladino literature before the 1870s.

Finally, there is one feature shared by the five adaptations of identified sources, excluding *Nantas*: all three rewriters completely overwrote the author's voice or that of his alter ego, substituting it with what I have called the collective voice of Sephardi westernizers, discernable in all Ladino fiction. This may be the most obvious sign of Ladino literature's premodern state even in the first third of the twentieth century.

*Part 3*  Theater

# ⑪⑪⑪ 5

# Sephardi Theater: Project and Practice

Sephardi Theater is one of the least documented and least studied sociocultural practices in the lives of Ottoman Jews. Since the extant memoirs hardly, if at all, mention it,[1] the only available source of information on Sephardi Theater is the Ladino press, which played an exceptional role in its development. Moreover, the conceptualization of Sephardi Theater offered and promoted by Ladino periodicals was an integral element of the whole project, indispensable for its proper realization, if not for its very existence. Outside the framework of the Ladino press, Sephardi Theater cannot be adequately construed, and the data related to it appear as an unstructured assortment of random facts.

It is, perhaps, its chaotic and peculiar makeup that accounts for the fact that, as a cultural phenomenon, Sephardi Theater has attracted the attention of very few scholars; the most important of them is Elena Romero, who dedicated a few years to its comprehensive description. Her doctoral dissertation[2] consists of Romanized (more precisely, Hispanicized) editions of fourteen Ladino plays with notes, detailed descriptions, and other bibliographic materials. Romero has also published a number of articles on Sephardi Theater and a valuable collection of the materials found in most extant Ladino periodicals on the shows performed by Sephardim in the Ottoman Empire.[3] Finally, a chapter of her monograph on Sephardi print culture[4] offers the first and only overview of Ladino theater.[5]

My own work to a great extent relies on the data provided by Romero, without which my study would have been a lot more time-consuming. Nevertheless, I do not accept Romero's approach, as it fails to distinguish between Sephardi Theater as a social practice and Ladino drama as a corpus of texts forming its repertoire. She treats Ladino serialized fiction and "Sephardi theater" as two groups of *texts* that emerged as a result of westernization. However, while the former is indeed a literary genre that appeared as a by-product of the Ladino press and was used by Sephardi literati both for commercial and educational purposes, the latter was conceived as a tool of education that required Ladino texts for its implementation. Therefore, the plays constitute only one of the components of Sephardi Theater.

I do not aspire to offer a comprehensive explanation of every piece of information pertaining to Sephardi Theater, but I will propose a new frame of reference for interpreting Sephardi Theater by treating it as a sociocultural practice rather than a corpus of texts. In this book, when referring to the object of my study, I capitalize both parts of the term "Sephardi Theater" in order to differentiate it from everything else that may be described by the same words. I do so not only for the sake of clarity but also as a way of giving a name to something that never had one and that, from a scholar's viewpoint, should be named and defined.

Ladino periodicals always referred to this new practice simply as "theater," since they obviously had no need to add "Sephardi." although Ottoman Jews did not require a special term for this social practice and evidently had no misunderstandings discussing it, today in order to describe this idiosyncratic phenomenon we have to define what exactly we are talking about. By "Sephardi Theater," I mean a popular practice of student and other amateur groups to stage Ladino plays and perform them on days off and holidays before a local public, usually with charitable goals. Sephardi Theater emerged in the early 1870s in the Ottoman Empire and continued to exist in some of its successor states until World War II. Sephardi immigrants transplanted it to American soil, where it continued to flourish.

Not only was Sephardi Theater never institutionalized, but the contemporaries had no idea that such a thing existed and that they participated in it. Moreover, we have no evidence showing that the local Alliance committees or other westernizers had a coherent plan of creating a Sephardi theater as a means of expanding their larger educational project, but it is clear from the Ladino press that, in the early 1870s, they came to the conclusion that European-style theater could be used for civilizing their coreligionists and thus reaching their higher objectives. This sociocultural practice and their ideas about it crystallized in all Sephardi centers around the same time, so that Salonican journalists described the same phenomenon as their colleagues in Izmir or Istanbul. Thus, we are dealing with synchronic efforts of Sephardi intellectuals to introduce their communities to modern theater and make it a venue of mass education and charity rather than simply a site of entertainment.

## Origins

The first extant notice of a Ladino show in the Ottoman Empire appeared on March 25, 1873, in *El Nasyonal,* and from then on similar notes and brief reviews regularly appeared in the Ladino press. Until then, Ottoman Sephardim did not have a Jewish theater of their own.

Iberian immigrants brought theater to the Ottoman Empire, where it was barely known before their arrival, and not only dominated it for some time but apparently even trained some of their successors, mostly Roma. However, later, they were "outclassed and outshone by Armenians."[6] Other exiles transplanted theater to Amsterdam where, in the seventeenth and eighteenth centuries, they staged plays in Spanish, Portuguese, and even Hebrew,[7] but this theater did not persist beyond its time and was unknown to Ottoman Sephardim. They were exposed to two kinds of folk theater: the Turkish shadow theater, Karagöz, which was extremely popular in all parts of the Ottoman Empire even in the twentieth century, and, once a year, the traditional Purim shows.

Karagöz ("Black-Eyed," named after the main character) is a folk puppet theater that was highly developed in Turkey by the sixteenth century. The shows were performed in front of the sultan's palace and in the harem but also in private homes, coffeehouses, and marketplaces, thus being accessible to everybody (more precisely, to all men). Karagöz has a few stock characters: good-natured Karagöz, his friend Turk Hadjivat, the Dervish, the Dandy, the Jew (represented as a merchant or a rabbi), and others, their main characteristics being different regional or ethnic accents.[8] Sephardi men could see Karagöz shows when they visited public places and would have understood them without difficulty due to the simple plots of the plays, which heavily relied on buffoonery. Moreover, Jews themselves participated in Karagöz, though it is not clear to what extent. A traveler claimed that, in Edirne in 1539 during Ramadan, Jews gave a few shows for the general public and, later, performed in front of the royal tent and in the imperial harem.[9] According to another writer, in 1675 in Istanbul, there were shadow puppet shows performed solely by Jews. One of Byron's companions on his trip to Greece in 1809 recorded in his diary seeing a Greek version of Karagöz in Ionia, put on by a Jewish puppeteer.[10] Still, though it is reasonable to assume that watching Karagöz shows would have affected some part of the Sephardi public by shaping its taste for farce and by encouraging certain patterns of behavior during performances, there are no grounds to consider Karagöz one of the precursors or sources of Sephardi Theater, as suggested by Romero.[11]

The only kind of theater familiar to all Sephardim was the *Purim-shpil,* which is commonly believed to be the most important source of Jewish theater. Yet, traditional shows per se, whether Jewish or not, could not serve Sephardi westernizers as a basis for their Enlightenment-inspired project, which saw theater as a venue of modern education rather than a site of celebration or entertainment. Ladino drama reveals no evidence of being influenced by Jewish folk sources, and thus *Purim-shpil* cannot be regarded as one of its precursors either.[12] Yet, there was no contradiction between the two kinds of theater when, once a year, they coexisted, fulfilling different but not mutually exclusive functions. One could both celebrate Purim in a traditional way at home or at synagogue *and* watch Racine's *Esther* at the Variétés Theatre in Sheres (*El Avenir,* March 19, 1909, 4) or Xavier de Montepin's *Bread Seller,* which, though unrelated to the holiday, was always performed on Purim in Izmir by the Society Ozer Dalim (helper to the poor) (*El Nuvelista,* February 15, 1907, 6). Sephardi intellectuals, and Zionists in particular, used Purim and other Jewish holidays to educate the public about them and to make them meaningful and appealing to westernized Jews who, according to one Ladino play, knew more about French novels than about their own heritage. This is why Purim shows of this kind considerably differed from traditional ones. Therefore, the fact that Purim (as well as Hanukkah and Passover) was often a subject of Ladino drama testifies not to the influence of the *Purim-shpil* on Sephardi Theater, but rather to the efforts of Sephardi leaders to make traditional Jewish celebrations attractive to secularized Sephardim.

Since Ottoman Jews had not been exposed to modern theater, Sephardi westernizers, who in the early 1870s decided to expand their educational project by means of a theater, were faced with the necessity to create a cultural practice hitherto unknown in their community. They had to import the concept of modern theater and its main genres from Europe in ready-made form and introduce them to the Sephardi public. But, I believe, the reception of theater as a site of collective learning might have been facilitated for Ottoman Jews by their experience of studying together in *meldados.* This hypothesis is suggested by the recommendations accompanying the publication of some early Ladino plays. For instance, the preface to the first extant Ladino play, *The Playful Doctor*[13] (an anonymous rewriting of Molière's *Flying Doctor*), explains that it can be performed by an organized group of amateurs as well as by all readers in their own homes: "We hope that *Sosyedad Instruktiva* [Educational Society] will put it on in winter and that families can perform it in their homes for entertainment."[14] David Joseph Hassid, in the introduction to his *Han Benyamin* (an adaptation of Molière's *Miser,* Salonica, 1884),[15] also recommends that "decent families" and circles of friends perform this "morally innocent" and at the same time enjoyable comedy.

These recommendations to put on plays in private homes by circles of relatives and friends are clearly reminiscent of Sephardim's practice of reading together *musar* literature, encouraged by the vernacular rabbis. Lehmann demonstrated that the *meldados* prepared the audience for the reception of Ladino press and fiction, and one can certainly add to this list Sephardi Theater.

## Periodization

The history of Sephardi Theater clearly falls into two phases, corresponding to the dominant ideologies that defined its goals and functions in each period. For the sake of convenience, I will consider the 1908 Young Turk revolution as the turning point in the history of Sephardi Theater, although the two prevailing tendencies coexisted some time before and after 1908. Thus, I propose the following periodization:

> 1873–1908: the time between the first extant mention of a Ladino show in the Sephardi press and the revolution that allowed Zionist organizations to act openly in the Ottoman Empire
>
> 1908–early 1920s: the time between the revolution and the end of Ladino theater in present-day Turkey as a result of its nationalist policy[16]

Though Sephardi Theater was started by local westernizers and supported by the Alliance's committees, essentially as an extension of its schools, when the organization began to lose its authority to Zionists, they took it over and turned Sephardi Theater into a means of winning more adherents, thus converting it into a site of politicizing. Therefore, I describe the first period as "theater as school" and the second as "theater as propaganda."

This periodization has little to do with Sephardi Theater's artistic development, but instead highlights larger sociopolitical changes as the main factor leading to its transformation. Furthermore, there is no evidence that its aesthetic principles as such transmuted over time nor that its organizers were ever interested in this question. It is, therefore, not surprising that I found only one statement on this subject in the Ladino press, yet it appears to be fundamental principle of Sephardi Theater as a project during both periods. A review in *El Nuvelista* (January 18, 1907, 44) covering a performance of *The Marranos* in Hebrew performed in Beirut unequivocally affirms the superiority of pragmatic goals over aesthetic values. According to the newspaper, the majority of the spectators did not understand Hebrew and cried merely because they were familiar with the subject, which is why the actual plot had to be recounted later in the periodical. Still, insists the reviewer, although the "aesthetic[17] feeling" was sometimes lost, "the emergence of Hebrew on the stage was a step ahead on the way to its revival," and thus the show was undoubtedly a success.

## 1873–1908: Theater as School

Sephardi Theater's formative period lasted about ten years, during which the westernizers' ideas about their project crystallized and were implemented. After the mid-1880s, Ladino periodicals no longer discussed the benefits of theater, but mainly informed their readers of the current shows. Yet, in the 1870s and the early 1880s, one of the subjects frequently discussed by the Ladino press was this new cultural practice, especially its functions and purposes as envisaged by Sephardi intellectuals. All periodicals agreed that Sephardi Theater, like the Alliance schools, fulfilled a civilizing mission and was called to serve as a medium of instruction. It was primarily meant to be a venue of moral education and enlightenment, a school open to everybody. In fact, during this first period, the frame of reference used by most Ladino periodicals to describe Sephardi Theater was "school," its opposite being "ignorance." *El Nasyonal's* "special correspondent" complained about the conservative groups in the Izmir Jewish community that had banned representations of a Ladino version of Molière's *Forced Marriage* at local schools, calling it indecent. According to the journalist, they were too ignorant to understand that "theater is much more than a big school" (February 25, 1874, 90).

A few days later, another journalist enthusiastically responded to the new show at the girls school in Galata. This declaration, which readily recognizes the ignorance of the Sephardi public and the need to enlighten it, expresses the general attitude of the Ladino press toward Sephardi Theater. Addressing the director, the author exclaims, "Bravo, sinyor! The way to banish from the face of the earth the ignorance that reigns among some of our coreligionists is to show that theater is not only entertainment but also a place where 'one learns about morality, education, and civilization'" (March 2, 1874, 914–915). Although the author of this note takes it for granted that one of theater's functions is to provide entertainment, he declares it to be a secondary goal, whereas its higher objective is to serve as a medium of promoting morality, education, and civilization. This may be considered Sephardi Theater's statement of purpose to which it fully adhered during the first period of its existence and which remained important throughout the second period.

The idea of creating a theater in the Sephardi community was appealing to the local westernizers because, on one hand, it promised to be a good means of teaching morality and, on the other, this cultural practice was popular in Europe. Such a view of theater is most fully expressed by Hassid in the preface to his *Han Benyamin.* He talks at length about the important role of theater in Europe and the "civilized countries," where it is considered to be "the first school" of moral education. According to Hassid, theater is a friendly advisor that shows people, in a gentle way that does not cause them embarrassment, what they have done wrong and why it makes others laugh at them. Theater thus encourages the spectators to discover and abandon the vices that they were not aware of before. Hassid's theater discourse is apparently in dialogue with the contemporaneous *musar* literature studied in *meldados,* which Sephardi Theater might have intended to replace. In any case, the affinity between the two practices is quite obvious. The following excerpt from Isaac Farhi's *Zekhut u-Mishor* (published in Izmir in 1850 and reprinted in Salonica in 1868 and 1887) conveys the same idea, except the tool of moral transformation recommended by the author is a *musar* book rather than theater (of which he is highly critical): "If one finds that someone is constantly committing a fault and wants to correct his ways, 'it is conceivable to invite him to his home . . . and as they are talking, he should take a *musar* book and read to him about what the other has been doing.'"[18]

Hassid's piece clearly refers to what, according to Lehmann, was an important characteristic of Ladino rabbinic literature: it almost always tried to talk to its audience with empathy and kindness in order to avoid any possible embarrassment. For example, Abraham Palachi (who published in the 1860s) describes the best way to teach *musar* in public: "if there is among those listening someone who has stumbled into a certain sin, and accidentally he comes to pass censure upon this matter, he should take care not to dwell on this too long, for he would embarrass [the other], but [should speak] briefly and in kind words."[19]

It is clear that, despite the differences in content and ideology, Hassid advocates methods of moral education similar to those of the vernacular rabbis. This continuity, however, is found in Sephardi Theater only in the first period of its history, when it focused on changing the public's worldview rather than the world itself. In its second period, Sephardi Theater, while maintaining its paternalistic stance, adopted different methods of indoctrination, which suited better its practical objectives.

Sephardi Theater was conceived by its creators as a school for all but, a great number of shows were in fact performed at educational institutions. The third extant note on Sephardi Theater in the Ladino press announced a show that was going to take place at Madame Arlod's girls school in Hasköy (*El Nasyonal*, April 8, 1873, 56). Indeed, especially at the beginning, the Alliance institutions and other modern schools were the most important participants in and champions of the new cultural practice. In the public's mind, theater soon became inseparable from the schools, including the Salonican Talmud Torah.

Usually, before a Jewish holiday or another festive occasion, the school director or a teacher would stage a play with children of all ages, which would be performed before parents, friends, sometimes local authorities, and wealthy members of the community. In the first period, a large part of the profits would go to the directors, thus making school theater a lucrative enterprise for them. All this caused protests from both local literati and parents, who felt that the students spent most of their time rehearsing one show after another and had too little time for the school curriculum. One contributor to *La Epoka* (who signed his article "Teacher") complained about schools being so busy preparing various performances that the children did not have enough time to study, and he reminded the directors that their main obligation was to teach students rather than put on shows:

> If our readers could imagine how much the directors have to dance around the authorities [i.e., censors] in order to get from them permission [to put on a show], the time they waste having the children learn the play and selling the tickets, they would share our concerns. All this requires no less than three or four months!! During this time the classes are almost completely suspended, and there is a lot of excitement at school. And what is all this for? So that the director can make a few grushes at the students' expense. (June 8, 1900, 8)

The other major sphere of Sephardi Theater was charitable organizations, which depended on amateur troupes to put on shows and thus raise funds for their respective causes. The second extant note on Sephardi Theater mentions a show to be performed by the Soseta de Instruksyon i Byenfesensya[20] (Society for Education and Charity) in Istanbul (*El Nasyonal*, April 8, 1873, 54–55). In this domain, Sephardi Theater realized its second purpose, namely, to encourage charity, which was constantly reiterated by Ladino newspapers. For instance, a description of one school show concludes on an optimistic note: "We hope that this [story] will not be the last one, and that later we will have the pleasure of seeing other stories the profit from which will make it possible to do a lot of charity, and thus we will not be inferior to other nations" (*El Nasyonal,* March 23, 1874, 958–959). In order to be considered progressive and civilized, a community not only had to have its own theater, but, no less important, it was required to use the profit from this theater for charitable purposes.

Since Sephardi Theater was expected to bring enlightenment to the community, its financial support was regarded as a patriotic duty. For example, *El Nasyonal* published a programmatic letter to the editor which, among other things, explained the importance of sponsoring Sephardi Theater as a means of fighting ignorance and promoting progress: "We must praise those who for the love of the nation contribute to this show by continuing to make small donations that promote charity and progress and diminish the misery and ignorance reigning in our nation because of the reluctance to sacrifice a small sum, which is nothing for the donor but brings great fruit" (October 8, 1873, 52).

Very soon, this function of Sephardi Theater became a given. However, by the early 1900s, charities became so numerous that people were often confused about their goals. So, while schools were criticized for performing too many shows, these countless charities with unclear goals also began to cause public irritation. One of *El Avenir*'s correspondents complained about the endless announcements in the Salonican press:

> Earlier, we knew that amateurs gave theater shows for the profit of charitable causes known for their important work, such as Bikur Cholim, Matanot la-Ebyonim [Gifts to the Poor], Ermandad [Brotherhood], etc. . . . but it seems that the times have completely changed. The performances are put on now . . . for the profit of "private charities" and "eminent humanitarian causes." Nobody knows what is hiding behind these pompous words. (*El Avenir,* May 22, 1906, 7)

By the turn of the twentieth century, the general public had internalized the idea that Sephardi Theater not only provided entertainment but was also a place of learning and of doing charity, which would eventually earn Sephardim the respect of other nations. From the very start, the Ladino press voiced the determination of the local westernizers to create a Sephardi theater in the hope that it would allow Ottoman Jews to become equal to other communities. The existence of theater in a community was regarded as an indication of its progressiveness that would be duly appreciated by foreigners. Thus, in the announcement of a school show, we read: "We were assured that many tickets have already been reserved by those non-Jews who know Ladino and by those who enjoy seeing progress in all communities" (*El Tyempo,* February 26, 1874, 2).

The local literati so much valued the opinion of those foreign visitors that, on one hand, they boasted about their rather absurd praise, often quoted by someone who presumably had overheard the comments, and, on the other, they were embarrassed by the possible vulgar conduct of their coreligionists. For example, *El Nasyonal,* advertising a second performance of *Josef Sold by His Brothers* played by the students of Mademoiselle Boton's school, explained why it was necessary to see the show again: "Those who attended the first performance tell us that many [spectators] from other nations, who honored us with their presence, assured them that they were very happy to see this show, because they had never seen anything similar, and it was exceptional" (March 18, 1874, 946). A note in *La Buena esperansa* (March 28, 1907, 1) informed readers that the upcoming show at the Talmud Torah would be attended by foreign visitors, and since the organizers wanted to ensure the "moral and financial success" of the event, the public was kindly requested not to eat fruit or other snacks during the performance, lest the foreigners disparage the Sephardim.

These and similar references to non-Jews and foreigners who understand Ladino, attend Jewish theater shows, and may be critical of Sephardim's rude behavior hardly reflected the reality. It is certainly possible that European residents of the city fluent in French might have attended some shows at Alliance schools, but—ironically—the only note mentioning this practice I was able to find angrily describes a failure to get non-Jewish guests. An Alliance school for girls in Rhodes invited some Europeans to see their show, but someone, presumably an enemy of the Jews, managed to persuade the non-Jews not to go (*El Avenir,* July 19, 1905, 7). In any case, it would have taken quite a lot of foreigners to reserve all the seats, not leaving enough tickets for the local spectators, as *La Buena esperansa* claimed. Thus, it is clear that the Ladino press did not refer to real visitors, but rather to those hypothetical Europeans who support progress everywhere and who would one day attend Sephardi Theater shows and report to the world that Ottoman Jews are truly civilized and that their five-year-old students act better than the best Parisian performers. Nevertheless, these notes are valuable, as they reveal the ideals and anxieties of Sephardi westernizers, who looked at themselves from the vantage point of imaginary Europeans existing only in their minds.

The terms "other nations" and "foreigners" were omnipresent in the Ladino press, whether it was talking about good manners or charity. The latter aspect became even more prominent in the second period of Sephardi Theater.

## 1908–Early 1920s: Theater as Propaganda

By the early 1900s, the Alliance's universalistic ideals and faith in human perfectibility, which had informed the goals of Sephardi Theater as a project in the first period, were replaced by a Zionist, pragmatic agenda that required immediate action—most important, recruiting new adherents in order to gain political power. While the first period of Sephardi Theater's history was a time of hope and of setting long-term and rather vague objectives, the second period may be described as a time of action and of achieving specific short-term goals. By the time Zionism had come into the open in the Ottoman Empire, the Alliance had considerably lost influence even though its school network continued to grow until 1914. The Alliance schools that had traditionally served as venues of Sephardi Theater were gradually taken over by Zionists, as their teachers, sometimes surreptitiously, converted to Zionism.[21] In addition, as Sephardi Theater turned into a site of propaganda, which was more effectively performed by adult members of new Zionist organizations than by seven-year-old children, the role of the schools significantly diminished. More and more shows were staged by Zionist clubs and sports associations. For example, Salonican Kadima put on its own dramatic shows.

When Zionist organizations turned to theater as a means of gaining influence, they found themselves in a much better position than the first westernizers had thirty-five years earlier. By 1908, Sephardi Theater was widely recognized as a laudable social practice; it had an audience aware of its functions; it had the experience of using schools and public buildings for shows; and there was a pattern of discussing theater in the press. As to the repertoire, some of the previously produced plays could still be performed, but many more had to be created in order to convey the new message, especially since the number of Zionist clubs and associations was growing rapidly, which required more plays. While in the first period Sephardi Theater organizers insisted that a community without a domestic theater cannot be considered progressive, their Zionist successors maintained that every nation must have a theater in its national language, because it serves as an excellent educational tool. A programmatic article on Zionist theater stated, "Everywhere, theater is one of the most popular entertainments and, at the same time, a means of efficient national education. Nowhere in the world today can one imagine a city or a large audience without a theater in its language" (*El Puevlo*, March 19, 1923, 2). This propagandistic statement was followed by detailed instructions on how a Zionist organization could attract more spectators.

The author begins by praising the Max Nordau Society for putting on plays in Ladino but criticizes it for performing Jacques Loria's *Dreyfus*, which had already been performed in Salonica a few times. In addition, the author gives recommendations to the committee of this society on how they must improve their work. This "encouragement," as the journalist calls it, is expressed in an authoritarian and harsh tone that was unfamiliar to Sephardi Theater in the first period, sounding very much like the directives of agitprop theater:

> It would have been better if they had picked a new play in order to awaken the curiosity of the audience and attract a larger public. Let them not tell us that there are no Jewish plays or that it is difficult to find those: this is not so. In Hebrew, German, English, and even French, one can find Jewish plays, which it would not be difficult to translate or adapt. All it takes is to make a small effort to get them. And there will not be a shortage of translators.

Unlike the theater project at the time of its inception, the emerging Zionist theater faced challenging competition from the existing theater and the necessity to draw the public to its side. After 1915, Salonican Zionists also had to compete with socialist organizations, whose theater performances aimed at the same audience, namely, the large working-class population. One of the strategies of Zionist organizations was to reach out to the poor through the theater, which would eventually make possible the direct and effective indoctrination of the uneducated Sephardi masses. In order to accomplish this mission, the Salonican Kadima planned to bring simple yet instructive distractions to the residents of a poor suburb, for which purpose they chose Molière's comedy *Doctor Despite Himself*, which was always extremely popular among Sephardim. The following note announced an upcoming show:

> "The young Zionist Society Kadima of the Baron Hirsh neighborhood prepares to offer a beautiful feast for the residents of this quarter, thus continuing to focus on one of the crucial points of its program, which consists in providing the poor population of this suburb with healthy and instructive entertainment" (*El Puevlo*, May 15, 1912, 2).

In the second period, the role of charity became so important that newspaper articles often would focus solely on this aspect of theater shows without even mentioning the play that was expected to bring profit. Frequently, a newspaper article covering a theater performance would begin or end with a sentence explaining the charitable purpose of the event and suggesting that readers who had not yet seen it should do so as soon as possible. The following note directly advises the public to make donations to Tomkhe Yetomim (Supporters of Orphans):

> The performance of the drama *Expiation* in Judeo-Spanish that will take place Sunday night on Passover week is going to be most brilliant. . . . One must especially remember that this great festive evening is given for the profit of the society Tomkhe Yetomim, which in the neighborhood of Kalamaria maintains a home where 50 orphans are provided for and taught. (*El Avenir*, March 25, 1912, 1)

## Repertoire

Romero was able to establish 803 titles and the actual texts of 84 Ladino plays.[22] A significant number of them, particularly those produced in the first period, were clearly intended to be read as well as performed. This twofold purpose of Ladino plays is manifest in some of the authors' comments in the texts, which otherwise would be unfeasible stage directions. Hassid insists that the public should read the plays before seeing them at the theater, or else the lesson might be missed. The preface to his *Han Benyamin* bears a didactic title, "Examples Very Much Help to Understand People," thus suggesting the right way of comprehending the play—lest someone might enjoy it simply as a comedy. *The Playful Doctor* is also preceded by a short introduction that ascribes to this simple farce, filled with slapstick and buffoonery, a moral lesson: the play presumably teaches one how to choose good friends. Obviously, one had to read the introduction in order to get the intended message.

Ladino plays often appeared in periodicals, sometimes in serialized form, and quite a few of them were not even meant for staging. Thus, the anonymous *Hardships of Laundry* (1900), which explains the advantages of laundry factories, was described in *La Epoka*, where it was published, as "scenes of life" and as a series of "amusing articles" (March 2, 1900, 4). Some authors evidently expected their texts to be merely recited. This is true for *The Language and the Jewish Nation* (1909) by Yakim[23] Ben David, a rather long play in verse without stage directions, which represents the contemporaneous language debate between the leading Ladino periodicals.

When Sephardi literati were putting together a repertoire for the new theater, they did not have any domestic texts to resort to and hardly knew about the emerging Yiddish theater (which at that moment would not have satisfied their needs anyway). Spanish theater, because of its linguistic advantages, could have served as an ample source of borrowing, but Sephardim were unfamiliar with Castilian drama. More than thirty years after the emergence of Sephardi Theater, in a letter to Angel Pulido, Sam Lévy expresses regret about Sephardim not having access to the Spanish theater of the Golden Age:

> The language known here more than Italian or French is Judeo-Spanish. Most residents of Salonica speak the idiom which resembles Castilian. Why don't Spanish troupes come to our part of the world? It would be wonderful to have them here. Everyone would be interested in seeing them. Many people who know only Judeo-Spanish would be happy to hear the actors coming from Spain. Respectable merchants as well as simple workers would be very glad to have a chance to attend real Spanish plays and to hear the return of *acá, allá,* and . . .[24] (*Le Journal de Salonique,* November 2, 1905, 1)

In the 1870s, for the same reasons they had to import French serialized fiction, Sephardi intellectuals had no choice but to turn to French theater for material to borrow. They had been exposed to French theater in the Alliance and other western schools or during their trips to France. Hence, there are many Ladino rewritings of French plays, mainly those based on biblical stories and of contemporaneous French drama. In the first group, one finds Racine's tragedies *Esther*[25] and *Athalia,* as well as Delphine de Girardin's *Judith* and Scribe's libretto for Halévy's opera *La Juive* (The Jewess).[26] No doubt, these plays were translated because they tell Jewish stories, but they shared another feature that might have influenced the Sephardi rewriters: all the title roles had been performed in Paris by Rachel or Sarah Bernhardt (or both of them).[27] There were rewritings of other tragedies based on the Bible, such as Lamartine's *Shaul,* and a large group of plays that had nothing to do with Jewish topics and included mostly entertaining pieces. Among them one finds classics of French comedy beginning with the medieval farce about Avocat Pathelin, Racine's only comedy, *The Litigants,* and works by Molière, who was by far the most popular foreign playwright in the history of Sephardi Theater. However, the majority of the entertaining pieces were contemporaneous comedies, farces, and vaudevilles that were meant to satisfy the taste of those Sephardim who wanted to see the plays that were being performed in Paris. The choice of texts was largely defined by what was available in the French theaters after the 1860s.

The list of the contemporaneous French plays translated into Ladino is at first glance surprising in terms of the writers' political and social positions, which contrast with the ideological homogeneity of the "Jewish" part of Sephardi Theater's repertoire. They include light farces by Eugène Labiche, the author of the famous *An Italian Straw Hat* and a future Academy member; soon-to-be-forgotten love dramas by Henry Bataille; social satire by the former anarchist Octave Mirbeau; social farces by the Dreyfusard Georges Courteline; and the comedy *Le Passant* whose author, François Coppée, was a notorious anti-Dreyfusard and a co-founder of the Ligue de la Patrie Française. These plays have one common feature: at different times, they were very popular in Paris, mainly in the boulevard theaters. (For instance, *Le Passant* brought the first great triumph to Sarah Bernhardt, who, in turn, made it famous.) The press hardly mentioned the entertaining Ladino plays, and Sephardi Theater organizers evidently did not try to control the sphere of pure entertainment, which is why we know next to nothing about it.

Though the repertoire of Sephardi Theater significantly relied on French drama, many local literati created original plays, turning to biblical stories and episodes of Jewish history and, later, to local situations. In the first period, Ladino plays were mostly composed for the Jewish holidays, such as Passover, Hanukkah, and Purim, and were not contextualized in any way. The most popular biblical stories were those about Queen Esther, the flight from Egypt, and Joseph and his brothers. In the Zionist period, Sephardi Theater leaders favored more dramatic and violent episodes where Jewish heroes and heroines demonstrated their patriotism and dedication to Judaism by saving the land and the people of Israel, for example, the stories about Yiftach, Debora, David and Goliath, Bar Kokhba, etc. Zionist authors tended to actualize and politicize these stories in a straightforward way by adapting the original message to the movement's needs. For instance, one of the versions of the Maccabees story (Istanbul, 1920, translated from Hebrew by David Elnakave) ends with the characters singing together "Ha-Tikvah."

In the early twentieth century, the repertoire of Sephardi Theater included more plays on Jewish life, especially in Eastern and Central Europe and Palestine, mainly translated from Hebrew, Yiddish, German, Dutch, and Russian—most of the latter via Hebrew. Benghiat was among the first authors to start writing plays about Sephardim's everyday lives, but only the socialist organizations in the 1920s–1930s dealt with this subject extensively. The majority of plays based on the Bible or Jewish history are so formulaic that it is hard to tell without a detailed analysis of each text whether a given play is original or an adaptation. Still, there is no doubt that the proportion of texts dependent on foreign-language sources in Ladino drama is lower than in the belles lettres. Some literati would both translate plays from other languages and compose their own on similar topics using the same patterns. Thus, the Bulgarian Zionist Yosef Avram Papo translated Alfieri's *Saul,* Racine's *Athalia,* and a few other tragedies, but also wrote his own plays, such as *Naboth's Vineyard,*[28] based on biblical stories.

Ladino drama is quite diverse, comprising texts radically different from each other not only in form and genre but also in terms of their artistic value, since among them there are translations of French classics as well as explanations of Jewish holidays put together ad hoc by schoolteachers. Though produced for the same public, these plays were intended to serve different purposes. Indeed, when a Ladino newspaper talks about a performed play (the title of which is often omitted), it is usually described as "amusing," "instructive," or "healthy," and, at the same time, "enjoyable" or "moving and moral." In other words, drama pieces are evaluated not in aesthetic categories but from a purely functional perspective: one play is meant to amuse, another to instruct, yet another to provide healthy entertainment.

From the point of view of the plays' functions, the Ladino press distinguishes two kinds : the first is best described as indoctrinating drama that aims at reshaping the audience's worldview, whereas the second group consists of entertaining plays whose main goal is to amuse the audience. From what we know about Sephardi Theater, one may conclude that the choice of "instructive" plays for staging—and, therefore, the authors' livelihood—depended on the functions they fulfilled rather than their potential success with the audience. It seems that, unlike the creators of serialized novels who, in order to earn a living, had to win the market by satisfying the demands of the audience, the majority of playwrights did not have to compete for the market and usually sought to satisfy the requirements of the Sephardi Theater's organizers and sponsors.

In the second period, Sephardi authors writing for the theater were often supported by Zionist organizations or clubs and even by individual sponsors. Thus, a well-known Zionist writer, Shabtay Yosef Djaen,[29] dedicated his drama *Devora*[30] to the "Belgrade lawyer" David Moshe Alkalay and his wife, Lika, whom he thanks for their "encouragement and support and for their friendship." This successful lawyer was a grandnephew of Judah Alkalay, while Lika was his granddaughter. David Alkalay, the founder and leader of the Zionist movement in Serbia, in 1897 was elected to the Zionist General Council. He was also the first publisher of Zionist literature in Serbia, which explains why Djaen's work was translated into Serbian and staged in Belgrade and Sarajevo. Of course, this was not a common case, but judging by the formulaic dedication, it was probably not the only one. At any rate, newspaper notes make it clear that certain wealthy people would attend Sephardi Theater shows mainly for the sake of supporting the theater.

Djaen's *Devora*, according to the notice on the title page, could not be reprinted, translated, or staged without the permission of the author or his heirs.[31] This was not unusual for the time, as even in the nineteenth century, some Sephardi playwrights began to regard their work as their property and sometimes insisted on being paid royalties. On the title page of *Han Benyamin*, Hassid indicates that this play cannot be performed without his permission and that he is to receive all the royalties. For the same reason, some authors were concerned about the typographical errors in their texts. Djaen felt so responsible for his text that, on the last page, he apologized for the printing errors. He explained that he was not in Vienna while the play was being printed there, the printer did not know Ladino, and the proofreader missed some typos. This note is followed by a list of misprints.

It is noteworthy that serialized Ladino novels always contained a great number of typos, which were not corrected even when the texts were reprinted as separate editions. This negligence is obviously covariant with the anonymity of Ladino fiction, as both indicate a lack of responsibility for the text on the part of its creators. However, the *musar* writers started using copyright as early as the eighteenth century. This suggests that the authors of educational Ladino drama not only adopted some of their methods of teaching but also, at least to some degree, shared their attitude toward their work.

## The Public and Actors

The case of Salonica, due to the high percentage of its Jewish population, presents the best picture of Sephardi theater life. Like other big Ottoman cities, it offered its residents and guests various kinds of entertainment, which were described in travelogues and in the local press. There are a few kinds of indirect evidence permitting the researcher to conclude that Sephardim actively participated in the city's cultural life. The most convincing evidence is the fact that all Ladino periodicals wrote about Salonica's theater shows, albeit much less frequently than *Le Journal de Salonique,* and advertised certain events that could be of interest for Sephardim. One of them was cinema, which, at the turn of the twentieth century, became quite popular in Salonica and Izmir. In fact, it is in Salonica that the first screening for the general public was held, on July 4, 1897, a year and a half after the Lumière brothers' historic screening in Paris. As it did not require knowledge of any specific language, cinema was accessible to all Sephardim. We find *La Epoka* a detailed review of a new cinema show:

> Saturday afternoon the hall of the Olympia is jam-packed. Only those who come early find good seats. Why all this rush? Because there, on the cinema screen, one can see beautiful actresses and ballerinas. . . . The film which is presently at the Olympia attracts a great number of spectators. One should see the enthusiasm with which the public applauds the scene of a battle between the Japanese and the Russians. One has the impression of watching the actual battle. (*La Epoka*, November 3, 1905, 1)

In 1900, Shalom Sholem published in *La Epoka* a series of humorous rhymed reviews of the city's theater life (which, symptomatically, never mentioned Sephardi Theater). These reviews mainly discussed musical shows held in public gardens and cafés, which had become very popular and were visited even by women of the higher classes. SS (this is how the poet always signed his pieces, in Latin characters) mentioned operas, trios, duets, and various types of dances, including the "snake dance" performed by an Arab woman. Dramatic shows that would require an understanding of the script were never mentioned, and speaking of Verdi's operas, the author almost brags about not knowing what they are about. He reiterates that now, unlike the old days, one finds all types of entertainment and can afford the tickets, some of which cost only one piastre. The way these reviews talk to the reader makes it clear that Sephardim indeed participated in the city's nightlife. SS begins his review published on June 8, 1900, by praising the popular Cavana duet: "If I were to make a list of real artists, there would be just one duo, and even this is a lot. Don't think I am arrogant if I tell you that Cavana is the only duo that deserves to be on my list. Is there anyone among you, dear readers, who has seen it and was not enchanted by their singing?"

There is another piece of evidence testifying to Sephardim's active participation in Salonica's cultural life, which, given the general context, appears to be trustworthy even if somewhat exaggerated. The article "Jews and Non-Jews" (*El Luzero*, July 4, 1905, 2) claims that every year Salonicans buy a great number of tickets for various festive events, such as school feasts, balls, shows, etc. While all of these events are attended by Catholics, Greeks, Germans, Austrians, and members of other communities, the highest percentage of spectators belongs to the "descendants of Abraham, Isaac, and Jacob."

Since the proportion of Sephardim in Salonica's theater audience must have been relatively high, general observations about the public shed some light on the situation in the Sephardi community. *Le Journal de Salonique* (March 29, 1900, 2), lamenting the poor attendance at the city's theaters, blames this on their directors, who disregard the fact that there are two distinct audiences: "The first one consists of educated and well-read Salonican intellectuals who travel to Europe." They are theater fans ready to pay any price for a good show and will not tolerate mediocrity, even if admission is free.

The second category includes naive, simple, and omnivorous spectators, who swallow all dishes if they are served to them Fridays, Saturdays and Sundays, the main issue being the price of the tickets. This public needs big houses with thousands of seats and troupes that provide great varieties of shows amusing to "the public's eye" more than anything else.[32]

We may assume that the same was true for Sephardi Theater, because the Sephardi audience was quite heterogeneous in terms of its socioeconomic status and education. Nevertheless, the Ladino press would never admit to poor attendance at Sephardi Theater shows and hardly ever explicitly acknowledged that different groups of spectators had different needs. Only Zionist periodicals, concerned about practical results, sometimes indirectly recognized the necessity of providing the uneducated masses with accessible entertainment (cf. Kadima's program for the poor).

We have no data on the attendance at Sephardi Theater shows, since the newspapers always talk about "thousands of spectators," as does the description of a show held at Salonica's *Talmud Torah ha-Gadol*, discussed below. This is certainly an exaggeration, since seating thousands of people would have required a very large hall. If the event was held outdoors, the public would not have been able to hear the children on the stage. As we know from *Le Journal de Salonique*, the city did not have halls sufficient for thousands of people. I found only one indication of a precise and realistic-looking number of spectators and actors at a Salonican show. According to *La Epoka* (September 21, 1900, 7), at an Italian show held in the newly opened theater at the Grand Hotel, there were fifty-four actors and more than four hundred spectators sitting close to each other.

The reason we have so little reliable information on the Sephardi Theater public and its response, in spite of the extensive coverage of some of the shows (sometimes, as many as three or four notes in one newspaper issue), is that the Ladino press never intended to report on the actual shows and, therefore, on the audience's real response. Instead, it aimed at creating the desired image of Sephardi Theater required to ensure its proper perception, which is why Ladino periodicals always described the audience's reaction as enthusiastic. Indeed, every review ends with the same conclusion formulated in slightly varying terms: "The public was delighted."

For the same reason, the Ladino press never mentioned any discontent of the educated public but occasionally discussed the misbehavior of the masses, which was invariably presented as a lack of education that could be corrected. Hence, the few notes criticizing the public's bad manners should not be taken as a full and accurate reflection of the situation; they certainly did not appear after every incident of this kind, which must have been quite frequent, at least in the early years of Sephardi Theater. I believe that such episodes were brought up only when the newspaper chose to talk about the importance of good manners. It is not surprising that the masses had no idea about theater etiquette and that the journalists wanted to enlighten them on this issue, but apart from that the press voiced the westernizers' persistent aspiration to look respectable in the eyes of imaginary foreigners. Evidently, spectators from the working classes were often impolite: they would bring young children to the theater, laugh at the wrong time, wear large hats, and talk in loud voices, since this is what they were used to doing during street shows. Conversely, better-educated and more affluent spectators would go to charitable events at theaters and schools and politely listen to long monologues in different languages, encouraging the actors. Sometimes, these events included balls. For example, the Institute Poli in Salonica suggested that women who have enough time on their hands should see a wonderful show performed by young girls and then participate in a big ball (*La Epoka*, September 15, 1899, 5–6).

The difference in the conduct of the two groups of spectators[33] is illustrated by the reviews published in *La Epoka* on April 8, 1898, describing the responses of two audiences that attended similar shows in different social settings. On April 4, 1898, at the *Talmud Torah ha-Gadol*, a big performance was organized to celebrate *halbasha*.[34] The other goal of the event was to raise money for the new *talmud torah* that would replace the old building. On April 6, the school, whose students were the beneficiaries of this action, put on a charitable performance with the same purpose. According to the newspaper, the first show was attended by thousands of spectators, who made a lot of noise fighting for the seats reserved for the distinguished guests. The noise did not stop even after the performance had started. The performance that took place two days later at the school was attended by a small audience, including a few wealthy families, and the journalist highly praised the spectators' behavior. One can infer that those were indeed two different types of public: on one hand, possibly a few hundred spectators, most likely workers at various Salonican factories or the port, who were not interested in watching plays or listening to monologues in unfamiliar languages on their day off, and, on the other, a rather small group of well-to-do spectators, including donors, who enthusiastically encouraged the young actors. Obviously, the two groups of spectators came to the performances with different expectations: to enjoy themselves, to socialize, to participate in a communal event, or to do charity. And even though both of them anticipated entertainment, they understood it and responded to it differently. We may assume that the masses were more used to puppet theater, other street shows, and cheap cabaret performances; theatergoing as a bourgeois cultural activity was hardly familiar to them.

The information we have about the actors involved in Sephardi Theater is extremely limited. We are constantly reminded that the actors were amateurs, which means they did not differ from the public in terms of their understanding of theater. They were young people of both sexes who, after getting married, would usually stop performing and join the audience.[35] In the first period of Sephardi Theater's history, the majority of actors were either students or graduates of the newly founded European-type schools, who soon began to organize theater troupes and associations that produced charitable performances for special occasions. These amateurs would gather in the evenings to rehearse the show and perform it in public theaters and gardens (such as the Eden and Alhambra in Salonica or the Variétés in Sheres) and later in clubs. Sometimes, they would be invited to perform the same piece in a few different places. The very first Sephardi show known to us took place in an Armenian quarter of Istanbul at the Armenian theater which was to receive all of the profits of the event (*El Nasyonal*, April 4, 1873, 48). During the second period, when Sephardi Theater was mainly sponsored by Zionist and socialist clubs, more people got involved in performances, but still there were no professional actors. By the turn of the twentieth century, all large centers of Sephardi life had at least one charitable organization (and often more) that had its own theater troupe.[36]

One of the most famous troupes in Salonica was La Bohème, founded in 1903 by Shem Tov Arditi. It staged mostly French and Italian plays in Ladino and closely collaborated with *La Epoka* in its campaign in support of Ladino, for which it was praised as "one of our best societies for charity and progress" (*La Epoka*, July 7, 1905, 9). The only reference outside the press to a Sephardi show that I have encountered talks about this troupe. In a letter to Angel Pulido, Sam Lévy speaks about the plays translated and staged by La Bohème:

How successful were the performances of these plays! What enthusiasm! What raptures! The eyes of hundreds of spectators flooded with happy tears! Graceful actresses received wreaths which had ribbons saying: "Long live Judeo-Spanish!," "For the mother language!," "Forward *La Epoka*!," etc., etc. Those lyre-shaped wreaths and baskets were a meter high and even larger.[37]

We can surmise from the same article in *La Epoka* that La Bohème had a contract with a group of benefactors supporting a poor family, and another newspaper accused it of violating the agreement, which, according to *La Epoka,* was slander. The troupe allegedly failed to announce that those unable to buy tickets should come anyway and support the enterprise by their applause. It is not clear, however, what the conditions of the contract might have been. Passionately defending the troupe, *La Epoka* formulates its concept of the amateur actors' mission.

[They are] young people who, sacrificing their leisure, spend most of their time helping the suffering and the miserable. One must be absolutely heartless and shameless to throw unabashed and mindless accusations in the face of the young people who become actors, i.e., those who expose themselves to the criticism of the audience (which is a lot) in order to serve those called their brothers and neighbors.

Amateur actors perfectly suited the purposes of Sephardi Theater, as the need for professionals would have arisen only if its leaders had been preoccupied with the quality of the acting and the aesthetic value of the shows. However, their chief concern was the event as such and the participation of local enthusiasts. In fact, one of the most striking things about the coverage of Sephardi Theater shows in the press is the absence of any critique of the actors' performances. All acting was praised indiscriminately, and the highest compliment for Sephardi actors was to say that they played no worse or even better than those of "other nations," even if the review talked about young children.

Though the Ladino press always praised the "wonderful performance" of amateur actors, it never explained what exactly this meant. Perhaps, since Sephardi Theater was envisioned as a large school, the very fact that children participated in those shows and recited their lines in different languages was considered an educational accomplishment worthy of praise. If the article was a little more specific, it emphasized the "realism" of the performance. Thus, we constantly find expressions like "real Muslim accent," "spoke like real Parisians," etc. Here is a comparison of this kind: "The students . . . began the play in Judeo-Spanish entitled *The Flight from Egypt* composed by the teacher r. Bekhor Avram Evlagon. . . . The girls were so wonderful that they seemed to be real Jews who had just fled from Egypt" (*El Nasyonal*, April 21, 1873, 73–74). How could young girls possibly resemble people who were exhausted and starving after enduring years of hard work and deprivation? Undoubtedly, the review simply tried to say that the students did a good job and deserved praise, the highest of which was to emphasize the realism of their performance.[38] This naive response does not mean that the local literati were not sophisticated enough to see the difference between Sephardi Theater performances and various foreign shows available even to those who never left the Ottoman Empire, but they had different expectations and aesthetic standards for Sephardi Theater. Besides, seeing it as an educational enterprise par excellence, they were interested in the progress made by the "amateurs." This is why the few reviews written in the first person and offering a seemingly subjective evaluation always talk about the acting of the amateurs in a patronizing tone and from a teacher's viewpoint. In fact, it is often impossible to tell whether the note is talking about five-year-olds or the adult members of a Zionist club. For instance, we read: "Speaking of all the efforts made by the amateurs, I cannot help praising sinyorina Ester Romano, a 10-year-old girl, and sinyor Ijak Azuz for interpreting their roles in a simple and natural way. . . . The small Jewish band also deserves special praise for the progress it was able to make in such a short time" (*El Imparsyal*, March 14, 1910, 2–3).

## The Image of Sephardi Theater in the Ladino Press

In the previous sections, I discussed Sephardi Theater's history, repertoire, actors, and audience using the Ladino press as a source of information. Yet, the significance of the press for a proper understanding of Sephardi Theater goes far beyond that. As was mentioned above, the Ladino press to a large degree constructed the desired image of Sephardi Theater, thus conferring on this new cultural practice a high social and moral status.

Aside from circulating plays, Ladino periodicals published two types of material related to Sephardi Theater: announcements of forthcoming shows, which often included information on the availability of tickets and their prices, and reviews of recent shows. It is obvious that the term *review* describes only the nominal purpose of these newspaper articles, since their true goal was not to analyze the staging of the play in question, the costumes, or the music, but to explain to the public the moral significance of the show, thus serving as an additional means of indoctrination. All such articles follow the same pattern with small variations, depending on the kind of shows they are discussing. Unlike many other articles in the Ladino press, they are never signed, even by initials, and despite appearing in newspapers of different orientation, they all seem to be written by the same person. In other words, these "reviews" form a genre of their own with a recognizable pattern. It has two distinct subcategories: reviews of "serious" shows and reviews of entertaining ones.

Reviews of serious shows use the following outline: "Play X (composed by Y) was performed at school (or club Z on the occasion O by amateurs, whose acting was superb. (It was followed by a comedy.) The audience was delighted." One can discern this model even in long and verbose articles, like the one quoted earlier, which described a charitable show during Passover week at a girls school in Istanbul:

> The students . . . began the play in Judeo-Spanish entitled *The Flight from Egypt* composed by the teacher r. Bekhor Avram Evlagon. . . . The girls were so wonderful that they seemed to be real Jews who had just fled from Egypt. . . . Each of them played her part with great success. . . . Later, they performed another play in French that made rejoice the hearts of all those who understood it. (*El Nasyonal*, April 21, 1873, 73–74)

As to the comedy that followed the main play, neither its title nor its author is indicated, and its subject is not mentioned. Moreover, it was not even considered important that everybody in the audience understand the language of the entertaining play.

All notes on comedies and other entertaining shows in the Ladino press are brief, usually three to seven lines, and rarely mention the play's title or author (unless it is Molière, though not always then either). The basic pattern of these reviews looks as follows: "Comedy X was performed at school (or club) Y on the occasion O, and everybody found it very funny. (The amateurs' acting was superb.)" here is one of the most elaborate reviews of an entertaining show: "On the occasion of Hanukkah, the night of 3 Tebet, the society Machaziqe ivrit [Supporters of Hebrew] organized an amusing literary evening for its members. The most brilliant piece on this special program was a play by Molière that made everybody laugh and that was performed by the amateur actors from this society" (*El Liberal,* December 21, 1914, 3).

Thus, the main difference between descriptions of serious and entertaining shows consists in a complete lack of interest in the play in the latter case. But there is an essential characteristic common to all reviews of Sephardi Theater performances: they are always complimentary without ever being specific in their praises. The hypothesis that they were positive because they were solicited by the theater directors, requested by the local Alliance committees, or resulted from a collaboration of the newspaper with the theater troupe would be plausible if there had been negative responses to Sephardi Theater shows, but all reviews were equally complimentary. For instance, though *La Epoka* collaborated with La Bohème, its reviews of the shows put on by other theater troupes were no less flattering. I explained above why the acting of the young amateurs was never subject to critique. The fact that all these reviews were complimentary is also accounted for by the very essence of Sephardi Theater, which was not an art project but an educational one carried out by Sephardi westernizers, including Zionists, who were fully cognizant of its objective. Hence, a theater troupe could be reprimanded for the wrong choice of plays for staging (as in the case of the Max Nordau Society), because this had to do with the message, but never for poor staging, ugly costumes, or unpleasant music. Furthermore, it is clear that all reviews of Sephardi Theater performances were written not by theater experts but by regular staff members (if not the editors themselves) whose task consisted in arranging the information they received, according to the existing pattern. And, as I have shown, the structure of this pattern, dictated by its pragmatics, is quite rigid not allowing for significant modifications. In fact, all analyses and personal opinions are beyond the scope of these reviews.

The idiosyncratic character of this genre is elucidated by a comparison of theater reviews published by Ladino and Francophone Sephardi periodicals, in particular, *La Epoka* and *Le Journal de Salonique*. The former chiefly aimed at the audience able to attend only those shows that did not require knowledge of foreign languages, i.e., Sephardi Theater and some entertaining shows such as cinema, musical performances, circuses, and Karagöz. *Le Journal* catered to Salonicans fluent in other languages and interested in various kinds of theater, which included both the readers who followed Sephardi Theater news in the Ladino press and those who had no knowledge of Ladino. *Le Journal de Salonique* hardly ever mentioned Sephardi Theater, and the following review of a Ladino show is the only one I found there.[39] Yet, it happens to be a most valuable sample, because it may be regarded as a translation of the paradigmatic Ladino review of a Sephardi Theater show adapted for Francophone readers:

> Last night at Eden Theater, a group of amateurs gave a show in Judeo-Spanish for the profit of a private charity.
> The choice of the play was most fortunate, and the performance of the young actors deserves the highest praise. *To be fair, one should cite the names of all those amateurs, but that would be too long. Nonetheless, we have the pleasure of mentioning in particular M. Misrahi, M. Botton and*

*Mlle Nahmias, whose acting was truly admirable. M. Misrahi played the part of the old man most perfectly; M. Botton showed exceptional vigor in his interpretation of the difficult role of the treacherous friend; and Mlle Nahmias was extremely good as the unhappy wife.*

The show was a most lively success. The audience was truly enthusiastic. The young actors were greeted by a long ovation.

*We sincerely join the passionate applause that last night [acknowledged] the excellent work of these amateurs.* (October 12, 1905, 2)

This review of a Sephardi Theater show offers the same kind of information as one finds in almost every account published in Ladino newspapers: it cites the date, place, and occasion; praises the choice of play (the title of which is not mentioned) and the amateurs' acting; and assures the reader of the play's success. However, the journalist makes two additions (see the italicized sentences) in order for the piece to match the genre requirements of a theater review in a French periodical. The first is a rather extensive analysis of the actors' performance, which are not described merely as "excellent" or "superb" but discussed in some detail, so that the reader gets an idea of the characters and their relationships. The second addition is the introduction of the reviewer's "personal" perspective: he identifies himself with the enthusiastic audience which enjoyed the show. He was so impressed by the troupe that he would like to talk about it at length, but, unfortunately, is unable to do so for lack of space. These two additions demonstrate what is missing in most reviews of Sephardi Theater performances as compared to those published in the contemporaneous Francophone press.

A note in *Le Guion* talks about the celebration of the Alliance's fiftieth anniversary: "After a pleasant dialogue delivered very well and with impeccable pronunciation by two students of the Alliance school for girls, [the public] was shown the famous farce about Avocat Pathelin, which amused the audience very much. The actresses, present and former students, were applauded and greeted with enthusiasm" (June 1910, 2–3).

*Le Guion* (Izmir, 1910) was a monthly published by the Alliance's Association des Anciens Élèves in Ladino and French. Unlike Sam Lévy's two papers, the two versions of this periodical addressed the same audience, fluent in both languages, so the whole project was a sort of linguistic game. The interesting thing for us here is that this French note could have been translated from or to Ladino verbatim and published in any Ladino newspaper. In any case, it does not belong to the genre of theater reviews found in regular Francophone periodicals, including *Le Journal de Salonique*.

Most of the time, *Le Journal* reviewed foreign shows brought to the city, and its accounts were always meant to be both informative and amusing. For instance, in its first issue (November 7, 1895, 2), *Le Journal* published a review of a show brought to Salonica by the French troupe directed by Lindey, who would later become a frequent visitor to the city:

> Always resilient, Mlle Lindey charms us by her impeccable enunciation and confident acting. . . . In the female world which gravitates toward her, we will mention Mlles Roger, Raville, and Doucet, and Mme Bégat, who do their best in the secondary roles trying to keep up with their leader. . . . One must recognize that in general the male roles are interpreted better. We noticed an excellent actor, M. Debray, who has the gift of provoking hysterical laughter by his funny mimicry and surprised expression.

It is immediately clear that the analysis of the actors' performance here differs from that in the piece on Sephardi Theater published in the same periodical, which is quite stiff and terse. Rather than stating that Mademoiselle Lindey's acting is wonderful, the journalist tells us that she is always "resilient" and that her performance "charms" the public due to her "impeccable enunciation" and confidence. The other actresses are trying to keep up with her, but in general the men are better. The reviewer particularly liked one of them, because of his funny manner. In other words, this description is specific and subjective.

The same was true for critical reviews. In fact, a few months later, on February 24, 1896, *Le Journal* criticized the same actress's performance, observing that she should have studied her role better (which made her very angry). Thus, *Le Journal de Salonique* published both positive and negative reviews that were always specific.

The goal of the complimentary review quoted above was not only to inform readers about a recent show and assure them it is worth seeing but, no less important, to entertain them while indirectly persuading them to attend upcoming shows offered by the same troupe. But even if they do not go, readers can enjoy the pleasant essay, which is never the aim of Sephardi Theater reviews, whose only purpose is to let the public know that a scheduled laudable event took place and, as usual, went very well. It is not surprising, therefore, that quite often such notes appeared in Ladino periodicals under the rubric "Local News," next to notes on tramways and fires, instead of under "Theater," because they were indeed communal events more than anything else.

As in the case of the travel accounts, discussed in chapter 2, the Ladino and the Francophone press used the same term to refer to different genres. Sephardi Theater shows did not lend themselves to any analysis beyond the rigid genre pattern that suited the needs of its organizers, whereas the

Sephardim able to attend Italian and French theaters did not need Ladino reviews of those shows and read the ones published in Francophone periodicals, whether Sephardi or other local papers.

The second type of publication related to Sephardi Theater is the notification of forthcoming shows. They follow the same basic pattern as the reviews, differing mainly in the verb tenses and adverbial modifiers of time. The following model makes it possible to turn an announcement into a review: "Play X will take (took) place on . . . (change of temporal modifier). Its goal will be (was) to support association (or club) Y. It will be (was) successful. The amateur actors will play (played) very well." For instance, here are an announcement of a charitable show and its review, published in two different newspapers:

> Two brilliant feasts will take place during Passover week. The second one will be a performance *for the profit of Tomkhe Yetomim,* which *will take place* next Sunday night. It will be extremely interesting, because one will see *amateur actors perform with amazing ability* their difficult roles. The drama *Expiation* is highly moving and moral, it will awaken healthy and lively feelings. (*El Avenir,* April 1, 1912, 1)

> The festive evening [given] *for the profit of Tomkhe Yetomim,* organized under the patronage of the honorable sinyor Shemuel Daniel Modiano, . . . *took place* Sunday night at the Eden Theater and achieved truly amazing success. . . . A very passionate drama . . . *was performed with admirable ability by amateur actors and actresses.* They say that the net profit of the feast came up to more than 70 Turkish liras. (*El Liberal,* April 7, 1912, 3

The first note predicts that wonderful things are going to happen, and the second one confirms that all these expectations were indeed fulfilled. Both notes (see the italicized words) indicate the time of the show and state that its profit goes to Tomkhe Yetomim, that the play is emotional, and that the amateur actors (will) perform(ed) their roles with admirable skill. In this case, it was enough to delete just one temporal adverb ("next") along with changing the verb forms. The two pieces are almost identical, which means that the journalist not only did not have to watch the show but did not even have to depend on others for information about it. Thus, we are dealing with two texts that differ from each other only in terms of their time relations.

Evidently, any positive review of an ongoing show functions as its advertisement, but this happens only because the facts are presented as the reviewer's own experience. In *Le Journal,* this was true for most of the articles on Mademoiselle Lindey's troupe, as well as for *La Epoka's* note on cinema, which was reviewing a show that was new to the cultural life of

Salonica and that could now be seen every week. It is written to sound like a first-hand account, although it does not use first-person verb forms. The reviews of Sephardi Theater performances function essentially as communal reports and are therefore written in an "objective" tone.

It is also useful to compare announcements of Sephardi Theater shows and those of guest theaters published in the Ladino press. For instance, on October 19, 1905, *La Epoka* published on the same page advertisements for a Ladino show and a French one. The announcement of the Sephardi Theater event talks about its charitable character without specifying the beneficiary, saying anything about the play, or indicating the time and place. Evidently, the note itself cannot persuade anybody to watch the show and does not offer sufficient information to those interested in seeing it. It is clear that the goal of this announcement is not to advertise a show, but rather to assure readers that Sephardi Theater is successfully doing its good work: "The society La Nueva Bohème is rehearsing a play which it is going to perform for the profit of one of the most useful charities."

The second announcement, like most other advertisements of guest performances, offers some information about the play and indicates the date and place. The only purpose of this note is to attract more spectators to the forthcoming show: "Mlle Emilie Lindey is continuing with success to play her series of shows at the Eden Theater. . . . We are assured that during the Sabbath matinee the troupe is going to show a very nice play specifically written for families." One finds here an element that is both an advertising technique and an expression of the newspaper's attitude that we never see in notes on Sephardi Theater events. The clause "We are assured that . . ." is used to convince the audience that the forthcoming show has been seen by an expert, who recommends it to the public. At the same time, this clause introduces another viewpoint, thus marking the editor's detached attitude toward the event. Here is another advertisement of a foreign theater that uses the same pattern: information about the performance, the date and place, and the same self-distancing clause that is supposed to add weight to the advertisement: "This week an Italian opera troupe began its shows at Alhambra Garden. We are assured that Salonica is very fortunate to have such a famous company, which has three talented prima donnas and such [good] actors as we have never seen before" (*La Epoka,* June 14, 1901, 4). Another note on a guest troupe uses a similar introductory phrase: "A lot was said about the high merit of these actors" (*La Epoka,* July 5, 1895, 8).

However, when it comes to Sephardi Theater shows, the press authoritatively states that the performance is going to be excellent and most successful, thus leaving no room for any other opinion. The following advertisement of a Ladino performance exposes the difference between *La Epoka*'s attitudes toward Sephardi Theater and guest troupes. Like other Ladino periodicals, it unambiguously identifies itself with the Sephardi Theater cause and treats its shows as part of communal life, while foreign theaters are perceived as cultural events and advertised as commercial items. Of course, the publication of advertising notes was profitable for the paper,[40] and the editor tried to make them effective. Here, the speaker is "in" the text and obviously dominates it by means of pronouns and modal and attitudinal words, which are italicized in the excerpt. These linguistic elements identify him as an insider wishing success to the Sephardi Theater enterprise rather than as an observer describing a new performance:

> A theater show in Judeo-Spanish put up for the profit of two needy families will *definitely* take place Sunday night at the summer theater in Beyaz Kule Garden.
>
> *Unfortunately,* earlier efforts to sell tickets did not bring the *desired* results, because recently *we* have had numerous charitable events. Despite these *modest* results, the performance *absolutely must* take place Sunday night. *We have no doubt* that Sunday night everybody will rush to the theater at Beyaz Kule in order to applaud the young amateurs, enjoy themselves, and at the same time contribute to a *good* charity. (*La Epoka,* June 19, 1908, 2)

Characteristically, this note mentions charity three times but does not say a word about the show, which once again demonstrates that the goal of such articles, composed by insiders, is not to attract readers' attention to the artistic achievements but to compel them to do charity, which is morally commendable. Thus, Sephardi Theater announcements are prescriptive and appeal to the people's sense of duty without trying to make charity attractive, which is what one finds in *Le Journal de Salonique,* which presents charity as an exciting and gratifying pastime. Here are the beginning and the end of a long article covering a literary evening held at a wealthy Salonican house:

> Yesterday, the large hall of the Villa Mon Plaisir was too small to host the numerous friends and guests of the de Charnaud family who came to the charitable evening given for the benefit of the orphans. In the back of the grand hall where the cream of Salonican society gathered, there was a modestly but tastefully decorated stage. . . . By midnight, the event was over, and the public left, happy to have spent a few wonderful moments and at the same time to have contributed to a very good cause. The voices of the orphans who are going to benefit from this evening will fervently rise in gratitude to the generous donors. These pure voices will affectionately thank particularly the hostess, Baronne de Charnaud, under whose auspices the feast was held. (*Le Journal de Salonique,* March 26, 1900, 1)

## Conclusions

All press materials related to Sephardi Theater, except for the articles discussing its purposes published in the early 1870s, performed the same function: to present every one of its shows as an important communal event of great educational and moral value that offered the public an opportunity to support a praiseworthy charitable cause while having a good time. This opportunity was usually advertised in an announcement, and after the show had taken place, its "moral and financial success" was triumphantly confirmed in a review. Hence, these announcements and reviews are variants of an invariant that can be called "Sephardi Theater's triumphs." In other words, in the Ladino press, there is essentially one genre of writing about Sephardi Theater, and due to its peculiar pragmatics, it does not match either of the two theater-related genres found in *Le Journal de Salonique* or any other French-language periodical.

An examination of the press discourse revealing its structure and the factual reality behind it indicates that, starting with the first announcement of a Ladino show and the introduction to the first extant Ladino play, all newspapers aimed at supporting and propagating Sephardi Theater as a laudable social practice primarily intended to indoctrinate Ottoman Jews in accordance with the dominant ideology and to encourage them to do charity. As a result, Ladino periodicals, with their formulaic announcements and reviews, produce an impression of a coordinated activity of a large group of people in different Jewish centers in the Ottoman Empire. No doubt, the authors of Ladino plays, at least the educational ones, were also part of this endeavor, which is why they and their works enjoyed higher prestige than serialized novels and those who produced them. Ladino fiction, the only market-oriented genre of Ladino literature, was commissioned by newspaper editors concerned about their financial situation and was meant to entertain readers. In contrast, educational Ladino plays were either commissioned by theater groups or schools or produced with the knowledge that they would be staged by them. Such shows were advertised in the press as important social events. It is remarkable that, unlike the novels, both Djaen's *Devora* and Hassid's *Han Benyamin,* for example, were printed in big clear letters on good paper and had few typos. These texts were, undoubtedly, meant to be used for "high" purposes, such as public education and charity, rather than merely for private reading around the family table. In short, the differences between Ladino belles lettres and drama are determined by the circumstances that brought each genre into being, by their *declared* goals, and by their *actual* social functions.

# ⫶⫶⫶ 6

## Ladino Drama: Case Studies

In this chapter, I will examine five Ladino plays that belong to different genres—comedy, high drama, and thriller—and combine elements of instruction and entertainment in varying proportions. The rewriter of *The Playful Doctor* remains unknown, while the four other plays are signed by their creators. The plays will be discussed in chronological order: the two adaptations of Molière's comedies, *The Playful Doctor* and *Han Benyamin*, appeared in Sephardi Theater's first period (1863 and 1884, respectively); both *Purim Eve* (1909) and *Devora* (1921) were created in the second period and explicitly aimed at indoctrinating Sephardim in Zionist ideology. *Dreyfus*, produced in 1902(?), reflected the Zionist agenda without making any direct statements. Overall, this selection of plays written within almost fifty years provides an adequate picture of Sephardi Theater's repertoire. I will not analyze any translations of contemporaneous French plays, since this would not add anything to our understanding of Sephardi Theater beyond what one learns from the list of their authors cited in the previous chapter.

> *The Playful Doctor*
> A play by Molière in one act of sixteen scenes
> *El Mediko djugeton*
> Pyesa en un akto de dyesiseys esenas de Molyer
> Editada en *El Tyempo*
>    Istanbul: 1863[1]

The Sephardi press usually referred to Molière as "the greatest French comic author," and six of his plays were adapted in Ladino, most of them at least twice. *The Playful Doctor* is a rewriting of Molière's *Le Médecin volant,* which is a farce about a clueless rich man and a clever valet who outwits him. The old man's daughter and her lover decide to convince her father to let them get married. In order to spend some time with his beloved, the young man asks his valet, Sganarelle, to visit the girl's house in a doctor's disguise and persuade her father, Gorgibus, to send her to their country house. Sganarelle succeeds in fooling the rich man, but a few hours later, now in his regular clothes, he meets the old man again, and tells him that he is the doctor's twin brother. Using different disguises and natural adroitness, Sganarelle pretends to be two people, until Gorgibus's servant realizes what is going on and explains to his master that he has been fooled. At this point, the young couple appears, and the father gives them permission to marry. The play's only goal is to make the audience laugh, which is often achieved through rather crude jokes, as well as by means of acrobatic tricks and slapstick.

In its Ladino version, the comedy is not abridged but significantly domesticated, beginning with the characters' names. Thus, the funny Latin Gorgibus becomes the Spanish Frederiko. But the most remarkable change is that of the central character's name: Sganarelle is now called Shelomo, and his invented twin is referred to as Eliezer. In addition, the anonymous rewriter attributes to the comedy a message in the spirit of the Alliance schools: ignorance and bad manners are presented as moral vices, which were presumably decried by the great French playwright. The introductory note, similar to the prefaces to some Ladino novels, explains that the comedy "in its moral part serves as a lesson to some people who pretend to be wise and good friends, while in reality they are ignorant and ill-mannered."

The rewriter attempts to modify the play's message through his transformation of the final scene. Molière's comedy closes with the words of Gorgibus, who forgives everyone, including Sganarelle: "Let's all celebrate this marriage and drink to the health of the whole company" (scene 16). In the Ladino version, however, Frederiko, instead of forgiving the impostor, says to the young couple, "May you have a good and happy life, but I do not want to see this scoundrel Shelomo again. Never mind what he did to me this time, let it be so. But may God protect him if I ever meet him again . . . and if he tries to approach me, let alone cheat me, you will see what I will do to him."

Most of the other changes, just like in the novels, are made for the sake of decency, a feature hardly compatible with the farce as a genre. For example, in scene 4 of Molière's comedy, when the fake doctor comes to examine the young girl, he first wants to see her urine, then he swallows it, and finally announces that she has a fever. In an effort to make the episode less vulgar, the Sephardi rewriter modified it, so that Shelomo only touches the urine and then asks for a blood sample, which makes the rest of the scene incomprehensible.

The rewriter is more successful in his representation of Shelomo's "learned" discourses, in which one finds a few instances of skillful contextualization. For example, Hippocrates is replaced with ha-Rambam. In scene 4 of Molière's comedy, Sganarelle tells Gorgibus that he is not an ordinary doctor: "I know the secrets. Salamalec, Salamalec. Rodrigue, do you have the courage? Signor, si, signor, no. Per omnia saecula saeculorum." In the Ladino version, certain phrases that would have been too difficult to explain to the Sephardi audience are deleted. For example, the quote from Corneille's *Le Cid* (II, 2: "Rodrigue, as-tu du coeur?") was probably familiar to everyone who attended school in France but would have been incomprehensible for most Sephardim. When Shelomo uses a corrupted Latin proverb that was probably familiar to the French public, the Sephardi rewriter makes sure his audience understands that Shelomo is speaking Latin by adding explanatory words: "I possess the secrets and the mysteries of life, *I know Latin*.[2] Look, sinyor: 'Per omnia saecula saecularium.' But I am wasting my time, you don't understand anything."

As a result of the rewriter's work, Sephardim received a play that was funny without being nearly as vulgar as Karagöz shows and could be performed in front of women and children. Moreover, the rewriter even tried to use *The Playful Doctor* for didactic purposes by adding a moral lesson to a rather immoral farce.

> *Han Benyamin*
> A very celebrated play
> Translated and modified by David Joseph Hassid
> *Han Benyamin*
> Teatro muy alabado
> *Istoriya de Han Benyamin*
> Tradusido i modifikado de David Joseph Hassid
>
> Salonica: Estamparia del jurnal *La Epoka,* 5644 [1884], 80 pages

In his preface to *Han Benyamin*, the earliest Ladino version of Molière's *Miser*,[3] Hassid contends that the main function of theater is corrective, and the desired "correction" should be achieved by enjoyable means. He also believes that his work will help to solve the technical problems that hinder the introduction of his coreligionists to European drama. It is noteworthy, however, that insisting on the importance of making translations, the rewriter never mentions the possibility of creating original plays in Ladino.

*Han Benyamin* is domesticated much more than *The Playful Doctor,* which was produced eleven years earlier. According to Romero, Han Benyamin was the name of a real person who once lived in Salonica and was notoriously avaricious.[4] Other modifications of the text also reminded Salonicans that the action takes place in their own city. For instance, when Han Benyamin gets mad at his cook, Daniel, for trying to prepare a large dinner, he angrily says that he is not going to invite all Salonicans (III, 1).[5] There are also a few mentions of specific places in the city, such as the Besh Chinar garden where Han Benyamin plans to take his guests to (III, 4).

Like in *The Playful Doctor,* all names are changed: meaningful in French but incomprehensible to the Sephardi public, so they are replaced with common Jewish names. Thus, La Flèche (Arrow), Brindavoine (Oat Sprig), and La Merluche (Cod) become Shelomo, Hayim, and Yakov, respectively. The police investigator is called Kemal Efendi, and his clerks are Mehmet and Abdula. Most items of clothing are replaced with modern ones, which gives Hassid an opportunity to advocate proper hygiene and European dress. Thus, in act I, scene 4, rather than ridiculing the silly fashions, as is done in the original, the ignorant Sephardi miser scolds his son for shaving three times a week instead of once a month and for wearing clean shirts and neckties.

Aside from employing the means of domestication used by most creators of Ladino novels, Hassid uses some other techniques that allow him to adapt the French play to local tastes. See table 6.1 for a comparison of the French and Ladino versions of a fragment of the closing scene (V, 6), in which three participants in the romantic story reunite after years of separation. In *Han Benyamin,* Molière's Valère, Mariane, and Anselme assume melodious names—Enriko, Matilde, and sinyor Eduardo—which the Sephardi audience would have found easier to pronounce and to remember.

This excerpt from the final scene of *Han Benyamin* reminds one of Ladino belles lettres rather than of a comedy. In fact, it should be understood as an inserted mini novel about a family who almost perished at sea but in the end miraculously reunites in Salonica (where the two women live in the Jewish neighborhood Maale de Rogos). Of course, this story is found in *The Miser* and contains the same facts, but in Ladino it is expanded by about 135 percent and told in such a way that it resembles a domestic novel which could be entitled, for instance, *A Disaster at Sea: A Very Moving Story.*

Table 6.1

| French | Ladino |
|---|---|
| VALÈRE. You are my sister? | ENRIKO. [To Matilde] *Oh God!* You are my sister!? |
| MARIANE. Yes, my heart is agitated since the moment you opened your mouth; and our mother, whom you are going *to make happy,* told me a thousand times about the misfortunes of our family. God did not let us, too, perish in that terrible shipwreck, but saved our lives at the cost of our freedom, and some pirates found us on a piece of the ship. After *ten years* of slavery, *good luck* returned us our freedom, and we went back to Naples, where we learned that all our property had been sold and were unable to find any news about our father. We went to Genoa, where my mother collected some small remainders of her inheritance that had been stolen, and from there, fleeing from the terrible injustice of her relatives, she came to this place, where she has been living a sad life. | MATILDE. Yes, *my dear,* I am your sister. My *soul* and my heart have been beating *hard, since the moment* you *began to* open your mouth. Our mother, *who will cover you with kisses and whom you will embrace and press to your heart,* told me many times about this misfortune . . . |
| | SINYOR EDUARDO AND ENRIKO. *How were you saved?* |
| | MATILDE. *Forgive me, joy does not let me speak. Here is what I will tell you. When we were thrown into the wide and raging sea,* God *took pity on us* and did not want to kill us in that shipwreck [*drowning in water*] but saved us by making us lose our freedom. [To Enriko] *Listen how it happened:* when the ship broke in two, mother and I continued floating on a piece of board, where some pirates found us and made us slaves. *In short,* after *very hard* slavery *of which I do not want to tell you in order not to make your heart sad, God took great pity on us and set* us free (*as I will tell you sometime later*). Then, we returned to Naples where we found that all our property had been sold to other people and were unable to learn anything about our *beloved father who God only knows where he is now and whether he is alive or dead.* [Matilde, Enriko, and sinyor Eduardo each shed two tears that they dry up with their smiles.] From there, we went to Genoa to collect the inheritance which mother had inherited from *our grandfather sinyor Roberto,* which (*inheritance*) was almost completely stolen. Then, wanting to escape from the terrible injustice of her relatives, she came to settle here, *in Maale de Rogos,* where she and I lead a *very hard and* miserable life. |

Table 6.1 *continued*

| French | Ladino |
|---|---|
| ANSELME. O God, how great is your power! And how clearly you show that only you can do miracles! Embrace me, my children, and both of you add your joy to your father's joy. | SINYOR EDUARDO. O God! *I cannot wait any more!* How great are your miracles! *O powerful Creator of the whole world! Creator of heaven and earth! Lord of waters! You turn darkness into light! Sorrow into joy!* [To Enriko and Matilde] Let's embrace each other, children, and add your joy to the joy of your father, *as I am your father.* |

Note: : In each version, I italicize words and sentences that do not find correspondence in the other one. I indicated only those discrepancies that convey different information or affect the style register

In order to make the mini novel more exciting and touching, Hassid inserts an additional cue—the men's question addressed to Matilde—as well as the stage direction on shedding two tears, which is obviously not meant to be followed by the actors but is appropriate for narrative fiction. Furthermore, the narrator interrupts her story twice to announce to her brother that she won't tell him everything, as it would make him sad, and then promises a detailed account, which creates suspense similar to what one finds in serialized fiction. This mini novel has another feature common to Ladino fiction: Hassid introduces a new word—*naufradjyo* (shipwreck—explaining it in parentheses for those who were going to read the play. Moreover, in one case, unsure whether "which" will be understood correctly, Hassid adds in parentheses its referent: "inheritance."

The Sephardi rewriter is evidently not satisfied with the simple moral lesson of the French comedy—"Do not be avaricious"—and at the very end adds another one: "Do not forget your God." We have seen this device used in *The Two Voyages of Gulliver,* where Benghiat makes the protagonist pray for salvation at sea.[6] Here, sinyor Eduardo's announcement of the great news is preceded by his praise of God, whom he thanks for the miraculous deliverance of his family. This addition can be described as a short psalm that employs liturgical language: "O powerful creator of the whole world! Creator of heaven and earth! Lord of waters! You turn darkness into light! Sorrow into joy!" In the original, God is also recognized as the source of miracles, but the respective passage is shorter and less elaborate.

Furthermore, in *The Miser* it is good luck that allows the two women to recover their freedom, whereas in *Han Benyamin* God once again takes pity on them and saves them from slavery.

Alongside adding and replacing words, Hassid inserts highly expressive phraseology that modifies the emotional climate of the text.[7] His reason for developing This scene into a mini novel was his awareness of the public's taste for melodramatic fiction. Besides, it was the only place in the comedy that offered him an opportunity to add a religious lesson.

In his version of *The Miser,* Hassid achieved the goals laid out in the preface: he succeeded in making the French comedy accessible to the Sephardi audience, thus introducing it to Molière's theater as a primary school of morality. *Han Benyamin* undoubtedly stands out as a remarkably skillful rewriting and thus is one of the few exceptions highlighting the general indifference of Sephardi Theater organizers to the literary quality of Ladino plays.

> *Dreyfus*[8]
> By Jacques Loria
> Drama in 5 acts and an apotheosis
> *Dreyfus*
> Por Jak Lorya
> Drama en 5 aktos i un apoteos
>     Sofia: 1903, 56 pages

Jacques Loria (1860–2948) is one of the best known Sephardi literati, whose life and work merit a separate study. He began his pedagogical career as a teacher at the Alliance school in Tatar Basary (Tatarpazardjik), eventually becoming its director. According to some sources, Loria later secretly converted to Zionism, which was discovered and led to his termination.[9] In 1914, he moved to France. Between 1919 and 1922, Loria was the editor in chief of *La Nacion,* the organ of the Zionist Federation of the Orient (Istanbul).

Loria first became known to the reading public in 1896 as the author of *The Mysteries of Pera,* a 932-page sensational novel published in Istanbul in serialized form.[10] Strauss points out that Loria's literary career may be regarded as "typically Ottoman."[11] Indeed, he wrote in French, Ladino, and Turkish under various pseudonyms, including Comte de Persignac and Prinkipo Bey. When his first novel was released, "Greeks and Italians both claimed that this talented but hitherto unknown author came from their own community."[12] In 1909, his new novel, *The Imperial Treasure of the Topkapi Palace,* appeared in Turkish.[13] Between producing his French novel and the

Turkish one, Loria created works in Ladino dealing with Jewish issues, especially with antisemitism, which he treated from a Zionist perspective, that is, as fundamentally ineradicable. The most popular of them were his thrilling novel *Matsa de sangre* (The Bloody Matza) and the play *Dreyfus.*

It is remarkable that, in spite of the extraordinary importance of the Dreyfus Affair for France, the literary response of French writers to this event was rather limited,[14] whereas in Ladino drama and belles lettres, it was quite significant. There were a few Ladino plays on the Dreyfus Affair,[15] and within a few years the Dreyfus show was canonized in Sephardi Theater just like the Purim show, the flight from Egypt, and the Hanukkah play about the Maccabees. All these shows were meant to celebrate victories of the Jewish people over its oppressors, but by the late nineteenth century the biblical events had lost their immediate relevance for most Sephardim. Dreyfus's story was significant not only because he had triumphed over his persecutors so recently, but also because it made many Jews redefine their Jewishness in modern terms, that is, in relation to contemporaneous antisemitism. In view of all this and the growing influence of Zionism, it is not surprising that in Sephardi Theater the Dreyfus story, alongside the biblical accounts of Jewish victories, became a genre of its own. Even many years later, Sephardi authors continued to use the Affair for their plays.[16]

It is evident from Loria's play that he was well informed about the details of the Affair and had read Dreyfus's memoir, *Five Years of My Life* (1901), either in the original or in the Ladino translation published in the same year. However, a significant part of the Sephardi audience was also quite familiar with the events of 1894–1899, the period covered by the play, which made it hard for Loria to keep the public in suspense. But, an experienced author of thrillers, he managed to produce a truly exciting play with a clear ideological message.

*Dreyfus* was meant both to be staged and read, which is evident from the stage directions, which are often quite descriptive and are meant for readers rather than spectators: "Esterhazy has the eyes of a bandit" (I, 2). At the same time, the author is concerned about the effect his play will produce when performed. Thus, one of the scenes is introduced by an explanation intended for the actors: "This scene is the most dramatic one in the play and should be performed with attention. Then it will make a great impression on the public" (IV, 4).

Most of Dreyfus's persecutors, some of them made-up grotesque characters, are outspoken antisemites who give different reasons for hating Jews. Major Fabres, Esterhazy's associate and Dreyfus's worst enemy, expresses the quintessential Christian antisemitism: "Judas Iscariot was a

Jew! If he sold our Lord Yeshu for thirty ducats, who is going to be surprised that another Jew sold his motherland?" (I, 6). Another character explains that he hates Jews: "When it comes to a Jew, one should believe every rumor! If someone tells me that a Jew has stolen the moon and swallowed Mount Levan, I will immediately believe it. Jews are capable of anything!" (II, 3).

For obvious pedagogical reasons, Loria adds to his play an ideological message conspicuously absent from *Five Years of My Life*. While the real Dreyfus does not use the word "God" even once, Loria's protagonist frequently talks to the "powerful and merciful God," asking him for the justice which he does not expect from human beings, and then thanks God for his salvation.

Loria's play has only one significant addition that has no referent in the real Dreyfus story, whose purpose is to make the happy ending more thrilling. Kept in solitary confinement in Devil's Island, Dreyfus stops receiving letters from his wife and is not aware of his supporters' efforts to have his case reopened. The new inspector of prisons sent from France visits him and brings him a box of pills which, he promises, will give the prisoner more energy. Alone in his hut, Dreyfus opens the box and finds there a letter from his wife in which she announces the imminent triumph of justice. Thus, while loyal to the Zionist agenda, Loria was no less interested in making profit, for which purpose he turned a dark episode of Jewish history into a thriller. Furthermore, this successful writer did not shy away from self-promotion. On the last page of the edition I used, the ingenious author announces his forthcoming novel, *The Bloody Matza*, and not only decries the practice of sharing books but offers his own ambitious plan of action: "In order to ensure the novel's success, eastern communities must organize reading groups that would warmly receive *The Blood Libel* [another title of the novel], which would encourage the author to begin its publication."

Due to the nature of Sephardi Theater coverage in Ladino periodicals, one can almost never establish whether a given Ladino play was successful or even whether it was staged at all. But we do know that Loria's *Dreyfus* was both reprinted and staged more than once. For instance, as will be remembered, twenty years after its first publication, the Max Nordau Society staged it in Salonica, and it attracted many spectators.

*Purim Eve*
Mordehai M. Monassowitz
A comedy in one act
Translated from Hebrew by Nissim Natan Katalan

*Neshef Purim*
Komedya en un akto
Tresladada de ebreo por Nisim Natan Katalan
Kazanluk: 1909[17]

Purim shows put on by Zionist organizations typically included short plays, songs, monologues, and dialogues in Ladino or Hebrew. From the newspaper reviews, it is clear that they did not resemble traditional Purim performances as a type of theater. For instance, the show put on by Biblioteka Israelita Kadima in Salonica in 1915 had a long program that included various songs, such as "Purim Purim Lanu" and "Ha-Tikvah," explanations in Ladino and Hebrew of the holiday, and the play *Mordehay and Esther* (*El Liberal*, March 5, 1915, 1). It is evident that the show, even though it included a play, was not a traditional celebration, but a concert aimed at educating the audience. No doubt, *Purim Eve*, too, was produced in Hebrew solely for the purpose of indoctrination. The play is meant to warn westernized Jews of the dangers of cultural assimilation and to restate the message of Purim as a reminder of this danger.

*Purim Eve* does not advocate emigration to Palestine but emphasizes the need for children's education to focus on Jewish history and traditions and on Hebrew as the true Jewish language. The argument of the play is straightforward: on Purim eve, a devoted Zionist, Shemuel Natan, and his twelve-year-old son, Hayim, come to the home of their relative Avram Levy and find that his children are not aware of what day it is and do not know anything about the holiday. Avram Levy is a well-off merchant of rugs who, given his occupation, probably lives in a port city and speaks some French. His children learn French and prefer translated adventure stories to books on Judaism.

Natan is shocked and scolds Avram and his wife, Aneta, for raising their children in complete ignorance about Jewish holidays and history. His son summarizes the book of Esther for everybody, and as he finishes, a group of actors who go from house to house performing the Purim story enters the room. When their show ends, the ignorant children, whom Natan even hesitates to call Jews, demand a Jewish education, and their parents promise to find them a teacher the next day. The delighted children announce that they want to be Jews.

The play reiterates the key Zionist claim: antisemitism is eternal and will always endanger Jewish existence in the diaspora. To illustrate this point, the author expands Haman's speech in Esther 3:8–9, adding to it some standard antisemitic clichés. Thus, when Haman tries to convince King Achashverosh to take immediate action against the Jews, he describes them as old "inner enemies" who are threatening the well-being of the kingdom by robbing it and by being disobedient and different from everybody else even in their appearance (an anachronistic concept, hardly applicable to the Persian Empire). The only way to save the population—insists Haman—is to annihilate the Jews and thus liberate the country. Monossowitz offers a propagandistic version of the Purim story, according to which Haman hates all Jews and has seriously thought about the "Jewish question":

> [T]his enemy did not come to our country today. It has been living among us for many years. The Jewish people ignore your decrees and *do not follow your laws.* This people has appropriated our best lands. It appropriated our goods and riches. *They have different laws,* different gods, and their faces differ from ours. They curse us, they despise us like worms, they mock us and make fun of our customs. . . . O great and merciful king, deliver us from them. Hurry to save your country from this cursed people. Drive them out of your lands![18]

While some of the children's lines in *Purim Eve* were meant to make the public laugh, this is not why the author labeled his play a "comedy": it is the idea of assimilation that he wants to present as ludicrous. Though *Purim Eve* came out in Bulgaria, where by 1900 Zionists had taken over the Alliance, the original Hebrew play obviously targeted westernized Jews everywhere and was probably intended to be translated into other languages. This would explain why some characters have Romance names (Aneta) and some German ones (Klerhen and Max).

> *Devora*
>
> A theater play in 3 acts and one picture
> Written by Shabtay Yosef Djaen
> The music and dances composed by professor Avram Suzin
> *Devora*
> Pyesa teatrala en 3 aktos i una estampa
> Eskrita por Shabtay Yosef Djaen
> La muzika i los danses fueron kompuestos por profesor Avram Suzin
>
> Vyena: Unyon Buchdruckerei, Tishrey 5682 [1921], 61 pages

Due to the rather high status of Sephardi playwrights in the second period of Sephardi Theater's history, we know the names of many authors of Zionist plays and often have some information about them. The most prominent Ladino playwright of that time was Shabtay Yosef Djaen (1886–1946), whose works about great Jewish heroes were staged in various Sephardi communities. Djaen always aspired to become a rabbi (which he eventually achieved, and, in 1928 he even became the chief Sephardi rabbi of Buenos Aires).[19] Aires).[19] His *Bar Kokhba* was staged in 1904, when the author had just turned

18. In 1921, his drama *Yiftach* was performed in Serbian by professional actors in Belgrade and Sarajevo.

Djaen's *Devora,* published in 1921 in Vienna, is a perfect example of a Zionist drama whose author not only received support from a Zionist leader but also donated 10 percent of the profits from the play to the Jewish National Fund. This drama is a straightforward expression of Zionist ideals and primarily aims at persuading Sephardim to go to Palestine. It does not talk about loyalty to Judaism or to God, but rather to the land of Israel. *Devora* also reminds Jews of their great past and encourages them to emulate their ancestors. The play is based on the story of the prophetess Devora related in Judges 4, which is only slightly modified by a few fictional elements.

In the opening scene, Israelites talk about the hard life of their people, who are oppressed by King Jabin and Sisera, the local commander of the king's army. This happened because God sold the people of Israel to Canaan to punish them for their transgressions. Devora encourages her husband, Barak, to go with his army to Mount Tabor. She promises Barak a complete victory and accompanies him to Kedesh, where he meets Sisera and his nine hundred chariots. He destroys Sisera's army, and the latter flees from the battlefield, reaches Yael's tent, and asks her for refuge. Instead, Yael gives him warm milk, which puts him to sleep, and then thrusts a tent peg into his temple. Thus, Djaen closely follows the biblical story, adding to it just three made-up characters.

There are two programmatic monologues in the play, both delivered by women: Yael's soliloquy in act II, scene 1, and Devora's song in act III, scenes 8–9. Yael represents the strong and wise Jewish woman whose authority is reaffirmed by her son's faith in her. Yael's monologue about her love for the land of Israel is a patriotic hymn as well as a tribute to courageous Jewish women:

> O blessed Holy Land! I admire your greatness, I am enchanted by the riches that God gave you. . . . The nights with shining stars, the days with the brilliant sun, you are full of gold and diamonds. . . . O Holy Land, where dwells God's glory! Alas! we are living in bad times. The children of Israel abandoned their fathers' ways. And their God turned away from them. Now they are fighting for their liberation and the prophetess Devora, a worthy daughter of Israel, and her spouse, Barak, are leading them to freedom. . . . O Devora! . . . You prove by your courage that a woman can rise above the trivial life to which the world destined her. (II, 1)

Devora's song in Djaen's play is close to the biblical text in Judges 5:

Listen, kings, give ear, princes,
I will sing to the Lord,
To the dweller of the clouds,
I will sing my songs of glory. (III, 8–9)[20]

Even this brief overview shows that Djaen's drama is not original in any sense, but it offers the actors an opportunity to remind the spectators that the land of Israel needs them. The detailed descriptions of the setting and dances, and the large number of characters (more than twenty), including those who are called "immigrants," make it clear that the author composed his drama for staging at a large theater or club. We do not know enough about the use of music in Ladino plays, but the catalogs show that quite a few performances used music. Even less is known about the staging of Ladino plays, but one can gather from the stage directions in some of them, including *Devora*, that the settings, costumes, and props could be rather elaborate.

## Conclusions

Ladino drama is a more heterogeneous corpus of texts than belles lettres. Unlike the serialized novels, which were produced for one purpose and governed by the same literary laws, Ladino plays were created under various circumstances to fulfill different functions and, therefore, did not adhere to one set of aesthetic norms, even when formally attributed to one genre category. *The Playful Doctor* and *Han Benyamin* have nothing in common with *Purim Eve*, which is also labeled "comedy," the latter being closely related to *Dreyfus* and *Devora* in terms of its agenda.

Though there is very little information about the circulation and distribution of Ladino plays or the remuneration of Sephardi playwrights, we know that often the welfare of the authors did not depend on the artistic merit of their work nor on its ability to attract the public. Some plays were published in periodicals and meant both to be consumed as narrative fiction and staged by families or friends (*The Playful Doctor*), whereas others appeared as separate editions and were specifically designed to be performed at big clubs (*Devora*). Loria's *Dreyfus* is obviously a rare and more complicated case: it was successful both as a serialized story and as a theater show. *Purim Eve*, on the contrary, was unlikely to bring any profit based on its literary merit and had to be performed at fundraising events.

It is evident that the term "Ladino drama"—unlike "belles lettres" or "*musar*"—cannot be used to designate a particular genre of Ladino literature, but only to refer to the corpus of texts generated by the needs of Sephardi Theater as a sociocultural practice.

# ❚ ❚ ❚  Conclusion

The history of Ladino print culture, still to be written from this perspective, is a story of intentional ruptures and fresh starts prompted by new social needs and perceived educational goals.[1] The nineteenth century witnessed its last beginning, the birth and flourishing of modern Ladino literature, a period of its great success which this book explains in specific terms previously not applied to its study. Interpreting past events on the basis of insufficient data is a risky enterprise, since a newly discovered piece of evidence may suddenly overturn a carefully constructed theory. Nevertheless, while I am aware of the tentative nature of my conclusions, I am convinced that they point in the right direction. Furthermore, this study provides a new starting point for an account of the demise of modern Ladino culture, which still needs to be written.

My book has attempted to understand the functions of Ladino literature in the process of westernization by questioning a few generally accepted assumptions and reconsidering some available data. I examined the three forms of modern Ladino cultural production as a unity, trying to establish connections between them and the particular role each of them played in shaping the worldview of Ottoman Sephardim. In terms of methodology, I chose to break large questions into a few specific ones and then test the validity of the answers by means of case studies. This allowed me to reveal the inaccuracy of certain claims made by my predecessors.

Among them is the belief that the press served as the most powerful tool of westernization because—despite the small circulations—it presumably reached almost everybody. Aiming to explain the initial failures and subsequent triumphs of Sephardi journalists, I began by asking what kept the circulations low, and then tried to assess whether a few hundred copies would have sufficed for reaching tens of thousands of Sephardim. Though it is clear that the situation varied from city to city and that all estimates are approximate, there is every reason to conclude that the newspapers, except for their entertainment parts, were not—and could not have been—read by many.

On the other hand, we can assume that their subscribers, attuned to liberal ideas and aware of the progress of science, were among the most committed supporters of reforms and westernization. No doubt, they were the parents who sent their sons and daughters to European-style schools. Later, some of those young people engaged in publishing while others chose to become, for a few years, amateur actors and to propagate new ideas and modern cultural practices by means of theater. Other newspaper readers changed their lifestyles in minor ways, for instance by attending theater shows or simply by switching to European clothes and diets. But even such innovations contributed to westernization.

Sarah Stein may be partly right when she says that, looking at the images in Ladino periodicals, their readers were "aware that a gulf separated them from Franco-Jewish elite culture, and that this gulf was as wide as that which distinguished them from the native of Madagascar."[2] Yet, as we have seen, this realization was by no means paralyzing. And even if some readers knew they could not emulate their French coreligionists, their cultural sympathies lay on the European side, which in itself was an ideological victory of the westernizing project. Thus, designed to advance westernization, the Ladino press indeed succeeded in connecting Sephardim to the larger world and promoting tolerance, secularization, and other liberal values, but its influence was to a great extent indirect.

In the course of my work, I have also discovered that, in order to see some "established" "facts" with new eyes, it is useful to understand how myths about the Ladino press were born. The idea that Ladino periodicals were read by the "ignorant masses" and that their editors were famous among all Ottoman Jews was introduced by the first Sephardi historians who, like Galante, were participants in the events, and this view was uncritically adopted by later scholars. One of the most popular myths was crafted by David Fresco, who presented himself as a hero in the pages of his own newspaper. An unsigned article followed by a rhymed panegyric claimed that "'a great Jew,' who is too modest to allow himself to be mentioned, was single-handedly responsible for reviving Jewish culture in Constantinople." The poem "sang praises of the 'heroic writer, David'" who lived "on the banks of the Bosphorus."[3] It will be remembered that this image was picked up and developed by Fresco's admirer Moïse Franco, who stated that Fresco was the most famous Jew in the Mediterranean archipelago. However, this contention was challenged by Elie Carmona, who believed that Sam Lévy, his brother-in-law, was the one who deserved this title.

Another misconception about Ladino literature discussed in this book concerns the belles lettres, which has been seen as an unnecessary part of Sephardi culture, something it should be ashamed of. Yet the novel was not only a full-fledged genre of Ladino literature, but also the most popular one, which made its production a lucrative business. As will be remembered, one Sephardi rewriter, Shelomo Ben-Sandji, in the preface to his collection of Ladino novels, reminds his readers that he is publishing it with the goal of pleasing his stomach and those of his relatives. In other words, he is a professional who makes a living by producing belles lettres and takes it for granted that his readers are aware of this fact. Ben-Sandji is a vendor par excellence, which is perceived in his tone; that is why, unlike Uziel with his idealism, he cannot accept financial losses. The commercialization of Ladino literature, of which his preface is the best proof, testifies to the success of westernization.

This also means that, in terms of its reach, the belles lettres was the most efficient, if unintended, means of westernization because, unlike serious periodicals—many of which did not last long—it was both accessible and attractive, even to the least educated and the least intellectually curious people, the proverbial ignorant masses. Of course, the majority of the novels did not contain anything but adventures and love stories, and most rewriters never intended to make them educational. Nonetheless, even this kind of literature showed Sephardim that in other countries life was different and more exciting than their own. In addition, Ladino belles lettres expanded the readers' vocabulary to include new words naming the things found in that enchanting world referred to by the word "Europe."

Needless to say, the image of the "West" created by this kind of read had little to do with reality. But, after all, westernization is always an emulation of an *imagined* West. The image of Europe as a place where banks close on Jewish holidays and where people are "every day" buried to the sounds of Chopin's funeral march, as presented by Sam Lévy, is also bizarre. In reality—and most important—it was the new mode of publishing and distributing fiction that was borrowed from Europe, together with the canon of novels for imitation.

The role of Sephardi Theater in westernizing Ottoman Jews cannot be properly assessed because we do not know how many people actually attended the shows. It is obvious, however, that, as a modern cultural practice and a new site of charity, it must have had a certain impact on people's lifestyles. As for Ladino drama, entertaining plays such as *The Playful Doctor,* no doubt, appealed to the reading public, but not many of those are found in periodicals. The light, entertaining performances in the French style must have had the same effect as the belles lettres, though such shows were not meant for mass audiences.

It is evident that all three forms of modern Ladino cultural production worked in the same direction, furthering westernization, and that their methods were determined by their goals rather than by the genre as such and were, therefore, changed ad hoc. Finally, it has to be emphasized again that, since the growth of literacy is a prerequisite for the development of print culture, the latter can be adequately understood only in the context of modern schooling. I believe that combining the study of schooling and publishing in one community might yield unexpected results. Even my brief study of the Salonican press, which takes into account the emergence of modern schools, sheds new light on the formation and development of the reading public.

I realize that this book may foster many doubts and that it contains more questions than answers, but I find it imperative to raise them, because most other works on modern Ladino culture make—or, rather, repeat—numerous claims that need to be reconsidered. At the same time, disappointing as it is, it has to be recognized that, due to the lack of sources, many of our questions will have to remain unanswered.

There is an aspect of this study which I have not yet mentioned, because it has never figured as such on my agenda. When, in May 2007, Nicolas Sarkozy became president of France and the media discovered that among his maternal ancestors were Salonican Jews,[4] a friend of mine who had been following my research on Sam Lévy sent me an email: "So what do you think about a Salonican Jew becoming President of France? Imagine how Sam would have kvelled . . ." It had never been my goal to revive Sephardi journalists, but I was thrilled to hear that one of them had become a real person, at least for some of my readers. In fact, other colleagues of mine have criticized Lévy and even made fun of him. I only hope that the images of him and the other Sephardi literati I have created in this book, without ever attempting to produce literary biographies, are true to life and do justice to them. So far, only Albert Kalderon has offered a full-fledged portrait of one of the most prominent Sephardi literati, in his biography of Avram Galante.[5] However, Galante's life is well documented. In any case, I would be glad to know that I was able to make the world of Ladino print culture alive and relevant for others by showing that it is a lot more than a pile of yellow newspapers or, worse, a pale microfilm.

# ⫘ Notes

## Introduction

1. Esther Benbassa and Aron Rodrigue, *Sephardi Jewry: A History of the Judeo-Spanish Community, 14th–20th Centuries* (Berkeley, 2000), 70.

2. It first appeared in English in 1995 (Oxford) under the title *Jews of the Balkans,* which did not include the prologue of the French original. In this book, I cite the full English translation, titled *Sephardi Jewry* (Berkeley, 2000).

3. Amelia Barquín,"Edición y estudio de doce novelas aljamiadas sefardíes de principio del siglo XX," Ph.D. diss., Universidad del País Vasco, Bilbao, 1997.

4. Strictly speaking, the first attempt at this kind of study was Robyn Loewenthal's dissertation, "Elia Carmona's Autobiography: Judeo-Spanish Popular Press and Novel Publishing Milieu in Constantinople, Ottoman Empire, circa 1860–1932," Ph.D. diss., University of Nebraska, Lincoln, 1994. However, this work is seriously flawEd. In any case, aside from the actual autobiography, Loewenthal uses only secondary sources. In this book, I will use her transliteration of Elia Carmona's "Autobiography," citing it as Loewenthal, "Carmona's Autobiography."

5. On the expulsion and its causes, see Henry Kamen, "The Expulsion: Purpose and Consequence," in *Spain and the Jews,* ed. Elie Kedourie (London, 1992), 74–91; Stephen Haliczer, "The Castilian Urban Patriciate and the Jewish Expulsion of 1480–92," *American Historical Review* 78 (1973), 35–62.

6. On the lives of Jews and *conversos* before and after 1492, see Haim Beinart, "The Conversos and Their Fate," in Kedourie, *Spain and the Jews,* 92–122.

7. See Benbassa and Rodrigue, *Sephardi Jewry,* xxxvii.

8. On the legal and the actual status of Ottoman Jews, see Minna Rozen, *A History of the Jewish Community in Istanbul: The Formative Years, 1453–1566* (Leiden, 2002), 16–34.

9. See Benbassa and Rodrigue, *Sephardi Jewry,* 9–10, 202–203nn27–40.

10. On the controversial dating of their first book, see A. K. Offenberg, "The Printing History of the Constantinople Hebrew Incunable of 1493: A Mediterranean Voyage of Discovery," *British Library Journal* 22 (Autumn 1996 [= April 1997]), 221–235.

11. Michael Berenbaum and Fred Skolnik, eds., *Encyclopedia Judaica*, 2nd ed. (Detroit, Mich., 2007), s.v. "Salonika."

12. Yosef Hayim Yerushalmi, *The Re-education of Marranos in the Seventeenth Century: The Third Annual Rabbi Louis Feinberg Memorial Lecture in Judaic Studies* (Cincinnati, Ohio: University of Cincinnati, 1980), 8.

13. See Abraham Yaari, *Hebrew Printing at Constantinople* (Jerusalem, 1967) (Heb.).

14. A detailed discussion of Ladino will follow in section IV.

15. Quoted in Yerushalmi, *The Re-education of Marranos*, 9. This comment confirms once again that, despite possible difficulties in oral communication, the Spanish and Portuguese immigrants were able to read the same texts. Aside from the fact that in the sixteenth century these two languages were closer to each other than they are now, many Spanish exiles had spent some time in Portugal, and most educated people in that country knew Castilian.

16. The Greek translation was meant for the local Greek-speaking Jews (Romaniot), who did not have a printing press of their own.

17. Moisés Almosnino, *Crónica de los reyes otomanos* (Barcelona, 1998).

18. It first saw light in 1638 in Madrid Martínez as a Romanized and significantly reworked adaptation entitled *Extremos y grandezas de Constantinopla*. See Pilar Romeu Ferré, introduction to Almosnino, *Crónica de los reyes otomanos*.

19. Benbassa and Rodrigue, *Sephardi Jewry*, 56.

20. In the Hebrew introduction to *Me'am Lo'ez*, Huli explains at length that the books of these two authors are too difficult and too short and, therefore, have to be replaced with his multivolume work.

21. Matthias Lehmann, *Ladino Rabbinic Literature and Ottoman Sephardic Culture* (Bloomington, 2005), 31.

22. *Me'am Lo'ez*, introduction to Genesis, 4, 5.

23. This term was introduced by Lehmann to refer to the eighteenth- and nineteenth-century rabbis who, being educators rather than scholars, produced most of their works, which were meant for mass readerships, in the vernacular. See his doctoral dissertation, "Judeo-Spanish *Musar* Literature and the Transformation of Ottoman Sephardic Society (Eighteenth through Nineteenth Centuries)," Freie Universität, Berlin, 2002.

24. Lehmann, *Ladino Rabbinic Literature*, 35.

25. Elena Romero, *La Creación Literaria en Lengua Sefardí* (Madrid, 1992), ch. 4; Romero, *Y hubo luz y no fue tan buena: Las coplas sefardies de Purim y los tiempos modernos* (Barcelona, 2008); Eleazar Gutwirth, "A Judeo-Spanish Planctus from the Cairo Genizah," *Romance Philology* 49(4) (1996), 420–428.

26. On Attias and his work, see Matthias Lehmann, "A Livornese 'Port Jew' and the Sephardim of the Ottoman Empire," *Jewish Social Studies* 11 (Winter 2005), 51–76.

27. On these blood libels and the intervention of European Jews, see Jonathan Frankel, *The Damascus Affair: Ritual Murder, Politics, and the Jews in 1840* (Cambridge, 1997).

28. This view was formulated by Daniel Schroeter in his essay "Orientalism and the Jews," *Journal of Mediterranean Studies* 4 (1994), 183–196. In fact, this most interesting article demonstrates that every encounter of Western European Jews with Sephardim was surprising, if not shocking, for the former. I believe that the two major factors leading

to the end of Sephardi history, i.e., a history separate from that of Ashkenazim, were the mass immigration of Ottoman Jews to both Americas and the Holocaust.

29. Julia Phillips Cohen offers an interesting discussion of the adoption and rejection of this myth by Ottoman Jews in the late nineteenth century. See Cohen, "The Past as a Foreign Country: Ottoman Sephardim and Their Changing Vision of Spain in the Modern Period," unpublished paper presented at the 37th Annual Conference of the Association of Jewish Studies, 2005.

30. See Aron Rodrigue, *French Jews, Turkish Jews: Alliance Israélite Universelle and the Politics of Jewish Schooling in Turkey, 1860–1925* (Bloomington, 1990), 1–16.

31. Private email, July 31, 2009.

32. Henceforth, the Alliance.

33. Aron Rodrigue, "From *Millet* to Minority: Turkish Jewry in the 19th and 20th Centuries," in *Paths of Emancipation,* ed. Pierre Birnbaum and Ira Katznelson (Princeton, 1995), 238–261, 248.

34. Sam Lévy, *Salonique à la fin du XIXe siècle: Mémoires* (Istanbul, 2000), 105.

35. Rodrigue, *French Jews, Turkish Jews,* xiii.

36. For more on these reforms and their impact on the lives of Ottoman Jews, see Benbassa and Rodrigue, *Sephardi Jewry,* ch. 3; Rodrigue, "From *Millet* to Minority."

37. Quoted in Rodrigue, "From *Millet* to Minority," 243.

38. Ibid.

39. For a strictly linguistic description, see Alonso Zamora Vicente, "Judeo-español," in his *Dialectología española* (Madrid, 1960), 349–377. This description, however, is not complete as it focuses mainly on Ladino's deviations from Castilian Spanish. A much fuller description was produced by Mark Gabinsky, a Romance linguist competent in Balkan and Semitic linguistics. Unfortunately, his book *Sephardic (Judeo-Spanish) Language* (Kishinev, 1992) is available only in Russian.

40. *Encyclopedia Judaica,* s.v. "Ladino."

41. For a detailed discussion of this subject, see Tracy K. Harris, *Death of a Language* (Newark, 1994), 53–65. It is hardly coincidental that the scholars using the term *Judezmo* support the idea that already in Spain Jews had a language of their own. Thus, David Bunis, who refers to the Sephardi vernacular almost exclusively as Judezmo, finds the earliest evidence of its existence in the eleventh and twelfth centuries. See his entry "Judeo-Spanish" in *The Encyclopedia of Jews in the Islamic World,* ed. Norman Stillman (Leiden, 2010) (henceforth, *EJIW*).

42. Harris, *Death of a Language,* 57.

43. Iacob M. Hassán, "La literatura sefardí culta: Sus principales escritores, obras y géneros," in *Judíos, Sefardíes, Conversos,* ed. Angel Alcalá (Valladolid, 1995), 319–330, 320.

44. Romero, *La Creación,* 18.

45. Isaac Jerusalmi, *From Ottoman Turkish to Ladino: The Case of Mehmet Sadik Rifat Pasha's Risale-i Ahlik to Judge Yehezkel Gabbay's Buen Dotrino* (Cincinnati, Ohio, 1990), 28–29.

46. See Haim-Vidal Sephiha, *Le Ladino: Judéo-espagnol calque* (Paris, 1973).

47. Jerusalmi, *From Ottoman Turkish to Ladino,* 29.

48. Pilar Romeu and Iacob M. Hassán, "Apuntes sobre la lengua de la *Crónica de los reyes otomanos* de Moisés Almosnino según la edición del manuscrito aljamiado del siglo XVI," *Actas del II Congreso Internacional de Historia de la Lengua Española* (Madrid, 1992), 2:161–169, 168. The cited section belongs to Hassán.

49. For a summary of this discussion, see David Bunis, "Modernization and the Language Question among Judezmo Speaking Sephardim of the Ottoman Empire," in *Sephardi and Middle Eastern Jewries: History and Culture in the Modern Era*, ed. Harvey E. Goldberg (Bloomington, 1996), 227–239. The opinions of individual participants can be found in Angel Pulido, *Españoles sin patria y la raza sefardí* (Madrid, 1905). In her pioneering study of the Ladino press, Sarah A. Stein offers an overview of the language debate in Ladino periodicals, but since her analysis is based mainly on the newspapers published by David Fresco, a vehement enemy of Ladino, the significance of this negative attitude is exaggerated. Stein, *Making Jews Modern* (Bloomington, 2003), ch. 2.

50. It is symptomatic that none of the scholars has resorted to a purely linguistic argument that Ladino cannot be considered a language but only a sum of regional dialects, none of which was standardized or equipped with "an army and a navy." In any case, this terminological discussion is an exercise in futility.

51. Bunis, "Modernization and the Language Question," 238.

52. Thus, Sephiha entitled a chapter of his book *Le Judéo-espagnol* (Paris, 1986) "La Noblesse de notre langue mite."

53. Joshua A. Fishman, "Bilingualism with and without Diglossia; Diglossia with and without Bilingualism," *Journal of Social Issues* 23 (1967), 29–38, 34.

54. Minna Rozen, "The People," in *The Cambridge History of Turkey*, vol. 3: *The Later Ottoman Empire, 1603–1839*, ed. Surayia Faroqhi (Cambridge, 2006), 255–271, 260–261.

55. See, for example, Almosnino's account of women's lives in Istanbul in the mid-sixteenth century in his *Crónica de los reyes otomanos*, (229–230).

56. Thus, it was a language of mass education rather than one of study or scholarship, as suggested by Stein, *Making Jews Modern*, 59. Elsewhere, I suggest that in the sixteenth century Ladino was considered suitable for high-culture purposes, which is why rabbi Almosnino produced a few works in this language.

57. Itamar Even-Zohar, "Aspects of the Hebrew-Yiddish Polysystem: A Case of a Multilingual Polysystem," *Poetics Today* 11(1) (1990), 121–130.

58. Quoted in Romero, *La Creación*, 47.

59. Shaul Shtampfer discovered that, while virtually all Jewish males in Eastern Europe were taught to read Hebrew and Aramaic for ten years, their literacy was still very low. See Shtampfer, "What Did 'Knowing Hebrew' Mean in Eastern Europe?" in *Hebrew in Ashkenaz: A Language in Exile*, ed. Lewis Glinert (Oxford, 1993), 129–140.

60. On traditional Jewish schooling in the Ottoman Empire, see Rodrigue, "Réformer ou supplanter: L'éducation juive traditionnelle en Turquie à l'épreuve de la modernité," in *Transmission et passages en monde juif*, ed. Esther Benbassa (Paris, 1997), 501–522; Rodrigue, *French Jews, Turkish Jews*, 35–38; Lehmann, *Ladino Rabbinic Literature*, 28–29; Alexandr Benghiat, *Suvenires del meldar: Estudyo verdadero de lo ke se pasava un tyempo* (Izmir, 1920) (Ladino, Rashi script).

61. The article by Julia Phillips Cohen and Sarah Abrevaya Stein—"Sephardic Scholarly Worlds: Toward a Novel Geography of Modern Jewish History," *Jewish Quarterly Review* 100 (Summer 2011), 349–384—irrespective of the authors' goals, allows one to trace the use of Hebrew and French by Ottoman Jews not only of different generations, but *also* from different parts of the empire.

62. Quoted in David Bunis, "The Earliest Judezmo Newspapers: Sociolinguistic Reflections," *Mediterranean Language Review* 6–7 (1993), 5–66, 33. The quote appears in Ladino and is followed by the author's English translation. Here, the translation is mine.

63. Bunis, *EJIW,* s.v. "Judeo-Spanish."

64. See Rodrigue, "The Ottoman Diaspora: The Rise and Fall of Ladino Literary Culture," in *Cultures of the Jews: A New History,* ed. David Biale (New York, 2001), 863–885; Harris, *Death of a Language,* ch. 13.

65. See http://www.helsinki.fi/~tasalmin/europe_index.html (accessed May 17, 2010).

66. See http://en.wikipedia.org/wiki/Belarusian_language (accessed May 18, 2010). This entry on Belorussian language in Wikipedia provides information not available elsewhere in English-language sources.

67. Stein, *Making Jews Modern,* 78–79.

## 1. The Emergence of Modern Cultural Production in Ladino

1. For example, Sarah Stein, *Making Jews Modern* (Bloomington, 2003), chs. 2, 4, 6; Amelia Barquín, "Un periódico sefardí: *El Meseret* de Alexandr Ben-Guiat," *Sefarad* 57(1) (1997), 3–31; Cristina Martínez-Galvez, "La prensa sefardí en Rumania: Contenidos del periódico *El Luzero de la Pasensia* (Turnu-Severin 1885–1888)," *Revista de Filología Románica* 26 (2009), 205–227; Borovaya, "Shmuel Saadi Halevy/Sam Lévy: Between Ladino and French: Reconstructing a Writer's Social Identity," in *Modern Jewish Literatures: Intersections and Boundaries,* ed. Sheila Jelen, Michael Kramer, and L. Scott Lerner (Philadelphia, 2010).

2. I am indebted to Kenneth Moss for his insightful comments on this subject.

3. Esther Benbassa and Aron Rodrigue erroneously indicate that in 1913 there were 389 Ladino periodicals in the Ottoman Empire. See their *Sephardi Jewry* (Berkeley, 2000), 112. The source they cite for this figure states that in 1913 the number of *all* periodicals published in the Ottoman territories reached 389. Avigdor Levy, "Ottoman Jewry in the Modern Era, 1826–1923," in *The Jews of the Ottoman Empire,* ed. Avigdor Levy (Princeton, 1994), 100. Given what we know about publishing in the Ottoman Empire, I doubt that any precise numbers can be established, regardless of what the official sources indicate. After 1909, the number of publishing licenses issued to the journalists at their request was larger than the number of actual periodicals. (See "Mechanisms of Press Control" below.)

4. Romero, *La Creación,* 180.

5. See Jonathan Frankel, *The Damascus Affair* (Cambridge, 1997).

6. On this subject, see Barukh Mevorakh, "The Influence of the Damascus Blood Libel on the Development of the Jewish Press in 1840–1846," *Zion* 23–24 (1958–1959), 46–65 (Heb.).

7. During this visit to Izmir on the way from Damascus to Istanbul, Montefiore met with influential members of the local community. See *Diaries of Sir Moses and Lady Montefiore,* ed. Louis Loewe (Chicago, 1890), 1:265. I thank Abigail Green for this reference.

8. Abigail Green, *Moses Montefiore: Jewish Liberator, Imperial Hero* (Cambridge, Mass., 2010), 294.

9. According to Dov Cohen, who did not mention his sources, Uziel was born in 1810 and died in 1879. Cohen informed me that a communal record of 1846 registers a donation made by "Rafael Uziel, el gazetero," and that later he had contacts with the Alliance.

10. The notion that his name was Pincherle or Uziel Pincherle, taken for granted by many authors, was challenged by David Bunis who, however, based his conclusion on indirect evidence. See Bunis, "The Earliest Judezmo Newspapers: Sociolinguistic Reflections," *Mediterranean Language Review* 6–7 (1993), 5–66, 38.

11. I am grateful to Alper Romano for his interest in my work and for helping me solve the Uziel-Pincherle problem.

12. On Francos, see Minna Rozen, "Strangers in a Strange Land," in *Ottoman and Turkish Jewry: Community and Leadership,* ed. Aron Rodrigue (Bloomington, 1992), 123–166.

13. Bunis, "The Earliest Judezmo Newspapers," 23–28.

14. Recorded in the minutes of Meeting of the Board of Deputies Held at Spanish and Portuguese Jews' Congregation, July 14, 1840 (5600), 225–228, ACC/3121/A/005/A.

15. Joseph Freiherr von Hormayr, *Taschenbuch für die Vaterländische Geschichte* (Berlin, 1846), 275–276. I thank Alper Romano for bringing this book to my attention.

16. The portrait was painted in 1848 by Solomon Alexander Hart.

17. Cited in Kemal H. Karpat, *Ottoman Population, 1830–1914* (Madison, Wis., 1985), 111.

18. These data are scattered in the contemporaneous press and IN travel accounts quoted in Laurence Abensur-Hazan, *Smyrne: Évocation d'une Échelle du Levant, XIXè–XXè Siècles* (Saint-Cyr-sur-Loire, 2004).

19. It was owned and published by a French merchant, Gustave Couturier, but edited by Bargigli, the consul general of Tuscany. See G. Groc and I. Çaglar, *La Presse française de Turquie de 1795 à nos jours: Histoire et catalogue* (Istanbul, 1985), no. 153. The poor quality of the available microfilm makes it impossible to identify the page numbers.

20. These are my reconstructions, sometimes made *ad sensum* when I could not guess which Rashi letter was used. Here are the originals:

> Y muchas vezes se meteran kozas de komplimyentos ke pokos de nuestra nasyon de estas partes estan pratiko[s] en eyas.

> Pero los savyos de nuestra[s] partes de Turkiya no se pyedren ni emplean sus tyempos en tal koza ni estudyan, y dita partikula[ridad] por kavza de el gran apryeto y la gran mankansa de moneda ke ay en estas partes.

21. See, for instance, Gaon, "Sha'arei ha-Mizrach," *Hed ha-Mizrah* (June 8, 1943), 7 (Heb.); Mevorakh, "Puertas de Oriente," *Alei Sefer* 6–7 (1979), 213–216, 213 (Heb.).

22. I was unable to establish exactly how the subscription to *La Buena esperansa* compared to that of *L'Écho de l'Orient,* because the latter indicated its rates in a currency forgotten today and, perhaps, not really used even then. Before 1883, there were a few concurrent monetary systems in the Ottoman Empire, some of them

found only in certain locations. In Izmir, the regular Ottoman piastre de G.S. (grand signore) coexisted with another one, piastre forte d'Espagne, which apparently was worth less.

The monetary reform of 1844 introduced the gold Ottoman lira, which equaled one British pound sterling. It was divisible into a hundred piastres (kurush or grush) and four thousand paras. See Şevket Pamuk, *The Monetary History of the Ottoman Empire* (Cambridge, 2000).

23. Abraham Yaari, "Hebrew Printing in Izmir," *Aresheth* 1 (1958), 97–222, 108 (Heb.).

24. Ibid., 109.

25. Bunis, "The Earliest Judezmo Newspapers," 32.

26. "A Sermon Delivered at the Great Synagogue of Smyrna on the Arrival of Sir Moses and Lady Montefiore in That City by the Rev. P. Segura, Haham Bashi of Smyrna, 5601," Core Collection, Montefiore Endowment, 03144. I thank Abigail Green for bringing this document to my attention.

27. It survives in a German translation, which appeared in *Der Orient*, no. 18 (April 16, 1840), 134–135.

28. Its frequent coverage of Jewish news and its particular interest in Montefiore following his visit to Izmir might suggest that Isaac Pincherle had some influence on the editor, who was *also* an Italian.

29. For comparison, in 1844 in Izmir, 1 oka (2.75 pounds) of bread cost 1.12 piastres. Charles Issawi, *The Economic History of Turkey: 1800–1914* (Chicago, 1980), 336.

30. Not a biweekly, as Bunis and Mevorakh indicate.

31. For various reasons, including their linguistic makeup, I do not believe they were borrowed from Ottoman periodicals, as suggested by Mevorakh, "Puertas de Oriente," 214. Besides, it is highly unlikely that Uziel would have known Ottoman.

32. As Giselle Elbaz has discovered, the "quote" from *The Almagest* used to legitimize Uziel's emphasis on the study of sciences (no. 4, 25) is not found in Ptolemy's work. Most probably, Uziel unknowingly borrowed it from another source.

33. See *The Targum of the Minor Prophets*, translated by Kevin J. Cathcart and Robert P. Gordon (Wilmington, Del., 1989).

34. I am grateful to Sergey Tishchenko for his explanation.

35. This message (as well as the title of Uziel's prospective newspaper, *La Buena Esperansa*) should be interpreted in the context of the messianic responses to the Damascus Affair, most notably Judah Alkalai's attempts to link traditional messianism with an optimistic view of Jewish emancipation. See Israel Bartal, "Messianism and Nationalism: Liberal Optimism vs. Orthodox Anxiety," *Jewish History* 20 (2006), 5–17. Uziel was, no doubt, familiar at least with Alkalai's *Minchat Yehudah* (1843), a panegyric on Montefiore and Crémieux.

36. Abigail Green, "Sir Moses Montefiore and the Birth of the 'Jewish International,'" *Journal of Modern Jewish Studies* 7(3) (November 2008), 287–307, 292.

37. See my translation of and commentary on this article in *The Sephardi Studies Reader, 1730–1950*, ed. Julia P. Cohen and Sarah A. Stein (Stanford, Calif., forthcoming).

38. Matthias Lehmann, *Ladino Rabbinic Literature and Ottoman Sephardic Culture* (Bloomington, 2005), 29. In Izmir, the *talmud torah* was a communal institution that provided free primary education for 200–300 boys from poor families. The *meldars* were private schools with smaller classes.

39. Gadi Luzzatto Voghera, "Italian Jews," in *The Emancipation of Catholics, Jews and Protestants,* ed. Rainer Liedtke and Stephan Wendehorst (Manchester and New York, 1999), 172–187, 180.

40. Perhaps it is not coincidental that in December 1846 another minority periodical closed in Izmir for lack of funds. It was the first Karamanlidika (Turkish language in Greek characters) newspaper and was *also* founded in 1845. Evangelia Balta, *Beyond the Language Frontier: Studies on the Karamanlis and the Karamanlidika Printing* (Istanbul, 2010), 109–110.

41. See Frankel, *The Damascus Affair,* 228, 230. Uziel's representative in Salonica was a Sh. Shelomo Modiano, obviously a member of the prominent Franco family which played a key role in promoting social reform and modern education in the community.

42. Gaon, "Sha'arei ha-Mizrach," 7.

43. On Crémieux's schools, see Aron Rodrigue, *French Jews, Turkish Jews* (Bloomington, 1990), 3–4, 47.

44. See *EJIW,* s.v. "*La Buena Esperansa* II."

45. Gaon, "Sha'arei ha-Mizrach," 7, came to this conclusion because Aron Hazan does not mention it in his article "El jurnalismo de Turkiya," published in the special issue of *La Buena esperansa* dedicated to its twenty-fifth anniversary (1896).

46. Bunis, "The Earliest Judezmo Newspapers," 41.

47. Romero, *La Creación,* 181.

48. Julia Phillips Cohen, "Fashioning Imperial Citizens: Sephardi Jews and the Ottoman State, 1856–1912," Ph.D. diss., Stanford University, 2008, 38.

49. Ibid.

50. In 1869–1874, the Salonican administration published *Selanik,* a monthly in Ladino, Greek, Turkish, and Bulgarian, but it was not a Jewish periodical. Moshe Gaon, *The Ladino Press* (Jerusalem, 1965), no. 204.

51. For more information, see Rodrigue, "The Beginning of Westernization and Community Reform among Istanbul's Jewry, 1854–65," in Levy, *The Jews of the Ottoman Empire,* 439–456; Benbassa and Rodrigue, *Sephardi Jewry,* 77–78.

52. Rodrigue, "Abraham de Camondo of Istanbul: The Transformation of Jewish Philanthropy," in *From East and West: Jews in a Changing Europe 1750–1870,* ed. Frances Malino and David Sorkin (Oxford, 1990), 46–56, 49.

53. See Moïse Franco, *Essai sur l'histoire des Israélites de l'Empire Ottoman depuis les origines jusqu'à nos jours* (Paris, 1897; reprint, 2007), 129–142.

54. Isaac Jerusalmi, *From Ottoman Turkish to Ladino* (Cincinnati, 1990), 10.

55. Rodrigue, "Abraham de Camondo," 52.

56. Romero, who erroneously dates *El Lunar* 1865, calls *El Trezoro* a literary supplement, which contradicts this advertisement. *La Creación,* 183.

57. Since many issues of the periodical are missing, I borrowed this information from Franco's *Essai sur l'histoire des Israélites,* 171, which does not provide the precise date or page number. The same is true for the following two references to the newspaper's materials.

58. According to *El Jurnal israelit* (February 11, 1867), it had 40,000 Jews, 30,000 of whom were Sephardim of Spanish and Portuguese descent, and the other 10,000 included Italian, Ashkenazi, and other Jews.

59. *EJIW*, s.v. "Gabbai, Ezekiel II."

60. Ibid., s.v. "*El Telegrafo.*"

61. On other families of Sephardi literati, see Julia Phillips Cohen and Sarah Abrevaya Stein, "Sephardic Scholarly Worlds: Toward a Novel Geography of Modern Jewish History," *Jewish Quarterly Review* 100(3) (Summer 2010), 349–384.

62. Quoted in Stein, *Making Jews Modern*, 60.

63. Quoted in Rodrigue, *French Jews, Turkish Jews*, 71–72.

64. On the transformation of the notion of Sephardi patriotism, see Cohen, "Fashioning Imperial Citizens."

65. Stein, *Making Jews Modern*, chs. 4 and 6.

66. Jennifer Phegley, *Educating the Proper Woman Reader: Victorian Family Literary Magazines and the Cultural Health of the Nation* (Columbus, 2004), 77.

67. For more information on these magazines, see Martyn Lyons, "New Readers in the Nineteenth Century: Women, Children, Workers," in *A History of Reading in the West*, ed. Gulielmo Cavallo and Roger Chartier, trans. Lydia G. Cochrane (Amherst, 1999), 315–324.

68. *EJIW*, s.v. "*El Telegrafo.*"

69. Lyons, "New Readers in the Nineteenth Century," 320.

70. I suggest that this method of teaching goes back to Huli's *Me'am Lo'ez,* which is full of such stories. For instance, the story of Noah's Ark is interrupted by little jokes about the conduct of various animals, some of whom bite Noah for not feeding them on time. See an English translation in Cynthia Crews, *Extracts from the Me'am Lo'ez (Genesis)* (Leeds, 1960), 36.

71. Unfortunately, Lehmann's study of the rabbinic educational enterprise does not provide enough information on its economic aspect.

72. Quoted in Lehmann, *Ladino Rabbinic Literature*, 68.

73. Jean Hebrard, "Les nouveaux lecteurs," in *Histoire de l'édition française,* ed. Roger Chartier and Henri-Jean Martin (Paris, 1985), 3:471–509, 498.

74. See Lehmann, *Ladino Rabbinic Literature*, 62.

75. The following is an approximate translation of the passage: "you will tire, you will achieve nothing, and if all of your days you strive, you will not reach the end. Days and years will pass, and all of your efforts will be for naught.

"For there is no end or limit to the creatures that the Holy One, God, has created" (trans. Olga Borovaya and Dina Danon).

76. See Paloma Díaz-Mas, *Sephardim: The Jews from Spain* (Chicago, 1992), 107.

77. Lyons, "New Readers in the Nineteenth Century," 313.

78. Ibid., 313–314.

79. Iris Parush, *Reading Jewish Women: Marginality and Modernization in Nineteenth-Century Eastern European Jewish Society* (Hanover, 2004), 94–95.

80. For example, speaking about Yiddish and Ladino literacy in the Russian and Ottoman empires, respectively, Stein states: "In both contexts, Jewish rates of literacy in these vernacular languages were extraordinarily high" (*Making Jews Modern*, 4). Even if one considers literacy in Yiddish "extraordinarily high" (which is questionable in itself), there are no statistics for Ladino literacy.

81. Sam Lévy, *Salonique à la fin du XIXe siècle: Mémoires* (Istanbul, 2000), 101.

82. Rodrigue, *Jews and Muslims: Images of Sephardi and Eastern Jewries in Modern Times* (Seattle, 2003), 15–21. The date for the girls school in Salonica (1874) is found in Rena Molho, *Salonica and Istanbul: Social, Political, and Cultural Aspects of Jewish Life* (Istanbul, 2005), 129.

83. Rodrigue, *French Jews, Turkish Jews*, 37.

84. Rachel Simon, "Jewish Female Education in the Ottoman Empire, 1840–1914," in *Jews, Turks, Ottomans: A Shared History, Fifteenth through the Twentieth Century*, ed. Avigdor Levy (Syracuse, 2002), 127–152, 135.

85. Paul Dumont, "Le français d'abord," in *Salonique 1850–1918: La ville des Juifs et le réveil des Balkans*, ed. Gilles Weinstein (Paris, 1992), 208–225, 210.

86. Hifzi Topuz, *Information internationale dans la presse turque* (Paris, 1960), 34.

87. Barquín, "Un periódico sefardí," 11–12.

88. According to Groc and Çaglar, *La Presse française de Turquie*, *Le Progrès de Salonique*'s (no. 402) circulation was 700 copies (no source cited) and that of *Le Journal de Salonique* (no. 272) was 1,000 (based on Lévy's own estimate).

89. Frankel, "Jewish Politics and the Press: The 'Reception' of the Alliance Israélite Universelle (1860)," *Jewish History* 14 (2000), 29–50, 30. These figures are found in Mevorakh, "The Influence of the Damascus Blood Libel," 56. However, Maurice Samuels indicates that "according to the lists of subscribers published in the journal, at its beginning in 1840, the *Archives* counted 450 subscribers. By 1843, this number had risen to about 1,000." Samuels, *Inventing the Israelite: Jewish Fiction in Nineteenth-Century France* (Stanford, 2009), 287.

90. Cited in Stein, *Making Jews Modern*, 238.

91. According to an article in *Le Journal de Salonique* (September 26, 1909, 3), which does not cite its source, in 1876 in Istanbul, there were seventy-one periodicals: sixteen of them in Turkish, one in Arabic, twenty in French, one in German, one in English, twelve in Greek, thirteen in Armenian, four in Bulgarian, two in Ladino, and one in Italian. The number of Ladino newspapers is indeed correct.

92. A. Djivéléguian, *Le Régime de la presse en Turquie* (Paris, 1912), 65.

93. Ibid., 64–65.

94. Paul Fesch, *Constantinople aux derniers jours d'Abdul-Hamid* (New York, 1907), 62.

95. Karpat, *Ottoman Population*, 149. The census did not include the Jews of foreign nationalities. Still, the figure cited in *EJIW*, s.v. "Istanbul"—100,000 Jewish residents— appears exaggerated, especially in comparison with the numbers found in *El Jurnal israelit* (see n. 57).

96. Avner Levi, "The Jewish Press in Turkey," in *Jewish Journalism and Printing Houses in the Ottoman Empire and Modern Turkey*, ed. Gad Nassi (Istanbul, 2001), 13–27, 19.

97. Stein, *Making Jews Modern*, 65.

98. Fesch, *Constantinople*, 68.

99. Topuz, *Information internationale*, 36–37.

100. *EJIW*, s.v. "El Tiempo."

101. This number appears exaggerated in comparison with the newspaper's total circulation, which is rather vaguely estimated in this article. Based on Halevy's figure for Salonica's Jewish population in the late 1870s (see n. 111), it is reasonable to conclude that subscriptions did not surpass two hundred copies.

102. This word means "paper money." However, Halevy seems to refer specifically to the banknotes issued by the Ottoman government in 1876–1877 to fund the war with Russia, which had very little value. For this reason, Halevy, as well as some other publishers, began to indicate the subscription price in mejidiye or other silver coins.

103. A pre-reform silver coin still in use through the end of the nineteenth century, it equaled 20 piastres.

104. Elia Carmona recalls that in 1885 his boss, the head printer at *El Telegrafo, El Tyempo*'s rival, which cost a hundred piastres per year, was making a hundred piastres per week. Loewenthal, "Carmona's Autobiography," 274–275.

105. On the consumption of meat by Ottoman Jews and the costs of kosher meat, see Minna Rozen, "A Pound of Flesh: The Meat Trade and Social Struggle in Jewish Istanbul, 1700–1923," in *Crafts and Craftsmen of the Middle East: Fashioning the Individual in the Muslim Mediterranean*, ed. Suraiya Faroqhi and Randi Deguilhem (London, 2005), 195–234.

106. On the food expenditures and their weight in the overall budget of the residents of Ottoman Istanbul, see Şevket Pamuk, "Prices in the Ottoman Empire, 1469–1914," *International Journal of Middle East Studies* 36 (2004), 451–468.

107. According to the population census cited in *El Meseret* (April 2, 1897), that year, there were 22,516 Jewish residents in Izmir. Quoted in Cohen, "'Zeal and Noise': Jewish Imperial Allegiance and the Greco-Ottoman War of 1897," in *Judaism and Islam in Medieval and Modern Times,* ed. Michael Laskier and Yaacov Lev (Gainesville, Fla., forthcoming), n. 3. *EJIW,* s.v. "Izmir," offers an unlikely number of 35,000 Jews at the end of the nineteenth century.

108. In 1850–1914, 1 franc equaled 0.044 lira, i.e., 4.4 piastres (Pamuk, *The Monetary History,* 209).

109. the metalik, another pre-reform coin, equaled ten paras.

110. Barquín, "Un periódico sefardí," 12.

111. *La Epoka* (December 8, 1879, 1) puts it at 70,000. *Encyclopedia Judaica* (s.v. "Salonika") cites 80,000 for 1900. The Ottoman Census of 1902 indicates 62,000. Cited in Molho, *Salonica and Istanbul,* 86.

112. See, for example, Paul Dumont, "The Social Structure of the Jewish Community of Salonica at the End of the Nineteenth Century," *Southeastern Europe* 5 (1979), 33–72. According to Sam Lévy, who estimates the Jewish population as 82,000 between 1880 and 1890, the Jewish proletariat of Salonica was more than 25,000. Lévy, *Salonique,* 38.

113. Lévy, *Salonique,* 57.

114. Ibid., 101.

115. Ibid., 101–102.

116. Ibid., 101.

117. Frankel, "Jewish Politics and the Press," 31.

118. Stein, *Making Jews Modern,* 66.

119. Even if *La Epoka* indeed had a double circulation, this lasted only for a few months and could not have affected the situation in general.

120. For instance, see Minna Rozen, *The Last Ottoman Century and Beyond* (Tel Aviv, 2005), 1:ch. 7; and her elucidating article "Salonica" in *EJIW.*

121. Robyn Loewenthal, "Jewish Censorship and Judeo-Spanish Popular Literature in

the Ottoman Empire," in *Studies on Turkish-Jewish History,* ed. David F. Altabé, Erhan Atay, and Israel J. Katz (New York, 1996), 181–191, 181.

122. Ipek K. Yosmaoglu, "Chasing the Written Word: Press Censorship in the Ottoman Empire, 1876–1913," *Turkish Studies Association Journal* 27(1–2) (2003), 15–49, 17.

123. Siren Bora, "Formation of the Jewish Press in Izmir: The First Jewish Newspaper, *Üstad,*" *Tarih ve Toplum* 127 (July 1994), 18–22, 19 (Turk.).

124. Here is my translation of this document:

> Recently, many unknown people, without asking or obtaining authorization of the sublime porte, have established presses in Constantinople, Smyrna, and other places where they print and publish what they want. This state of affairs contradicts the principles of the Ottoman government. Although there is no doubt about the importance of the press, this must not [be allowed to] continue causing serious negative consequences. Hence, it is necessary to keep only the presses belonging to the Greek and Armenian patriarchates and a small number of other presses known to the government. It has adopted regulations to suspend the work and to close all similar establishments not included in these categories as well as prohibiting all other [presses] that have not been previously authorized. Therefore, we are handing the French ambassador this official memorandum and asking him to stop the operations of the two printing presses listed in the attached note which, as we heard, belong to French subjects and which were established without permission.

I was unable to find the "attached note."

125. Yosmaoglu, "Chasing the Written Word," 17–18.

126. Ibid., 18.

127. Yosmaoglu is unaware of this fact, which is why she cites *Muhbir* as "the first example of punitive censorship following the 1864 Regulation." It was closed on March 8, 1867. Yosmaoglu, "Chasing the Written Word," 18.

128. Moshe Gaon, *Eastern Jews in Palestine* (Jerusalem, 1938), 463–464 (Heb.)

129. Djivéléguian, *Le Régime de la presse,* 64.

130. Topuz, *Information internationale,* 25. Yosmaoglu offers slightly different dates in "Chasing the Written Word," 19.

131. Quoted in Yosmaoglu, "Chasing the Written Word," 19.

132. See, for example, Djivéléguian, *Le Régime de la presse,* 61; and Fesch, *Constantinople,* 54.

133. Yosmaoglu, "Chasing the Written Word," 22.

134. Until then, *El Meseret* appeared on Thursdays. For a few years, from that moment on, the first page (rather than half) of the periodical was in Turkish and contained international and business news.

135. Lévy, *Salonique,* 134–135. Lévy does not cite the year, but this incident must have happened sometime after Herzl's final audience with Abdul Hamid, which took place on May 17, 1901. The text of the cable is found in "Daout Lévi," *Les Cahiers séfardis* (September 30, 1947), 323–328, 325.

136. See, for example, Robert Justin Goldstein, "Censorship of Caricature in France, 1815–1914," *French History* 3(1) (1989), 71–107.

137. It was meant to be sung to the melody of "Complainte de Fualdès" by Jehan de la Brebaume. The tune can be found at http://www.cipoo.net/music_a.html ("Ancient-Anonymous") (accessed June 5, 2008). I thank Derek Vanderpool for this reference.

138. Communiqué of the General Secretariat (Yildiz Palace), art. 7. Quoted in Fesch, *Constantinople*, 52. No date is provided.

139. On foreign post offices in the Hamidian period, see Yosmaoglu, "Chasing the Written Word," 27–28.

140. Quoted in Rozen, *The Last Ottoman Century*, 1:102.

141. On these events, see, for example, Bernard Lewis, *The Emergence of Modern Turkey* (Oxford, 1968), ch. 6.

142. Communiqué of the General Secretariat, art. 1.

143. Manolis Kandylakis, *The Newspapers of Thessaloniki* (Thessaloniki, 1998), A:405 (Greek). I am grateful to Paris Papamichos Chronakis for summarizing the relevant parts of the book.

144. Yosmaoglu, "Chasing the Written Word," 34.

145. Ibid., 35.

146. Benbassa, "Associational Strategies in Ottoman Jewish Society in the Nineteenth and Twentieth Centuries," in Levy, *The Jews of the Ottoman Empire*, 457–484, 463.

147. On the Zionist press in the Ottoman Empire, see Benbassa, "Presse d'Istanbul et de Salonique au service du sionisme (1908–1914)," *Revue Historique* 276 (1986), 337–365.

148. See Rodrigue, *French Jews, Turkish Jews*, 42.

149. Stein, *Making Jews Modern*, 61.

150. Loewenthal, "Carmona's Autobiography," 275.

151. Fresco did not become the director and editor in chief of *El Tyempo* until 1894. See *EJIW*, s.v. "Fresco, David."

152. Avram Galanté, *Histoire des Juifs de Turquie* (Istanbul, 1985–1986), 9:213.

153. Ibid., 3:75.

154. See Stein, *Making Jews Modern*, 61; Loewenthal, "Jewish Censorship," 184. In any case, the two journalists could not have been persecuted by Hayim Palachi, as Loewenthal claims, because he died in 1899.

155. Albert E. Kalderon, *Abraham Galante: A Biography* (New York, 1983), 28.

156. Quoted ibid., 29.

157. Ibid., 31.

158. Aron Rodrigue, "From *Millet* to Minority: Turkish Jewry in the 19th and 20th Centuries," in *Paths of Emancipation*, ed. Pierre Birnbaum and Ira Katznelson (Princeton, 1995), 238–261, 242.

159. Rozen, *The Last Ottoman Century*, 216–217.

160. Loewenthal, "Carmona's Autobiography," 355.

161. Galanté, *Histoire des Juifs de Turquie*, 3:75.

162. This may be a reference to Sultan Abdul Mejid's declaration of March 7, 1845, in which he expressed his desire to banish "ignorance, the source of much evil . . . from among the people." See Rozen, "The Hamidian Era through the Jewish Looking Glass: A Study of the Istanbul Rabbinical Court Records," *Turcica* 37 (2005), 113–154, 128.

163. For the first time, its Ladino version was included in the Sephardi *siddur* in 1868. I thank Avner Perez for this information.

164. 1 Chron. 22:9; Isa. 16:5.

165. "I will always ask God / in my humble voice / to give life and glory to Sultan Hamid II."

166. "Sultan of lands, *hakan* of seas, son of sultan of sultan . . ."

## 2. The Press in Salonica

1. Heath W. Lowry, "When Did the Sephardim Arrive in Salonica? The Testimony of the Ottoman Tax-Registers, 1478–1613," in *The Jews of the Ottoman Empire,* ed. Avigdor Levy (Princeton, 1994), 203–214, 207.

2. On this policy, see Joseph R. Hacker, "The Sürgün System and Jewish Society in the Ottoman Empire during the Fifteenth to the Seventeenth Centuries," in *Ottoman and Turkish Jewry: Community and Leadership,* ed. Aron Rodrigue (Bloomington, 1992), 1–65.

3. Lowry, "When Did the Sephardim Arrive in Salonica?," 209.

4. Ibid., 208.

5. Ibid., 206.

6. On the ethnolinguistic composition of the new Salonican community, see Minna Rozen, "Individual and Community in the Jewish Society of the Ottoman Empire: Salonika in the 16th Century," in Levy, *The Jews of the Ottoman Empire,* 215–274, 218–219.

7. Pamuk, "Prices in the Ottoman Empire," 451.

8. Rozen, *The Last Ottoman Century and Beyond* (Tel Aviv, 2005), 1:141.

9. Rena Molho, *Salonica and Istanbul: Social, Political,and Cultural Aspects of Jewish Life* (Istanbul, 2005), 127–128.

10. Marc Baer, "Globalization, Cosmopolitanism, and the Dönme in Ottoman Salonica and Turkish Istanbul," *Journal of World History* 18(2) (2007), 141–169, 151.

11. Rozen, *The Last Ottoman Century,* 143.

12. Ibid., 144.

13. For a detailed discussion of the Alliance schools in Salonica, see Rena Molho, "Education in the Jewish Community of Salonica in the Beginning of the Twentieth Century," 127–138; and Molho, "Female Jewish Education in Salonica at the End of the 19th Century," 139–150, both in her *Salonica and Istanbul.*

14. Esther Benbassa and Aron Rodrigue, *Sephardi Jewry* (Berkeley, 2000), 83–84.

15. Rozen, *The Last Ottoman Century,* 147.

16. Baer, "Globalization, Cosmopolitanism, and the Dönme," 152.

17. Molho, "Le Renouveau de la communaute juive de Salonique entre 1856 et 1919," in her *Salonica and Istanbul,* 85–98. Only the families that paid the communal tax (i.e., 1,300 families out of 13,000) were eligible to vote.

18. Ibid., 91.

19. *Encyclopedia Judaica,* s.v. "Salonika."

20. See Halevy's obituary in *La Epoka* (January 16, 1903), 1.

21. Moshe Gaon, *Eastern Jews in Palestine* (Jerusalem, 1938), 463; *El Avenir* (February 1, 1899), 1.

22. Rozen, *The Last Ottoman Century,* 145.

23. Ibid.

24. Aron Rodrigue, *French Jews, Turkish Jews* (Bloomington, 1990), 47.

25. Ibid., 49.

26. On the establishment of the first Alliance schools in Salonica and Juda Nehama's role in this endeavor, see *A Jewish Voice from Ottoman Salonica: The Ladino Memoir of Sa'adi Besalel a-Levi*, ed. Aron Rodrigue and Sarah Stein, trans, translit., and glossary Isaac Jerusalmi (Stanford, Calif., 2011), ch. 22.

27. Isidore Singer, ed., *Jewish Encyclopedia* (New York, 1901–1906), s.v. "Neahama, Judah."

28. Benbassa and Rodrigue, *Sephardi Jewry*, 76.

29. Julia Cohen and Sarah Stein, "Sephardic Scholarly Worlds: Toward a Novel Geography of Modern Jewish History," *Jewish Quarterly Review* 100 (Summer 2010), 349–384.

30. I thank Elbaz, my student at Johns Hopkins University (class of 2010), for allowing me to use her unpublished paper, written in May 2008, on the representation of science in the Ladino press.

31. Matthias Lehmann, *Ladino Rabbinic Literature and Ottoman Sephardic Culture* (Bloomington, 2005), 13.

32. Ibid., 177.

33. Quoted ibid., 191.

34. *El Tyempo* (October 11, 1873), 4. Quoted in Lehmann, *Ladino Rabbinic Literature*, 187.

35. See their introduction to *A Jewish Voice from Ottoman Salonica*.

36. Ellipsis in the original. It is often used in the Ladino press for suspense.

37. Rodrigue and Stein, introduction to *A Jewish Voice from Ottoman Salonica*.

38. Sam Lévy, *Salonique à la fin du XIXe siècle: Mémoires* (Istanbul, 2000), 20.

39. *La Epoka* (October 3, 1877), 4. I thank Julia Cohen for sharing this information with me.

40. Not to be confused with Elia Carmona, editor in chief of *El Djugeton*.

41. "Rachel-Elie Carmona," *Les Cahiers séfardis* (January 1, 1948), 321–323. On the couple's term in Tetuan, see a letter from Dr. Berliawsky to the president of the Alliance, accusing the Carmonas of having an Arab cook, eating non-kosher meat, showing "contempt for the Jewish religion," and using corporal punishment. According to the author, the directors' conduct caused a conflict with the local community, which led to their transfer to another city. (Archives of the Alliance Israélite Universelle, France, VI.B.25.36, October 22, 1903.) I am grateful to Frances Malino for making this document available to me.

42. We know that one of them became the wife of Asher Yakov Shalem, a member of the Salonican Tribunal of Commerce and *La Epoka*'s contributor on financial matters. *El Meseret* (May 18, 1900), 6, congratulates him on assuming this position. He seems to have been related to Shalom Sholem, a Salonican poet and Lévy's close friend.

43. This information is found in *La Epoka* (September 4 and October 16, 1876), quoted in Julia Cohen, "Fashioning Imperial Citizens: Sephardi Jews and the Ottoman State, 1856–1912," Ph.D. diss., Stanford University, 2008, 64–65. However, Cohen erroneously suggests that Halevy's eldest son is Daout.

44. Most notably, the article describing the celebration of *La Epoka*'s twenty-fifth anniversary (November 2, 1900, 3–5) indicates that all four of its founder's sons were present there and were honored for their work, but only three of them—Daout, Bezalel, and Sam—are mentioned by name.

45. "Daout Lévi," Les Cahiers séfardis (September 30, 1947), 323–328, 324.

46. Ibid.

47. Ibid., 328.

48. This circumstance has caused confusion for some scholars, who somehow assume that the father continued to be the newspaper's publisher long after his death.

49. Lévy, Salonique, 24.

50. Ibid.

51. There is no evidence suggesting that they were related to David Florentin, the editor of El Avenir.

52. Lévy, Salonique, 25.

53. See ibid., 18–21; Rodrigue and Stein, A Jewish Voice from Ottoman Salonica, ch. 8, 25.

54. See Rodrigue and Stein, Memoirs of an Ottoman Rebel, ch. 21.

55. Lévy, Salonique, 26.

56. On Shaul Amariyo, see Zikhron Saloniki [A Memoir of Salonica], ed. David A. Recanati (Tel Aviv, 1971), 2:456 (Heb.).

57. See Rodrigue and Stein, A Jewish Voice from Ottoman Salonica, chs. 4, 5, 7, 8, 11.

58. See Isaac S. Emmanuel, "A History of Salonican Jews," in Recanati, Zikhron Saloniki, 1:132.

59. Lévy, Salonique, 38.

60. Vassilis Dimitriadis, The Topography of Thessaloniki during the Turkish Rule, 1430–1912 (Thessaloniki, 1983), 7 (Greek). I am grateful to Paris Papamichos Chronakis for this reference.

61. Klimis Mastoridis, Casting the Greek Newspaper: A Study of the Morphology of the Ephemeris from Its Origins until the Introduction of Mechanical Setting (Thessaloniki, 1999), 301.

62. Moshe Gaon, The Ladino Press (Jerusalem, 1965), no. 20.

63. Lévy, Salonique, 101.

64. Margalit Matitiyahu, "The Jewish Press of Salonica," Qesher 3 (May 1988), 43–48, 45 (Heb.).

65. This information was provided by Julia Cohen.

66. Lévy, Salonique, 74.

67. Ibid., 77–78.

68. On these novels, see Hélène Guillon, "Les Feuilletons dans Le Journal de Salonique," in Les Sépharades en littérature: Un parcours millénaire, ed. Esther Benbassa (Paris, 2005), 107–120.

69. His right eye is partially covered by the frame of his glasses, which makes his blind eye less conspicuous. Halevy lost vision in this eye as a result of an unsuccessful surgery performed by a doctor from Athens on Allatini's advice thus, no later than 1882. By the end of the 1890s, Halevy had become almost blind in the other eye as well.

70. In his first extant picture (dated 1904), Lévy has a beard, "the most beautiful decoration of [his] face"; he vowed to shave it off after getting married (Le Journal de Salonique, April 29, 1901, 2), which happened sometime in 1904.

71. This photo, which was cut out of a bigger one owned by his descendants in which he appears next to his wife, was published with his obituary in La Epoka.

72. On this subject, see Ebru Boyar and Kate Fleet, *A Social History of Ottoman Istanbul* (Cambridge, 2010), 174–182; Minna Rozen, *A History of the Jewish Community in Istanbul: The Formative Years, 1453–1566* (Leiden, 2002), 16–33; Esther Juhasz, *Sephardi Jews in the Ottoman Empire: Aspects of Material Culture* (Jerusalem, 1989), 120–172. The rabbis, for their part, encouraged Jews to dress differently from Christians and Muslims in observance of the biblical injunction: "You should not do as they do" (Lev. 18:3).

73. P. Risal [Joseph Nehama], *Salonique: La ville convoitée* (Paris, 1914; reprint, Istanbul, 2004), 187. Joseph Nehama (aka P. Risal; 1880–1971), an Alliance teacher, historian, and author of a famous Ladino-French dictionary, was Juda Nehama's son. See Abraham Elmaleh, "Un Serviteur fidèle de l'Alliance et des lettres," *Mahbereth* (April 1965), republished in Joseph Nehama, *Ducateur, crivain, historien et homme daction,* available at http://www.aiu.org/bibli/ils_ont_fait/Joseph_%20Nehama.pdf (accessed August 20, 2009). On the ways Jews dressed in Salonica, see Rodrigue and Stein, *A Jewish Voice from Ottoman Salonica,* ch. 27.

74. See Isaac Jerusalmi, *From Ottoman Turkish to Ladino* (Cincinnati, 1990), 6. The fez was made mandatory for the army and government officials by Mahmud II in 1829. See Donald Quataert, "Clothing Laws, State, and Society in the Ottoman Empire, 1720–1829," *International Journal of Middle East Studies* 29 (1997), 403–425.

75. Lévy, *Salonique,* 40.

76. Ibid., 48–49.

77. Ibid., 135.

78. See Sarah Stein, *Making Jews Modern* (Bloomington, 2003), ch. 6.

79. Lévy, *Salonique,* 27.

80. Hélène Guillon erroneously states that Lévy was expelled because of his refusal to convert to Islam. She misrepresents his attitude toward both Islam and the Ottoman culture by repeatedly claiming that he belonged to "three cultures." Guillon, "Sam Lévy, un intellectuel salonicien," in *Itinéraires Sépharades,* ed. Esther Benbassa (Paris, 2010), 193–203, 195.

81. On the Dönme schools in Salonica, see Baer, "Globalization, Cosmopolitanism, and the Dönme," 154.

82. Quoted in Guillon, "Les Ambitions d'un jeune journaliste séfarade: Les Carnets intimes de Sam Lévy (1894), future rédacteur en chef du *Journal de Salonique* (1895–1911)," *Yod* 11–12 (2006–2007), 271–288, 276.

83. Ibid., 284.

84. Ibid.

85. Ibid., 284–285.

86. Ibid., 278.

87. Lévy, *Salonique,* 77.

88. Zemun was famous for its "proto-Zionist" rabbi, Judah Alkalay. Now it is *also* known as the birthplace of Theodor Herzl's father.

89. The synagogue survived World War II, but in 1997, when the city council was taken over by the nationalist Serbian party, it was sold to be used as a restaurant. I thank Ivana Vučina Simović, for this information.

90. For prices, see table 1.1.

91. Although Sam Lévy's wife (like his mother and sisters) is never mentioned by name,

he later refers to her as his collaborator (*Salonique*, 133). In 1900–1901, she took classes at the Sorbonne. During that time, she stayed with her aunt in Paris, where her future husband visited her a few times. Apparently, one goal of his trip to Paris via Vienna discussed below was to accompany her back after a vacation. See *La Epoka* (October 11, 1901), 1.

92. Paul Haberland, "Literary Censorship in Austria since 1945. Part One: A Survey," *Germanic Review* 65(2) (1990), 76–81, 77. In 1850, Alexander Bach, the minister of the interior, introduced a set of guidelines to be followed by all publications, which were not abolished until 1926.

93. The political side of this conflict and Lévy's disagreement with the Young Turks on the Macedonian question are discussed in his book *Le Déclin du Croissant* (Paris, 1913).

94. I am grateful to Devin Naar for this information.

95. F.O. 286/589, Foreign Office archive, London. I am grateful to Paris Papamichos Chronakis for sharing with me this valuable information.

96. Paul Dumont, "Le français d'abord," in *Salonique 1850–1918: La ville des Juifs et le réveil des Balkans*, ed. Gilles Weinstein (Paris, 1992), 208–225, 217.

97. I thank Devin Naar for bringing this text to my attention.

98. On the Alliance's responses to the emergence of Zionism, see Rodrigue, *French Jews, Turkish Jews*, 126–144; Benbassa, *Une diaspora sépharade en transition (Istanbul, xixᵉ–xxᵉ siècles)* (Paris, 1993), 110–115, 137–139.

99. Benbassa suggests that Sciuto's political engagement significantly depended on the funding he received (*Une diaspora sépharade*, 84).

100. All biographical information cited here is from the following three sources, which do not contradict one another: "In Memory of the Great Activist David Florentin, the Leader of Greek Zionists," in *Saloniki, Mother-City of Israel* (Jerusalem, 1967), 267 (Heb.); "David Isaak Florentin," in *Documents on the History of the Greek Jews*, ed. Photini Constantopoulou and Thanos Veremis (Athens, 1999), 422; "David Florentin," in *Jubilee of Tsur Moshe: A Story of a Cooperative* (Tel Aviv, 1987), 8–10 (Heb.). I thank David Florentin's grandson Moshe Florentin for providing the third source.

101. For more information on Kadima, see Molho, "The Zionist Movement in Salonica Up to the First Panhelenic Zionist Congress," in her *Salonica and Istanbul*, 165–186.

102. Elena Romero, *La Creación literaria en lengua sefardí* (Madrid, 1992), 184.

103. Benbassa, *Une diaspora sépharade*, 94.

104. *La Boz del puevlo* of Salonica should not be confused with the periodical of the same name published in Izmir by Joseph Romano, and Florentin's *La Vara* should not be confused with the famous *La Vara* directed by Galante in Cairo.

105. Romero (*La Creación*, 184) and Benbassa (*Une diaspora sépharade*, 94) erroneously cite 1926 as the year of his emigration.

106. This street is situated in the Florentin neighborhood, but the latter was named after Salomon Florentin, who is not related to David. I thank Moshe Florentin for this explanation.

107. An excerpt from this speech is quoted in Rodrigue, *French Jews, Turkish Jews*, 80.

108. Gloss in the Ladino text.

109. G. Groc and I. Çaglar, *La Presse française de Turquie de 1795 à nos jours* (Istanbul, 1985), no. 362.

110. For more information on this periodical, see Matitiyahu, "The Jewish Press of Salonica," 46–47.

111. Nehama, *Salonique*, 185.

112. See Baer, "Globalization, Cosmopolitanism, and the Dönme," 154–155.

113. See Dragan Subotić, *A Historical-Bibliographical Supplement to the History of the National Press: Serbian Books and Press in Macedonia in 1869–1941* (Belgrade, 1998), 75–77 (Serb.); Boro Mokrov and Tome Gruevski, *An Overview of the Macedonian Press, 1885–1992* (Skopje, 1993) (Serb.).

114. Given that by 1895 Halevy's eyesight had significantly deteriorated and that he did not know French, it is reasonable to assume that the actual work of editing and publishing *Le Journal de Salonique* was done by Daout and Sheridan. Nevertheless, Saadi Halevy deserves full credit for the idea of creating a Francophone Jewish newspaper and getting a license for it.

115. On the various functions of French in Salonica, see Dumont, "Le français d'abord."

116. See Molho, "'Le Cercle de Salonique' (1873–1958): Club de Salonique," in her *Salonica and Istanbul*, 151–164.

117. Rozen, *The Last Ottoman Century*, 145.

118. Molho, *Salonica and Istanbul*, 135.

119. Cited in Rodrigue, *Jews and Muslims: Images of Sephardi and Eastern Jewries in Modern Times* (Seattle, 2003), 186. This information is *also* found in "Alliance Israélite Commission d'Inspection," *Le Journal de Salonique* (January 10, 1909), 6. Moise Benghiat was the brother of Alexandre, the editor of *El Meseret*. In late 1908, he was appointed interim director of the oldest Alliance school in Salonica. Moise Benghiat, like his older brother, was a frequent contributor to *La Epoka* and *Le Journal de Salonique*, signing as M.B.

120. Among them were three Dönme schools: a primary school (established in 1873) and two secondary instittutions. (Sam Lévy was a graduate of one of them.) All three taught French. Baer, "Globalization, Cosmopolitanism, and the Dönme," 154.

121. Dumont, "Le français d'abord," 210.

122. Lévy, *Salonique*, 77.

123. On these events, see Molho, "The Zionist Movement in Thessaloniki," in her *Salonica and Istanbul*.

124. The first attempt to compare *El Avenir* and *Le Journal de Salonique* in terms of their ideology was Adamo Antoniadis, "Die jüdische Gemeinde von Thessaloniki Ende des 19. Jahrhunderts: Innerjüdische Konflikte, untersucht in den Zeitungen 'El Avenir' und 'Journal de Salonique,'" Ph.D. diss., University of Basel, 2007.

125. Rodrigue and Stein, *A Jewish Voice from Ottoman Salonica*, ch. 26.

126. Manolis Kandylakis, *The Newspapers of Thessaloniki* (Thessaloniki, 1998), A:404–407 (Greek).

127. Protis was the legendary Greek founder of Marseille, c. sixth century BCE.

128. Mastoridis, *Casting the Greek Newspaper*, 303.

129. Kandylakis, *The Newspapers of Thessaloniki*, 406. This novel claimed that the Jews helped foreign powers to undermine the integrity of the Ottoman Empire.

130. The only direct evidence of this I have seen is *El Luzero* (August 9, 1905), 2. One of its contributors, complaining about the indifference of Salonican Jewish newspapers, refers to *Le Progrès* as one of "our" journals, the others being *El Avenir, La Epoka,* and *Le Journal de Salonique*.

131. Benbassa, *Une diaspora sépharade,* 125.

132. *El Nuvelista* congratulates him on this occasion (May 11, 1908, 2). I thank Julia Cohen for sharing this note with me.

133. Kandylakis, *The Newspapers of Thessaloniki,* 406.

134. Gaon, *The Ladino Press,* no. 14.

135. On this school, see Rodrigue, "Jewish Society and Schooling in a Thracian Town: The Alliance Israélite Universelle in Demotica, 1897–1924," *Jewish Social Studies* 45(3–4) (1983), 263–286.

136. Angel Pulido Fernández was a Spanish senator who at the turn of the twentieth century became interested in the Sephardim and started a campaign to promote Spanish-Sephardi rapprochement. Among other things, his book includes contributions from some Sephardi intellectuals.

137. This ideology is reflected in the Alliance's educational policies. Julia Cohen discusses it in her "The Past as a Foreign Country," unpublished paper presented at the 37th Annual Conference of the Association of Jewish Studies, 2005. Cohen cites specific instructions on this matter, which are reproduced in Paul Silberman, "An Investigation of the Schools Operated by the Alliance Israélite Universelle from 1862–1940," Ph.D. diss., New York University, 1973, 256.

138. Hence, there is no contradiction between Lévy's Ladino cause and his proclamations about Sephardim's moral obligation to learn Turkish as a second language. For a discussion of Lévy's language polemics with David Fresco, see Stein, *Making Jews Modern,* ch. 2. It should be noted, however, that Stein mistakenly attributes some of Lévy's articles to Saadi Halevy, who had stopped contributing to *La Epoka* before the discussion started.

139. See Rodrigue, "Totems, Taboos, and Jews: Salomon Reinach and the Politics of Scholarship in Fin-de-Siècle France," *Jewish Social Studies* 10(2) (2004), 1–19.

140. See Irith Dublon-Knebel, *German Foreign Office Documents on the Holocaust in Greece (1937–1944)* (Tel Aviv, 2007), 84–95. Cited in Devin Naar, "Reformuler l'identité, réinventer la patrie: Juifs judéo-hispanophones en Amérique, entre Salonique et Séfarad," in Benbassa, *Itinéraires Sépharades,* 63–78, 75.

141. I am grateful to Michael Silber for helping me to identify this synagogue.

142. Lévy, *Salonique,* 116.

143. Ellipsis in the original.

144. On Haim Nahum's mission to Ethiopia, see Benbassa, *Haim Nahum: A Sephardic Chief Rabbi in Politics, 1892–1923* (Tuscaloosa, Ala., 1995).

145. Five years later, Lévy promptly responded to the Seventh Zionist Congress by mocking the delegates' speeches: "Today in Basel took place a congress of Jewish nationalists. We do not yet know the results of this convention which is going to be like all the other ones where they listen to speeches, applaud, congratulate themselves, and shout, 'Viva Zion!'" *El Luzero* (July 29, 1905), 1.

146. This literary device was certainly not new and had been used by French-Jewish authors to ridicule their assimilated compatriots. In 1844, writing in *Les Archives Israélites,* Ben-Lévi described a fictional land where the Jews had completely integrated into society and attained high positions in the government, while still maintaining various Jewish institutions. See Maurice Samuels, *Inventing the Israelite: Jewish Fiction in Nineteenth-Century France* (Stanford, 2009), 74–75. The following year, *L'Univers Israélite* published

a made-up letter that describes the customs of the "red-skinned" American Jews, which was meant to satirize the ways of emancipated French Jews (ibid., 112–113). Unlike his predecessors, who were concerned about the dangers of modernity, Sam Lévy creates fantastic states to demonstrate that assimilation is both possible and beneficial for the Jews.

147. Lévy, *Salonique*, 64.

148. On the coverage of pogroms in the French-Jewish press, see Eliyahu Feldman, *Russian Jews at the Time of the First Revolution and the Pogroms* (Jerusalem, 1999), 115–116 (Heb.).

149. On Frank, see *Encyclopedia Judaica*, s.v. "Zagreb"; http://hr.wikipedia.org/wiki/Josip_FrankKategorija (accessed June 15, 2009).

150. On the history of this motto, see Lisa Moses Leff, *Sacred Bonds of Solidarity: The Rise of Jewish Internationalism in Nineteenth-Century France* (Stanford, 2006), 171.

151. Quoted in Benbassa, *Une diaspora sépharade*, 85.

152. Ibid.

153. Rodrigue, "From *Millet* to Minority: Turkish Jewry in the 19th and 20th Centuries," in *Paths of Emancipation*, ed. Pierre Birnbaum and Ira Katznelson (Princeton, 1995), 238–261, 253.

154. For a more detailed comparison of these texts, see Borovaya, "Shmuel Saadi Halevy/Sam Lévy: Between Ladino and French: Reconstructing a Writer's Social Identity," in *Modern Jewish Literatures: Intersections and Boundaries,* ed. Sheila Jelen, Michael Kramer, and L. Scott Lerner (Philadelphia, 2011).

155. That is, 8 PM.

156. Boris Uspensky, *The Structure of the Artistic Text and Typology of a Compositional Form,* trans. Valentina Zavarin and Susan Wittig (Berkeley, 1973), 85.

157. See *Dictionnaire de l'Académie française,* 6th ed. (1832–1835) and 7th ed. (1932–1935).

158. Phyllis Cohen Albert, *The Modernization of French Jewry: Consistory and Community in the Nineteenth Century* (Hanover, 1977), 53.

159. *El Liberal* (Madrid) (July 18, 1904). I thank Julia Cohen for bringing this text to my attention.

160. Quoted in Rodrigue, *French Jews, Turkish Jews,* 80.

161. Pierre Loti, *Voyages 1872–1913* (Paris, 1991), 329. This excerpt is translated by Alan Astro.

162. Quoted in Rodrigue, *Jews and Muslims,* 144.

163. Loti, *Voyages,* 316.

164. Guillon, "Les Feuilletons dans *Le Journal de Salonique,*" 120.

165. Lévy, *Salonique,* 76.

## 3. The Serialized Novel as Rewriting

1. See Curt Leviant's introduction to his translation, *King Artus: A Hebrew Arthurian Romance of 1279* (New York, 1969).

2. See its description and summary in Zvi Malachi, *The Loving Knight: The Romance Amadis de Gaula and Its Hebrew Adaptation* (Petah-Tikva, 1982).

3. *Me'am Lo'ez,* Hebrew introduction, 3.

4. See Alla Markova, "Un fragmento manuscrito de una novela de caballerías en judeoespañol," *Sefarad* 69(1) (2009), 159–172.

5. It is possible that there were more of such texts than is usually believed, because a great number of novels never appeared as separate editions and were either lost with the periodicals that have not survived or are waiting to be discovered by scholars in extant Ladino newspapers. I thank Aviva Ben-Ur for pointing this out to me.

6. I first suggested these terms in Borovaya, "Translation and Westernization: *Gulliver's Travels* in Ladino," *Jewish Social Studies* 7(2) (2001), 149–168.

7. See, for example, Gideon Toury, *Descriptive Translation Studies and Beyond* (Amsterdam and Philadelphia, 1995); and André Lefevere, *Translating Literature: Practice and Theory in a Comparative Literature Context* (New York, 1992).

8. See Borovaya, *Modernization of a Culture: Belles Lettres and Theater of Ottoman Jews at the Turn of the 20th Century* (Moscow, 2005) (Russ.); Borovaya, "The Role of Translation in Shaping the Ladino Novel at the Time of Westernization in the Ottoman Empire," *Jewish History* 16(3) (2002), 263–282; Borovaya, "The Serialized Novel as Rewriting: The Case of the Ladino Belles Lettres," *Jewish Social Studies* 10(1) (2003), 30–68.

9. For instance, Rosa Asenjo talks about Ladino texts as rewritings (*reescrituras*) in her article "Narrativa patrimonial y de autor," in *Sefardíes: Literatura y lengua de una nación dispersa,* ed. Iacob M. Hassan, Ricard Izquierdo Benito, and Elena Romero (Cuenca, 2008), 375, 376.

10. Romero, *La Creación literaria en lengua sefardí* (Madrid, 1992), 221–263.

11. Amelia Barquín, "Edición y estudio de doce novelas aljamiadas sefardíes de principio del siglo XX," Ph.D. diss., Universidad del País Vasco, Bilbao, 1997; Barquín, "*Martirio, cenas de la vida*: Un folletín de Sam Lévy," in *Jewish Studies at the Turn of the Twentieth Century,* ed. Judit Targarona Borrás and Angel Saenz-Badillos (Leiden, Boston and Köln, 1999), 2:451–456; Barquín, "La aventura de la novela sefardí," *Neue Romania* 22 (1999), 9–24.

12. See, for example, David Altabe, "The Romanso, 1900–1933: A Bibliographical Survey," *Sephardi Scholar,* ser. 1 (1977–1978), 96–107.

13. See Aron Rodrigue, *French Jews, Turkish Jews* (Bloomington, 1990), 111–120.

14. The students who left the Ortaköy school (Istanbul) in the academic year 1883–1884 had spent an average of 1.4 years there. The average for the same year for the Alliance school in Galata, where the Jewish population was better-off, was 3.4 years (ibid., 113). Carmona was a student at the Ortaköy school in 1881–1885. Robyn Loewenthal, "Elia Carmona's Autobiography: Judeo-Spanish Popular Press and Novel Publishing Milieu in Constantinople, Ottoman Empire, circa 1860–1932," Ph.D. diss., University of Nebraska, Lincoln, 1994, 267 (henceforth "Carmona's Autobiography").

15. See Avner Levi, "Aleksander Benghiat and His Contribution to the Ladino Press and Belles Lettres," in *The Heritage of Sephardi and Mizrachi Jewry,* ed. Issachar Ben-Ami (Jerusalem, 1982), 205–212; Barquín, "Un periódico sefardí: *El Meseret* de Alexandr Ben-Guiat," *Sefarad* 57(1) (1997), 3–31; Olga Borovaya and Julia Phillips Cohen, "Alexander Ben Ghiat" and "*El Meseret,*" both in *The Encyclopedia of Jews in the Islamic World* (henceforth *EJIW*).

16. Barquín, "Edición y estudio," 46–47.

17. Levi, "Alexander Benghiat," 206.

18. Avram Galanté, *Histoire des Juifs de Turquie* (Istanbul, 1985–1986), 3:76. For comparison, a feuilleton published by *La Epoka* cost its subscribers one piastre.

19. Quoted in Romero, *La Creación*, 236.

20. Loewenthal, "Carmona's Autobiography," 305.

21. Ibid., 309.

22. Alyssa Quint, "Yiddish Literature for the Masses? A Reconsideration of Who Read What in Jewish Eastern Europe," *AJS Review* 29(1) (2005), 61–89.

23. Ibid., 63.

24. Ibid., 70.

25. Loewenthal, "Carmona's Autobiography," 305.

26. Johann Strauss erroneously interprets Carmona's statement to mean that "Judeo-Spanish was read by the lower classes." Strauss, "Who Read What in the Ottoman Empire?" *Arabic Middle Eastern Literatures* 6(1) (2003), 39–75, 55. Strauss would have better understood Carmona's statement if he had seen its correct translation. The journalist mentions children and old *women* (rather than *people*) to emphasize that he wrote for the least educated Sephardim.

27. Jurnal politiko de literatura / ke lo entyende mizmo una kriatura.

28. This is how *El Kirbach* advertised Florentin's version of Dumas's *La Dame aux Camélias,* which was reprinted in Salonica in 1922. Quoted in Elena Romero, "Nuevos aspectos de la narrativa judeoespañola," in *Proyección histórica de España en sus tres culturas* (Junta de Castilla y León, 1993), 177–191, 188.

29. Quoted in Romero, *La Creación*, 234.

30. Ibid., 235.

31. I am grateful to Julia Cohen for sharing this text and for her apt observation.

32. Preface to *El Jiro del mundo kon sinko metelikes de autor franses Pol Dubua* (Salonica, 1905), 1.

33. Ellipsis in the original.

34. Romero, "Nuevos aspectos," 183. On its other rewritings in the Ottoman Empire, see Strauss, "Who Read What," 63.

35. Itamar Even-Zohar suggests that, in "weak" literatures, where translated literature occupies the central position, the texts for translation "are chosen according to their compatibility with the new approaches and the supposedly innovatory role they may assume." Even-Zohar, "The Position of Translated Literature within the Literary Polysystem," in *Literature and Translation: New Perspectives in Literary Studies,* ed. J. S. Holmes, J. Lambert, and R. van den Broeck (Leuven, 1978), 117–127, 119. This observation has to be reconsidered or further elaborated for the case of serialized fiction imported by weak non-European literatures wholesale as a canon. Clearly, compatibility is not the only criterion of selection, unless this concept is redefined in broader terms to include extraliterary parameters.

36. For instance, in 1912, the girls school in Tripoli had almost all the novels that will be examined in the next chapter, albeit mainly in Italian translation. I thank Frances G. Malino for this information.

37. Strauss, "Who Read What," 39–40.

38. Ibid., 40.

39. On the serialized novel in various languages, see, for example, Marc Angenot, *Le roman populaire: Recherches en paralittérature* (Montreal, 1975); Anne-Marie Thiesse, "Le roman populaire," in *Histoire de l'edition française*, ed. Roger Chartier and Henri-Jean Martin (Paris, 1985), 3:454–469; Juan Ignacio Ferreras, *La novela por entregas, 1840–1900 (Concentración obrera y economia editorial)* (Madrid, 1972); Geoffrey Brooks, *When Russia Learned to Read: Literacy and Popular Literature, 1861–1917* (Princeton, 1985); and John O. Jordan and Robert L. Patten, eds., *Literature in the Marketplace: Nineteenth Century British Publishing and Reading Practices* (Cambridge, 1995).

40. On French, German, and Jewish serialized novels, see Maurice Samuels, *Inventing the Israelite: Jewish Fiction in Nineteenth-Century France* (Stanford, 2009); Hans Otto Horch, *Auf der Suche nach der jüdischen Erzählliteratur: Die Literaturkritik der "Allgemeinen Zeitung des Judentums" (1837–1922)* (Frankfurt, 1985); Dan Miron, *A Traveler Disguised: The Rise of Modern Yiddish Fiction in the Nineteenth Century* (Syracuse, N.Y., 1996).

41. Francis Lacassin, preface to *Le Juif errant* by Eugène Sue (Paris, 1983), 3. Cited in Samuels, *Inventing the Israelite*, 74.

42. Here and in the following chapters, the numbers in parentheses following quotations indicate the pages in the respective Ladino editions.

43. This novel is cited in all catalogs as anonymous. I am convinced that it is a compilation of Carolina Invernizio's serialized novels, but I have not established which ones exactly, because this research would require reading her 128 novels and identifying every part of this complicated story as a possible borrowing from them.

44. For the tropes used in Ladino ballads, see http://www.sephardifolklit.org/flsj (accessed on June 6, 2008).

45. Communiqué of the General Secretariat (Yildiz Palace), art. 2. Quoted in Paul Fesch, *Constantinople aux derniers jours d'Abdul-Hamid* (New York, 1907), 52

46. Barquín, "*Martirio*," 454.

47. See an annotated English translation in *Jewish Travellers: A Treasury of Travelogues from 9 Centuries*, ed. Elkan Nathan Adler (New York, 1966), 4–21.

48. According to Lehmann, the most popular *Me'am Lo'ez* volumes were Huli's commentary on Genesis (nine editions between 1730 and 1897) and his commentary on the first part of Exodus (seven editions between 1733 and 1868). *EJIW*, s.v. "*Me'am Lo'ez*."

49. Romero, "Nuevos aspectos," 183, erroneously attributes this rewriting to Florentin who, according to her, published it in 1924. She probably refers to a reprint, since the original edition came out in 1905. I was unable to identify the original novel or its author.

50. Reza Dudovitz, *The Myth of Superwoman: Women's Bestsellers in France and the United States* (London, 1990), 47–48.

51. Juan Ferreras, *La Novela por entregas, 1840–1900: Concentración obrera y economia editorial* (Madrid, 1972), 78.

52. Ibid.

53. I thank Matthias Lehmann for this explanation.

54. According to Barquín, "Un periódico sefardí," 18, the original belongs to Léon Gozlan (she erroneously spells his name as "Gozlar"), a prolific French writer of Jewish descent. It is noteworthy that she did not find the French original, but only its Spanish translation.

55. Avram Galanté, *Les Juifs d'Anatolie* (reprint, Istanbul, 1975), 1:119; my italics.

56. Hence, we should not assume that every novel attributed to a certain rewriter was, indeed, produced by him (if he happened to be a newspaper editor).

57. Romero, "Nuevos aspectos," 190–191.

58. It is not legitimate to call the rewriters "plagiarists" nor to describe their work as "shameless," which is what Romero does in "Nuevos aspectos," 191.

59. Loewenthal, "Carmona's Autobiography," 306.

60. Paloma Díaz-Mas, *Los Sefardíes: Historia, lengua y cultura* (Barcelona, 1993), 171.

61. Barquín, "*Martirio*," 454–455.

62. Ibid., 455.

63. Quoted in James Etmekjian, *The French Influence on the Western Armenian Renaissance* (New York, 1964), 207.

64. Quoted in Silvia Coll-Vinent, "The French Connection: Mediated Translation into Catalan during the Interwar Period," *Translator: Studies in Intercultural Communication* 2 (1998), 207–228, 209.

65. Even-Zohar, "The Position of Translated Literature."

66. Ibid., 121.

67. Ibid.

68. Pavel Grintser, "Dve epokhi romana" [Two Epochs in the History of the Novel] in his *Genesis romana v literaturakh Azii i Afriki* [The Genesis of the Novel in African and Asian Literatures] (Moscow, 1980), 3–44, 33 (Russ.).

69. Preface to *El Jiro del mundo*.

70. Kenneth B. Moss, "Not *The Dybbuk* but *Don Quixote*: Translation, Deparochialization, and Nationalism," in *Culture Front: Representing Jews in Eastern Europe*, ed. Benjamin Nathans and Gabriella Safran (Philadelphia, 2008), 196–240.

71. Ibid., 199.

72. Ibid., 225.

73. Even-Zohar, "The Position of Translated Literature," 124.

## 4. Ladino Fiction

1. Interestingly, this title is not a translation but a transliteration of the French one.

2. In the nineteenth century, many of the French classics that entered the canon of serialized fiction, including some of those discussed in this chapter, *also* were used for nonliterary adaptations, namely, for opera and ballet librettos. In fact, already in the 1790s, Lesueur composed the operas *Paul et Virginie* and *Télémaque*; Dumas's play *La Dame aux Camélias*, based on his novel, served as the libretto for Verdi's *La Traviata* and Saughet's ballet *La Dame aux Camélias*. Abbé Prévost's *Manon Lescaut* inspired two operas—by Massenet and Puccini—and a ballet by Halévy, who *also* composed an opera based on Sue's *Le Juif errant*. In the twentieth century, some formulaic French novels earlier popular as serialized read, were made into movies in various countries. It is certainly not coincidental that the strategies used for producing these scripts and librettos are essentially the same as those employed by Sephardi rewriters.

3. Alexandre Dumas fils, *La Dame aux Camélias* (Paris, 1998), 222.

4. Spelling per the original.

5. According to Romero, this rewriting, produced by David Florentin, appeared anonymously sometime before 1901, when it was reprinted in *El Meseret* under the title *Anjelina del Amor: La vida de una desgrazyada*. Romero, "Nuevos aspectos de la narrativa judeoespañola," in *Proyección histórica de España en sus tres culturas* (Junta de Castilla y León, 1993), 177–191, 188. Abraham Yaari cites a later edition of the same text—"*La dama alas kamelyas: Romanso muy pasyonante* por Alexandre Dumas fils, adaptado por Isaak D. Florentin, 2nd ed. (Salonica, 1922)"—in Yaari, *A Catalogue of Ladino Books at the Library of the Hebrew University of Jerusalem* (Jerusalem, 1934), no. 494 (Heb.).

6. Cited in Yaari, *A Catalogue of Ladino Books*, no. 445. The title of Florentin's rewriting as cited by Romero—*Angel of Love: The Life of an Unfortunate Woman*—is the next step along this road.

7. In Ladino belles lettres, *romanso (muy) ezmuvyente* (a [very] moving novel) practically became the designation of a subgenre. Curiously, Benghiat's rewriting of *Manon Lescaut* discussed below indeed appeared with this label (but this happened later).

8. This name is obviously borrowed from *La Traviata*. Barquín demonstrates that the novel *La Maldisyon del djudyo* has two sources: Hugo's drama *Le Roi s'amuse* and Giuseppe Verdi's opera *Rigoletto*, the libretto of which is based on this play. See Amelia Barquín, "Edición y estudio de doce novelas aljamiadas sefardíes de principio del siglo XX," Ph.D. diss., Universidad del País Vasco, Bilbao, 1997, 323–333. Both *La Traviata* and *Rigoletto* were brought to Izmir and Salonica by foreign troupes.

9. I quantified this observation by counting the number of characters on the page. It should be kept in mind that French words are usually longer than Ladino ones.

10. Abbé Prévost, *Manon Lescaut* (Greenwich, Conn., 1939), 25–26 (translator unknown).

11. For a brilliant analysis of this scene and the two levels of narration, see Erich Auerbach, *Mimesis: Representation of Reality in Western Literature* (Princeton, N.J., 1953), 397–398.

12. Prévost, *Manon Lescaut*, 22.

13. In Turkish, "good manners" is *terbiye*.

14. In these lists, the italicized words are the new terms glossed in parentheses.

15. In Turkish, "to insist" is *inat etmek. Meter inat* is a typical composite Ladino lexeme, consisting of Romance and Turkish elements.

16. These terms were coined by Aleksandr N. Veselovsky. See his *Izbranniye raboty* [*Selected Works*] (Leningrad, 1939), 42.

17. For a more detailed analysis and a different interpretation of this novel, see Borovaya, "The Serialized Novel as Rewriting."

18. See Romero, *La Creación*, 247.

19. Jacques-Henri Bernardin de Saint-Pierre, *Paul et Virginie* (Paris, 1839), 31.

20. Ibid., 66.

21. Ibid., 302.

22. Quoted in Rena Molho, *Salonica and Istanbul* (Istanbul, 2005), 140.

23. For instance, in 1911, the bulletin of the Alliance schools complained about parents and teachers not making even a tiny effort to discuss this subject with children in order to protect them from "real and serious dangers." "Éducation sexuelle des enfants," *Bulletin des Écoles* (1911), 109. I thank Frances G. Malino for the reference.

24. See my transcription and translation of this novel at http://www.stanford.edu/group/mediterranean/seph_project/index.html.

25. The following can be taken as direct proof of this: "*En las tenyevlas de la noche* [*In the Darkness of the Night*]. Romanso. Imitado por Aleksandr Benghiat, adaptado del ingles por David Fresko (Jerusalem: Estamparia de Shelomo Yisrael Sherezli, 1911 or 1912)." In other words, Fresco, who indeed knew English, translated the novel from this language, and Benghiat adapted it in a certain way. Romero *also* believes that Benghiat used a French source for his rewriting of *Gulliver's Travels*, but she does not explain her reasons for this assumption. *La Creación*, 250.

26. For a more detailed discussion of this novel, see Borovaya, "Translation and Westernization: *Gulliver's Travels* in Ladino," *Jewish Social Studies* 7(2) (2001), 149–168. However, my interpretation of this rewriting has changed significantly since that article was published.

27. Cf. the discussion of children's versions of *Gulliver's Travels* in Zohar Shavit, *Poetics of Children's Literature* (Athens, Ga., 1986), 116–117.

28. My italics.

29. Jonathan Swift, *Gulliver's Travels* (London, 1994), 12.

30. Shavit, *Poetics of Children's Literature*, 112.

31. This conflation results from the Greek translation of the Hebrew *dag gadol* (big fish) as *ketos* (sea monster, huge fish) in the Septuagint.

32. This story was reprinted from *El Avenir* which had borrowed it from Ben Yehuda's *Ha-Hashkafa*. I do not know which of *El Meseret*'s Jewish predecessors nicknamed the sailor a new Jonah, but this reference is not present in the original account of the whaling ship *Star of the East*. See http://www.bbc.co.uk/dna/h2g2/brunel/A471548 (accessed September 17, 2008).

33. *Sefer Eldad ha-Dani* in *Ma'asiyot maraviyozos* (Salonica, 1812), *bet*. This Ladino text differs from the Hebrew original used by Adler for his translation. See his *Jewish Travellers*.

34. In his analysis of the Hebrew adaptation of an Arthurian novel, Curt Leviant points out that the rewriter "Judaizes" it by using biblical phraseology, which allows him to direct "the Jewish reader's attention to various biblical stories." For instance, a description of the king's feast is meant to bring up the book of Esther. Curt Leviant, ed. and trans., *King Artus: A Hebrew Arthurian Romance of 1279* (New York, 1969), 18.

35. See my transcription and translation of this novel at http://www.stanford.edu/group/mediterranean/seph_project/index.html.

36. In Sherezli's catalogs, the title is expanded to *Hasan-pasha el terivle, gran vizir*.

37. Benghiat mistakenly refers to him as "bey." "Dey . . . was the title given to the rulers of the Regency of Algiers under the Ottoman Empire from 1671 onwards." *Encyclopedia Britannica* (1996), s.v. "Dey." It is unlikely that this error originated in Benghiat's French source.

38. In the eighteenth century, the Ottoman government was responsible for protecting French ships in the Mediterranean from the corsairs who were, therefore, considEred the empire's enemies. In order to avoid persecution during their visits to the empire, they had to bribe Ottoman officials rather than present letters of recommendation. Hasan failed to pay the bribe and ended up in prison. I am indebted to Bruce Masters for this explanation.

39. However, it is erroneously cited as the date of Selim III's ascension.

40. There are just two Ottoman terms that are not translated into Ladino or glossed: *seraskir* (minister of war) and *kapudan pasha* (minister of the navy), but they are often found in the Ladino press. At the same time, the Ottoman silver coin akçe is referred to by the European term *asper.*

41. It is characterized by excessive use of the "cleft" construction (It + be + noun or pronoun + that or who + relative clause), which is common in French but not often used in Ladino. For example, we read: "En akeyos tyempos . . . era kon naves de todas las granduras ke los vyajes por mar se azian" (5).

42. The real Hasan had a pet lion,but this episode might have been made up. There is a monument to Hasan with a lion in the town of Çeşme: http://en.wikipedia.org/w/index.php?title=Cezayirli_Gazi_Hasan_Pasha&oldid=183207040 (accessed March 28, 2008).

43. See Selcuk Aksin Somel, *The Modernization of Public Education in the Ottoman Empire* (Leiden, 2001), 200–202. Unflattering European maps of the Ottoman Empire were censored, and even during "the transition period from Hamidian to Young Turk rule . . . Greece, Egypt and the Balkan states were colored as belonging to Turkey." Benjamin C. Fortna, "Change in the School Maps of the Late Ottoman Empire," *Imago Mundi* 57(1) (2004), 23–34, 24, 29.

44. James Wood, ed., *Nuttall Encyclopedia* (England, 1907).

45. On the Turkicization project upheld by *El Tyempo* at the turn of the twentieth century, see Sarah Stein, *Making Jews Modern* (Bloomington, 2003), 70–71.

46. On Sephardi Ottomanism, see Esther Benbassa, *Une diaspora sépharade en transition* (Paris, 1993), 105–110; Cohen, "Fashioning Imperial Citizens."

47. For instance, in 1910, *Le Journal de Salonique* published a series of articles on Turkish literature.

48. See Romero, *La Creación,* 206.

49. According to ibid., 289, *Thérèse Raquin* was adapted for the theater, but Romero does not provide any further information.

50. Émile Zola, *Nantas,* in his *Contes et nouvelles* (Paris, 1973), 115–146, 146.

51. Ibid., 129. The English translation is as follows:

> That morning, Nantas was overrun with business. A prodigious activity reigned in the offices he had set up on the ground floor of the house. There was a whole world of employees, some motionless behind their gratings, others continually coming and going, slamming the doors; there was a continuous ring of gold, open bags running over upon the tables, the music ever sounding of a strong-box whose waves seemed as if they would flood the streets. (Émile Zola, *Married for Money* [New York, 1911], 44)

52. In the French text, I counted prepositional combinations like *au* or *d'or* as two words. In the Ladino text, I did not count the parenthetical glosses.

## 5. Sephardi Theater

1. The only mention of Sephardi Theater outside the Sephardi press I was able to find is Sam Lévy's letter to Angel Pulido, which will be quoted below.

2. Romero, *El Teatro de los sefardíes orientales* (Madrid, 1979), 3 vols.

3. Romero, *Repertorio de noticias sobre el mundo teatral de los sefardíes orientales* (Madrid, 1983).

4. Romero, *La Creación literaria en lengua sefardí* (Madrid, 1992), 265–312.

5. A number of articles on Sephardi Theater have appeared since the publication of Romero's dissertation, but most of them, except linguistic ones, render parts of her work without offering anything new. Rena Molho attempts to use three Ladino plays published by Romero as sources of historical evidence. See her "Le théatre judéo-espagnol à Salonique: Une source de l'histoire sociale des juifs locaux," 263–274; and "Judeo-Spanish Theater on the Themes of Tradition and Change in the Early Twentieth Century," 275–284, both in Molho, *Salonica and Istanbul* (Istanbul, 2005).

6. Bernard Lewis, *The Jews of Islam* (Princeton, 1984), 131. I thank Aviva Ben-Ur for this reference.

7. See Haydee Litovsky, *Sephardi Playwrights of the Seventeenth and Eighteenth Centuries in Amsterdam* (Lanham, 1991); Harm den Boer, *La Literatura sefardí de Amsterdam* (Alcalá de Henares, Spain, 1995), 307–345; Bartolomé de Torres Naharro, *Aquilana*, trans. Avner Perez (Maale-Adumim, 2005).

8. In one of the few transcribed Karagöz plays, Karagöz owns a swing and makes money by swinging other characters in it. Curiously, he promises to charge the Jew less if he speaks the "correct language." See *Jeu de la Balançoire* in *Le Théatre populaire*, ed. L. Schmidt (Paris, 1965), 492–493.

9. Ilhan Başgöz, "The Waqwaq Tree in the Turkish Shadow-Play Theater: Karagöz and the Story of Esther," in *The Jews of the Ottoman Empire,* ed. Avigdor Levy (Princeton, 1994), 549–556.

10. Ibid.

11. Romero, *La Creación,* 266.

12. Ibid., 266–267.

13. See the analysis in chapter 6.

14. Quoted in Elena Romero, *El Teatro de los Sefardíes Orientales* (Madrid, 1979), 888.

15. See analysis in chapter 6. This is how the rewriter's name is spelled in Latin characters on the title page of the play, above its Hebrew version.

16. In other former Ottoman territories, Ladino theater survived until World War II.

17. This is the only instance of this word being used in Ladino that I have seen.

18. Matthias Lehmann, *Ladino Rabbinic Literature and Ottoman Sephardic Culture* (Bloomington, 2005), 82.

19. Quoted ibid., 63.

20. This may be the same as the Sosyedad Instruktiva, which was mentioned by *El Tyempo* as an amateur group that might be interested in staging *The Playful Doctor.*

21. One such case, that of Jacques Loria, is discussed in chapter 6.

22. Romero, *La Creación,* 268.

23. This is how the author's name appears on the title page of the play. In *The Guide to Ladino Materials in the Harvard College Library,* prepared by Aron Rodrigue (Cambridge, 1992), 97, it is erroneously cited as "Nisim."

24. "Here" and "there" in both Castilian Spanish and Judeo-Spanish. Hence, I assume thatLévy is referring to the difference in pronunciation between the two languages and

274 ||| NOTES TO PAGES 208–224

welcomes the "return" of the Castilian pronunciation. The third term is covered by an ink stain on the newspaper.

25. For an analysis of the rewriting of *Esther,* see Tamar Alexander, *"Esther:* A Judeo-Spanish Traditional Play (Salonika, 1932)," in *The Jewish Communities of Southeastern Europe from the Fifteenth Century to the End of World War II,* ed. J. K. Hassiotis (Thessaloniki, 1997), 23–53. It is clear that Jews perceived Racine's *Esther* as a "Jewish" play. Thus, *Le Journal de Salonique* (February 16, 1903) informs its readers that, although this tragedy is "very seldom staged in Paris these days," it is still appreciated, especially by the Parisian Jews who are celebrating the anniversary of its 1689 premiere.

26. This is mentioned only in Moïse Franco, *Essai sur l'histoire des Israélites de l'Empire Ottoman depuis les origines jusqu'à nos jours* (Paris, 1897; reprint, 2007), 275.

27. This was suggested to me by Maurice Samuels. In fact, Girardin wrote *Judith* specifically for Rachel who, in the eyes of French society, represented the quintessential Jewish heroine. See Scott L. Lerner, "Jewish Identity and French Opera, Stage and Politics, 1831–1860," *Historical Reflections/Réflexions Historiques* 30(2) (2004), 255–281, 278. Needless to say, the Sephardi press claimed Sarah Bernhardt as a Jewish actress and followed all her triumphs and travels in detail.

28. For a Romanized edition of this play, see Yosef Avraam Papo, *La Vinya de Navot: Drama bíbliko en sinko aktos en versos,* ed. Avner Perez (Maale Adumim, 2003).

29. On the third page of *Devora,* his name is spelled in Latin characters as "Djain."

30. See the analysis in chapter 6.

31. On the same page, Djaen announces that 10 percent of the profit from the performances of the play goes to Keren ha-Yesod (the Jewish national bank that bought land in Palestine).

32. While it is generally true that, for the uneducated public, the visual side of a show is more important than the words, the need to emphasize this fact in a Salonican newspaper may have been prompted by the complex linguistic situation in the city, where members of different speech communities often watched the same shows.

33. I talk about two groups mainly for the sake of convenience, because we have very limited information on this subject. Besides, this is how the Sephardi press presents the situation.

34. This is a communal holiday during which clothes are distributed among the poor. In Salonica, it was held during Passover week.

35. Romero, *La Creación,* 275.

36. Ibid., 297.

37. Angel Pulido, *Españoles sin patria y la raza sefardí* (Madrid, 1905), 117.

38. Elsewhere, Sam Lévy offers a definition of "realism" in literature. He contends that "the first principle of a realist novel is to tell the truth, even if this truth does not suit some readers." Quoted in Amelia Barquín, *"Martirio, cenas de la vida*: Un folletín de Sam Lévy," in *Jewish Studies at the Turn of the Twentieth Century,* ed. Judit Targarona Borràs and Angel Saenz-Badillos (Leiden, Boston and Köln, 1999), 2:451–456, 454.

39. It is hardly coincidental that this review was published in 1905, which can be characterized as the periodical's most "Jewish" year in terms of the materials it published and the attitudes it expressed.

40. For example, on June 14, 1895, *La Epoka* published a nine-line announcement

of the performances of a foreign circus on its last (and least expensive) page. At three piastres per line, it cost twenty-seven piastres, while a ticket to the show cost four piastres. In 1908, *La Epoka* charged for advertisements as follows: on page 1, fifteen piastres per line; on page 2, ten piastres; on page 3, seven and a half piastres; on page 4, five piastres.

## 6. Ladino Drama

1. I am using the transliterated edition of this play prepared by Elena Romero in *El Teatro de los sefardíes orientales* (Madrid, 1979), 888–896.

2. My italics.

3. It was rewritten in Ladino a few times under various titles, including *Eskarso* and *Deskarso*. See Romero, "Más teatro francés en judeoespañol," *Sefarad* 52(2) (1992), 527–540.

4. Romero, *El Teatro,* 165–175.

5. As the division of each of the five acts into scenes in the Ladino version does not always correspond to that of the French original, for the sake of convenience, I will indicate only the numbering in Molière's text.

6. There is a striking similarity between this episode and Eldad's salvation.

7. He achieves the desired effect through expansion of nucleus nouns, verbs, adverbials, and whole sentences. Thus, instead of responding to Enriko's first question with a simple "yes," Matilde adds words of endearment (*my dear*). And it is not just her heart that beats but *also* her soul, and they do not just beat but do so *strongly,* and they do not do so when Enriko opens his mouth, but as he *begins* to open it.

8. See my transcription and translation of this play at http://www.stanford.edu/group/mediterranean/seph_project/index.html.

9. Esther Benbassa, *Une diaspora sépharade en transition* (Paris, 1993), 101. However, Loria's great supporter Sam Lévy offers a different version of his relationship with the Alliance in *El Luzero* (June 30, 1905), 1. He recounts that Loria was unjustly accused of writing erotic novels, coming to class late, and being a spy. In reality, Lévy claims, Loria's students made excellent progress, and he did many good things for the community, including establishing a mutual aid fund in Bulgaria and Salonica. Insulted by the rumors, says the article, Loria wrote to the Alliance leadership asking for permission to resign, but the Central Committee refused and appointed him director of a large school in Tunis. Later, Loria became director of the Alliance school in Salonica, but in 1908 he was fired from this position and replaced by Moise Benghiat. In his letters to the editor of *Le Journal de Salonique* (November 3 and 5, 1908), he defends himself against accusations of wrongdoing, blaming his colleagues and *Le Progrès de Salonique* for all his troubles.

10. As was mentioned earlier, Sam Lévy intended to publish its Ladino version first in *El Luzero* and then in *La Epoka*. I was unable to establish whether any parts of this novel came out.

11. Johann Strauss, "Who Read What in the Ottoman Empire?" *Arabic Middle Eastern Literatures* 6(1) (2003), 39–75, 64.

12. Ibid.

13. Ibid. I believe that Strauss's translation of this title—*The Imperial Treasure of the Topkapi Serail*—is incorrect.

14. See Susan R. Suleman, "Entre histoire et 'roman de concièrge': L'Affaire Dreyfus dans l'imaginaire populaire des années 1930," *Cahiers Naturalistes* 76 (2002), 157–176; Suleman, "The Literary Significance of the Dreyfus Affair," in her *The Dreyfus Affair: Art, Truth, and Justice* (Berkeley, 1987), 117–139.

15. Romero, *El Teatro*, 510–520. However, some plays were published several times under different titles.

16. For instance, an immigrant from Izmir, Nissim Danon, composed the play *Dreyfus* (as well as *Queen Esther*) in Romanized Ladino while already living in Palestine. I thank his grandchildren Dina and Eitan Danon for providing this information.

17. I am using the transliterated edition of the play prepared by Romero, *El Teatro*, 975–982.

18. I have italicized the few words in Haman's monologue that correspond to his discourse in Esther 3:8–9: "their laws are different from those of every other people, and they do not keep the king's laws, so that it is not appropriate for the king to tolerate them."

19. Romero, *La Creación literaria en lengua sefardí* (Madrid, 1992), 280.

20. Cf. Judges 5:3: "Hear, O kings / give ear, O princes / to the Lord I will sing, I will make melody to the Lord."

## Conclusion

1. For an outline of such a history, see Borovaya and Lehmann, *EJIW*, s.v. "Judeo-Spanish Literature."

2. Sarah Stein, *Making Jews Modern* (Bloomington, 2003), 141.

3. Ibid., 240.

4. His great-uncle was Moshe Aaron Mallah, the co-founder of *El Avenir*. See Raanan Eliaz, *Jewish World Review* (May 7, 2007), http://www.jewishworldreview.com/0507/sarkozy.php3.

5. Albert E. Kalderon, *Abraham Galante: A Biography* (New York, 1983).

# ⫶ Index

OLGA BOROVAYA was born in Russia, where she received an M.A. in Romance linguistics and a Ph.D. in cultural studies. Since 1998, she has been doing research and teaching at the University of California at Davis, Stanford University, and Johns Hopkins University. Her first book—*Modernization of a Culture: Belles Lettres and Theater of Ottoman Jews at the Turn of the 20th Century*—came out in Moscow in 2005.